This ethnographic study of political life in the department of the Yonne, in the Burgundy region, explores a still richly Balzacian provincial world. The author, a French anthropologist, has extensive field experience in Ethiopia. Deploying the insights and methods of social anthropology by drawing on local history, interviews and participant observation, Abélès describes politicians at every level, from municipal officers to Members of Parliament and Ministers. He provides a clear picture of the process of 'decentralisation' initiated by the Socialist government in 1982, and undermines the simplistic notion of 'centralist France'. This book, which develops a fresh perspective on political life in France, past and present, illustrates more generally a new approach to modern political phenomena, from the point of view of anthropology.

Cet ouvrage est publié dans le cadre de l'accord de co-édition passé en 1977 entre la Fondation de la Maison des sciences de l'homme et le Press Syndicate of the University of Cambridge. Toutes les langues européennes sont admises pour les titres couverts par cet accord, et les ouvrages collectifs peuvent paraître en plusieurs langues.

Les ouvrages paraissent soit isolément, soit dans l'une des séries que la Maison des sciences de l'homme et Cambridge University Press ont convenu de publier ensemble. La distribution dans le monde entier des titres ainsi publiés conjointement par les deux établissements est assurée par Cambridge University Press.

This book is published as part of the joint publishing agreement established in 1977 between the Fondation de la Maison des sciences de l'homme and the Press Syndicate of the University of Cambridge. Titles published under this arrangement may appear in any European language or, in the case of volumes of collected essays, in several languages.

New books will appear either as individual titles or in one of the series which the Maison des sciences de l'homme and the Cambridge University Press have jointly agreed to publish. All books published jointly by the Maison des sciences de l'homme and the Cambridge University Press will be distributed by the Press throughout the world.

Cambridge Studies in Social and Cultural Anthropology

79

Quiet days in Burgundy

A list of books in the series will be found at the end of the volume

QUIET DAYS IN BURGUNDY

A study of local politics

MARC ABÉLÈS

Translated from the French by Annella McDermott

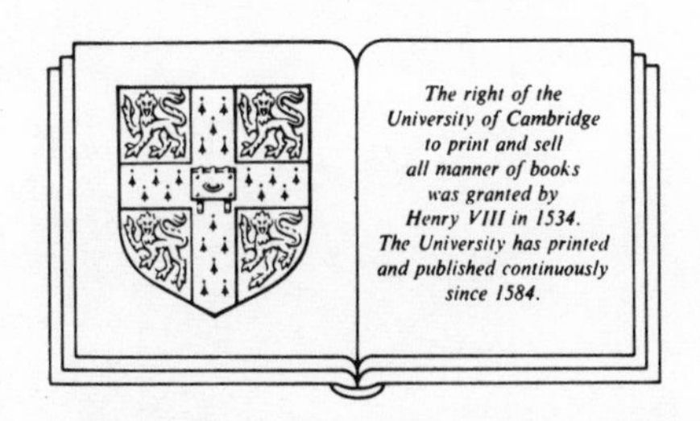

CAMBRIDGE UNIVERSITY PRESS
Cambridge
New York Port Chester Melbourne Sydney
EDITIONS DE
LA MAISON DES SCIENCES DE L'HOMME
Paris

Published by the Press Syndicate of the University of Cambridge
The Pitt Building, Trumpington Street, Cambridge CB2 1RP
40 West 20th Street, New York, NY 10011, USA
10 Stamford Road, Oakleigh, Melbourne 3166, Australia
and Editions de la Maison des Sciences de l'Homme
54 Boulevard Raspail, 75270 Paris Cedex 06

Originally published in French as *Jours tranquilles en 89: ethnologie politique d'un département français*
by Editions Odile Jacob 1989

First published in English by Editions de la Maison des Sciences de l'Homme and Cambridge University Press 1991 as *Quiet days in Burgundy: a study of local politics*

Printed in Great Britain at Redwood Press, Melksham Wiltshire.

British Library Cataloguing in publication data

Abélès, Marc
Quiet days in Burgundy: a study of local politics
1. France. Politics
I. Title II. [Jours tranquilles en 89. *English*]
320.944

Library of Congress cataloguing in publication data applied for

ISBN 0 521 38302 1 hardback
ISBN 2 7351 0397 8 hardback (France only)

SE

Contents

Preface to the English edition

This book is an ethnographic account of the workings of local politics in France. It focuses on the power and activities of elected officials, and also seeks to explain how political legitimacy is constructed and transmitted.

The current political and administrative system in France dates back to the French Revolution. In 1790, the nation was divided up into departments and communes (which can be compared to counties and municipalities respectively). This division has never been seriously challenged since its introduction.

Communes and departments are still the main arena for local politics in France. There are altogether 36,000 communes in France, ranging from small villages and the surrounding countryside to major cities, such as Paris or Lyons. These are grouped into 96 departments. The commune is the electoral district for the mayor and town councillors. Members of Parliament are elected to represent the department. The canton is an administrative unit made up of several communes and serving as the electoral district for the department's General Council. The region, a relatively recent creation, unites several departments.

For a long time, departments were governed by prefects appointed by the central government. The departmental assembly, the General Council, debated issues but could not make decisions. All this changed with the decentralisation reform of 1982, when the prefect's powers were transferred to the president of the General Council. Nevertheless, this reform, which also established a Regional Council elected by universal suffrage, did not affect the division into departments and communes. This book focuses on one such department – the Yonne.

The Yonne is one of the four departments in the Burgundy region. Located in the northern part of the region, and with an area of 742,804 hectares, it is the twelfth largest department in the country. Its 'county seat',

Auxerre, is 166 km south-east of Paris and 155 km north-west of Dijon. The population of the department is 311,000; Auxerre has 39,000 inhabitants; Sens, the major town to the north, 26,000; and Avallon, to the south, 9,000. In area and number of inhabitants, the Yonne is a typical French department.

Farming is the major economic activity in the Yonne. Fields and pastures cover six-tenths of the area, and forests occupy much of the rest. Soil, climate and altitude vary. As you travel across the department, landscapes change as one type of farming gives way to another. The farms around Sens are characterised by open fields producing abundant yields; in the wooded Morvan area in the south, there is little agricultural activity. Many areas are covered with vineyards, and the Chablis wines from the west of Auxerre have a reputation worldwide. Cereals are grown in the north, while in the south, livestock farming predominates.

Industry has developed mainly around Auxerre and Sens, both located along the rail and road link between Paris and the south of France. In recent years, the service sector, particularly retail businesses and tourism, has experienced the strongest growth. There are many well-known tourist attractions, ranging from prehistoric sites such as the caves at Arcy-sur-Cure to famous buildings like the Basilica at Vézelay and a number of castles, some of which date back to the Renaissance. Many Parisians have country homes in the area.

While I was doing my fieldwork, and even more after the book's publication in France, I was frequently asked why I had chosen the Yonne for my research. Did I come from the department? Did my family live there? No: I am a Parisian, and regarded as a stranger by the locals. Before I started my research, I knew very little about my own country. I did, of course, venture occasionally into the countryside for the odd weekend or holiday. I had visited Vézelay and, like many Parisians, crossed the Yonne on my way south. My choice of research area was not determined by any prior knowledge of this area, but by the fact that there was good demographic, economic, sociological and political information available on the department.

I began the fieldwork in 1982, and soon discovered what life was like in the provinces – and how different it was from Paris! In the Yonne, I encountered many customs and forms of behaviour rather like those described by Balzac in his *Scènes de la vie en province* (*Scenes from Provincial Life*). Of course, I am not suggesting that society has not changed considerably since Balzac's time. Modern technology has transformed French society, the department has not gone unscathed by two world wars, and there have been major economic changes. After all, the Yonne is not far from Paris, and it is certainly not isolated from the outside world. Yet the atmosphere in the district is utterly typical of provincial life. People take their time. Local events clearly take precedence over national ones. The newspaper *L'Yonne Républicaine*, distributed only within the department, is widely read. Even on the day of the national election, people hurry to buy it rather than the national dailies, such as *Le Monde* or *Le Figaro*.

The political history of the Yonne since the late nineteenth century is similar to developments in other parts of France during this period. Like many other areas, the Yonne was strongly marked by the clash between Church and State when the latter decided to secularise the schools. Two political currents – one Radical and one moderate – flow strongly through local politics. The Communist Party, which emerged after the First World War, and the Popular Front, dating from the mid 1930s, have left their mark. The Communists succeeded in gaining control at the communal level after the Second World War because of their key role in the Resistance against the German Occupation. And for reasons connected with the national situation during the Fourth Republic, the Gaullists of the RPF Party also made a breakthrough in the department, although their influence was shortlived. Even after de Gaulle's comeback in 1958, his supporters were unable to take over the department, which remained faithful to political traditions going back to the late nineteenth century. The most famous contemporary local politician, Jean-Pierre Soisson, still proclaims his attachment to these traditions.

Despite the Yonne's adherence to past traditions, national trends are fully reflected in the department. I had hoped to find a research area in which local politics followed national trends, and this proved to be the case in the Yonne. When this book was published in France, many readers from other parts of the country remarked on how the situation I described resembled that in their own departments. The effects of the decentralisation reform in the Yonne – in particular, the way in which the president of the General Council gained power – were also paralleled elsewhere. Fortuitously, the decentralisation reform was instituted during the period of my fieldwork, and I was able to witness and record the impact of this important transformation in local power.

The ethnographic approach clearly suits the provincial way of life. People like to take their time. They enjoy commenting on local events, and they usually remember these events with great clarity. This is especially helpful to anthropologists. Also, since I did research over a relatively long period, I was able to collect a large amount of information and to win the trust of my informants. I talked to most of the local politicians, and managed to interview some of them several times. I was able to follow the election campaigns closely, and kept up with the activities of several town councils and of the General Council.

Preface to the French edition

Post-code 89: the department of the Yonne. Its political profile mirrors that of France itself, since the territory is basically divided between the Socialists, the Rassemblement pour la République and the Union pour la démocratie française. The Communists still have some influence in their traditional strongholds, such as Migennes; the National Front also has a presence nowadays, and is particularly influential in the north of the department.

When I first went to the Yonne I was not interested in party political rivalries. My starting-point was a long-standing fascination with politics, as a profession and also as a game. My main interest lay with the people who are active in politics, with the way they go about things and their obstinacy in continuing long after history appears to have slammed the door in their faces. Moreover, their passion appears to be contagious, despite periodic declarations from the French people to the effect that they are becoming less interested in politics. Energy is spent in the pursuit of office; money too, perhaps, though this is difficult to find out. People are as silent on this last point as they are generous with their presence in the great spectacle of State. Politics is not an easy subject to write about; everyone immediately expects backstage revelations, the real truth about public figures. In fact, it is naive to think that the people who govern us will suddenly reveal themselves off the record. However, they do like to give the impression, and this is by no means the least of their vanities, that in their public lives they only show us one small facet of their characters. They like us to enjoy the slight frustration engendered by the tantalising mixture of the universal – the public figure – and the familiar – someone like you or me – as presented by the media.

It was only after a detour abroad that I began to understand these issues. During the seventies, I developed a passion for anthropology, and through the kind offices of the Social Anthropology Laboratory, I was able to go and study a traditional Ethiopian society.[1] There I found a world which had retained a strict sense of hierarchy and where each local society was eager to protect its autonomy from the centre. Meanwhile, the whole society was collapsing, and the regime, having shown its complete inability to resolve the country's serious economic problems and overcome famine, was succumbing to the joint attacks of popular discontent and the military. I lived through these events in an area far from Addis Ababa, amongst a people from the south of the country. It was a place where politics was an everyday occupation; like the ancient democracies, Ochollo had its exluded ones, the artisans and the women, but for those who had the status of citizens, life was punctuated by frequent assemblies where each man could freely express his point of view and affect decisions.

One day, someone came to tell me that from now on everything was to be different. 'Ochollo is no longer Ochollo', one of the respected elders told me. 'There will no longer be assemblies, only committees, and we must integrate all those whom we did not formerly consider complete citizens.' There followed a discussion between us: 'Ochollo is in Ethiopia, and they say on the radio that Ethiopia is now Socialist. You foreigners seem richer than us: is that because you're Socialists?' I said that it was not, but that we too had had a revolution, a long time ago. Searching for the most appropriate term, I said: 'We are a republic.' 'Ah', said one, 'so the republic comes after Socialism.' Not everyone was convinced: they wanted details about what exactly a republic was. The conversation continued, but I felt dissatisfied: did I after all have a very good understanding of my own people's political customs? How would they look, seen from the point of view of the Ochollo?

Having just spent many long months trying to understand the concept of politics held by people in Ethiopia, I could not be content with the level of knowledge which had hitherto informed my life as a citizen of my own country. It must have been at this point that I first felt the desire to cast an anthropologist's eye over political life in France. The idea slowly took shape as other field-trips followed my Ethiopian initiation: East Africa again, then Spain . . . till one day I took the plunge. It was an odd experience at first, to be thrust into such a familiar universe! Whereas in Ochollo I had to devote myself to long and patient observation in order to arrive at a coherent description of their system of assemblies, in France I had no great difficulty in distinguishing the different roles of the municipal council, the General Council and the National Assembly, or in finding out the frequency with which elections to them were held. When you are in a society as different from your own as that of Ochollo, the greater part of your work consists in identifying the protagonists. For example, who are these notables who smear their heads with butter and wear multi-coloured trousers? Why must a man offer great feasts if he is to aspire to this prestigious rank? Do these grandees have any particular power over their fellow-citizens? These are the sort of questions to which the anthropologist must find an answer when faced with an opaque and largely mysterious universe.

As can be imagined, I experienced no such difficulties in my travels through France: like everyone else, I was more or less familiar with the duties and prerogatives of a mayor or a member of the National Assembly. If I needed to know more at any point, there were a large number of books which would more than fill the gaps in my knowledge . . . whereas a large part of my work in Ochollo had consisted of translating exotic customs and beliefs into my own language, I now faced a very different task, and one that offered many more surprises: I was now observing a society which I understood intimately. After all, wasn't I supposed to know the rules of the game? I had voted many times, and I had certain ideas about politicians and the different ideological battles they have been fighting for so many years. So there was no exoticism here, no question of butter in our notables' hair, no point in dreaming any significance into our leaders' cars. If anything, I was disturbed by the very familiarity of the words used – the 'right' and the 'left' – and the nature of the activities, particularly the innumerable meetings which take up most of the time of elected representatives.

So I decided to go and have a look, taking all these questions on board, and well aware that I might have to swallow some of my illusions. Why the Yonne? One good reason was that I did not know the department, which was essential if the inquiry was to be impartial. I also had the feeling that the Yonne was a good example of the provincial heartland of France, where political careers originate. Once predominantly rural, the department had undergone a period of change similar to that of many others; thus, after the Second World War the chief town, Auxerre, suddenly swelled with groups of people who were leaving the land in search of other jobs. Above all, I wanted to attach my inquiry to a specific place, to escape from the web of statistics and polls, in an attempt to gain a better understanding of how politics is experienced at the level of daily life. It was true that I would not see everything, and that the validity of my work, its 'relevance' to the country as a whole, would be questioned. This would be a loss for social science . . . but a gain for my project, if I should glimpse some truths about our own way of practising and talking about politics. I had the good fortune, during the years I was working there (from the presidential elections of 1981 to the general elections of 1988) to observe the effects of a very significant reform in local government, namely decentralisation. I was also able to observe closely the activities within the department of two leading politicians: Nallet, who 'parachuted in' to Tonnerre, and Soisson, the deputy and mayor of Auxerre, who became a Minister under the new policy of *rapprochement* between the Socialists and the centre-right . . .

Decentralisation was more than just a backdrop to my investigations, because of the questions it raised about the redistribution of roles between the State and elected representatives. It was also a major event for many mayors and members of the General Council who were being made to question the nature of their powers with the passing of a way of life in rural France. Decentralisation provoked a spontaneous process of self-analysis in these elected representatives. My discussions were enriched by the uncertainty the reform created amongst a group of people who had hitherto experienced the State as a well-oiled machine about which one grumbled, of course, but where everyone knew his or her place. Hitherto, the brightest star in the political firmament of each department had been the prefect: nothing could be done against his will, or indeed without his cooperation. Even political figures who were well known at national level had to win over the prefect and the heads of the various departmental technical services.

The changes made hardly any impact on the public at large. This gap between the relative passivity of the citizens and the agitation observable among their elected representatives was itself a matter for inquiry. Nowadays, most researchers are only interested in political competition at the national level, but it is worth remembering that politics also operates on a local scale. This is particularly so in the French system, where it appears to be almost impossible to achieve national prominence without having first served your time as town councillor, mayor or member of the General Council. Until very recently, it was considered good form to hold three or four different elected offices simultaneously. However, it must be admitted that when the departments and regions were governed by representatives of the State, the tasks of members of the General and Regional Councils were in fact limited.

In any case I had no wish to decide right from the beginning to concentrate on this or that type of local politician. It seemed better to make an anthropological study of a whole group that had its own customs and rituals and whose members, despite their well-publicised disagreements, maintained strong social links. Why not devote myself to a study of these relationships? In order to do this, I had to find a number of individuals who would illustrate, each in his own way, the splendours and miseries of being an elected politician. I therefore took up my pilgrim's staff, with no clear idea as yet of the welcome that would greet a traveller whose only baggage was a boundless curiosity. The point of departure seemed obvious: Auxerre, the chief town, where the prefecture and the main administrative offices are to be found. I could make some contacts there and meet the protagonists. On the other hand, this plan presented certain disadvantages: the department seen from Auxerre would be a little bit like France seen from Paris. It was better to avoid this distorted, 'centralist' viewpoint, even if it meant taking a few side roads. I decided I would be like a boy playing truant from school, taking my time and letting the images sink in: such were the basic precepts of my provisional philosophy.

I therefore decided to begin my investigation by going off to the least populated canton of the Yonne, in the extreme south of the department. I could think of no better way to form a picture of local political life than going and asking the inhabitants of this region what they thought about politics. I had been warned by political scientists that the heart of rural France is often depopulated, and that political activity has suffered as a result of this demographic decline, so that I should not expect to find any spectacular level of participation in public life down there, or even a very striking illustration of the cleavages in the country as a whole. However, I felt the best thing was to go and take a look, and I must say that the discovery of Quarré-les-Tombes and its surrounding canton on the edge of the Morvan made my journey worth while. That is where my travels began: I stayed in Quarré longer than intended, and it was in travelling around these rural communes and conversing with the elected representatives and inhabitants that I formed the majority of the hypotheses developed in this work concerning the profession of political representative and the customs associated with election in our modern democracies. I had the feeling that I was seeing there in an almost pure state certain types of behaviour and certain ways of thought which can be found in other contexts, but in forms too complex to permit detailed analysis.

After this prolonged stay in the highlands of the Morvan, I was drawn to the milder skies of the valley of the Yonne. It was time to go to the chief town, to plunge into the labyrinth of narrow streets which still constitutes the town of Auxerre today. The mayor and his officials had provided me with information and access to archives; they also agreed to answer my questions. Gradually I was able to meet informants representing the main tendencies of thought in Auxerre. At the same time, I was taking an interest in other types of political situation, and I was constantly visiting the four corners of the department, not only rural areas like Puisaye or wine-growing areas like Irancy and Chablis, but also urban and industrial centres like Sens and Migennes. Little by little I pieced together in my mind a picture of politics at the everyday level which I was convinced was valid for many other regions, with its mixture of declared indifference to the great ideological divisions, sudden bursts of energy during electoral periods, and beneath it all the steady resolve of public figures to keep their status and improve their positions of power.

This book is intended, then, to tell the story of a journey to the heart of French provincial life. You will find in it some very engaging and entirely real people. The fact is that I have decided to break with the usual tradition of the social sciences, justified though it is in many circumstances, and to give the real names of my informants. As many of them said to me: 'We are public figures, and there is no need to conceal our identity.' All the elected representatives I met agreed very readily to cooperate. They answered my questions and gave me every opportunity to observe their activities. I am very grateful to them, for without their practical help I would have been trapped in many a cliché. It might perhaps be useful to compare my approach to other ways of viewing political phenomena. First of all, sociology and political science: for a long time these two disciplines have specialised in studying electoral behaviour, and the institutions and organisations which dominate public life. With their aim of detecting patterns, and constructing all-encompassing models and typologies, they present a macroscopic view. Statistical analyses and correlations within carefully chosen parameters are brought in to back up theories and predictions which then have a direct impact on the political strategies of our leaders.

The anthropologist, on the other hand, places more emphasis on the specific place, the individuals concerned, and the relationships between them: no graphs, no questionnaires, no sampling, no opinion polls. The anthropologist takes his time. He cultivates the floating attention common in psychoanalysis. He fixes it on ways of speech and forms of behaviour so everyday and so banal that their meaning has become lost on the principal people concerned. The anthropologist is interested above all in the transfer of power within our societies, the conditions in which legitimacy is acquired and transmitted by those to whom the citizen entrusts the task of representing them. In the field the anthropologist acquires a detailed knowledge of political networks and the bonds which unite a group of people to those whom they elect.

In a way, an anthropologist is like a journalist, immersed in real life and in the present. However, the journalist must always be up to date, even to the point of anticipating the future. The anthropologist, on the other hand, sees in any one event a starting-point from which to grasp the pattern and meaning of other events which may belong to earlier periods. Urged on by the needs of the moment, the journalist is in a hurry. The anthropologist is more of a loiterer. He has to establish some distance, stand back a little from the present. He is thus in a strangely ambiguous position: both inside and outside, participant and observer, contemporary and yet at a remove. In his attempt to put the reality of the moment into perspective, history can be an invaluable tool. Memory is the unconscious drive behind many political customs. However far away the great debates which shook public life a century or two ago may appear now, they have left definite traces behind. It is essential to grasp this principle of continuity in politics in order to understand the persistence of networks and the methods of transmission of power.

The historian seeks in the past explanations of the present, yet he only turns his attention to the present with the greatest of caution, fearing he will lack objectivity. My attitude was completely different: I became the chronicler of the native political memory, retracing lines of continuity, and emphasising the extraordinary impact on the present of certain events which have become founding myths. I found in historical discourse the means our society has of understanding itself, in the same way as those societies 'with no history' which the anthropologist usually studies have recourse to mythologies. The time in which we live is in fact composed of a sort of simultaneity, not an absolutely strict chronological succession: hence the need to retrace in the past those forms, real or symbolic, which can reveal the true shape of the figures and events of the present.

Abbreviations

CDS The Centre des démocrates sociaux (Centre of Social Democrats), created in 1976, contains Centrists who used to belong to the MRP.
CGT Founded in 1895, the Confédération générale du travail (General Labour Federation) long dominated the French labour movement. After the Second World War, the CGT split between supporters of the Communist and Socialist Parties, with the latter setting up another union, Force ouvrière. Since 1947, the CGT, the strongest labour union in France, has stayed close to the French Communist Party.
CNI Created in 1948, the Centre national des indépendants (National Centre of Independents), with liberal or conservative leanings, brought together 'notables' who were farmers or came from the middle and upper bourgeoisie. It played a major role under the Fourth Republic. One of its leaders, Antoine Pinay, was Prime Minister in 1952. This party, tiny though it is, still exists, but currently its leanings are to the far right.
ENA The Ecole nationale d'administration (National School of Administration), set up after the Second World War, trains the French administrative elite. Several politicians are among its alumni.
FGDS The Fédération de la gauche démocrate et socialiste (Federation of the Socialist and Democratic Left) was created in 1965 with François Mitterrand as president. This federation was an alliance of non-Communist leftist parties who opposed de Gaulle's policies. The FGDS broke up after the events of May 1968.
FO Force ouvrière (the Workers' Union) is a labour union founded in 1947 by members of the CGT who rejected the Communist Party's hold over the CGT. Strongly organised in the civil service and among office employees, the FO has always adopted moderate positions.
FTP The Francs tireurs et partisans (Free Partisans and Partisans), an organisation of the French Resistance, was set up in 1942. It played a major role in the Yonne. At the national level, it was headed by Communists.

HEC The Ecole de hautes études commerciales (School of Higher Business Studies) is the most famous business school in France.
HLM Habitations à loyers modérés (moderate-rent housing): French public housing, reserved for low-income families. Such housing units are directly managed by the communes or specialised offices.
MRP Created in 1945, the Mouvement républicain populaire (Popular Republican Movement) was a Christian Democratic Party that, after a breakthrough at the polls in 1945 and 1946, declined to less than 15 per cent of the vote in 1951 and thereafter. Though leaning towards the left, the MRP later became liberal right wing. It always supported the Common Market. Among its most famous leaders were Robert Schumann, Pierre Pfimlin and Jean Lecanuet, who ran against de Gaulle in 1965. In that year, the MRP became the Democratic Centre, and in 1976, the CDS.
PCF The Parti communiste français (French Communist Party) was formed in 1920 after the Tours Congress when Communists separated from Socialists, who refused to join the Bolshevik Third International under Lenin's leadership.
PS The Parti socialiste (Socialist Party) was created in 1971 to replace the SFIO. It chose François Mitterrand as leader. Since 1981, this party has been the major component in the so-called presidential majority.
PSU Socialists who opposed Guy Mollet's, and the SFIO's, Algerian policy formed the Parti socialiste unifié (Unified Socialist Party) in 1960. The PSU was headed by Michel Rocard before he joined the Socialist Party in 1974. The PSU, which was dissolved in 1990, was never more than a tiny group on the far left.
RPF The Rassemblement du peuple français (Rally of the French People) was founded by General de Gaulle in 1946. That year, it did well in the polls, with more than 30 per cent of the vote in municipal elections. In the 1951 parliamentary elections, however, it won only 21 per cent of the vote; and from 1953, some of its deputies left to join others on the right. In 1953, de Gaulle decided to withdraw from politics, and the deputies still loyal to him set up the Centre des républicains sociaux (Centre of Social Republicans), which received only 4.4 per cent of the vote in 1956.
RPR Created by Jacques Chirac in 1976, the Rassemblement pour la République (Rally for the Republic) brought together Gaullists who had formerly belonged to the UDR. The RPR is one of the two major parties on the democratic right.
SFIO Founded in 1905, the Section française de l'Internationale ouvrière (French Section of the Workers' International) united all French Socialists till 1920. After the Tours Congress that year, only Socialists who did not accept Bolshevik tenets remained in the SFIO. Headed by Léon Blum and then, after 1945, by Guy Mollet, the SFIO played a leading role in politics under the Third and Fourth Republics.

UDF The Union pour la démocratie française (Union for French Democracy) was created in 1978 by Valéry Giscard d'Estaing to unite his supporters with Centrists and Radicals. This party and the RPR are the two major parties on the democratic right.

UDSR The Union démocratique et socialiste de la résistance (Democratic and Socialist Union of the Resistance) was a party formed out of the Resistance against German occupation during the Second World War. Since it often had a swing vote in parliament under the Fourth Republic, its role was much greater than its influence at the polls. Among its leaders were René Pleven, who was Prime Minister, and François Mitterrand, who often served as Minister.

UNR The Union pour la nouvelle République (Union for the New Republic) was a Gaullist party formed in 1958 after de Gaulle came back to power. It was the majority party during the first ten years of the Fifth Republic.

A note on French elections

The electoral system

The principle underlying the *majority election system* is that the candidate coming in first should win. Normally, there are two rounds: candidates receiving less than a legally determined percentage of the vote in the first round are not allowed to stand in the second, and other minor candidates usually withdraw and offer their support to the winner or the runner-up.

The principle underlying *proportional representation* is that a party should receive a proportion of seats equal to the number of votes its list of candidates has won.

In France, the majority system, when used, has usually been *uninominal*: in other words, there is one seat to be filled per election district, and voters choose a single candidate. If there are several (say *x*) seats to be filled in a single district, the majority system will be either *plurinominal* or will have recourse to party lists, each list containing up to *x* candidates fielded by a single party. If it is *plurinominal*, all candidates run individually; and the *x* front runners will be elected. If lists are used, there are two possibilities. If ticket-splitting is allowed, voters choose a party list but may cross out certain names on it and choose an equal number from other lists. The winners will be the *x* candidates who have received most votes. If ticket-splitting is forbidden, all *x* candidates on the list receiving most votes will be elected under a majority system.

Given the principle underlying the proportional system, there are party lists with, normally, one round of voting.

It is important to bear in mind that, regardless of the system used, the French parliamentary election district has always corresponded to a department or has been carved out of one.

The election of deputies

The Third Republic (1870–1940) alternated between a two-round, one-district-one-seat majority system and proportional representation. From

1875 to 1914, the former prevailed. The Dessaye Act of 1919, which applied to parliamentary elections in 1919 and 1924, combined both into a system based on lists at the departmental level. Accordingly, if a list won an absolute majority in a department, all candidates running on it were elected; otherwise, seats were distributed proportionally. Starting in 1927, the two-round majority system with one seat per district was reintroduced.

Under the Fourth Republic (1946–58), a one-round proportional system was used with lists in districts corresponding to departments.

The Fifth Republic, from 1958, when it was founded, returned to a two-round majority system with one seat per district. In compliance with an act of 10 July 1985, however, the 1986 parliamentary elections took place in one round under a proportional system with party lists in districts corresponding to departments. Since 1987, France has come back to the two-round, one-seat-one-district majority system, which was used during the 1988 parliamentary elections.

The election of senators

A two-round majority system with the department as electoral district is used to elect senators; but this election is not open to universal suffrage. Instead, senators are elected by the members of an electoral college made up of deputies, general councillors and town councillors from the department.

The election of town councillors

In communes with fewer than 3,500 inhabitants, town councillors are elected under a two-round majority system, and ticket-splitting is allowed. In towns with more than 3,500 inhabitants, they are elected under a two-round proportional system, and ticket-splitting is not allowed. In all cases, the mayor is elected by the town councillors.

The election of general councillors

General councillors are elected under a two-round majority system with one seat per district, the district corresponding to a canton (which groups several communes). They elect the General Council's president.

The election of regional councillors

Regional councillors are elected under a proportional system with the region as a whole corresponding to the electoral district. Voters are not allowed to split lists or indicate a preference for certain candidates. The president of the Regional Council is elected by the regional councillors.

Map of the department of the Yonne

1

Who is eligible?

The story of a local notable
2 August 1982
It is a beautiful summer afternoon and there is a large crowd in the village hall at Saint-German-des-Champs. The mayor of the village, M. Louis Devoir, is to receive a medal today, as are two municipal councillors and two members of the fire brigade. The atmosphere is relaxed but serious. The whole of Saint-Germain is there, of course, and many friends have come from other communes in the canton. The familiar faces of local dignitaries can be seen: the general secretary of the sub-prefecture, the head of the fire brigade, several mayors and people like M. de Chastellux, the 'lord of the manor' of the canton, and the descendant of a great Burgundian family. For M. Devoir is an important person: aged eighty-eight, he is the perfect example of an elected representative strongly attached to his commune, of which he has been the mayor since 1945. Well known to all, and a man of sound opinions, he has played an active part not only in local politics, but also in the various agricultural bodies of the department.

The president of the General Council and senator for the Yonne, M. Jean Chamant, has come in person to present the medals. He is a long-standing friend of the mayor of Saint-Germain. Formerly a Minister, under Georges Pompidou, he is himself a native of the Avallonnais and represents the canton of Quarré-les-Tombes on the General Council. Silence falls, and M. Chamant begins his speech on Louis Devoir. He draws a comparison between the oak trees of the forests of the Morvan and the mayor who is 'built to last a hundred years'. The senator then refers to the heavy demands of public service: elected representatives must always be available to listen to their fellow-citizens; they have to manage their commune and make sure its facilities are improved. They must mediate with the authorities. M. Chamant also mentions Louis Devoir's qualities of mind and heart. A true son of the Morvan, he has the ability to think deeply, he weighs his words and has the priceless virtue of loyalty to friends. The senator ends by expressing his gratitude for M. Devoir's constant loyalty to himself. He then pins the gold medal on M. Devoir's chest and presents the silver and vermeil medals to the municipal councillors. Then it is the turn of the Saint-Germain firemen to receive their medals, and in this speech M. Chamant emphasises the altruistic dedication shown by the firemen, mentioning the department's commitment to civil defence, with the establishment of first aid centres and the provision of the necessary human and material resources.

M. Devoir is next to speak: he thanks the senator and states that he is particularly touched by the award of this medal, which he is very proud to receive. 'Other distinctions which have been conferred on me are more important in the eyes of the world, but this medal is more precious to me because it is the concrete expression of the friendship and trust you have placed in me for so long and which I will never forget.' The speaker then informs his fellow-citizens of his decision not to stand for re-election in 1983. This is therefore the last ceremony in which he will participate as mayor. He is visibly moved, and the same emotion can be seen on the faces of those listening. The ceremony ends with the presentation by the mayor of Quarré-les-Tombes of a gift in the name of the mayors belonging to the association of communes of which he is president. It is two fine volumes of art history published by the monks of the Abbey of La-Pierre-qui-Vire, which is also in the canton. The guests of honour leave the dais; it is time for the reception. Possibly because of the heat, the excitement of the ceremony, or the emotion aroused in all by the announcement of M. Devoir's retirement, everyone is anxious to quench their thirst; drinks are brought round, and people begin to chat.

This was one of the first ceremonies I attended in the canton of Quarré. I had already met some elected representatives in the chief town and in the nearby villages, and was gradually discovering the forested landscapes and the austere majesty of this granitic region. 'Neither a good wind nor good men ever came out of the Morvan', says the proverb. This distrust is revealing: one has the impression that for a long time the geological contrast between the Morvan and the surrounding plains was the cause of the isolation of the inhabitants of the massif. The people have frequently interiorised the prejudices of which they were the object, to the point of describing themselves as withdrawn, as trapped in a natural landscape which is hardly an invitation to innovation and dynamism. They stress the difficulties experienced by stockbreeders in this terrain which is not rich enough to fatten beasts or develop cereal crops. The other agricultural region of the Avallonnais is known as the plain, and the people of the Morvan cast an envious eye over it, without, however, concealing their almost ancestral dislike of its inhabitants. Quarré-les-Tombes is a small market town whose surrounding territory mainly consists of the forest belonging to the private estate of the Dukes. Early stock-rearing is practised. Traditional economic activities associated with the floating of logs down the river came to an end about fifty years ago. Farmers, shopkeepers in the market town and retired people make up the majority of the population of the canton.[1]

M. Devoir's house stands a few yards from the town hall, next door to what was once the priest's house. He usually arranged to see me in his office at home, where he keeps the books and documents to which he refers when speaking of the Morvan, his commune and his family memories. M. Devoir frequently published short items about the history of Saint-Germain in the regular municipal bulletins. In a way he was the living memory of this history, and he recounted it willingly, with a fund of anecdotes and stories about local figures who have known a moment of glory. That is why when I first began my work I was naturally sent to see this man, whose wisdom and knowledge were recognised by everyone in the area. As I listened to my new mentor, and watched him in action, I could not help but notice the enthusiasm he showed for a certain form of public life, even though the questions I asked him about his politics seemed to leave him curiously indifferent. Like most of the mayors of the canton, my informant could be classified as right wing, and he and his family were church-goers. He seemed happy with the term 'moderate': candidates who had stood for the town council outside the mayor's list were generally considered leftists.

Louis Devoir had always won by a comfortable majority ever since he first took up his seat as mayor of the commune. On several occasions he did not even have any opposition list at the municipal elections. 'The result was a foregone conclusion', I was told by several inhabitants of Saint-German who had toyed at some time with the idea of presenting a rival list. This had not prevented the appearance of independent candidates, hoping to benefit from the practice of voting for candidates from more than one list, rather than just the set list from one party. However, for thirty years the mayor's team had regularly emerged the winner. When I asked M. Devoir how he first became mayor, he replied that he was a member of the town council from 1925. He became assistant mayor, a post in which he remained until the elections of 1935, when he decided not to stand for re-election. At this time he had taken over the family farm and had enough to do. Moreover, rival lists had appeared; he himself had grown somewhat distant from the mayor, but he had no wish, though he was urged to do so, to join the adversaries of the mayor, who in the event was re-elected and remained in office until 1945. M. Devoir therefore went through the war years without compromising himself with the Vichy regime, unlike many local representatives. As for the retiring mayor, there was absolutely no question of his standing again in 1945.

'There were three opposing lists', M. Devoir related. 'Despite many pressing invitations, I did not join any list. Only three candidates were elected. Although I was not one of them, I did win a impressive number of votes. At the insistence of several friends, I decided to stand again at the second ballot. The ballot-papers I had printed carried only my name.' And the miracle happened. In M. Devoir's own words: 'I was pleasantly surprised by the number of votes I obtained – 75 per cent, sixty votes more than my nearest rival.' That is how M. Devoir became mayor, persuaded, as it were, by public opinion, in a sort of plebiscite. Moreover, when he referred to the subsequent stages of his political career, the mayor of Saint-Germain continued to emphasise the commune's enthusiasm for his management of the town's affairs: 'At the next election, which in this particular instance was held two years later in 1947, all those who had been elected in 1945 were on my list; there were no other lists, and they were all elected. We were united again.'

To be the man who brings people together, and who puts an end to the antagonisms of the past (we must not forget that the war was not long over) was M. Devoir's constant ambition from then on.

> In six subsequent elections, I only had a rival list once. No one from it was elected. At each election I had the largest number of votes, except for one occasion, when another candidate got two votes more than me. The last time I stood, in 1977, I got 231 out of 310 votes. The candidate immediately behind me got 224 and the third, 162. I am proud to say that in the thirty-eight years that I have been mayor, I have stood for unity and mutual understanding.

I have taken these words and the earlier remarks from a small volume of memoirs which M. Devoir has written for his family: *Au fil des jours et des ans* (*Down the Days and the Years*).[2] They could have been written by many of the rural mayors I met. In them, the mayor of Saint-Germain establishes a strong connection between his desire for consensus and the uncontested nature of his victories. He implies that he does not represent a faction, since a majority of the votes automatically go to him. It is not out of vanity that the mayor insists on the strength of his vote in comparison with his nearest rival. If the difference were to decrease, alarm bells would ring: it would mean that the mayor's name had lost its magic, that it was no longer a magnet drawing people together.

I place great emphasis on the importance given to the *name*, for it worked as a sort of Open Sesame during M. Devoir's electoral career. He refused to join any side in the first round of the elections in 1945. He ended up, as we saw, standing in the second round, but being careful to put forward only his name. No manifesto, just one crucial detail: the identity of the candidate. It was more significant than a manifesto or any amount of empty polemics. The name carried the secret of the candidate's legitimacy. From my interviews with M. Devoir, there had in fact emerged an important dimension to the figure of the elected representative, unrelated to his managerial abilities or his political allegiances. I slowly came to realise that in this case the candidate represented not merely himself, but the continuity of a distinguished family line. Moreover, when he told his story, my informant gave little emphasis to his activities as a farmer, but was much more forthcoming when it came to his predecessors in the office of mayor.

A distinguished family line

M. Devoir spoke to me at length about his father and his ancestors in general. He had drawn up a family tree going back to the eighteenth century, with the birth in 1715 of a peasant named Claude Devoir, who later married Claudine Villain. Amongst their direct descendants was a grandson named Thomas, who as well as being a husbandman, worked as a schoolmaster. He had taken over this role from Etienne Dizien, who died young, leaving two sons, Jean and Etienne. Later Thomas married his predecessor's widow. Four children were born to then. Louis-Philippe, the mayor's grandfather, became a farmer. A second son, Philippe, loved adventure and went off to Brazil, where he was an engineer working on the installation of the railways: he would return for brief visits to his family. Called up in 1914, he was killed in action soon after. Another brother, Auguste, chose the military life, and settled later in Lunéville, where he ran the officers' club. Médéric followed in his father's footsteps and became a schoolteacher. He later left Saint-Germain, became Secretary at the Education Offices in Bordeaux and ended his career in Sens, his wife's native town, where he was the bursar of the poorhouses. His son became a doctor and his daughter married a teacher in a *lycée*.

Only one of Thomas's sons, then, had chosen to stay on the land: admittedly, their father, who had obtained his certificate (*certificat d'études*) and worked as a teacher since 1833, must have had some influence on the choices of the other three. Thomas Devoir had also brought up the two sons of Etienne Dizien. There is a strong resemblance between their careers and those of their half-brothers. Jean Dizien sat his higher certificate at Auxerre and became first a teacher, then deputy head of the teacher training college in that town. His brother Etienne joined the army, and took part in the Crimean campaign, for which he was made a Knight of the Legion of Honour. Returning ill from Algeria, where he was involved in the pacification, Captain Dizien died in his native village. Like the Devoirs, the Diziens were proud to be loyal servants of the State, whether in the army or as schoolmasters. The brother of Thomas Devoir's predecessor taught at the school in Cure, a village near Vézelay. He married Claudine Devoir. One of his sons was headmaster for many years of the primary school at Avallon, and the second entered the Church and became first of all vicar-general of Sens, then Bishop of Amiens. The Army, Education, the Church: these great national institutions are highly valued amongst such families, with their solid peasant roots. There was not, at the end of the nineteenth century, that rejection of religion observable in other schoolmaster families. Anti-clericalism, which as we shall see spread like wildfire in this area, seems in this case to have come up against a family tradition in which the Church and education were very closely associated as dispensers of knowledge and pillars of the same culture. After all, had not Thomas Devoir, appointed as primary school teacher in 1833 by an order signed by François Guizot, received his licence to teach some years earlier from the Cardinal of La Fare, Archbishop of Sens and Auxerre, Primate of the Gauls and Germany?

The name of Devoir is therefore associated on the one hand with the development of education in the commune of Saint-Germain. However, Louis Devoir's infancy was spent with stories ringing in his ears of the feats of Captain Dizien, hero of Sebastopol, to whose memory a monument was erected. The town council agreed unanimously to grant a plot of land in perpetuity to the family so that the monument could be built: the memory of this soldier who set off in search of glory appealed to the imagination and contributed to the prestige of the Devoir family. At the end of the last century, those of the family who remained in the village and dedicated themselves to the land benefited in a sense from this symbolic capital accumulated by their relatives in the service of the nation. Médéric, the father of M. Devoir, was a farmer who had a smallholding and a few animals and whose daily life was little different from that of other inhabitants of the region:

We had a team of two oxen and a horse. The reaping and gathering in had to be done every year, so my father bought a mechanical reaper in 1912. The threshing was done with a very simple piece of equipment: a threshing-machine worked by a horse walking round. Then the winnowing had to be done with another primitive machine.[3]

Unlike many other peasants, however, Médéric Devoir, after getting his primary leaving certificate, continued with his studies for some time; he was sent as a boarder to the higher elementary school in Avallon, where he obtained his elementary diploma. He owed this extension of his education to his cousin Etienne Dizien, the headmaster of the school.

Médéric was ten years old in 1870; the defeat and then the collapse of the Empire, followed by the proclamation of the Third Republic, began one of the most troubled periods in the history of Saint-Germain. The arguments between republicans and Bonapartists shook the commune. Families who had been friendly quarrelled; one family decided to leave the place because of the harassment they suffered. In the patriotic atmosphere of the time, 'scholar battalions' were formed: training took place at the school and Médéric was made instructor in 1883. The mayor, Barbier, a fervent Bonapartist, had been appointed in 1874; his predecessor, who had been more favourable to republican ideas, had had to resign when his political enemies managed to have him brought before the courts on the pretext of an irregularity, in fact well intentioned, in his administration. Barbier was a timber merchant who had some land in the area. An incident which gave rise to a quarrel between him and Médéric was to alter the political life of the commune. As military instructor, Médéric had a right to exemption from military service, but he had to have a certificate from the mayor testifying that he had indeed carried out periods of instruction. Barbier refused the certificate, alleging that he was not sure whether the instruction had taken place. Médéric therefore had to do his military service, but the injustice suffered was the main reason why he decided to stand in the 1888 elections. He won, and was to continue as mayor until 1910, when he retired voluntarily from public life.

It was a splendid period in the life of the commune, distinguished by public works and by the installation first of all of the telegraph and then of the telephone, the first in the canton. Médéric Devoir gained a reputation for efficiency and competence. He acted as an expert adviser in cases of disputed ownership of agricultural lands. A little later he was appointed deputy magistrate of the chief town. His fame also won him some political friendships that went beyond the limits of the commune. For Médéric had declared his opposition to the Law of Separation of Church and State, and had formed a friendship with Etienne Flandin, the member for Vézelay of the General Council, who regularly stood against the Radical-Socialist Albert Gallot. (They alternated with each other between 1893 and 1914.) Until his death in 1936, Médéric remained a respected and influential figure locally. Whether or not his decision to stand for election was motivated by anger, as the anecdote has it, his political success was in no sense the result of chance. The position of the Devoir family, and the education which the future mayor of Saint-Germain received, predisposed him to some extent to his future role. Still, it was he who really brought the name to prominence, and one can understand why, in 1945, once again troubled times, the electors should naturally have turned once more to the bearer of this name.

Louis Devoir, then, can be seen as the natural successor to Médéric. He had come to renew a tradition. His father had earlier re-established harmony in the commune, then a troubled period of wars and political antagonisms came round once more. Remember that M. Devoir withdrew in 1935, rather than take part in factional struggles. However, his father's successor had made Louis Devoir his assistant mayor. Thus the flame was not extinguished, especially since Louis Devoir found himself appointed an adviser in questions of land-ownership and a magistrate, just like his father Médéric before him. Nor was that all. When, after the war, new agricultural organisations were set up, with the disappearance of the Peasant Corporation, the future mayor of Saint-Germain was approached to join the Departmental Agricultural Action Committee composed of eight members appointed by order of the prefect on 2 October 1944. He represented the Avallonnais and remained on the committee until the reappearance of the Chambers of Agriculture. He was then elected to the Chamber of Agriculture of the Yonne, of which he became the first vice-president, remaining in this office for fifteen years. Thus we see how M. Devoir became what is commonly known as a local notable. He also sat on the army recruiting board, and on various other bodies:

I was president of a union of potato seedling producers for the whole of the Morvan. It was while I was president that the silo at Quarré was built. I was a member of the departmental management committees of agricultural mutual benefit insurance companies and mutual aid societies, and I was vice-president for several years of the regional committee for the study and development of the Morvan, set up and chaired by M. de Vogüë.[4]

Over the years, the bonds between the mayor and his electors grew stronger: M. Devoir had enough influence in the department to ensure the success of his interventions on behalf of his community. He also managed to obtain subsidies for useful public works to be carried out. One can see the result of this activity in his manifestoes, where he details the successful projects he initiated. There is a detailed list of these in his 1953 election manifesto: public buildings, roads and highways, telephone facilities, water, local finances. 'DRAW YOUR OWN CONCLUSIONS', the pamphlet tell voters: 'If you believe we have fulfilled the mission you entrusted to us, and we deserve to continue, VOTE for the list we present. If you think we have failed, and that others can do better, VOTE for them. We will give way to them without bitterness, wishing them GOOD LUCK.'[5] Here you can see in a condensed form the whole political style of the mayor of Saint-Germain: the emphasis on management, the 'apolitical' stance, the aim of improving conditions in his commune. Not so very different from that of the majority of rural representatives, and therefore a highly significant attitude. The retiring officers claim their legitimacy has been reinforced by the actions of which they boast, and challenge their rivals to do better.

In our conversations, M. Devoir placed much emphasis on friendships he had formed beyond the boundaries of Saint-Germain with political figures from the department. The name Flandin recurred, and we shall hear more of it, for this family has played an important part in the life of the Yonne. We saw that Médéric was involved with Etienne Flandin: like Flandin, Médéric considered himself a republican, but shunned Radicalism. He took an active part in Flandin's electoral campaigns. Remember that Etienne Dizien had settled in Cure, the village where Etienne Flandin lived. The latter, an important figure in the locality, would visit Médéric, and he set great stock by Médéric's advice. In 1914, the seat fell vacant and Etienne Flandin was elected senator for the French Indies and Médéric was asked to advise on the suitability as a candidate of the young grandson of the retiring deputy. He was only just over the legal age, and was still undecided, and Médéric Devoir was 'one of those who did most to persuade the young Pierre-Etienne Flandin that he should put himself forward as a candidate, and to get him accepted'.[6] When Louis Devoir decided to anticipate the call and enlist in 1913, the Flandins reappeared once more. 'Young Pierre-Etienne Flandin had come to my father's house a few days earlier, and offered to take me along, which he did.' Pierre-Etienne and his wife were, of course, invited to the wedding of the future mayor, and 'insisted on being present despite a recent death in the family'.

Between the two world wars, Pierre-Etienne Flandin was without question the best-known politician in the Yonne: he was a Minister several times, and Prime Minister, so he was the outstanding public figure in the department. However, I shall be turning to this man and the story of his political career later; for the moment it suffices to note that Louis Devoir's loyalty to him never faltered, even after Flandin had left the public stage.

Similarly, the mayor of Saint-Germain always loyally supported Jean Chamant, the deputy for the Avallonnais since 1945. We saw that it was Chamant who awarded the medal of honour of the commune and of the department to M. Devoir, who was one of those who suggested the name of Chamant to replace in the General Council the mayor of Quarré, who had died in 1964. Devoir could have put himself forward, as many of his fellow-citizens urged him to do, but he felt it was wiser to remain on the sidelines. It is always an asset to have as the member of the General Council a politician who is influential at national level, and rural representatives use all their skill to extract maximum advantage from this kind of situation: the presence of a Flandin or, later, a Chamant helped to ensure that manna in the form of subsidies fell on the canton and more particularly on the communes of which their friends were mayors. From the deputy's point of view, the support of a man like Devoir was invaluable, and it was no coincidence that when Chamant found himself in need of a substitute at the time of the general election of 1958, he should turn to the mayor of Saint-Germain: 'My first thought was to ask you to be my substitute deputy. It would be first of all an honour for me and secondly a source of satisfaction throughout the region, for your fame reaches beyond the limits of the Avallonnais', the deputy for the Yonne wrote in a note.[7] However, M. Devoir did not agree to the request: as he later humorously pointed out, if he had accepted he would have had to sit in the Chamber of Deputies when Chamant subsequently became a Minister.

Some fifteen years earlier, Chamant, then a young deputy for the Yonne, tried on behalf of a group of Independent Republicans to persuade the mayor of Saint-Germain to stand for election to the General Council. In his letter, the deputy referred to conversations he had had on the subject with the president of the General Council, the deputy and mayor of Auxerre, Jean Moreau, and the senators:

> M. Jean Moreau himself has decided to make a last appeal to you. We believe you can hardly refuse, under these conditions.
>
> As you know, I am entirely at your disposal, to take you all round the canton in my car: I shall drive, and we shall soon accomplish our mission. Dr Plait and M. de Raincourt have also asked me to say that if their presence is of any help you only have to ask.
>
> Our joint efforts cannot help but end in a triumph which will be a fitting demonstration of the esteem in which you are held throughout the canton.[8]

M. Devoir, however, turned down the chance of standing in this cantonal election of 1949. He seems to have had no wish to take up any political position outside the bounds of the commune. Though quite at ease in his role as spokesman for the peasant world at departmental level, he felt unwilling to go any higher; his concept of the roles of member of the General Council and deputy led him to favour candidates who had an entrée into political and governmental circles in the capital. This was how M. Devoir saw it, and this desire to remain in his place, ignoring the siren voices of political ambition, goes a long way to explaining his constant re-election and the fame he acquired in the Avallonnais.

In 1983, after nearly half a century as an elected representative, M. Devoir decided to retire from public life. For a successor, he turned to his principal assistant mayor, Louis Dizien. The latter belongs to a family which has had close links with the Devoirs for generations. If we go back in time, we find, for example, a marriage between Jean Dizien and Marie Devoir in 1767. They had seven children, among them Etienne, one of whose sons was none other than the schoolteacher of Saint-Germain whose widow was to marry Thomas Devoir. Another of Etienne's sons, a teacher at Cure, married, as we have seen, a Claudine Devoir, granddaughter of Claude. Jean Dizien, son of a brother of Etienne, also married a Devoir, Anne. The granddaughter of this Jean Dizien was none other than the wife of Médéric Devoir, the mother of Louis Devoir. One of the latter's daughters married Jean Dizien, who is the grandson of a brother of Médéric

Devoir's wife. If we add that Louis Dizien, the designated successor to the mayor, is the brother of the latter's son-in-law, we can see the extent to which the transmission of political office is a family affair here: Médéric and Louis Devoir have together clocked up fifty-five years as mayor, but the latter has had no male issue. The obvious thing therefore is to pass the municipal torch to a Dizien. It is worth noting, incidentally, that apart from a Dizien who once filled the post of assistant mayor, this family had never played a central role in local public life. It is nevertheless clear that the Devoir–Dizien alliance has been operating for almost a century to ensure the pre-eminence of one of the names in the commune.

It was with a certain sadness that I realised in the course of our conversations that M. Devoir, who would soon be ninety, was the last of his line. He could boast of a large number of descendants, but the words spoken by his uncle on the day of his wedding had to some extent been spoken in vain: 'So, my dear Louis', the latter had said, 'you are the only one who can carry on the name of Devoir. Without you the name will be lost as the distaff side marry. Do your duty . . .'[9] His uncle was making a pun on the meaning of the word *devoir* ('duty'), and this feeling for the family name and its connotations shows through in many documents, like this letter from Léon Dizien, who had been brought up, as we saw, by his step-father Thomas Devoir, to his half-brother Médéric Devoir, when he was appointed Bishop of Amiens: 'My dear Médéric, I rejoice more for my family than for myself at this great honour which carries with it a heavy burden. God grant that I may be always a Devoir and know my duty.' There is certainly no risk of the name Devoir being wiped from the memory of the inhabitants of Saint-Germain. Will the Dizien name shine with same lustre in its annals? One thing we can say with certainty is that the new mayor of Saint-Germain continued to work closely with his predecessor. Moreover, when I was at M. Devoir's house there were always many other visitors, for as people said: 'he is a real authority'.

Getting elected

'Authority', in the Latin sense of *auctoritas*, is one who incarnates legitimacy. This is the particular quality which permeates the words and deeds of the grand old man of Saint-Germain. In this part of the world, legitimacy is transmitted as part of the heritage of a distinguished family. It is as though the name were enough to 'authorise', to confer on its bearer fitness to assume local responsibilities. Local roots and membership of a family which is historically 'distinguished', in both senses of the term, are, it would seem, indispensable in order to win election. Similar situations can be found in many local communities, where the same names recur again and again among elected representatives. Of course, we are not talking about the divine right of kings: the local electorate do have a say from time to time in the choice of local administration. Indeed, it is noticeable that in Saint-Germain, as in the rest of the canton and in the majority of rural communes in France, local council elections consistently achieve a high level of participation by voters. About 85 per cent of the electorate took the trouble to vote in the canton of Quarré-les-Tombes in 1983. There is a paradox here, in that one also notices an apparent absence of emotion in political life, as one would expect from the existence of a small poll of candidates. For one thing, everyone knows that there is not a great deal at stake: voters are fully aware of the fact that their local representatives are subject to unavoidable constraints, such as decisions made at national level, and policy decisions to favour certain sectors, whether agricultural or social, whose effects are felt at the level of the commune, but which the commune is powerless to influence. All a local representative can do is seize the opportunities offered by these circumstances. So, is there apathy at local level? Do our politicians live in the kingdom of the Sleeping Beauty? I did get that impression, more or less, when I first landed in Quarré. People were forever telling me that they had no interest in politics. 'We don't get involved in politics here', I would be assured by farmers who nevertheless expressed very decided views on what I can only call the politics of milk prices and quotas. And how could I explain the sudden burst of ardour I observed a little later at the time of the local elections? During this period, the cafés resounded with animated discussion. There were the mini-dramas which always blow up at regular intervals in this particular period in the life of a community. Gossip is the stuff of memorable election campaigns: everyone is on the look-out for rumours along the lines of 'the present mayor won't be standing this time', or 'so-and-so isn't on the mayor's list this year, because he's become a liability'. Then you get the anecdotes: 'The other night in the bar, Albert said to the lads: "OK, you're on. I'll stand." But I bet he chickens out.' This effervescence is symptomatic, as is the rash of candidates one observes on these occasions. What is it that leads people to solicit the votes of their fellow-citizens? Obviously, one could reply that sitting on the local council in a rural area offers a man the chance to obtain some advantage for his village, such as the tarred and surfaced road they've asked for so often and never got. However, such a pragmatic answer is incomplete. We must not neglect the symbolic aspect: to be an elected representative is also to be recognised by others. In M. Devoir's account of why he first stood, we have the recurring motif of his being approached by others, first of all by the reigning mayor, and later by his friends: if he stood, it was in response to a demand emanating from others. Many elected representatives make similar claims: 'I didn't want to stand, but I was approached by several people', or 'Sometimes one has to make a sacrifice.' We find a similar retrospective version of events at a higher level also, amongst professional politicians. It is as though spontaneously seeking political responsibility was in some way unseemly, or even indecent. Now, these claims hardly seem justified by the facts. Once elected, the chosen ones readily agree to prolong their sacrifice. Very few vacate the position at the next election. The usual thing is to occupy the office several times in succession, three on average for the mayors in our canton. This protested reluctance which surrounds the story of entry into electoral life can be interpreted in two ways. Politics is not a job like any other, in that standing for office involves committing oneself, even in a situation represented as highly apolitical. It is also an expression of ambition. By attributing the decisive impulse to others, one minimises these factors. At the same time, this type of formulation suggests that representing others has a rather mysterious side to it. An election is in fact a magical process from beginning to end. The expectations of others have come to be fixed on one man who is thereafter to embody the group. There is no guarantee that he will be elected; but he is already out of the ordinary in being *eligible*. This notion of eligibility is highly significant, and it is worth noting that it has never been taken on board by political scientists. One can sense its presence in the claims of elected representatives, which give the impression that entry into competitive politics was a dramatic moment in their lives, one difficult for that reason to put into words, except in the terms cited, whose equivocal nature is obvious. The very act of offering oneself as a candidate is throwing oneself to the lions; there is no guarantee that one will be accepted. The candidates' subsequent emphasis on the fact that they were 'approached' is intended to lend credence to the idea that their name was able to evoke at least a preliminary consensus. However, all this tells us nothing new about the conditions required in order to be eligible. It is not very difficult to adjust to being a municipal councillor, or mayor of a commune, as I was able to verify by a simple inventory of persons who have assumed these functions: in Quarré, between 1900 and 1919, we find that twenty-three individuals occupied the 63 seats contested in the course of four elections; of these twenty-three, more than a third were elected twice in succession, and over a quarter, three times. Two-thirds of our candidates, therefore, attracted the votes of the electorate at least twice. More recently, in the period from 1945 to 1977, we find forty-four individuals for 91 seats. Membership of the council is still the prerogative of a minority which has managed to retain its privileges from generation to generation. This permanence is illustrated by the dynasties of elected representatives, of which we had an example earlier. So we have an insistence on the absence of politics, and a small pool of candidates, both of which suggest an image of tranquil conservatism, which will come as no surprise to anyone who has travelled into the heartland of France.

And yet people vote! Rival lists are drawn up, and independent candidates appear. This is the fact which demands an explanation, since one would expect that only national elections, where there are clear issues at stake, would excite the inhabitants of these rural communes. Is it a case of artificial rivalries? Or is it a case of declared political apathy masking a more profound relationship with politics, one that cannot be readily assimilated into the categories used by pollsters and political scientists? There is a mystery here, and I would challenge a specialist in political science as normally constituted to explain why electors should feel a preference, for example, for the 'Union for the Defence of Communal Interests' list rather than for the 'Municipal Union' list, when both profess to be free of political bias and anxious only to serve the community. Both lists seem anxious to gloss over any fundamental differences, leaving only technical issues: improvements in road maintenance, better facilities, making it easier for young couples to set up home or continue to reside in the community. Yet the electors have no difficulty distinguishing between them, and making very decisive choices, as I was able to observe during the municipal elections of March 1983.

That year there were two opposing lists in the commune of Quarré-les-Tombes. On the one hand there was the list of the outgoing mayor, who presented himself as apolitical and dedicated to good management; on the other, a list aiming to bring in 'new men in the service of the commune'. The organisers of this list were a teacher from Avallon, a native of the Yonne who had been living in the commune for the last few years, and a retired primary school teacher who had spent his whole career in Quarré, where he enjoyed a certain popularity. Opposing them were the outgoing mayor, also retired, previously in charge of the infrastructure in Auxerre, first elected in 1971, and priding himself on the managerial skills he had acquired in the course of his professional life. Apart from these two lists, there were a number of independent candidates. The mayor had a clear advantage since he was tried and tested: as a specialist in highway maintenance in a region where the scattered nature of the hamlets, combined with the rigorous winters, makes constant road repairs a necessity, M. Legros had won the hearts of his electors. At the first round, he and almost everyone on his list were elected or re-elected. Only three seats remained to be filled, and the rivalry grew fiercer. In a tract distributed between the two rounds, those still in the running from the 'new men' list set about their rivals: the latter had no serious plans for the future – all they had to propose was the opening of an old people's home in Quarré. A more virulent criticism was added: the apolitical stance of the mayor and his friends was a front. The tract ended with these words: 'Men and Women of Quarré, you have been deceived. How else can one explain the fact that a so-called "apolitical' list came through your letter-boxes on the eve of the elections inside a regional newspaper totally dedicated to right-wing propaganda?'[10]

The accusation revealed something about the stance of the writers; in fact everyone knew that the two teachers were left-wingers, but up to that point they had avoided displaying their allegiance. On both sides, the presentation had been apolitical, but their poor showing in the first round had no doubt persuaded the opposition to change their tactics. However, their offensive hardly seems to have had any influence on the electors' decisions. Only one candidate was elected from the 'new men' list: the retired schoolmaster got enough votes to win a seat on the council. The comments I heard on the point were all along the same lines: 'I voted for him, because I've known him for a long time. He's a decent man; I know all about his politics, but I also know he'll work for the commune.' Nor did people seem particularly surprised at the failure of the other teacher, despite all his efforts at the time: 'He's not really from round here; he might have had a chance if he'd been a bit less pushy.' People felt he had tried to hog the limelight.

In contrast to the poor score obtained by this teacher and the rest of his list, there is another result which is worth a second glance: of the three candidates elected, one was an Independent. He had merely put his name on the ballot-strips, with no other information. Why had he, a lone figure, done as well as the candidates from the two main groups? To the untutored eye, Jean-Philippe Truchot had no obvious quality which would lead the voters to single him out in this way. Socially, the new councillor seemed to be just an average farmer. He had shown no particular tendency to innovation in keeping his animals, nor was he exactly a pillar of the farmers' union. Aged about thirty, Truchot would generally be considered a 'youngster' in an area that seemed to prefer its representatives to be more mature. He had always confessed himself uninterested in politics, and seemed anxious to maintain this neutrality. Nothing, then, seemed to predestine this candidate to attract the votes of his peers. In fact, the case seemed to raise an important question: are some representatives elected by chance? Are these choices random, or are they evidence of an electoral logic which escapes the observer? Whatever the final answer to this question may be, my analysis of this particular situation was able to throw some light on the behaviour of the voters.

Shortly after the election, as I was sharing my astonishment at Truchot's success with one of my informants, the man told me: 'Well, you know, politics runs a little bit in that family.' Jean-Philippe's father showed very little interest in public life, but I was not to forget that his grandfather had actually been mayor of Quarré. Although young and inexperienced, Jean-Philippe had been elected 'because of his name'. He was in fact the descendant of a veritable dynasty of representatives who had formerly championed the cause of Radicalism. Each voter could therefore immediately identify the candidate as the heir to a *political heritage*. What we must understand here by the words 'political heritage' is not only the memory of the political offices held by different ancestors, but also a distinctive ideological element, in this case anti-clericalism, which, it is assumed, has been transmitted down the line. To be endowed with such a heritage is not, of course, a guarantee of success. One has to know how to use it properly, and even to advantage, in the political stakes. That is what Jean-Philippe Truchot did, though not in any obvious fashion. Far from pushing himself forward, the candidate showed great restraint. He chose to solicit votes on his own behalf, when he could easily have got himself on to one of the lists. To be on the outgoing mayor's list might seem from the outside to be an advantage, but here the logic of the heritage comes into play: although Truchot was not 'political', it would have been unthinkable for him to appear on the apolitical list. That would have been a betrayal of everything his family stood for, a squandering of his inheritance which the voters would have been duty bound to punish. At the other extreme, there could be no question of his joining a list clearly organised by two 'outsiders', for neither of the two teachers had their roots in Quarré. Under these circumstances, the only proper course was the one Truchot finally adopted: to compel recognition of the legitimacy of his name. This example throws several phenomena into sharp relief: firstly the role of political heritage as a condition of eligibility: the voters, far from choosing at random, take account of this factor in the candidate. There may well be a gap of one or two generations between the candidate and his elected forebears. Nevertheless, the traces are there, and they affect public response. Another observation on the ambiguities of apoliticism: leaving aside explicit antagonisms of the present, like the rivalry between the two Quarré lists where we eventually see the emergence of the left/right divide, there are also other cleavages which are not altered at all by the apolitical stance vaunted in public. The memory of ancient loyalties is still very much alive, certainly alive enough to draw a dividing-line between candidates at election time. We have another case which is highly significant in this respect, that of M. Richard, a farmer from another commune in the canton, Saint-Léger-Vauban. He stood in two successive local elections in 1977 and 1983, at the head of a list, but with no political label. At the first election, where he presented a complete list, he was beaten, together with his whole list, by the 'Union for the Defence of Communal Interests', which included, as one might expect, the mayor and the majority of outgoing councillors. In 1983, Richard stood with only five fellow-candidates on his list. This time he got on to the council with two others from his list. Is one to attribute this success to a change in public opinion? The fact is that the candidates distributed no manifestoes and claimed allegiance to no party. Their only distinctive trait was youth, which gave them a moderate protest status in comparison to the outgoing council. Within the commune, Richard's success was given a more subtle interpretation. When he stood for the first time, in 1977, he was seen primarily as the husband of the granddaughter of Collas, a former mayor who had distinguished himself in battle with the pro-clericals. Moreover, Richard was not himself a native of Saint-Léger; before he took over his father-in-law's farm, he was a butcher. So from many points of view he was an outsider whose ambition could be considered suspect: and then, the fact that he was presenting a whole list, not just himself, meant he was totally opposed to all the Saint-Léger representatives.

All this changed in 1983, when success crowned his enterprise. According to my informants, a different interpretation was given to his actions on the second occasion. This time the cues were reversed; his connection with the Collas family was seen as an asset, as it gave a sort of 'diachronic' legitimacy to his candidacy and was a counterweight to the objection that he was an outsider. The candidate's eagerness was no longer a sign of ambition, but of enthusiasm. Why the change? The explanation is quite simple: he presented only a partial list, which implied that he had accepted his position as part of a minority on the council. Thus the balance of power in favour of the outgoing council was not challenged. Under these circumstances, it seemed right that the tendency led by Richard should be represented on the council. Not that the newly elected representative had ever shown any particular sympathy towards the left; but it seems his fellow-citizens had silently but definitively attributed this 'nuance' to him, by comparison with the mayor, and by reference to the opinions held by his wife's forebears.

Starting from a limited number of cues, the local memory rebuilds a system of relationships which give meaning to the various individual candidacies. Thus the latter acquire a value: the candidate is marked right from the start as 'good' or 'bad' according to his affiliation to one of the polarities which structure the field of local politics. From this affiliation the political colour of the candidate is deduced. Let us not forget, however, that in communes where the dominant discourse stresses the absence of politics, this demarcation remains in the realm of the implicitly understood. A list in opposition to the council will invoke morality and the common interest: 'Perhaps you are confused by the large number of candidates; if so, the answer is to choose men who have demonstrated their honesty, integrity and loyalty. Forget personal rivalries, consider the general interest. We are not saying "Vote for us", but we are saying: 'Vote for the right people."'[11]

Beneath this avalanche of words, everyone knows what is being alluded to: what is discreetly called a 'personal' or a 'long-standing' rivalry carries the mark at a deeper level of an ancient ideological antagonism, which has been transmitted down through the generations. The voters' choice is guided, sometimes without their knowing it, by recourse to these cues. This is how, from the multiplicity of candidates, there emerges the group of eligible individuals who have some hope of laying claim to a future in politics. Even in communes where candidates are at liberty to stand independently, and the practice of voting for candidates from several lists instead of one opens the way to a balanced representation of different tendencies, the number of credible candidates is still limited. Is there amongst these eligible candidates any who are truly independent? The answer has to be no, for as we have seen, we must recognise the existence of a web of relationships underlying political life at the local level. Voting, by definition, means making a choice (from the Latin *eligere* ('to choose'). However, the choice is not exhausted in the precise operation consisting of selecting a ballot-slip in the booth and placing it in the box. Before that there is a task of sketching the map that enables one to place the candidate by reference to a network of relationships. The candidate's affiliation to the network may be real or supposed. In the case of Truchot, the link was real, since he descends directly from the former mayor. So far as Richard is concerned, there is, shall we say, reason to believe that he enjoys such a link. As for the networks themselves, in Quarré, as is usual in rural milieux, they do not have the consistency of a structured organisation. The network is not an ideological grouping or a political party, but rather a series of links forged by reference to certain shared values and ancient allegiances. A network is thus defined by the distinctive opposition it maintains towards other similar networks.

If we look on voting as essentially a relational phenomenon, we shall be less surprised to see certain people who regularly stand for election being consistently beaten. These are not cases of individual bad luck; similarly it would be quite wrong to attribute these failures to the particular personality of the candidates. It seems that eligibility, a quality shared, in theory, by all those who fulfill the legal conditions of age and nationality, is in fact conferred only on a minority. And we are talking here about the lowest rung of the political ladder, where the game is extremely simple, in contrast to urban contexts, where access to a political position may require also specific skills, membership of a party, and so on. What struck me most forcibly from my observation of political behaviour at Quarré-les-Tombes was the gap between the aspirations of certain candidates who seemed to have absolutely no hope of ever getting elected and the finality with which their fellow-citizens decided between the rival candidates. In vain the teacher launched himself eagerly into the electoral campaign with his list of candidates in opposition to the outgoing mayor: he was soundly beaten in the end by Truchot, who had not even felt the need to make any public statement. 'He was the obvious choice', people said. I was reminded of M. Devoir. Eligibility is not questioned; it is seen as a 'natural' quality in the individual. Examine what is natural, however, and you will soon find networks. And thus I found myself retracing the whole history of the republican conquest of Quarré, and indeed of the whole department.

Some historical landmarks

In the autumn of 1789, when France was divided into new administrative areas, the canton of Quarré-les-Tombes was created. In attaching to the district of Avallon the eight communes which made up the new canton, the members of the Constituent Assembly were basically imitating the ancient taxation division or *recette* of Avallon. The only place which belonged to a different tax division was Chastellux, which stands on the left bank of the Cure and came under the jurisdiction of Vézelay. The river forms to some extent a natural boundary separating the departments of the Yonne and the Nièvre, just as formerly it was the border between the provinces of Burgundy and Nivernais. When Chastellux was attached to the canton of Quarré-les-Tombes, in defiance of its administrative and geographical position, account was in fact taken of another factor, namely the centuries-old history of Burgundy. At Chastellux is the castle of the Counts of the same name who distinguished themselves in the service of the Dukes of Burgundy. Hercule de Chastellux was the elected representative of the nobility at the States General of Burgundy in 1618. In 1503 in an inventory and evaluation of the fiefs of the bailiwick of Auxois cited by V. B. Henry, we find that 'the lord of Chastellux had in fiefdom from the Duke of Burgundy his castle, Quarré, les Granges Rateaux, Saint-Germain-des-Champs' and other towns in the Avallonnais.[12] The domain of Chastellux included lands in the two provinces of Nivernais and Burgundy. As Baudieu explains, '[seigneurial] jurisdiction formerly embraced the five parishes in the area, that is Chastellux, Quarré-les-Tombes, Marigny-l'Eglise, Saint André and Saint-Germain-des-Champs'.[13]

Saint André and Marigny found themselves attached to the Nièvre in 1790, since these parishes stood on the left bank of the Cure. Chastellux, on the other hand, remained linked to Quarré. A document signed by the commissioners of Nivernais and Burgundy on 27 December and headed 'Boundaries of Nivernais and Burgundy' lists the parishes attached to the Nièvre. Opposite Saint-André-en-Morvan is the following note: 'Chastellux to Burgundy'.[14] This formulation and others of the same sort indicate that an exchange took place. Saint André in point of fact included several hamlets on the right bank of the Cure; all these hamlets were given to Nièvre, as well as the town situated on the left bank. In return, Chastellux remained linked to the Avallonnais, and it seems reasonable to suppose the recognition of Chastellux's historical links with Burgundy played a large part in the decision. Moreover, the traditional bonds between Quarré, the only important town in the earldom, and the castle obviously affected people's ideas; the local nobility had every interest in preserving the unity of a territory over which they still exercised hegemony. We have no evidence regarding the negotiations which led to the formation of the canton of Quarré. All we know is that Saint-Germain, which was not included in the Yonne in a map drawn on 13 January 1790, was nevertheless brought within the department because of its position on the right bank of the Cure. The same principle prevailed when Marigny-l'Eglise and Saint-André-en-Morvan were included in the department of the Nièvre though they themselves would have preferred to remain within the district of Avallon.

Thus the canton was born: its shape and the establishment of its boundaries were not entirely free of political considerations. A deep-rooted local tradition was taken into account: namely the existence and the importance on the one hand of the castle, and on the other, of the town. The inhabitants of Quarré have been free since 1554. Yet the memory of their subordination to the Chastellux still remains even today. The inhabitants of the hamlets on the edge of the manorial forest remember that their ancestors, soldiers who fought with Olivier de Chastellux, received from him cultivated lands on condition that they cleared them, built their houses, paid a tax to the Counts and took part in guard duty at the castle. These original settlers put down roots in the Thiérache, and their descendants still flaunt this ancient link with the castle, as if it conferred on them a touch of nobility. A common history links the 'woodlanders', as the people of Quarré call them, living on the least suitable land in the commune for rearing livestock, to the Chastellux. The landed property of these great landowners consists primarily of forest, and the inhabitants of the hamlets on the edge have had confrontations at times with their powerful neighbour. From time to time there have been disputes between the noble family and a population anxious to exercise freely their ancient grazing right and rights of use.

On their return from emigration, the Chastellux family recovered the pre-eminent position they had previously occupied in the Avallonnais. The castle and its lands had been sold as the property of the State during the Revolution, but the Count's faithful steward, Etienne Doullay, bought them for the respective sums of 4,550 and 8,589 francs. Back in France in 1810, the heir to the name, Henri-Georges-César, recovered all his property and placed his sword at the service of the monarchy: although promoted to brigadier during the Peninsular War, M. de Chastellux did not neglect his responsibilities at home. He was president of the electoral college of the Yonne, and was elected deputy for the department in 1820, a position which he retained until the events of 1830. The Count remained faithful to the elder branch of the royal family, so from that date onwards he devoted his time to the restoration of his castle and the upkeep of a domain which extended over 1,500 hectares in the canton and included 5,000 hectares of woodland. Henri-César and his nephew the Marquis Amédée, who were the wealthiest men in the Avallonnais, remained aloof from local political life until 1848: the Marquis at that time became mayor of his commune and member of the General Council. The seizure of power by Louis-Napoléon Bonaparte marked a turning-point in relations between the Legitimists of the Yonne, who had hitherto supported the party of order represented by the Prince-President, and the latter's Bonapartist supporters. Chastellux condemned the coup d'état and as mayor refused to publish the government's proclamations. The sub-prefect rapidly took steps against the Legitimist resistance: having suppressed the departmental newspaper, *L'Yonne*, he revoked Chastellux's functions as mayor. This initiative on the part of the sub-prefect was backed by a massive yes from the Avallonnais to the plebiscite of 20 December 1852.[15]

In the cantonal elections of 1852, the Legitimist candidate in Avallon chose to stand down in favour of a republican in order to defeat the government candidate. The Marquis de Chastellux found himself standing in the constituency of Quarré against a landowner from Saint-Germain, Houdaille, who though an Orleanist, was favoured by the sub-prefect. The latter tried to influence the Justice of the Peace in favour of his candidate. More seriously, irregularities occurred in the voting: the number of slips found in the ballot-boxes was higher than the number of votes. In the end, Houdaille and Chastellux were found to have an equal number of votes. Nevertheless, Houdaille was declared the winner. In his correspondence with the prefecture, however, the sub-prefect, Amelin, recognises the unreliability of the result. On the one hand he attributes to the Marquis considerable influence over the peasants. This was based on his position as the owner of large forests who could therefore control not only access to the woods for purposes of right of use and pasture, but also activities related to the timber trade, such as the recovery of logs floated down the first part of the river and their transformation into rafts or loading on barges for transportation to Paris. On the other hand the sub-prefect admits that the election was 'doubtful' and worries about the possible political uses that may be made of this somewhat 'artificial' result.[16]

The Marquis was not slow to respond with an appeal to the Council of State. The election result was annulled, to the great displeasure of the local administration. At the new election, M. de Chastellux recovered his seat, and the population of Quarré fêted him in triumph.

Singing and festivities were organised; one of M. de Chastellux's agents even came to ask the mayor to ring the church bells, a request which the mayor promptly refused. A deputation of young girls presented a basket of flowers to M. de

Chastellux, and paid him a compliment in verse. The Justice of the Peace's daughter was one of those presenting the basket. The Justice admitted as much today, but alleges in his defence that he only found out afterwards about his daughter's role. It is unlikely that he was unaware of it before. The presence of his daughter made a dreadful impression

writes Amelin, with no attempt to conceal his bitterness.[17]

This episode demonstrates quite clearly the durability of the relationship linking the peasants to the lord of the manor. Situated within the administrative unit of the constituency, the castle remained its political centre, and the representative of the government failed in his efforts to take control of the situation. After the premature death of the Count in 1857, no other member of the Chastellux family would ever occupy any official position of any importance again. All traces of Legitimism seem to disappear gradually after the eventual election of Houdaille to the General Council in 1885. Houdaille, with an income of 25,000 francs, was held to be 'devoted to the government'. 'A straightforward and honest character', the sub-prefect's note continues, 'and always zealous in the interests of the canton'. In 1855, the Count of Chastellux had a lawyer, Petitier-Chomaille, elected to the *arrondissement* council in preference to the outgoing candidate, but as the sub-prefect indicated at the time: 'M. Petitier-Chomaille's candidacy is in no way a political act: it is nothing more than a power-struggle between himself and M. Mary, also a lawyer in Quarré and the son-in-law of M. Chatelain, the outgoing councillor.'[18] The decline of Legitimism was not therefore halted by the councillor for the *arrondissement*, whom in any case we find twenty years later as mayor of Quarré and a republican.

The activities of Henry-César and his nephew Médée were not, however, without consequences: one act in particular greatly affected the political future of the canton. In order to increase his domain, the Count had bought some forests within the commune of Saint-Léger. In 1844, Father Muard, who was looking for a site to build a monastery, was captivated by the spot. The Chastellux family made him a gift of fifteen acres of woodland, where the different living quarters and sacred buildings of the Abbey were subsequently built. The spiritual influence of the Abbey in the region was soon considerable. 'The Abbey of La-Pierre-qui-Vire arouses great interest throughout the area. This institution produces very distinguished preachers. The very strict rule followed by the monks earns them great respect. They confine themselves exclusively to their duties', remarks the sub-prefect who at the same period was expressing mistrust of other religious institutions of this kind, such as the Saint Vincent de Paul Society.[19] The fact none the less remains that the establishment in the commune of a monastic enclave, symbolic of the alliance between the throne and the altar, and the arrival of a group of outside missionaries could not be received with indifference. It had the marks of a feudal imposition, and was a potential source of trouble in a peasant community that prized its independence.

As it happens, the political stability of the surrounding communes does not seem to have been affected, to judge by the remarkable durability of its mayors: Santigny in Saint-Brancher from 1848 to 1869, Tripier in Saint-Léger from 1840 to 1870 and Petitier-Chomaille in Quarré from 1860 to 1875. However, this long period of calm was to give way to some very different events which we must retrace: in them we will see the emergence of the main ideological oppositions and the corresponding networks which were to govern the political life of the canton from then on.

Two notorious affairs

On 9 October 1871, the mayor of Saint-Léger wrote to the schools inspector to tell him that Mlle Giraud intended to open a girls' school in his commune.[20] This school would be housed either at the town hall, at that point on the edge of completion, or at the boys' school. An apparently trivial announcement, but one which provoked a violent reaction from the administration. On 2 November, the sub-prefect and the schools inspector went to Saint-Léger and saw that the girls' school was already open, in disregard of the one-month delay prescribed by law. The two government officials noted a certain number of irregularities: the public notice was incomplete, the premises (a private house) did not correspond to the premises mentioned in the notice, and the latter was on public display, not at the town hall, but on the shutters of the mayor's house. However, the main reason for the officials' anger was the avowed nature of the plans of Mlle Giraud and Truchot, the mayor. Education had been provided previously by nuns: now, the municipal council, in a resolution accepted some days previously, was declaring its intention of replacing the nuns with a lay teacher. The prefect had asked the mayor to postpone action until the law on public education, then in preparation, was voted on in the National Assembly. The mayor had not complied, hence the administration's rapid response.

The visitors, that is, the sub-prefect and the schools inspector, were given a cool reception, to say the least. '[Mlle Giraud is] the daughter of a man with a bad reputation . . . she does not go to church and does not practise her faith.' The writer of these words, the sub-prefect, makes no attempt to disguise his antipathy to the schoolmistress: 'She had admitted to me', the official adds, 'that in opening an independent school, her aim was to get the nuns out of the village, and that once her aim had been achieved she would hand over to someone else.'[21] True enough, a few weeks later 'Mlle

Giraud's independent school' became the village school and quite simply replaced the religious school. That autumn of 1871, a rumour went round the canton that the schoolmistress was connected to Protestants. Had not the minister from Avallon given a lecture at Saint-Léger? When the school was moved to new premises in the town hall by the mayor, the priest's supporters did not hide their discontent. 'Insults and some blows were exchanged between the so-called Catholics and Protestants', the police sergeant who was sent to the spot records in his report.[22]

Faced with the mayor's intransigence and the tensions among the population, the authorities dropped their conciliatory attitude. Truchot was suspended for a time: he had behaved in a highly disrespectful way towards the officials on their visit to Saint-Léger. 'Amongst other compliments, he accused us of wanting to ruin the commune, and called us lackeys of the rich. He went so far as to say, in response to some remarks of mine, that we could be bought with a dinner.'[23] The sub-prefect could not help suspecting that the mayor was under the influence of Mlle Giraud's father, who was one of the village's councillors.

A few years went by; in 1877 the newspapers carried reports of a spectacular scandal in Saint-Léger-Vauban. Republican cartoonists had a field day with the exploits of a certain 'Sister Burn Bum' who was reported to sow terror in the village households. It was alleged that she had punished two of her pupils by making them sit down on a white-hot stove. One of the girls was said to be badly burned. The sub-prefect, following an inquiry, decided to dismiss the nun, Sister St Léon, but the municipal council of Saint-Léger and the mayor got up a petition, signed by eighty-six parents, questioning the allegations. They stressed the good qualities which the nun had displayed for twenty years in her care of the children. The prefect responded by stripping the mayor, Marchand, of his functions, accusing him of having wilfully understated the facts: he had not only denied the gravity of the burns, but had written to the newspapers.[24] In no time the department was agog with the affair, which very soon took a political turn.

There were questions in the Chamber of Deputies, and an official inquiry was set up: the Radicals vigorously denounced the barbarity of the pro-clerical faction. The conservative press used the results of the government inquiry, which finally concluded that the burns were not serious, to denounce the republican adversaries' libellous use of ill-founded accusations. 'As we see, the Radicals have once again wasted their time', remarked *Le Pays*. Marchand wrote to the Prime Minister protesting that he never got involved in politics, and was not even sympathetic to the conservatives. He also accused the sub-prefect of persecuting him for no reason and remarked that the latter seemed curiously unconcerned by the mysterious deaths of children in care, of which there had recently been many in Saint-Léger.[25] When he learned of Marchand's letter to the Prime

Minister, the sub-prefect counter-attacked; once more he drew attention the statements taken by the police, an inquiry by the inspectors for children in care, and 'Sister St Léon's confession'.[26]

It would appear that the sub-prefect's missive did not convince the authorities, for the decree stripping the mayor of his functions was annulled in October 1877 and Marchand took up office again. Admittedly, in the mean time the Ministry of the Interior had changed hands, and the mayor felt free to express his real feelings. 'All true conservatives', he wrote to the Minister, 'are anxious to see me reinstated as mayor, and are very surprised that this act of justice and atonement has not yet taken place.'[27]

These tumultuous events in the commune of Saint-Léger should be seen in the wider context of the establishment of the Republic in the ten years that followed the war of 1870. The problem of the relationship between Church and State had developed into a major political debate. At governmental level, the struggle between conservatives and republicans had not yet been resolved in favour of the latter. The local representatives of the State (prefects, sub-prefects and schools inspectors) therefore followed successive contradictory political tendencies, but this did not prevent them from exercising detailed control over mayors, who were appointed and could be dismissed at the discretion of the government. In the two affairs described, the schools question, to which both the population and their representatives were particularly sensitive, produced a different reaction. In the case of the plan for a lay school, the prefect's attitude, initially one of wait and see, was rapidly transformed into resolute opposition. On the other hand, in the affair of Sister St Léon, the administration made no secret of its aversion for clerical institutions; yet conservatism was strong enough to offer the mayor of Saint-Léger unexpected reinstatement.

Confronted with vigorous interventionism from the administration, elected representatives revealed their political identity. Truchot proferred insults, and Marchand petitioned the Prime Minister and publicised the disagreement in the newspapers: the methods differ, but in both cases we have a mayor refusing to back down. Their attitude is very different from the passivity of the mayors of the canton during the Second Empire. However, the change should not be attributed to the events of 1870 and the country people's re-encounter with the Republic. Truchot's fierce anti-clericalism had more precise motives. The Abbey of La-Pierre-qui-Vire had been growing steadily over the previous twenty years. More than the activities of the village priest, the presence of the monks was for the mayor and the people he represented a symbol of conservatism, the ideology of 'the rich'. The monastery only existed, after all, by virtue of the will of the Chastellux family; it was a living reminder of an unjust order resented by many.

The attitude of the municipal council in 1871 marked the beginnings of a conflict which was to last for more than half a century between on the one hand the monks of La-Pierre-qui-Vire, who were citizens and voters in Saint-Léger, and their supporters, and on the other that section of the population antagonistic to pro-clerical ideas. The second 'affair', the one which caused such agitation in 1877, should be seen against the background of the visceral hatred between the two camps. Marchand had been appointed mayor three years earlier, at a time when anti-clericalists were still suspect. The incarnation of conservatism, he was the man chosen by the monks, the only guarantors of his legitimacy. Yet though the political winds seemed at the time to turn in favour of the dismissed mayor, his victory turned out to be shortlived. At the 1878 elections, Marchand disappeared from the scene to be replaced by a team favourable to the Radicals.

This ferment in local politics was not confined to the commune of Saint-Léger. However, the republican breakthrough required more effort in the surrounding areas.

Although republicanism won out in the villages at the beginning of the 1880s, it did not put an end to conflict, which from then on would pit Radicals against moderates. The political life of the department would be marked by the rivalry between Flandin, representing the moderates, and Gallot, the proprietor of the newspaper *L'Yonne* and a supporter of Radical ideas. In a pamphlet dated 5 August 1883, the Democratic Republican Cantonal Committee, formed on the occasion of the cantonal elections, picked up the national programme of the Radicals, which called for the revision of the constitution with a view to abolishing the Senate and above all separating Church and State. The same document gives the minutes of a meeting at which the committee decided not to support the candidacy of the lawyer Chevillotte, mayor of Quarré, to the seat on the General Council but to present their president, a doctor from the town. We should note, incidentally, that the mayor of Saint-Léger was among the Democratic Republican candidates in the *arrondissement* ballot.

There is no need to linger on the results of these different elections, but simply to note that they were all favourable to the moderates. The mayor of Quarré became a member of the General Council; a few years later his assistant mayor joined the *arrondissement* council. Both were regularly confirmed in their respective mandates. The limited influence of Radicalism in the canton of Quarré reflects the state of opinion in the Avallonnais at large. As the sub-prefect wrote in 1970: 'The usual thing is to say that the Avallonnais is a little Switzerland, but the political temper of its inhabitants makes it more like a little Vendée.'[28] This situation was due to three principal causes: the area was relatively cut off from outside influences, there were internal quarrels in the Radical camp, and the pro-clerical faction pursued an active campaign of propaganda. The administration, henceforth flying the lay flag, found itself isolated:

The action of the administration is of necessity limited, because the population are quite comfortable: the people of Avallon have no need of anything and ask for nothing . . . This ambiguous situation is complicated further by the horror instinctively felt by the population for anything that comes from outside. Thus the officials form a separate social group in Avallon, and are scarcely integrated with the native population.[29]

The general impression of conservatism one receives from a reading of the electoral results must, however, be qualified. An analysis of the political situation in each of the municipalities sheds a different light on the subject and shows up some important contrasts. In two communes, Quarré and Saint-Germain, the most densely populated in the canton, the moderate camp held sway and was in power for long periods. In Saint-Germain, the year 1889 saw the instatement as mayor of Médéric Devoir, who had beaten a Bonapartist. However, in Bussières and Sainte-Magnance, neighbouring communes in the Côte-d'Or, the Radical option became established in the last decade of the century. The same holds true for the commune of Chastellux, whose inhabitants were to prefer a Radical candidate to the Count in the municipal elections of 1912. Ancient peasant reflexes of resistance to the supremacy of the nobility prevailed over another deep-rooted tradition whereby the heir to the castle and its lands tended to inherit the office of mayor also.

The communes of Saint-Brancher and Saint-Léger offer a less clear-cut situation. In the former, the Radicals predominated for about twenty years. A Radical mayor was chosen in 1900, and this tendency was to prevail until the end of the First World War. Saint-Brancher went in precisely the opposite direction: the conservatives who had been in the majority ever since the institution of the Republic were succeeded in 1902 by a Radical team led by a man closely allied with the deputy Gallot. The new mayor, Boijard, was re-elected without exception until his death in 1929, at which point the moderates took the lead again.

In looking at the nuances of local political opinion in the canton of Quarré, we cannot, of course, ignore sociological factors. On the one hand we have an area characterised by small-scale holding of poor-quality land on the edge of forest – this would include the communes of Bussières, Saint-Léger and Chastellux – and on the other, part of the territory of Saint-Brancher and Quarré, which was land more suitable for stock-breeding and farming and where the holdings were medium-sized and in some cases large: Saint-Germain, the north of Quarré, and Villiers-Nonain, one of the hamlets of Saint-Brancher, are examples of this situation. Applying the theories of André Siegfried, one could establish a relationship between these landholding profiles and the dominant currents of thought. Thus one would see a parallel between the distribution of land and the political tenor of an area, the first type of area described corresponding, as we have seen, to the Radical tendency, and the second to the moderate. Moreover, the growth of a commercial petty bourgeoisie in Quarré, a commercial centre situated on the edge of the Morvan, favoured the development of a staunch conservatism. The two successive mayors of this town were also to occupy the seat on the General Council until the Second World War. The overall moderate vote in the canton reflected to some extent the demographic weight of the Quarré-Saint-Germain-Villiers-Nonain axis and the preponderant influence of certain social groups, based on ownership of land or success in certain walks of life such as shopkeeping and the liberal professions.

While a right/left split and its economic and sociological basis can be seen here without too much difficulty, we must not forget the more delicate, but to my mind equally fundamental, issue of the stabilization of these categories, the ways in which they become an everyday feature of local politics. The statement that there is a link between politics and social and economic data is insufficient to explain the way things work at a local level to determine how people identify with what to the outside observer looks like a 'political ideology', but to the people involved feels more like belonging to a 'family' or at the very most to a vague political territory: 'more or less left wing', 'a bit of a right-winger' – these are the terms people favour. The opposition between moderates and Radicals was embodied from the beginning in networks. Certain names were to leave an indelible mark on the century, and certain families were to emerge whose direct descendants and allies are still prominent in local political life.

Some key figures

In 1902, Alfred Boijard, a member of the municipal council of Saint-Brancher, on which he represented the hamlet of Auxon, was elected mayor of the commune, following the resignation of Germain Santigny. Santigny had indicated his divergence some time earlier from the views of the other municipal councillors by abstaining on a motion to congratulate the Combes government on its energetic struggle against the pro-clericals.[30] Santigny's successor, on the contrary, embodied the new ideas: born in 1864, Boijard was appointed teacher at Saint-Brancher, and subsequently decided to settle there. He had developed an enthusiasm for politics early in life, and had acted as secretary to the Radical deputy Gallot before coming to live in the canton. He was said to be a freemason, and he himself avowed his attachment to republican principles. A few years later, the future mayor left the teaching profession; he subsequently sold grain and wine and even wood on occasion. He lived in the hamlet of Auxon. Politics remained the real focus of his interest. In 1898, he stood for the *arrondissement* council as a Radical, to annoy the moderates.

Boijard was beaten on that occasion, and was never to succeed in politics beyond the level of the commune. Nevertheless, he had a very real influence on the Radical current of thought in the Avallonnais. In 1923 he was president of the left-wing cartel for the department of the Yonne. He was therefore the natural choice as the cartel's candidate in the general election in 1924. Once more his hopes were dashed; yet Boijard did not abandon his local responsibilities. Re-elected mayor in 1925, he remained in office until his death in 1927. His son succeeded him on the municipal council and a few years later became mayor himself. The son seems to have been less fanatical about politics; he owned a threshing-machine and hired out his services to farmers, and as a young man, he also played the fiddle at local dances.

So the Boijard family occupied a prominent place for half a century, yet their fellow-citizens had mixed feelings about them. A reading of the election results shows that Boijard usually got just enough votes and no more, even in his own hamlet. It is true that Saint-Brancher had a curious voting system. Voting was by sections, each corresponding to one or more hamlets. I had some difficulty discovering the origin of this division. Some of my informants claimed that it went all the way back to the Revolution, and others alleged that as mayor, Boijard had invented this system to carve out an electorally reliable territory for himself. However, both these versions proved inaccurate: the creation of the sections did take place long after the Revolution, but it was not the work of the Radical mayor. As far back as 1841, Villiers-Nonain was demanding division into sections. At that time the sub-prefect rejected the demand, despite the fact that it conformed to article 45 of the law of 21 March 1837, because he considered it unnecessary: according to him, the voters of Saint-Brancher had decided the number of councillors appropriate to the population of each hamlet on their own initiative. But Villiers-Nonain returned to the attack and finally achieved the creation of two electoral sections; Saint-Brancher-Auxon and Villiers-Nonain. All this happened in 1880: two years later, a third section came into being at the request of the hamlet of Auxon, which was anxious to display its own political profile.

The division into sections made official a political cleavage which was already very ancient, between Villiers-Nonain – whose conservative tendencies were mentioned earlier – and Saint-Brancher, where an impoverished peasantry displayed a fierce anti-clericalism. Auxon fluctuated between these two extremes. People say that Boijard was sometimes obliged to have himself elected in the section of Saint-Brancher, where he owned some fields, to keep his mandate as mayor. He certainly had to play very skilfully on the opposition between the interior hamlets and the more prosperous area to obtain a majority on the municipal council. Boijard's stance, atheistic and pro-republican, was in strong contrast to the Catholic and conservative beliefs of the Santignys, the wealthy landowning family from Villiers-Nonain from whose ranks the Radical mayor's predecessor had come. Léon Santigny, the heir to the name, was later to succeed Boijard's son as mayor of the commune. The contrast between these two families is revealing: they represent the two opposite poles between which the voters of Saint-Brancher swung. Moreover, Boijard's career seems to me to afford a good example of the way republican ideas made inroads into the countryside through the agency of schoolteachers from outside, with all the ambiguity that implied: while they were acknowledged for their culture, Boijard's family nevertheless remained outsiders to some extent, no doubt because of their links with an urban political network and a taste for new ideas which marked them out from the conformism of the surrounding culture. Boijard was in fact the first to buy a steam-driven thresher. Later, his daughter married a man both of whose parents had been brought up in an orphanage, and who in turn became the mayor of Saint-Branchard.

A comparison can be made between Boijard, this early example of an 'urban drop-out', and another important figure in local Radical politics: Achille Collas, the mayor of Saint-Léger. Here we have a completely different situation: Collas was a small farmer, who seems not to have been driven by any political ambition. All his life, he fought but one battle. His enemy: the monks of La-Pierre-qui-Vire, whose presence was a daily reminder of the intrusion of religion into the life of the village. Some very old people who knew him describe him as irascible, and even violent. This picture is confirmed on reading the motions passed by the municipal council during his time as mayor and written in his own hand: Collas has not left behind him the memory of a man in love with ideological subtleties. He chose his side and waxed indignant according to a few black-and-white principles. He was a member of the republican camp from an early age; his family origins no doubt played a part in this. His grandfather was appointed teacher in Saint-Léger, and settled down in the commune; his father was a wine merchant.

We find here some similarity with Boijard's history. The typical Radical politician was not a countryman through and through. Although he was a farmer, Collas did not inherit land; hence, perhaps, he had a clearer sense of the hardships which pressed on the small-scale peasantry. Some time after his election, the municipal council took advantage of a failed assassination attempt on Emile Loubet to vote on a significant motion:

> The members of the municipal council of Saint-Léger-Vauban wish to express to Monsieur Loubet, President of the Republic, their outrage at the cowardly attempt

on his life at Auteil. They hope that the government will take all necessary measures to defeat the efforts of the clerico-monarchic faction to overthrow the Republic.[31]

The message is clear: for Collas and his friends at the turn of the century, the Republic was in danger. The mayor was a man with a mission: to hound the monks constantly and to maintain an atmosphere of political tension. This attitude seems to have palled at times on the inhabitants of Saint-Léger, for Collas's municipal career includes as many electoral setbacks as it does successes: he lost his mandate as mayor in the 1900 elections; re-elected councillor in 1904, he was beaten in 1908, then elected again in 1912. He did not return to the town hall until 1921, when he led a fierce campaign against the reinstatement of the monks at La-Pierre-que-Vire. However, the Abbey flourished once more; the mayor was to oppose without success the inclusion of the monks in the electoral rolls. The year 1929 marked a decisive turning-point: Collas's list was beaten by a team led by Dr Chevillotte, son of the former mayor of Quarré, and a wine merchant. Subsequent ballots confirmed the doctor in office. Collas retired in 1935, leaving his son to head the Radical lists; but that list was soundly defeated. The moderate tendency was thereafter in the majority at Quarré. It might seem that the Collas family had definitively left the local political scene, but it was not so. Many years after, in 1983, the election of M. Richard, husband of a granddaughter of the Radical mayor, was interpreted in the village as a sort of posthumous revenge. The new mayor was seen as the heir to the legitimacy long enjoyed by his ancestor by marriage.

Collas in Saint-Léger, Boijard in Saint-Brancher: at first glance it looks as though each commune produced its political leaders separately. That would fit with the 'parish pump' spirit displayed by the inhabitants of the different villages. Most people do not know the names of the municipal councillors of the neighbouring communes, 'and don't want to know', as one man assured me. And yet, we have seen that as far back as 1883 there was a Democratic Republican Committee which coordinated local initiatives; there were therefore regular contacts between the members of the committee. Links were created, or existing links strengthened, between families from different villages. Apart from the meetings in Quarré, the Collas family visited the Truchots, and they also had friends in Chastellux and Saint-Brancher, particularly a teacher from that commune, M. Fabureau, a close friend of Boijard. The fact is that the Truchot family was the centre of a vast political network.

For more than half a century the Truchots and the Rostains were the two families who dominated public life in Quarré: Ferdinand Rostain, who represented the moderate tendency in the wake of the lawyer Chevillotte, climbed the rungs of the ladder of electoral politics without any great difficulty. Originally assistant mayor, he succeeded the mayor on his death in 1908. He was constantly re-elected mayor of Quarré and member of the General Council until his death in 1939, when his son Maurice replaced him at the head of the municipal council and on the General Council. Maurice continued as mayor throughout the war years. Like many elected representatives who lived through those troubled times, he was brushed aside after the war. The history of the Rostain family is one of economic prosperity as the reward of hard work. One of their ancestors, originally from the Alps, and a pedlar, like many migrants from that area, settled in the Côte-d'Or. His son moved to Quarré, where he set up a timber business, then extended his activities to the grain and wine trade. The business flourished, and Ferdinand, son of the founder, became one of the first suppliers of chemical fertilisers in the Morvan. He thus became one of the biggest grain and wine merchants in the region, and a leading figure in the town of Quarré.

Facing Rostain was Louis Truchot, the driving spirit behind the Radical opposition: like the mayor, Truchot was a wine and grain merchant, but he came from a long line of farmers. His father and his cousin had sat on the council before him. Elected in turn in 1904, Truchot was to be a municipal councillor until the elections of 1912, when he suffered a setback: he then regained his seat in 1919 and was re-elected in 1925. After an initial defeat, he was voted on to the *arrondissement* council in 1919, where he remained as the canton's representative until his death in 1931. Truchot's brand of Radicalism was more flexible than that of a Boijard or a Collas. Thus we find him appearing twice, once in 1908 and again in 1929, on a list headed by Rostain. It is true that in 1908, just for the period of the ballot, Rostain had no hesitation in borrowing the label of Radical. Four years later, the men had separated again, and this time Truchot presented his own list.

The candidate's manifestoes set out to be rigorously apolitical: 'First of all we declare that we will clearly separate politics from administrative matters. When it comes to the interests of the commune, party politics should be left aside and personal rivalries forgotten.'[32] But the tone quickly turned polemical again; 'Our candidates' sole aim is to allow you to choose, and not have imposed on you, the men you want to take charge of your affairs.'[33] The outgoing mayor's response was biting:

> If you want to continue to be represented by men freely chosen from among yourselves, vote for us. If, on the other hand, you would rather be led by outsiders who despise you, who refer to you in public as 'those damned people from the Morvan' . . . vote for our rivals. Only M. Truchot is unable to follow his colleagues' example . . . Outside influences take precedence over his personal wishes and desires. We profoundly regret this tyrannical interference; we regret it for his sake and the sake of the spirit of unity which should guide us.[34]

The outgoing mayor's statement seems to have convinced the voters, for Truchot was defeated. Re-elected after the war, his Radical list suffered a stinging defeat in 1925, so four years later he made common cause with the mayor and thus returned to the municipal council. On his death in 1931, his brother Arsène succeeded him as municipal councillor and member of the *arrondissement* council. Professing a more moderate Radicalism, he swapped the label of Radical-Socialist for that of Social Republican at the elections to the *arrondissement* council in 1934. On the eve of war, Arsène died and his son was in turn elected to the municipal council. That same year, as we saw, Ferdinand Rostain died and his son Maurice became mayor. But there the parallel ends. The political destinies of the two families were reversed after the Liberation: the Rostain family faded out as the Truchot family rose. Georges Truchot was elected to the General Council in 1945, and became mayor in 1947; he classed himself as an 'Independent Socialist'. Without betraying his family's Radical links, he seems to have been interested above all in running the municipality efficiently. His administration of the commune was thus inspired by the same principles which had previously guided Rostain.

Was this 'irresistible rise' of the Truchot family based on its private property? Or was it due to the individual charisma of some of its members? According to the information I gathered, none of the Truchots seems to have made any great impression on his fellow-citizens; certainly the Truchots, like many other farmers, did make quite a bit of money and increased their lands. But this development seems to have taken place after George Truchot's period in the town hall, from 1947 to 1965. From the sociological point of view, the situation of the Truchot family before that is interesting. Apart from the family farm, a grain and wine business was passed down the generations until the beginning of the 1960s. In this way the family stood at the crossroads of two dominant professional activities in Quarré: commerce and agriculture. Obviously such a position is a strategic one in a chief town like Quarré, where the main businesses in the area are located. It is significant that Louis Truchot's main political rival, the mayor and member of the General Council Rostain, should also be a grain and wine merchant. This profession constitutes an excellent base from which to act as mediator between the different social groups and attain a position in local politics.

However, the Truchot family's success in politics can be seen from another point of view, particularly if we turn our attention to the family tree. If we look first of all at the marriages contracted by certain members of the family group, we find that Arsène Truchot, the father of Georges, was married to Achille Collas's sister. So the two families, who saw each other regularly and shared the same political ideas, cemented these links by a marriage. Similarly Fabureau, the schoolteacher from Saint-Brancher, exalter of lay ideas and another intimate of Truchot, married Louise, a sister of Arsène. Let us turn to more remote ancestors. The Truchot forebears were from Saint-Léger. At the end of the nineteenth century, Charles settled in Quarré; but Joseph, the son of Charles's uncle, remained, unlike his cousin Michel, in Saint-Léger. He was a municipal councillor in this commune for years, then became mayor in 1871. This particular Truchot was the obstinate supporter of lay schooling who confronted the schools inspector and the sub-prefect.

Eligibility and networks

Let us return now to the present: the name Truchot, as we saw, reappeared in 1983 in local public life. We can now readily appreciate how at the end of such a long family chain the 'independent' candidature of the young Jean-Philippe at the municipal elections came as no surprise to the voters in Quarré. It is by no means certain that the young man himself was aware of the weight of this history. 'The past is past', he seemed to imply, and my inquiries must have given him food for thought, since he claimed to be proposing to 'change things'. However, as far as his fellow-citizens were concerned, he first stood out as eligible because he belonged to a respected family.

The reason why this family can thus regularly produce eligible candidates is that it occupies a particular position in the centre of a web of threads which goes beyond the strict limits of the commune. It then comes as something of a surprise to hear people exalting the commune as a unit, and claiming that their horizons are limited to the 'village' or the 'town', for it is clear that as genealogical memory drifts back through time, it recalls links forged many years ago between families who hold positions of power in their respective communes. The gap between the image of a local political life evolving entirely within the limits of municipal territory and the more complex reality of networks occupying a much larger area deserves some thought: for, more than individual qualities, it is the link with a network, whether direct, as in the case of Jean-Philippe Truchot, or through marriage, as in the case of M. Richard, that determines a candidate's credibility and, even more, his election. It seems that even before the election, and whatever its outcome, the claims of certain candidates to occupy municipal posts are accepted as legitimate by their fellow-citizens.

For the observer, this legitimisation of power is the most remarkable aspect of the question. That certain families should monopolise local offices over time is seen by people as a factor conducive to the perpetuation of a coherent and harmonious order, an oasis of peace in a time of agitation and worry. When my informants 'talked politics', they never, of course, referred overtly to these networks which make election possible; they simply recalled anecdotes about the families of the councillors and the opinions they were believed to hold. And yet there persisted amid the tranquillity of a willed apoliticism an undisguised interest in electoral rivalries, a continuing antagonism, whose roots lay in the last few decades of the nineteenth century. The assignation of roles and the broad lines of the script have hardly varied since then. The ideological ferment has gone, but allegiances have grown stronger; links of friendship, strategic marriages, mutual help in agricultural tasks all help to strengthen political networks which cross the frontiers between communes.

I have been stressing elements of continuity. Does that mean that we are looking at a reassuringly bucolic picture of rural France? The reality is much more complex, as this plunge into local history has clearly shown. The political links which give rise to networks are rooted in a precise historical situation. There are certain key events, such as the bitter confrontation between Church and State which marked the beginnings of the Third Republic. At times like these, certain personalities emerge, and to some extent 'take power'. They influence others, pass round new ideas, bring people together and create networks. These people, the Collas, the Truchots, the Rostains and the rest, play a vital role: they embody significant changes, and interrupt the reign of traditional ideas. In short, they create new notions of legitimacy; they disappear, and passions subside, but they have founded families and in so doing have created dynasties of eligible candidates. Beyond Quarré, the history of the department shows the same traits: there are moments of drama and long periods of quiet. Dramatic moments are the period just mentioned and later the Resistance and the Liberation, when new people and new allegiances appear. Periods of calm are the times when oppositions seem to blur, when people co-exist more easily: for example, the time we saw Truchot and Rostain managing municipal affairs in harness, which did not prevent the former emerging later as the obvious alternative when the latter was swept away by the force of events.

In stressing that eligibility is a quality derived essentially from family relations, we must now, however, underestimate the importance of the individual actors, those we have already met and others we will encounter later, and who each in his own way plays a part in this story. One of the great privileges of the anthropologist is that he bases his analysis on the observation of social phenomena, but above all on constant conversations with other human beings. To say that local political networks exist, therefore, is not to point to fixed entities which determine the actions of individuals. On the contrary, everything seems to indicate that these networks are extremely malleable, and the changes they have undergone in the course of history show signs of being the work of particular individuals who are sometimes difficult to identify. It would be more helpful, therefore, to talk about a continuous process of integration of the protagonists into the networks and a mutual interaction between the two. The anthropologist's task is precisely to describe this double process of integration and interaction. It is his job to pinpoint links which are not necessarily explicit, or even conscious, but which connect the players on the local political stage: links which may be completely of our time, but which from another angle can be seen as rooted in diachronic time and demand from the researcher a detour through a blurred and hazy history. The anthropologist works like a beaver: he must accumulate a large amount of information through oral testimonies and observation of political activity, he must keep an eye on current affairs and must burrow in some rather dusty archives. The work can seem unrewarding, its outcome uncertain. Yet to my mind it affords the surest means of reconstructing the true origins of things which appear natural and obvious, such as the position within a hierarchy and therefore the local 'power' of an individual, and even of a whole family.

Since I am venturing into some rather general considerations, I would like to make one last point before I describe the next stage of the research, the initial outlines of which have already been sketched. My immersion in the political life of a canton seemed to me to throw light on two characteristics of the French political system. First was the existence of a web of relationships which was deployed in the context of traditional constituencies, but was not confined to them; it was affiliation to one of these networks which, as we saw, guaranteed access to political office. Second, I noticed the discriminating function of memory, which allowed people to locate each candidate spontaneously, despite his air of apoliticism, in relation to older political cleavages; here we are in the realm of the implicit, or even the unconscious. The excitement one observed at the time of the municipal elections was essentially related to the reactivation of these clues, which offered the surest means of locating each individual, whether a lone candidate or the head of a party list. Although I am an anthropologist, I had had to become a historian for a time, put on my detective's hat and follow the clues back to the moment of conflict which had shaped the political life of the canton for close on a century.

2

Dynasties

In exploring the political life of a rural canton, I had discovered networks with surprising ramifications, at least for a non-specialist. I had been able to reconstruct the origins of these networks far back in the history of the Republic. But I felt this journey back in time was not enough: I now had to take the measure of the networks. I had been given instances of bonds linking elected representatives belonging to neighbouring villages; I had also been told of political figures whose influence reached out to the whole of the department. In order to draw a complete map of the system, I had to follow all its meanderings, leaving Quarré-les-Tombes, and drifting gently towards other regions, trying to envisage other possible links. I was curious, though unsure where such a journey might lead. I had already observed certain oppositions: when I was at Quarré, people were always going on about the Morvan. On my visits to Auxerre also, I had been told: 'Remember you are working in the Morvan; it's a very closed area, different from other places . . . Nothing much has ever happened there.' The people I talked to would often extol the beauty of the Morvan landscape: 'But we don't get there often; it's so far away!'

To my friends in Auxerre, it was at least perfectly understandable that one should practise anthropology in such an isolated area. There were local customs which were certainly worth studying. Later, when I popped up again in the town with the firm intention of pursuing my researches there, they were rather surprised. Anthropology was something they associated with other people, peasants in outlying areas. In fact all I had been doing in Quarré was taking a close look at local politics. The Morvan is less cut off than it might appear to be from the viewpoint of the Icaunais, as the people of the Yonne are known. Surprisingly, although everyone says disparagingly that this granitic region is still living in the Middle Ages, it seems to be a favourite spot for some very high-ranking politicians. Not so long ago, the deputy for the part of the Morvan situated in the department of the

Nièvre was a certain François Mitterrand. Château-Chinon remains to this day one of the key places in the presidential epic. Of course, it will be objected that Mitterrand's link with the Morvan is purely accidental, as he was not born in the area; but that would be to ignore the extraordinary bond that ties him to the constituency, which he constantly revisits to meet supporters and friends. One thing is true, however: there is no Mitterrand dynasty in the Morvan. None of his sons will carry on the torch as a deputy: and the very fact that he has no property in the region except a pond (the President used to have his headquarters at the hotel in Château-Chinon) is significant. The most famous son of the Morvan has not put down roots there.

Turning to the Yonne, we find another name which has become famous all over the country: Flandin. We have already met the Flandins in M. Devoir's reminiscences. They have represented the Morvan for generations. At the same time, the influence of the family goes well beyond local frontiers. If I may say so without disrespect, the Flandins are, as they say in the guide books, 'worth stopping for'. In fact they demand our attention, for as the generations pass, this family, who were at first just rural notables, grow more and more prominent and end up occupying a central position in the networks of power. Here we have a true dynasty, one of those families with their roots in the soil that we associate with a certain image of rural France. But let us begin at the beginning.

Roots

In the eighteenth century, we find an Etienne Flandin, a doctor practising in the town of Lormes. His son, Gaspard-Etienne, was born in 1776: he became a timber merchant in the hamlet of Les Aubues in the parish of Lormes in Vézelay. His brother Jean-Louis owned land in Neufontaine. A third brother, with the nickname Dominique, also features in the annals of the family: he too was a doctor, but he had gone to Paris and lived in the rue Saint-Dominique, hence his nickname. So we have here a family of local notables, with a certain amount of landed property. Gaspard-Etienne Flandin married a Mlle Marie-Jeanne Marion who was the daughter of M. Jean Marion, also a timber merchant living at Villurbin in the parish of Saint-André-en-Morvan. In 1790 Jean Marion's widow, Jeanne Houdaille, daughter of the clerk to the court at Domecy, was the 'principal farmer of the lands and seignories of Bazoches', at that time the property of the Angran d'Allery family.[1]

In the sale of confiscated property which took place a year later, the Marion family became the owners of several new properties. They acquired the Abbey of Cure, a monastery built at the end of the tenth century not far from the river of the same name, the presbytery of Domecy, the mansion house of this parish which was later resold to a family from Avallon, and farming land in the surrounding area. Jean Marion had three sons, but they died without issue; so the property went to their sister, the wife of Gaspard-Etienne Flandin. Thus the latter's descendants had two residences, the mill and the Abbey at Cure. This geographical factor is not without significance; when the departments were created, Lormes was included in the Nièvre, whereas Domecy-sur-Cure became part of the Yonne within the canton of Vézelay. Thanks to this inheritance, the Flandins were prosperous and highly respected in the region; their sons went to study in Paris. The elder son, Louis, read law; the younger, Charles, was sent to follow his uncle's example and study medicine.

While pursuing their careers in the capital, the Flandin brothers did not neglect local politics. They remained very attached to their village on the banks of the Cure, and spent as many holidays there as their occupations allowed. Louis Flandin made his career in the higher reaches of the law, as Deputy Procurator Fiscal in Corsica, Public Prosecutor and Assistant Procurator Fiscal to the Court of Appeal in Paris and Councillor at the Imperial Court in Paris. He married Elizabeth Renard from Saint-Père, a neighbouring commune to Domecy, and they had two children: Paul, born in 1840, who was later to become Adviser to the Court of Appeal in Paris, and Marie, seven years younger, who was to marry a colonel in the artillery. Louis's branch of the family has no present-day descendants.[2] It is on his brother Charles's side that the family has prospered. Charles was the scientist in the family; he showed equal enthusiasm for chemistry and medicine, and undertook sometimes risky experiments. He was also the author of a treatise on poisons. Louis Flandin, on the other hand, was more of a historian: in particular, he published in the *Annuaire de L'Yonne* a history of the Abbey of Saint-Martin-de-Cure. In the mid nineteenth century, the Flandins were a typical example of a new cultured bourgeoisie who preserved very strong local connections while still enjoying a position of eminence in the capital. They could not remain indifferent to the political destinies of a region where they were held in such high esteem.

Louis Flandin was elected to the General Council for the first time on 6 December 1839. He was at that time a lawyer at the royal Court in Poitiers. He was a staunch Orleanist, and was to be continually re-elected until the end of the reign of Louis-Philippe. In 1852, cantonal elections were held after the accession to power of Louis-Napoléon. Having joined the latter's supporters, Flandin was the government candidate, facing a Legitimist, the Count d'Estutt, mayor of Tharoiseau. The Count d'Estutt enjoyed the support of the Count of Chastellux, whose local influence was discussed earlier; it is important to remember that the canton of Vézelay adjoins that of Quarré-les-Tombes. Despite a very active campaign by the Marquis and the Avallon Legitimist Raudon in favour of Estutt, Flandin was re-elected. He was to remain on the General Council without interruption until the end of the Empire: he was voted in again in 1858 and 1867. He was also held in high esteem by the local administration: 'An excellent individual, very keen on the interests of his canton. Able and intelligent. Good character for a magistrate', the sub-prefect remarks of him in 1867.[3] Although he was among the prominent individuals in the department, his income was much lower than that of the great families of the department: it was estimated in 1852 at 8,000 francs, as compared with 15,000 and 20,000 for M. Chastellux and M. de Labrosse, who represented neighbouring cantons.[4]

On the death of Louis Flandin, his brother took up the torch and became in turn mayor of Domecy in 1871 and member of the General Council. Charles Flandin had publicly expressed republican views under the Empire. In the general election of 1871 he got several hundred votes, but Raudot was elected. In the 1876 election, he was again eliminated in the first round; this time it was a Bonapartist, Garnier, who was elected for the constituency of Avallon. Charles Flandin never won a seat in the National Assembly, but he remained until his death the member for Vézelay of the General Council. He married late in life, in 1851, the daughter of General de Sonis, who bore him one son, to whom he gave the same name as one of his forebears: Etienne.

A 'moderate' republican

Born in Paris in 1853, Etienne studied at the Lycée Saint-Louis and chose law as his profession. He had a brilliant career: having obtained his doctorate in law, he was in turn part-time lecturer at the University in Algiers from 1880 to 1882, then Assistant Procurator Fiscal in Pau for the next five years, then Deputy Assistant Procurator Fiscal in Paris from 1887. He was appointed Public Prosecutor in Algiers in 1889. Like his father, the younger Flandin remained faithful to the land of his ancestors. It seems he was not content to rest on his Paris laurels. He soon became very interested in politics and decided to try his luck in the Avallonnais. He stood for the first time in 1884 under a republican label, but was beaten in the first round. Right from the time of this first attempt, Flandin was seen as a moderate attached to republican institutions. At the time the constituency of Avallon was the scene of a fierce battle between the Bonapartist Garnier, ex-prefect under the Empire who had already, on two brief occasions, represented the region in the Assembly (1876–77 and 1884–5) and a Radical candidate, Hervieu, an ex-sub-prefect and member for Avallon of the General Council. Hervieu, supported by two influential local newspapers, *L'Yonne* and *La Constitution*, was elected in 1887. Garnier won in 1889; however, this election was annulled because of irregularities, and Hervieu was re-elected at the by-election.[5]

At this time Flandin was a lawyer in Algeria. He had not, however, lost interest in local politics, and decided to try his luck again in the general election in 1893. This time the rivals in earlier elections had left the stage, and the lawyer was standing against a newcomer, the printer Albert Gallot from Auxerre. Gallot was the Radicals' champion; as we know, he published an influential local newspaper, *L'Yonne*. A second ballot was necessary, and was won by Etienne Flandin. This was the beginning of a long battle between the two men, typical of the political antagonisms of the time. Gallot was a staunch champion of rabidly anti-clerical ideas, for which his newspaper was a forum. To sketch in the background to the respective positions adopted by the two men, we must go back a little in time: at the end of the Empire, in 1869, two of the three deputies for the Yonne had beaten the government candidates. 'The Yonne', wrote François Goguel, 'seems to be a department that belongs to the left.'[6] This tendency was subsequently confirmed. Strong personalities were to dominate the first years of the Third Republic, in particular Victor Guichard, Charles Lepère, and above all, Paul Bert. Victor Guichard was a veteran: already under Louis-Philippe he had led the republican opposition in Sens. He was elected mayor of that town during the Revolution of 1848, but the following year he suffered from the general ebb of democratic ideas and retired temporarily from politics. He came back in 1871 as deputy, the oldest member of the National Assembly, and there he was to end his days: 'As president of the fourth section of the Chamber, he had just sat down and declared the session open, on 11 November 1884, when he collapsed and died, victim of a cerebral haemorrhage.'[7] Guichard's junior by twenty years, Charles Lepère was a lawyer in Auxerre who had been elected first of all to the municipal council and then to the General Council for that city at the end of the Empire. He was beaten for deputy in 1869, but represented his department in the Chamber from 1871 onwards. He was the leader of the Radical left and in 1879 became Minister of Agriculture. Paul Bert, born in Auxerre, first pursued a scientific career: a lecturer at the Faculty of Science in Bordeaux, he was appointed to the Chair of General Physiology at the Sorbonne in 1871. He became a member of the Academy of Science in 1885. On the fall of the Empire, Paul Bert rallied to the defence of his republican beliefs; he was appointed General Secretary of the Yonne, his department of origin, then prefect in Nord. He resigned when Gambetta left the National Defence Government. Elected deputy for the Yonne in 1872, he sat without interruption until his appointment as Resident General in Annam and Tonkin in 1886. Paul Bert attacked religious education ferociously: his book *Le Cléricalisme* is a lengthy attack on the ideas of the Church. But his main claim to fame was as Minister for Public Education in the Gambetta cabinet (1881–2) and promoter of the law instituting free, obligatory, lay primary education, passed on 20 March 1884.[8]

Under the influence of Paul Bert and his friends the Radical tendency gradually established itself in the whole of the department. In the 1889 elections, marked by the restoration of the *arrondissement* ballot, the six seats in the department went to six Radical candidates. The left was firmly established from then on; only the south of the Yonne seems to have remained more moderate, confirming the judgement of a prefect at the end of the Second Empire: 'The department, with the exception of the part of the Morvan included in the *arrondissement* of Avallon, is essentially irreligious.'[9] The difficulties experienced by the Radical Hervieu in his attempts to gain a foothold locally, at a time when the Bonapartists were still relatively influential, are significant. In the wake of Hervieu, and with his political friends holding the department, Albert Gallot might have been able to win in 1893, but he had a serious rival in the shape of Flandin, who was an important lawyer, and descended from an old Avallonnais family, whereas Gallot was from Auxerre, a big handicap for anyone wanting to represent the people of the Morvan and the plain.

The Radical candidate did not lose heart, however, and in the general election of 1898 he beat the outgoing deputy by just under three hundred votes. They swapped places at the next election: this time Flandin got in with six hundred votes more than Gallot. The rivalry between the two men had become a big local attraction: this struggle between Flandinists and Gallotists took place against a national background of fierce fighting between pro- and anti-clericals. It was at the end of this period that the Prime Minister, 'old man Combes', as he was affectionately known, gave his famous speech on the separation of Church and State. The Republic was launching an attack on the clergy; in fact, it was a declaration of war. It is important to remember that this event took place at Auxerre. A lavish banquet was organised inside the covered market, which was being inaugurated that day. The market has since been demolished, but the inhabitants of the town can easily recall that the location was chosen so that the building would mask the view of the Cathedral. The planners had thought of everything . . .

The predominance of Radicalism in the Yonne was uninterrupted until the First World War: in 1906, Flandin, who had kept the republican label, whereas all his colleagues had adopted 'Radical Socialist', was nevertheless re-elected; a new factor at this point was the appearance in all the constituencies of Socialist candidates who criticised Radicalism, saying it was now institutionalised and had gone soft. In fact, Etienne Flandin does not seem to have adopted policies that were any different from those of his fellow-deputies for the Yonne. A report of the sub-prefect of Avallon dated December 1907 moreover reflects some perplexity concerning the real allegiances of those who had voted for the deputy for Avallon.

The fact is that the deputy for the *arrondissement*, although classified as left-wing republican in official statistics, owes part of his majority to the pale or even reactionary communes in the *arrondissement*; it is also true, however, that some republican communes voted for him. It would be difficult, for the reasons explained, to draw any very clear conclusion about the political temper of the population of Avallon.[10]

It tended to drift, a bit to the left at one election, and a bit to the right at the next. What about the deputy himself? Can we draw any 'clear conclusion', as the prefect put it, about his political disposition?

All we know is that in Paris Etienne Flandin sat in the Chamber with the Republican Union group, of which he was one of the leaders. He took an interest in the debates on the relationship between Church and State, and in 1904 was appointed head of the commission set up to study the abolition of religious education. He asked for an adjournment of questions on 'the attempt to bribe the Prime Minister'. This attempt was alleged to consist of the offer of 2 million francs to ensure that no abolition measure would apply to the Carthusians. The commission was unable to establish the truth of the matter, and it seems that Flandin was mainly employed in calling for calm, no easy request at the time. Although he was a moderate, the deputy for Avallon participated in 1905 in the discussions on the Law of Separation of Church and State, and voted in favour of the measure. Opposed to the stance of his rival Gallot, considering it too extremist and polemical, Etienne Flandin nevertheless refused to compromise with those he considered the enemies of the Republic. In voting for this law, he felt, like many other deputies classed as conservatives, that he was strengthening the authority of the State in an area which he considered vital. If we look at the behaviour of the other deputies for the Yonne at the time, it seems that there were fewer differences between Flandin and Bienvenu Martin, deputy for Auxerre since 1897, leader since 1904 of the Radical-Socialist Left group and from 1905 Minister for Fine Arts and Religion, than between the latter and his Socialist rivals, even though they would be classified as on the left like himself. Moreover, the two men respected each other, and Flandin's well-attested competence accorded well with the ambitions of the Radical politician, who was more anxious to take up government office than to pursue an interminable war of ideologies.

We do not know whether it was the result of tiredness, or the attraction of a greater distinction, but in 1909 Etienne Flandin decided to resign his seat and stand for Senate. At the age of fifty-six he became senator for the

French Indies: he therefore ceased to represent his department in the Assembly. At the by-election which followed in the Yonne, Gallot easily regained the seat he had lost seven years earlier. Flandin, who was re-elected senator for the Indies in 1920, directed his activities in this period more towards foreign policy. As president of the Muslim section of the Parliamentary Committee on Overseas Development and Secretary to the French Development Committee on Syria, he became a specialist in North African affairs. It will be remembered that he had been a lawyer for several years in Algeria, and curiously his life came full circle, for in 1918 he was appointed Resident General in Tunis on a temporary basis. It was to be his last public office, as he died in Paris the following year.

Prodigal sons

The biography of Etienne Flandin suggests some of the complexity of such a man, and offers a contrast to our somewhat stereotyped image of the local politician. We rely mainly, of course, on ideas we get from the novels of Balzac about provincial families like the Flandins, who over the course of several generations rose to prominence in the little world of the Avallonnais. They carefully cultivated a network of relationships with the important figures in the area, great and small. With their mixture of republicanism and respect for sacred traditional values, the Flandins were splendid representatives of a peaceful traditional society which was not, however, entirely indifferent to the Radicalism in the air. The Flandins were the most prominent family in Domecy-sur-Cure, in the canton of Vézelay, but they were not merely local notables. For some time their vision had gone beyond the foothills of the Morvan and the neighbouring sub-prefecture. Charles and Louis, after all, had made their names in Paris. Local recognition was largely the reward for their success in the capital. In fact, there is something of the prodigal son in the figure of the local notable in their case. Underlying the image of 'local roots', an excellent argument if required against any political rival who should venture on to their territory, was a remarkable ability to keep on the move; they had to leave their territory, and yet always return, a movement which appealed to the imagination of their fellow-citizens and voters, who were inclined to judge the extent of a man's abilities by the amount of business awaiting his attention in Paris.

This mixture of closeness and distance exactly defines the Flandin dynasty. Their destiny took a more political turn with Etienne's entry into the National Assembly, but the path had already been mapped out by his ancestors, though the system of political appointments under the Third Republic was a great advantage to this kind of figure. There were to be no more authoritarian appointments, no more officially designated candidates: the prize would now go to men who could demonstrate an aptitude for public speaking, and whose abilities were attested by a university degree. Gone was the 'Republic of Dukes': teachers, doctors and lawyers now had pride of place. The Flandins' time had come. Although a commoner, Etienne was not, of course, a man of the people: but, unlike the de la Brosse or the Chastellux family, his roots were pure traditional peasantry.

So he was an ordinary man, except for two things: one was his height, for he was exceptionally tall, and the other his access to influential circles in the chief town and the capital. At any rate, that is how people saw him. Here is one anecdote of many I was told:

A crafty peasant goes into M. Flandin's office. 'Good morning, M. Etienne.' 'Good morning, friend.' 'I'm So-and-So, and I've lost my snuff-box in the Crot de Boeuf... People tell me you have a long arm... Could you come and help me look for it?' 'My dear friend, as you can see, I am extremely busy... Here is some money. Off you go to Domecy to old Mrs Guyot's shop and buy a new box full of snuff.'

There were also a number of stories about M. Flandin's 'long arm' in the literal sense – one story was that he had saved a child of thirteen from drowning. Several people also mentioned his willingness to intervene with the administration on behalf of his constituents. Marie Noël, a poet from Auxerre, has one particular memory of M. Flandin:

We are in the village hall at Cure, and it's prize-giving day for the local schoolchildren. Mélie comes up to get her prize, in a nice white bonnet. Papa [the teacher] presents it. He is sitting in an armchair, or perhaps it is just a chair, next to a gentleman with curly hair whom all the peasants greet, addressing him as 'Monsieur Etienne'.

Flandin did not, it would seem, encourage familiarity, as we can appreciate from the reminiscences of one of the children from Cure who later became a monk at La-Pierre-qui-Vire and who recreates the atmosphere of the time vividly.

Young Maurice [the narrator of the anecdote] had some family connections with Monsieur and Madame Flandin. During the summer holidays, he had to take an enormous bunch of honeysuckle to Madame Pauline every Thursday, and do some jobs in the garden of the house, for which he was paid.

He had often met Monsieur Etienne on the banks of the Cure, taking his daily walk between five and six o'clock or going through the woods in search of mushrooms. One day he was given a message for Monsieur Etienne. Having been trained by the servants, he knew that one should only speak to Monsieur and Madame using the third-person pronoun. Well, this time he forgot his instructions. In the urgency of the moment he blurted out: 'Monsieur Flandin, Madame Flandin would like to see you immediately.' Naturally, he was reprimanded. That was not how one should speak to Monsieur![11]

There is no need for comment: the story shows better than a long analysis the social position of a local notable at that time. The monk remembers that Monsieur Etienne's wife was a lady of strong personality in her own right, whose attachment to strict moral principles is still a legend in the family. Pauline Flandin, like the other women in the family, went to church and carried out other religious observances. This was probably seen as women's business, for her two sons, Charles and Pierre-Etienne, were not to show any great attachment to religion later. Moreover, 'Madame Pauline' was herself from a profoundly republican family: she was the daughter of Hippolyte Ribière, one of the most popular politicians in the department, because of his activities as a fierce opponent of the Second Empire and his role in the Franco-Prussian War of 1870.

The mention of this alliance between the Flandin and the Ribières brings us to an essential factor in local political life. Up to now, we have been able to glimpse the local ramifications of a network; at the other extreme, we have had a glimpse of the Parisian situation of the deputy for Avallon. But in order to understand Etienne's success, and later that of his son, we needed this vital link, for with the Ribières we go beyond the political world of the sub-prefecture and move on to a more complex operation which takes place in Auxerre and in which this family has been involved for some time. Once more we must follow Flandin's footsteps: notice that the prodigal son did not choose a Parisian for his bride, but someone from his native heath. This was in fact a strategic move.

The Ribières

From time to time, the present-day municipality of Auxerre organises functions in a superb eighteenth-century mansion: its last owner, Marcel Ribière, left it to the town hall several years ago. The Ribière mansion is something of a symbol of the past splendour of this distinguished family, whose detailed genealogy has not yet been established, at least not very far back. For my purposes I need go back no further than the bill of sale of the mansion dated 4 March 1847; by that time the purchasers, the Ribières, had attained an enviable situation. Pierre Hippolyte was the notary royal in Champlay. He was the son of Pierre Nicolas Ribière, bailiff to the civil court at Joigny, and Catherine Geneviève Coin. In 1821 he married a young lady from Auxerre, Rosalie Savatier-Laroche, resident in the rue Haute-Perrière. The owner of the mansion was a certain M. de Gislain de Boutin. The latter has left no trace in the history which concerns me, but we do know that the Savatier-Laroche family was prominent a year later, at the time of the events of 1848. Savatier-Laroche was the leader of the Socialist Democrats, who in July took control of the municipal council of Auxerre; he also became a member of the General Council in August of the same year.[12]

The influence of the Democrats was so strong that although the council was dissolved a year later, they were unanimously re-elected at the election which followed. However, normalisation was not long in coming. After a second dissolution in March 1851, the prefect Hausmann, who had divided the city into nine sections to prevent the re-election of the Democrats, saw his efforts rewarded. The defeat of the Democrats was to be long lasting: the Bonapartists ruled over Auxerre until the collapse of the Empire. Hippolyte Ribière, the notary's son, was a well-known lawyer at the Auxerre bar; he was twenty-six years old in 1848, and made no attempt to hide his sympathies for the republican side. At the proclamation of the new regime, while war was still raging, he was appointed prefect of the Yonne; as we know, he made his friend, Paul Bert, his assistant. By December the Germans were at the doors of the city, which they were to occupy for a brief period. Despite a revival of the Democrats, there was no insurrectional movement in Auxerre, and the Paris Commune found little echo there. On the other hand, the men who presided over the city's destinies, particularly Paul Bert, Lepère and Hippolyte Ribière, acquired considerable popularity.

The Ribière family's entry into politics dates from this time: Hippolyte, who represented the canton of Toucy on the General Council, later stood for senator for the department; he was elected in 1876 and again in 1882. This is how the introduced himself on that occasion to the voters, with his colleague Charton:

Ever since 1848, and even earlier in the case of my colleague [Charton had sat in the Constituent Assembly in 1848], in administrative and political office, in elected bodies, in popular education societies, in written or spoken expressions of our opinion, everywhere and at all times, we dare to affirm that our public life has been witness to our constant efforts on behalf of the triumph of the Republic and democracy.

The positions defended by Charton and Ribière were guided by their determination to ensure the triumph of republican ideas, but they rejected extremism in any form: 'The future lies', they wrote,

quite simply, in rational solutions to problems rationally formulated at the present time. What are the issues? The revision of the Constitution; separation of Church and State; reform of the judiciary; military service; the right of assembly and association; the law on public education. We will vote for the revision; we will vote from today, on the following measures, required from today: abolition of the irremovability of senators; extension of the right to vote; precise demarcation of the prerogatives of the two Chambers in respect of voting on financial and tax matters.

They did not, however, advocate the abolition of the Senate; for they felt that the Senate was changing, after the results of the previous first election in 1879: 'We can expect a majority which will be truly republican and must therefore be clearly anti-clerical.'[13]

I have quoted this manifesto because it reveals the beliefs of its authors.

In the presentation of this whole programme we see that the stakes are eminently political. They are trying in effect to strengthen the bases of a new type of State and to thwart the plans of those whom they see as the enemy within. The social content of the republican programme is not to the fore. The heirs of the Socialist Democrats of the Yonne have kept only the second part of the name, as their conclusion indicates: 'In short, all for the Republic, all for democracy.' The main issue at this time was the struggle against the 'notables': the Garniers, the Raudots, Bonapartists or Legitimists of any kind. Our two senators had not hesitated to intervene four years earlier in active support of the republican candidates when the monarchist De Broglie dissolved the Chamber. De Broglie in the famous 'Republic of Dukes' refused to apply the law of 10 August 1871 under which half of the members of the General Councils must submit to a new election. De Broglie is the man who suspends and dissolves republican councils: such was the gist of an appeal to voters by Charton and Ribière at the 1877 election.

So this was their enemy, this representative of the old aristocratic France: and in the years which followed the triumphal elections of 1877, Ribière was one of the public figures in his department resolved to change the composition of the political class and win widespread acceptance for anti-authoritarian and anti-clerical ideas. He died in 1885, but the succession was not broken. He had chosen for his son-in-law a man who was a lawyer like himself, a keen politician belonging to a long line of republicans: this marriage between the Ribières and the Flandins created a single network which spread over the greater part of the department. For Hippolyte's son had also picked up the torch: the year after his father's death, he got himself elected member for Toucy of the General Council, at a by-election caused by the death of Paul Bert. Marcel Ribière was twenty-six years old: he had a degree in law and practised as a lawyer, and already had some experience of the world of politics in Paris. This he owed in part to his father's connections, but apart from that, the ex-prefect had inspired in his heir a feel for politics and the desire to play a leading role in the changes which were now beginning. Even before his election, the young man had served his apprenticeship as Principal Private Secretary to the Minister of Agriculture.

Etienne Flandin and Marcel Ribière came on to the General Council at the same time; both combined a strong attachment to their native heath with the ability to move with ease in Parisian circles. Each had his personal fief, a rural canton which give him unswerving loyalty. Marcel Ribière was to be the councillor for Toucy for thirty-five years, but like his brother-in-law, he aimed higher. The family had a strong base in Auxerre, where the young lawyer was the editor of a newspaper, *La Constitution*, which defended the ideas of the moderate left. This influential position encouraged Marcel to seek a mandate from the town, and he set his sights on the town hall of Auxerre. In the municipal elections of 1892, he headed a 'Democratic Union' list standing against both the reactionary candidates and the 'Working-Class–Radical' list sponsored by the ubiquitous Albert Gallot, editor of *L'Yonne*.

The struggle was Homeric, if we are to believe contemporary observers. The outgoing mayor was a friend of Gallot, and there were sporadic accusations that the town had been taken over by the *L'Yonne* clan. Here is one account, chosen from many, of the atmosphere of tension that reigned in the election meetings at which the candidates faced each other:

> By eight o'clock, numerous groups had already formed in the hall. As I walked around, I could hear a lot of talk about Gallot's 'firm' collapsing, and people joking about the excuses some of the councillors were going to have to make. The councillors came in one by one, and did not seem too happy to see the large crowd which pressed up against them. The mayor told his little group of followers that he had a cold and could hardly speak.

Ribière chaired the meeting at the crowd's request. The time came for the mayor to speak: 'He gave an account of his term at the town hall in a distant fashion, with no feeling, and he was constantly interrupted by cries of "Speak up!" The recital was boring the voters . . . M. Ribière asked the crowd if they were satisfied with the mayor's account. "No, no, no", they all cried.'[14] Ribière and his friends won the election. 'For some time now', the prefect noted, 'a certain number of disenchanted Radicals have been trying to break away from what they call Gallot's "firm."'[15] However, because of numerous dissensions, Ribière never managed to establish himself as mayor. He was elected to the office in 1894, but lasted less than a year. Officially the reason for his resignation was his objection to 'a vote of the municipal council regarding the fees of the architect who submitted drawings for the design of the girls' school'.[16] He continued to sit on the municipal council, was re-elected in 1900 and became vice-president of the General Council, but it was not enough. As soon as the occasion presented itself, he stood for election to the Chamber of Deputies, joining his brother-in-law there in 1906. He was re-elected and then in 1913 he gave up his seat for a seat in the Senate which had fallen vacant because of a death; he was returned again in 1920 and on 11 October 1922 'death put an end to this successful career', as we read in his parliamentary biography.[17]

Once again the parallelism between the careers of Ribière and Flandin is striking. They both ended up as senators, neither having achieved political prominence at national level. Ribière never failed to support his brother-in-law's campaigns against their common political enemy, Albert Gallot: *La Constitution* provided Flandin with an excellent forum in which to respond to the attacks in *L'Yonne*. But Ribière remained faithful to a practical, Gambetta-style Radicalism: a member of the Radical Left in the Assembly, he remained faithful to this choice in the Senate, and enrolled in the Democratic Left group. Loyal also to his anti-clerical ideology, he was president of the Federation of Educational Mutual Benefit Societies of the Yonne and of the Auxerre League for the Rights of Man and the Citizen. Ribière can be seen as representative of the new kind of local politician: in the Yonne 'The Republic Embattled' was already giving way to 'The Republic in Power'. The anti-clerical left to which the member for Auxerre belonged was open to the ideas being developed by a Socialist Party whose impact was already being felt. When he first stood in 1906, Marcel Ribière was forced to a second round by a 'Unified Socialist' candidate.

But for the moment moderation was the thing: leaning sometimes a bit to the right (Flandin), sometimes a bit to the left (Ribière), the new men established their hold on the local political fabric: they had to accommodate a tradition of protest against the Church, in which the memory of 1848 was still vivid:

> The political climate of the department of the Yonne, during the first years of this century, was such that anyone who had electoral ambitions was obliged to support, verbally at least, the Radical tendency, which left its adherents a good deal of freedom, so long as they respected the tradition of lay ideas or somewhat vague anti-clericalism which had characterised it since the time of Paul Bert.[18]

As enlightened lawyers, Ribière and Flandin saw their role as representatives of the people, and pillars of a legitimate State which protected a certain number of fundamental freedoms; from their writings there clearly emerges the idea that the role of the deputy, like that of the civil servant, is to perfect the functioning of such a State. Both rejected extremist ideologies and the excesses to which they give rise, and stood firmly in the middle ground, professing a soundly 'Centrist' approach.

A new generation

The path had thus been traced for the successors to the two brothers-in-law. From now on, their names formed part of the historic patrimony of the department. The two senators had formed many links with lower-ranking local politicians; and the two families had their entrée into Parisian circles. It is hardly surprising, then, that two of Etienne Flandin's sons chose the careers in which their ancestors had been so successful: law and medicine. The third led a more adventurous life in business in North Africa. The eldest had the same name as his grandfather, Charles, and like him, he studied medicine and began a brilliant career as a doctor; he became a consultant in the great Paris hospitals, Ambroise-Paré, Bichat, Broussais and Saint-Louis. Pierre-Etienne, the second eldest, inherited his father's name and also his passion for politics. But at the time politics was not a profession; in fact it was scarcely an additional source of income. He therefore studied law at university, took a diploma in the School of Political Science and became a lawyer; but he remained very attached to the family stronghold in the Avallonnais, and could often be seen there accompanying his father on his electoral campaigns. He was no stranger to local political circles.

Sometimes circumstances lend a hand: some years before, Etienne Flandin had resigned. His rival Gallot immediately grabbed the vacant seat. Now we come to spring 1914: in a few days, Pierre-Etienne would be celebrating his twenty-fifth birthday. The subject on everyone's lips at the time was the general election due to be held on 26 April: who was to be the moderate candidate in Avallon? A suggestion came from the local mayors: what about 'young Flandin', as he was called by Rostain, the member of the General Council for Quarré? Médéric Devoir, whose advice was always sound, made the same suggestion, as we know. The Flandins turned it over in their minds. Uncle Marcel approved. So now we get the arrival on stage, facing an elderly Gallot, of a new generation, one that came too late for the fight for lay education, but was to see a war, a real one this time, in which many were to die. Pierre Etienne won by just 200 votes: he had stood as a 'Progressive', and was the youngest member of the Chamber.

Overall the left was beaten: also, in three constituencies the representative of the left at the second ballot was no longer a Socialist-Radical as always before, but a candidate from the Socialist Party. It was the end of the Radicals' hegemony; a commentator in *L'Yonne* had no hesitation in describing the defeats of Javal at Sens and Gallot at Avallon as 'the rising tide of reaction'.[19] Whether that rather rhetorical description was accurate or not, young Flandin's political career began under the most favourable auspices. Another friend of the family, Pierre Perreau-Pradier, wearing the colours of the 'Radical Left', had been re-elected in the neighbouring *arrondissement* of Tonnerre, beating a Socialist and a Socialist-Radical. Like Flandin, Perreau-Pradier was the heir of an old Yonne family: his father, Charles, was a farmer and wine-producer from Tonnerre, who had been first mayor of that town, then a member of the *arrondissement* council and later of the General Council, before being elected in 1910 as an Independent Radical deputy. He died three years later, but his son was then ready to profit from the political capital which had thus slowly accumulated. Pierre Perreau-Perrier attended the high school in Dijon, then continued his studies in Paris, where he obtained his doctorate in law. He began as an adviser to Paul Doumer: Charles Perreau-Pradier had been a friend of the latter ten years earlier, when Doumer was elected deputy for the Yonne. Pierre later became Assistant Principal Private Secretary to the

Under-Secretary of State for War, then entered the prefectural corps, with the rank of General Secretary: so he had served his apprenticeship and had no trouble taking over the political succession when his father died. Side-by-side with Flandin, he sat in the Chamber until 1940.

Pierre-Etienne's entry into politics coincided to within a few months with France's entry into the war. The newly elected deputy had obtained his pilot's licence two years earlier, and it was in this 'noble' though still young arm of the service that he took part in the Yser campaign in AF 33 Squadron. In 1915, the authorities turned to the young deputy as one of the few specialists in aeronautics: he was appointed official representative at the Ministry of War, then in 1917 became head of the inter-allied section of the newly created office of the Junior Minister for Aeronautics. Young Flandin's choice of aviation was not unimportant in his later political career. It points up some of the ambiguities within this bourgeois family: like his ancestor who had been wildly enthusiastic about medicine and chemistry, Pierre-Etienne was placing himself right from the beginning at the forefront of modern ideas; but at the same time he was a man with a heritage, the son of 'Monsieur Etienne', faithful to the moderate stance and the values of a bourgeoisie threatened by the rise of the Socialists and the upheavals in the Empire of the Tsar to the east. By the end of the war, Flandin, who was not yet thirty years old, had forged two firm convictions for himself: politics had to serve technological progress, which meant that the elected politician must be technically competent; and each individual had to choose which side he was on. Flandin's belief that capitalism was the best guarantee of freedom was never to waver.

Nevertheless, he advocated strict State control of the aviation industry: he rejected laissez-faire methods and attacked particularly the weak guarantees offered to the State by the contracts signed with manufacturing industry specifying the quality and price of items of equipment; he tabled a private bill aimed at ascertaining responsibilities and imposing the required sanctions. In other words he refused to countenance any compromise with the owners of capital which could harm the public interest: he was always a servant of the State, in the classic sense. However, he felt that the State should provide incentives: so after the war he pressed for the development of a civil aviation worthy of the name, and managed to obtain a reduction in the military budget so that the money could go instead to the building of civilian aircraft. With the return to normal political life, elections were held. Faithful to the Avallonnais, Flandin stood there again in 1919; he was on the moderate or Republican Union list, along with his friend Perreau-Pradier, and Milliaux, the outgoing deputy for Auxerre. This list easily beat its Socialist-Radical and Socialist rivals.

The 'sky-blues' thus had a majority in the Chamber, and it was at this point that Flandin obtained his first ministerial post, as Under-Secretary of State for Aviation, which curiously enough was attached to the Ministry of Public Works at that time. Flandin continued his efforts on behalf of civil aviation, and a number of airlines were created at this period. In 1921, the Leygues government fell, and Flandin went back to being a humble deputy. At the same time he was head of a legal firm specialising in business law: politics was still a luxury then, as it did not bring in an assured income. The majority of deputies, if they did not have a ministerial post, continued to practise their normal profession. Flandin maintained a close interest in aviation, chairing a congress on aerial navigation in November 1921, and later becoming president of the Aeroclub of France. He was also trying to strengthen his political base nationally: he was a member of the Democratic Republican party, which was to give birth to the Democratic Alliance. Flandin joined the executive of this group in 1922 and took an active part in the preparations for the 1924 elections.

'Young Flandin' thus began to make headway: his fellow-citizens in Domecy elected him mayor, and he carried on the family tradition of sitting on the General Council. The family were supporters of the Poincaré government: Pierre-Etienne's cousin, Marcel Ribière, the son of the senator, was in fact Principal Private Secretary to the Prime Minister. But, unlike Flandin, Marcel preferred to be behind the scenes. Though just as keen on politics as his cousin, he preferred not to risk the electoral route. But he was a useful ally, a typical networker, and a very prominent personality, who was heeded in the corridors of power. He had a successful career in Paris, rising to senior member of the Council of State, without, however, abandoning the little world of Auxerre. He kept the family mansion all his life, and when towards the end of it he presented the house to the town, he was closing a chapter of history. However, in 1924 none of this had happened. As an intimate of the Prime Minister, Marcel was one of the most influential men in the department. Flandin, standing against the Left Cartel, again managed to bring his list out on top in the Yonne. This time Flandin got the majority of the votes and only one Socialist, Boully, was elected. However, his opponents formed a majority in the Chamber, and until the Cartel was dismantled he had to be content to be a member of the opposition: he became one of the leaders of the parliamentary right, and that position assured him unquestioned pre-eminence in the department. Let us follow him for a moment on one of his trips to his native heath, where electoral concerns had to take precedence over any thoughts of a holiday.

Campaigning in the Yonne

The house stands on the river bank, a large mansion with the entrance at ground level and former stables which are now used as a garage. It is here that the Minister receives his visitors: on one side there is a waiting-room, and on the other a small office into which Pierre-Etienne's tall figure fits with difficulty. Taking advantage of parliamentary recesses, the deputy for the Avallonnais comes to the *arrondissement* as often as he can, temporarily leaving aside his work as a lawyer. Some days the waiting-room at Domecy is crowded. Nearly everyone has some request to make: one man wants the pension he feels has been unjustly refused him, another wants his son's national service deferred, and a third would like a job in Paris. Others, however, appear without any specific request. They tell him some family problem, or they complain about the difficulties they are experiencing as farmers: prices have fallen yet again: the Minister keeps changing; what on earth are they up to in Paris? Pierre-Etienne listens in silence. That is actually his main function: to listen, take note, be attentive. He is rather aloof, maybe; at least, that is the impression people get. The atmosphere in the study is quite scholarly, with all those books, which make a vivid impression on most of his visitors. There is always the mixture of familiarity and distance which is by now characteristic of 'Monsieur Etienne'. Flandin has known this rural world since childhood and is perfectly at ease in it, but it is important for him to preserve an air of mystery: people consider him a 'man of the world'.

Was he rather aloof? 'He gave that impression when you met him for the first time', replies M. Schiever, the mayor of Avallon. 'I told him one day that someone had remarked he was rather high and mighty, and M. Flandin told me: "Well, you know, nature made me tower head and shoulders above everyone else, so I don't know about mighty, but I have to accept I am high."'[20] During all the years when he was gaining a reputation in Paris as a politician free of demagoguery, Flandin was paying scrupulous attention to his constituency work. This is clear from a glance at the notebooks in which he listed for each commune in his *arrondissement* people who had some political influence, because they were mayors, or had some strategic occupation, such as inn-keeper, or publicly declared their opinions. All this was carefully noted in detail . . .

He put the same care into his electoral campaigns. In the 1928 campaign, Poincaré was back in power, after the failure of the Left Cartel experiment. The position was clear: 'A vote for Flandin is a vote for Poincaré.' Flandin's party, the Democratic Alliance, advocated a 'neutral and impartial' State, which would encourage private enterprise. Gone were the old dissensions which had been a gift to Radicalism. 'The time for metaphysical discussions and religious quarrels is over.'[21] In the constituency of Auxerre-Avallon the campaign was lively: Flandin's rival, a Socialist-Radical named Girard, was not of the same calibre as Gallot, but the left and the extreme left were nevertheless very influential in certain cantons. Flandin multiplied the number of meetings; every afternoon he went to several villages, and every evening at eight o'clock there was a rally in one of the more densely populated communes. Nor were the small hamlets neglected: for example, Flandin took the trouble to book a hall at Le Beugnon and wrote to the mayor of Lucy-sur-Cure about his plan. The latter replied: 'Yes, it is a good idea to give a lecture there, for it has at least thirty voters.' Another mayor advised him to go to Sceaux: 'I feel it would not be a waste of time to hold a meeting at Sceaux. This has perhaps never been done before, as the town hall is at Maison-Dieu.'[22]

What happened at these meetings? Everyday issues were of course aired: everyone had a tale to tell about the poor condition of the roads, the electrification work that needed doing, government neglect . . .

At Essert, the meeting was chaired by the mayor, who took advantage of the opportunity to point out to M. Flandin the poor state of the roads. A voter, thanking M. Flandin for coming to Essert, added that he hoped M. Flandin would continue to represent the new constituency of Auxerre-Avallon for as long as possible; to which the deputy responded with a smile that that was mainly up to the voters.[23]

That same day he went to Le Beugnon, as promised: 'Several issues were raised, particularly the filling-in of a pond that was a danger to health, and delays in building a road which would let the inhabitants of this important hamlet make their way to Joux-la-Ville or Nitry without having to go all the way down to Arcy-Sur-Cure.' In Joux-la-Ville, a voter protested that 'the body charged with building roads between villages is making people who want to pay the tax in kind break stones, when most people would prefer to pay in transportation'.[24] M. Flandin promised to intervene. But he was not to be let off so lightly: a second request came, from the mayor this time, asking him to help them with their plans to have water laid on.

In other cantons, the atmosphere was very different, politics taking precedence over local issues. At Etais, a commune well known for its Communist sympathies, voices were soon raised:

M. Poirier, the mayor, was nominated chairman. However, he made a point of stating that he still had the right to intervene and ask questions. And hardly in fact had M. Flandin begun his speech when he was interrupted by M. Poirier, and they argued back and forth for the next hour and a half, frequently interrupted by cries and imprecations from the audience, so that the meeting lost all sense of direction.

The mayor of Etais attacked Poincaré's policies and advocated the abolition of all taxes on agricultural profits; members of the public also intervened, one to protest against the imprisonment of the Communist deputies. Flandin responded that he would have considered it unacceptable

if those who incite soldiers and sailors to mutiny, for which they receive heavy sentences, should themselves go free thanks to their parliamentary immunity. When he added a remark about freedom of opinion in Russia, it was greeted with shouts of 'Kill him' and 'F—— off', which give some idea of the tone of the meeting and the level of argument.[25]

There was a large crowd at the Etais meeting, and this was not unusual: entertainment was limited at this time, for radio was just beginning, and a political meeting was an excellent opportunity to combine pleasure with instruction. People were keen to witness an oratorical contest, even if the arguments swiftly degenerated to a very low level. On this occasion, M. Poirier launched into a diatribe against the colonialist army and attacked in particular recruiting posters 'which tempt our young men with pictures of black women with firm, naked breasts'. M. Flandin commented that M. Poirier, having lived in Madagascar for several years, was no doubt an expert on black women, which raised a laugh in the hall. M. Poirier, not one for jokes, stood on his dignity. Between debating points and banter in sometimes doubtful taste, the minutes flew by; soon it was time to close the meeting and go off to the next town; there the deputy 'was listened to with sympathy and attention'.[26]

Flandin never seems to have lost his composure on these occasions; some people even compared him to an Englishman because of the phlegm he displayed. Attendances were always high, which seems strange to us today, when for even the most important meetings it is sometimes necessary to go and round people up from their homes with specially chartered coaches. In 1928, people flocked to meetings and the questions came thick and fast. The candidate was asked at one meeting for his views on home distillers: 'M. Flandin recalled that in the Chamber he belonged to a group for the defence of home distillers, of which, incidentally, he was one himself, and he assured all distillers that he would be vigilant in defence of their rights.'[27] Others attacked the government's foreign policy. Flandin had become the spokesman for a policy of peace under the auspices of the League of Nations. One interlocutor accused him of supporting Fascism, whereupon Flandin reminded him that he did not advocate a military alliance between France, Italy and Spain, merely an agreement which would be of great benefit to farmers. Others questions led him at times to long explanations of the financial policies of the Poincaré government. In short, boredom was not a problem during the campaign. One meeting gave rise to a motion:

The voters of Merry-sur-Yonne, approximately fifty in number, at a meeting in the town hall, having heard M. Flandin give an account of his time in the Assembly and sketch the broad lines of his future programme, approve his statements and welcome his candidature in the general election of 22 April.[28]

In the intervals between these meetings, Pierre-Etienne returned to his office at Cure. He worked there with the faithful Arthur, a former gas-worker who came over from Auxerre to help out during all his campaigns. There was always a huge bundle of correspondence awaiting him: some of it was Paris business, of course, but there were also numerous letters from mayors arranging the details of future meetings, or begging another favour; for example, one mayor who, after thanking Flandin for improvements made to the postal service, adds:

> May I take advantage of the opportunity to bring to your attention the following request? Young X of the class of 27, whose military service has been deferred for a year, asks to be posted either to Dijon in anti-aircraft defence, or if Dijon is impossible, to Troyes in the artillery.[29]

There follow various explanations and justifications.

Other letters came from voters pledging the support of associations to which they belong. Here, for example, is a missive assuring Flandin of the support of an ex-servicemen's association, the Ralliement Français, a 'focus of anti-Communist political activity' of which Field-Marshall Lyautey was a patron. The writer in this case is an engineer who intends to come to the meeting arranged at Chatel-Censoir.[30] That was a stormy meeting, with no shortage of hecklers; one of them launched a violent attack from the right side of the hall. But Flandin was forewarned, because one of his supporters had written to him after a turbulent session in another commune, giving him some details:

> The man in question is C., a Communist who is in charge of the dredger carrying out work on the canal at the present moment. He has got himself enrolled on the electoral register. I am writing to tell you this because he has said he is going to give you a few problems next Thursday. You could probably get a few more details from the prefecture . . .

The deputy thanked his correspondent and reassured him: 'I shall find out all about him, but I do not think he need worry us unduly.'[31]

Apart from the everyday business of the campaign, there was the question of giving the necessary support to moderate candidates in other constituencies where the political situation was less stable. Flandin was asked to take part in meetings organised at Auxerre and Sens, and he was urged to intervene with the local newspaper, which was lending worrying support to the rival candidate: 'We are sorry to see *Le Bourguignon* giving the impression it supports Boully in the Sénonnais. I remonstrated strongly with M. Bouquigny about this yesterday evening . . . Please let him know what I have been saying to our people about this.' This last letter came from a distiller in Gurgy who also urged Flandin to take a trip to the north of the department: 'Come to Auxerre, Sens or Joigny for the second ballot: your presence is needed to lend personal support in word and deed to a friend in peril . . .'[32] The writer was not an elected representative, but one of the prime movers in the moderate network, one of those people who are indispensable in a campaign, but always work behind the scenes.

The length and the precision of Flandin's reply show the importance he gave to his correspondent's views. First of all he reviewed the situation: 'Everything is going well for me here in the Avallonnais. I have been to nearly all the communes, with just a few left to visit. I have had a warm welcome everywhere, and been assured that I will have a handsome majority next Sunday.' They still had to ensure that Perreau-Pradier got in at the first round: 'We absolutely must make a very big effort on this, and prevent a second ballot.' Even the candidate at Auxerre ought to win at the first round, according to Flandin, if their supporters got out and voted as they should. As for the question of *Le Bourguignon*, the explanation was simple: 'It is the intervention of M.F., a close personal friend of M. Boully, which has given rise to M. Bouquigny's ambiguous attitude.'[33] Overall, the results of the election did not contradict Flandin's optimism: he was re-elected without difficulty, as was his friend Perreau-Pradier, though in the case of Auxerre his forecast was wrong, as it was a Socialist who was elected. Elsewhere, the right came out on top: 'The Yonne voted for Poincaré even more decisively than France as a whole.'[34]

Flandin as Prime Minister

On his return to Paris, Pierre-Etienne could congratulate himself on a job well done. His friends held the reins of power in the department, and the moderates had a majority in the country. Poincaré was ill, and he was soon to step down, but the government was assured of a certain continuity in the figures of two men: Tardieu and Laval. At last Flandin's time had come; when Tardieu formed his second government, he called on Flandin's services as Minister of Commerce and Industry, a post which he kept for a year. The government was forced to resign in December 1930, in the aftermath of the Oustric affair, but a little later one of Tardieu's ex-Ministers, Laval, formed a government of a similar political complexion. Here we find Flandin once again, in the prestigious post of Minister of Finance. Meanwhile the economic situation had worsened, unemployment was increasing and rumours of scandals were beginning to poison the political atmosphere.

It was at this time that Flandin was firmly taken to task for his connections with Aéropostale, a firm for which he was consulting barrister before he became Minister and which was going through a difficult patch financially. The Socialists led a press campaign against the Minister of Finance, claiming that he intended to support in the House a project in which his former clients had an interest. Called to account by Léon Blum, Flandin did not lose his composure, but recalled that he had always supported civil aviation, long before he became Minister. He pointed out that 'almost all issues relating to the responsibilities of civilian carriers land on my desk', and he counter-attacked by saying that his adversaries were not exactly scrupulous about avoiding the errors they were denouncing. He turned on Blum, who was a lawyer like himself: 'Fees are not always paid in cash: sometimes they are paid in political support, contributions to electoral expenses, an interesting or well-paid job for a son, a brother or a friend.' He finished with a transparent allusion to the fact that two textile magnates, Boussac and Lederlin, had purchased the services of Léon Blum and Joseph Paul-Boncour, leading lights in the Socialist SFIO.[35]

Flandin's vigorous response forced his adversaries to define their concept of the proper relationship between the profession of lawyer and that of deputy, a concept which was in fact in line with the Minister's. But above all it put an end to the attacks on him. Flandin kept the Ministry of Finance through a second Laval and a third Tardieu government. Removed temporarily from power by the success of the left in the 1932 elections, he returned two years later as Minister for Public Works. In November of the same year, at the age of only forty-five, he finally attained the post which crowns a great political career: that of Prime Minister. With hindsight, the Council of Ministers of the time was an odd coalition, in which the Socialist-Radicals, led by Herriot, joined forces with the right.

The new government faced a tense international situation. Hitler revoked the military clauses of the Treaty of Versailles on 16 March. In response, the French government tried to strengthen its links with the United Kingdom and draw closer to Italy; this was the aim of the Conference of Stresa, which was to be followed by a second diplomatic initiative, the signing of the Franco-Soviet pact. But the Flandin government, facing rampant inflation and an enormous budget deficit, could not restore stability. The recommended remedies – deflationary policies and a lowering of interest rates – proved useless. Attacked by Paul Reynaud and criticised by the left, the government fell on 31 May 1935, but Flandin continued as a member of the governments which preceded the accession to power of the Popular Front. Ex-delegate for France to the League of Nations, he became head of the French diplomatic service under the fourth Laval government.

As Minister for Foreign Affairs, it was he who had to support in the House the ratification of the Franco-Soviet pact: one of the paradoxes of history, for here was Flandin jeered at by the right and applauded by the left. But events quickened. First came the invasion of Ethiopia by the Italians; Laval tried to bargain again, offering two-thirds of Ethiopia in exchange for peace. This compromise, which was rejected by Mussolini in any case, was the object of harsh criticism, and the government collapsed.

Flandin kept his post under the Sarraut government. Hitler remilitarised the Rhineland in March 1936. Once again, after a debate in the Council of Ministers, the majority voted against a military response; they would limit themselves to lodging a complaint with the League of Nations. What exactly was Flandin's stance? According to his version, he proposed immediate mobilisation, which was rejected because the elections were only six weeks away. Paul-Boncour, his colleague, confirms that only Sarraut, Mandel, Flandin and he himself opposed the defeatists. A Radical Minister, Jean Zay, gives a somewhat different version:

The Council of Ministers opened with a statement by M. Flandin . . . Now, M. Flandin made no proposals. What he did was to list all the possible solutions, from the most energetic to the most abstract, from immediate mobilisation and entering the Rhineland to a mere diplomatic protest, with a mention in passing of the possibility of recourse to the League of Nations. His only conclusion, delivered in a cold, emotionless voice, was as follows: 'These are the options open to us. The Council must decide.'[36]

Sarraut was to read out a speech on the radio that very evening. One sentence of it has remained famous: 'We will not leave Strasburg at the mercy of German guns.' The sentence was in fact written by Flandin, which would give grounds for believing that he was in fact on the side of those who advocated a tough response. In the end, France went no further than a diplomatic protest. By now it was election time.

Spring-time

Easter Sunday, five o'clock in the afternoon . . . It is cold, and the villages are deserted; I arrive just after the start of the meeting, and already the fairly large room in the town hall at Quarré-les-Tombes is full to bursting, the audience spill out into the hall and I have to be very discreetly obstinate to slip into the hall and estimate the attendance. A religious silence reigns. Calmly seated behind the table around which are the elders of the canton, Pierre-Etienne Flandin speaks without raising his voice, with the same clear, courteous, thoughtful tone we know from the Chamber . . . But today it is an audience of peasants that the Minister for Foreign Affairs of France is addressing on a great problem which concerns all: war or peace?[37]

The writer is a journalist from Paris; for Pierre-Etienne was now an important man, who brought the French press in his wake. In the struggle between the right and the Popular Front, Prime Minister Flandin was one of the figures whose reactions were sought, particularly concerning the deterioration in the diplomatic situation. Back now in the Yonne, he faced a very different situation from the one he had known in 1928. At the general election in 1932, the Radicals and Socialists had obtained the majority of the votes; the municipal elections of 1935 had confirmed this tendency, with the Popular Front obtaining good results in numerous communes. In the south of the department, it was true, Flandin had an undisputed lead; and his friend G. Schiever, an Independent Radical, had been re-elected in Avallon. But Perreau-Pradier had problems in Tonnerre: he returned to the Chamber, but only after a second ballot in which he stood against the Socialist Robert Lévy, and his list had been beaten at the last municipal elections by the left.

Flandin was therefore resolved to make his local campaign the occasion for a detailed justification, addressed to journalists as much as voters, of his policies in government. This of course included a fierce diatribe against the old enemy, Communism. *Le Petit Journal* described the Democratic Alliance as 'the reincarnation of M. Thiers, whose motto was: "The Republic must be conservative or cease to be" . . . and of the typical national and liberal spirit of the nineteenth-century bourgeoisie, with their implacable repression of everything connected with the Revolution'; but the same publication aligned Flandin with that tendency in the party which 'is linked not only to the moderate Radicalism of M. Marchandeau, but also to the Centrist Radicalism of M. Herriot, thus laying the foundations for the next parliament of a republican alliance in which many people place great hopes'.[38]

In the event historical circumstances no longer favoured centre-right groupings, and the Radicals were to make common cause from then on with the Socialists. In his own constituency, the ex-Prime Minister's speech was well received, and his rivals, with Girard at their head, were impotent. Mindful of the fact that he was addressing an audience of rural voters, Flandin recalled at every meeting that his government had taken measures to eliminate the 20 million quintal wheat surplus so as to raise the price. Also, at the local level, promises had been kept. Re-electing the outgoing deputy meant fighting four evils: 'Class struggle; the squandering of financial resources; the political abuse of jobs for the boys; harassment from the tax-man'.[39]

But it always came back to foreign policy and assessment of the successive governments to which the deputy had belonged:

> Here we are, for example, at Vassy-Etaule, a small commune in the canton of Avallon, on a Saturday night. M. Flandin has just explained that long before the signature of the Franco-Soviet pact, Germany had been preparing her invasion of the demilitarised zone . . . However, it has not escaped the notice of our villagers that Chancellor Hitler's blow was accompanied by new offers of peace to us. How sincere are they? 'It is the wolf who for his own ends comes disguised as a lamb', replies M. Flandin.

Questions come thick and fast on the issue of links with the United Kingdom; and why remain an ally of Italy? Once again Flandin explains government thinking:

Some people urge us to break with England; others say break with Italy. Now, we have no wish to break with anyone. Against the spirit of aggression we see approaching, we wish to build a barrier composed of all those people who desire peace in Europe.[40]

The success of his speech was more or less guaranteed for the Minister, who had his arm in a sling after a serious car accident on one of his trips round the Yonne. He had a link with his voters going back twenty-four years. Nevertheless, if one reads the local press of the time, one readily perceives the worries underlying these meetings. It is quite remarkable how well informed the inhabitants of the villages were, and how closely they had followed developments in the international situation. We are far from the stereotyped image of a rural France wrapped up in its own concerns and cut off from the rest of the world. But people hardly seem to have believed what was happening. Pierre-Etienne was elected yet again: he was now 'the famous' Flandin, having won his stripes as a statesman. The largest towns in the department were to give a majority to Socialists from this point on: the Popular Front was victorious in Sens, Joigny, Migennes, Auxerre and everywhere except Tonnerre. However, Perreau-Pradier had a tough rival in Lévy, a Socialist lawyer from Paris, who had nearly unseated his rival at the previous elections.

All sorts of attacks and denunciations were launched against Lévy, who was not a native of the Yonne. Perreau-Pradier's manifesto did not hesitate to predict that Lévy and his friends would play the part of Kerensky, 'who by his demagoguery, his compliance and his weakness smoothed the way in a few short months for the arrival of Bolshevism in Russia'.[41] There followed an indictment of Communism, taken from a recent speech by Doriot, who was being held up as an expert on the subject. *L'Avenir Tonnerrois* reminded its readers that Lévy owned three blocks of flats in Paris; and as a parting shot there was a paragraph entitled 'M. Lévy's 3 votes': 'We all know the story of the Wandering Jew's five coins. Now we have M. Lévy's 3 votes. The "commonfront" candidate is claiming at his meetings that he came within three votes of fulfilling his life's dream: a seat in the National Assembly.'[42] The allusion is clear, and the tone a herald of things to come. It would appear that the campaign bore fruit, for Lévy and the Communist Froissart were eliminated in the first round.

However, the Popular Front won nationally, and Flandin became one of the leaders of the opposition; he continued to follow developments in foreign policy, but never returned to power, brushed aside by the assorted coalitions which followed the decline of the Popular Front. He wholeheartedly approved of the Munich agreement, and this led him to perform an action which caused a great stir. Following the agreement, he wrote a telegram congratulating the signatories on 'saving peace', beginning with the German Chancellor: Flandin's name was to be associated for a long time to come with this famous 'telegram to Hitler'. How could he be so blind? Flandin was typical of a whole group of politicians who slid gradually from pacificism to defeatism. Never again to have to live through the experience of the Popular Front, that was the main concern of the conservatives, summed up in the slogan 'Peace and Order'. The rest of the story is well known: full powers were voted to Pétain, and Flandin went back to work for a few months from December 1940 to February 1941, as Minister for Foreign Affairs, when Pétain decided to get rid of Laval. The latter was soon back, appointed by the Germans. Flandin, who had resigned and retired to his villa at Saint Jean-Cap Ferrat, crossed to Algeria at the end of 1942, but was arrested. He was tried in the High Court in 1946, and was cleared of collaboration with Pétain, but visited with national degradation. Churchill, Roosevelt and Leahy intervened to clear him of the charge of collaboration. However, the law stated that those visited by national degradation were not eligible for election, even if cleared of the penal charges against them, so he could not stand again.

Back to the Morvan

I have no wish to linger on events which are the province of History with a capital 'H', and I leave it to specialists to discover the truth about the ex-Prime Minister's behaviour. The declaration of ineligibility closed to Flandin not only the National Assembly in which he had so often spoken, but even locally elected bodies. So did the prime politician in the Yonne disappear completely? Was this the end for a dynasty which had gradually widened its sphere of influence from its village to the nation as a whole, over the course of more than a century of participation in public life? The answer is no. The family still retained its prestige in Cure. At the cantonal elections Dr Charles Flandin succeeded his brother as member for Vézelay of the General Council. Charles could boast that he had rejected the policy of collaboration. In any case, he had always been further to the left than his brother. Also, Pierre-Etienne's son had fought in the war as an airman alongside the British. The family as such was thus in no way disqualified, for its member could hardly be accused of wholesale collaboration. Pierre-Etienne himself explained at his trial that he had always favoured the Allied camp, and he mentioned a letter in which Churchill wrote to him: 'I was delighted when you entered the government in 1941.'[43] If he decided to resign in February 1942, he argued, it was precisely to avoid further involvement with the Germans.

Flandin continued to be an influential figure: it is true that the Democratic Alliance was now a mere relic, but friends of the former Prime Minister, particularly Antoine Pinay and the Group of Independents and

Peasant Farmers, were to play a prominent role in politics. Flandin may not have appeared in public, but he was nevertheless one of Pinay's unofficial advisers when the latter came to power in 1952. The moderate camp needed rebuilding in the Yonne, and Pierre-Etienne set about the task, though always in an unofficial capacity. According to information I was given, he intervened personally to ensure that one of his political allies, the former mayor of Auxerre, Jean Moreau, headed the Independents' list in 1947, and had no hesitation in suggesting names of younger men he thought could be elected. In short, Flandin continued to direct local political life by trying to ensure the continuity of the political tendency to which he remained loyal.

Could he ever hope to return to public life? Part of his local network had been decimated. Perreau-Pradier was ruled out, having voted for giving full powers to Pétain: he had been an intimate of Flandin, and had accompanied him in his rise to power in Paris, being in effect Under-Secretary of State at the Ministry of Finance, and then at the office of the Prime Minister when Flandin held these respective positions.

There was also the Ribière family: Uncle Marcel had been succeeded as member for Toucy of the General Council by his younger son Roger. Like his elder brother, Marcel, a senior member of the Council of State close to Poincaré, Roger had made his career in the upper reaches of the civil service; beginning as a tax inspector, he became head of the National Savings Bank. He did not play a major role in local politics. After the war, he was one of the old guard replaced by men who had been in the Resistance. Exit the Ribières? Not quite: the sister of Roger and Marcel had married Léon Noël, himself the son of a senior member of the Council of State whose roots were in the Yonne. Léon Noël's father remembered playing as a child with Marcel in the gardens of the prefecture, which was then under the direction of Hippolyte Ribière. Léon did not break with the family tradition: he also became a servant of the State, becoming an adviser at the Council of State, then Prefect and Head of the Criminal Investigation Department; Laval made him his Principal Private Secretary. Then he entered on a diplomatic career; his cousin Flandin – they were about the same age – also called on his services, appointing him General Secretary to the Office of the Prime Minister, then Ambassador to Poland.

However, in 1940, Léon Noël, who had just been appointed Vichy government delegate in occupied territory, resigned after ten days and joined General de Gaulle. The decisive step had been taken: unlike Flandin, or his cousin Marcel Ribière, who was prefect of Nice under the Vichy government, Léon Noël remained a fervent Gaullist until the end of his life; he agreed to testify in the High Court against the cousin to whom, as Flandin's friends remarked, he owed his posting as Ambassador. Worse still, he went into local politics, and in 1951 led the Rassemblement du peuple français list against Moreau and his friends and managed to get himself elected deputy. But Noël's heart was not really in constituency work; when the RPF adventure was over, he did not persevere in the electoral stakes, and was not even a candidate in the general elections of 1956. The family property at Toucy was always a secondary residence. Léon Noël was first and foremost a faithful follower of de Gaulle, and the latter on his return to power made him president of the newly created Constitutional Council. Léon Noël was certainly an important figure in the Yonne, but he did not have a lasting influence in local politics. As for the Ribières, they played only a very minor role; Marcel's son René, the only heir to the name, went into the prefectoral corps and became a Gaullist, but he left the department: he was elected Union pour la nouvelle république deputy for Seine-et-Oise and had a seat in the Assembly from 1958 to 1967.

But let us return to the early fifties. Pierre-Etienne Flandin was not content to sit back and live on his memories, but was keen to make a political comeback; he was only about sixty years old when in 1952 an opportunity arose in the form of election to the Senate, and in he plunged, in defiance of the declaration of electoral ineligibility, which meant that he could not have voting-slips with his name in the voting-booths, or hold public meetings. He was beaten in the first round; the name of Flandin was no longer enough to mobilise the mass of voters. Flandin felt this defeat keenly; but after all, he had not even been an official candidate. In 1955 his brother Charles fell ill and could not stand in the cantonal elections. Flandin had by this time recovered his civil rights and was once again eligible to stand.

Once more he threw himself into his campaign, organising lunches with mayors and leaving nothing to chance. He had to rally the farmers' representatives to his cause: 'I shall be at Cure from 1 April onwards and I shall come to the fair at Avallon, where I may perhaps have the pleasure of seeing you', he wrote to Louis Devoir, who at the time was President of the Chamber of Agriculture. 'Would you care to have lunch with me on that day? If you bring along some representatives of agricultural bodies I shall be very pleased to invite them also. I will telephone you on Friday. We could have lunch at the Hotel du Commerce at midday.'[44] The lunch took place, and a few weeks later Flandin was back on the General Council. He went no higher, however, and died three years later, in 1958. The accidental death of his son Rémy at the controls of an aeroplane affected him badly. With the death of this son, a tax inspector, he lost his natural successor, for Rémy was cut out for a career in politics.

On Pierre-Etienne's death, yet another Flandin, Paul, Charles's son, took over the seat on the General Council. Since the war, he had frequently acted as a link between his uncle and the elected representatives of the department. He was to be re-elected several times without interruption, and took an active part in the creation of the Morvan Regional Nature Park, intended to promote the development of this depressed region. Paul Flandin is today the head of the Park and chairman of the finance committee of the General Council in Auxerre. From 1839 to the present, therefore, the canton of Vézelay has been constantly represented by a Flandin. The present mayor of Domecy is also a member of the family: his mother is a daughter of Paul-Etienne and his father the nephew of the aeroplane manufacturer Louis Bréguet.

Politicians on the move

It seemed reasonable to tell something of Flandin's life as M. Devoir and his colleagues, the mayors of the Morvan, had spoken so much of him. I also met the present-day holder of the name on several occasions. 'Popaul', as he is affectionately known in the area, is, apart from his role as head of the Park, a key figure in the political life of the department. He can be seen regularly officiating at various ceremonies, such as large meetings of representatives of the Morvan, lunches in honour of particular individuals, smaller meetings of members of the General Council, and so on. He himself expressed some worry about the future; would there still be a representative of the family to take up the torch after him? According to my informants, the Flandins were part of the local heritage. People could not resist telling anecdotes about them: I have been doing it myself, because it seems to me that this allows us to go beyond a rather outdated concept of tradition, and perhaps reach a better understanding of the way local politics works in France.

The American historian Eugen Weber quite properly posed the question how it came about that political oppositions significant for an elite of Parisian politicians were nevertheless taken quite seriously deep in the rural heartland of France.[45] The answer lay, according to him, in the tremendous development that took place in the second half of the nineteenth century in technical, economic and cultural areas, and created an equal interest in political questions over the whole of the country. Politicisation as the end-result of a process of acculturation: this, roughly, is the explanation offered. It may be objected that earlier rural society was less isolated than this view suggests. Surely the Revolution had already begun the process of politicising local life? This is the objection formulated by certain historians, particularly Vigreux, who has made a close study of the republican experiment of 1848.[46] Weber's proposition no doubt neglects some important aspects of the reality of the time. On the other hand the question he asked does serve to show up a remarkable characteristic of life in the French provinces under the Third Republic: public interest in national political and ideological oppositions. Obviously this was due to an unprecedented cultural mutation, linked to the development of public education in the countryside. But there is another side to the phenomenon, too frequently ignored, and which concerns not the voters but those elected. Looked at from this point of view, and not simply as a fascinating anecdote, the rise of the Flandins merits serious attention.

The Flandins were an old local family who had benefited, like many others in France, from the forced redistribution of wealth under the Revolution. But the descendants of the Lorme doctor rapidly distinguished themselves from their fellow-citizens by establishing the basis of their social situation in Paris. Subsequently they made excellent use of their double attachment, to the village and to the capital. Two places, and of course two levels of discourse. I do not mean to imply any duplicity: I am referring simply to their ability at any given moment and with a given voter to move from the register of local problems into that of national issues. I noticed a particular insult which crops up frequently in debates at the beginning of the century: politicians would be called Frégoli after an actor whose rapid changes of costume and role – up to sixty in one performance – had made him famous. The Flandins, however, were quite the opposite of these 'Frégolis' down from Paris who were suspected of trying to 'hoodwink simple country people'. The Flandins were well known in the capital, and they had proven ability – they had studied law at university – and in village and town they were expected to deliver a coherent view of current events. They were also expected to maintain a local paper: Flandin maintained *La Revue de L'Yonne*, for example, and Ribière, *La Constitution*. At the same time they enjoyed the legitimacy conferred by the fact that they were natives of the region, like their families before them.

In the case of the great provincial notables who blossomed under the monarchy and the Empire, and for whom the first years of the Third Republic, the 'Republic of Dukes', marked the end, it was enough to exhibit a position in the social hierarchy in order to control the levers of local politics. With Etienne Flandin and his son we see the emergence of a new relationship between the elected representative and his fellow-citizens. The politician establishes a certain distance, but far from being dissolved, the links between himself and his constituency are strengthened. Initially, he has to succeed at a 'political' level: we see this very clearly in the case of Pierre-Etienne, who is incidentally a prime example of the politician of the first half of this century, who advances his career by the skilful deployment of all his talents, in this case not only as a lawyer, but also as an expert on aviation. Paris is the place where all the wheeling and dealing takes place, where the politician makes his way inside a political grouping, and we saw that he became party leader and leader of the Democratic Alliance. In this sense it is true that the elected representative is far away from his voters, during this long haul to the top. Yet he must keep in touch with his people, in his department. Not only must he respond to a wide variety of requests, but he is expected to guide the political debate at local level.

For there was a real debate going on in the villages and towns; we saw the sort of excitement that reigned during Flandin's election campaigns. At that time, the rival candidates faced each other publicly at meetings. They contradicted and questioned each other. In this way the population learned to grasp the main points of the national debate. The deputy played a central part in this process of politicisation. Whether he was merely close to the central power, or actually a member of government, it was his duty to respond to the voters on questions of the day. At the same time, the voters were of prime importance to the politician's future career: his very political existence depended on their votes. He might be Prime Minister, or Minister for Foreign Affairs, but he still had to take up his pilgrim's staff sometimes. In the days before mass communications, the politician was a mass medium in himself: Flandin would repeat before his voters the same speeches he had read to the Assembly. It was just as though he were addressing his colleagues in the Chamber, yet it was only a village meeting! That was exactly why people went.

The population were eager to engage in this way with the big political issues of the day, those that were treated at international conferences, or in big debates in the National Assembly. Promises and favours of all kinds were insufficient for the voters, as Flandin understood very well: hence the frequent meetings he organised on his patch. The politician was the product of a subtle dialectic between two very different worlds: the high spheres of central government in Paris and the here and now of local realities. He must be here and there at the same time, playing first the Yonne card and then the Paris card, practising his skills at the centre, and taking the lead on the periphery. He had to enable his electors to dream a little: the fact that the deputy was a Parisian as well as a farmer was no handicap – far from it! Everyone knew he met all sorts of important people up in Paris, and everyone pictured him at glittering receptions; the odd celebrity had even been spotted paying him a visit at his home on the banks of the Cure. We should not underestimate the importance of the ability of the public figure to fire the local imagination. From this point of view it is an advantage for him to be continually moving in a circle from his home to Paris and back to his home. This circular movement reinforces his power: representation becomes movement to and fro; as a focus for the imagination, the elected representative acquires the prestige of the mediator and the medium, and is a centre of interest and a carrier of new ideas.

There is another important point to be considered in studying the irresistible rise of the Flandins. So far, I have put most stress on the new relationship between the voters and their representative: the local career of a public figure consists of enlarging the horizons of the local people, giving them, as it were, a national outlook. But the strategy of representation has another side to it: as well as the relationship between voters and representative, there is the question of his relations with the local elite. To reinforce political success, it is a good idea to enlarge one's circle and establish a range of horizontal relationships with other elected representatives and influential figures. A good example of this is the importance for the political destinies of Flandin and his son of the alliance with the Ribières. The interlocking paths of the two local dynasties shape the map of local political life. Is this just a case of birds of a feather? It is true that the parallels between the careers of the cousins and those of their descendants are immediately obvious – the careers in the upper reaches of the civil service and the blossoming in the shade of Poincaré, the great moderate of the Republic, and saviour of the franc.

But perhaps it would be more interesting to note the differences: whereas Pierre-Etienne developed an early taste for electoral politics, Marcel seemed anxious to remain aloof. Léon Noël let himself be tempted, but late in life and to no lasting effect. If we turn to another figure, the same contrasts can be seen: Perreau-Pradier, also a provincial who moved to Paris, was nevertheless anxious to retain his pre-eminence in the Tonnerrois, and hardly seems to have been tempted by national politics. In fact, they are complementary because of these differences. Taken one with another, they form the basis of a network of relationships which Flandin patiently built up, and which was the foundation of his influence and legitimacy at departmental level.

This brings me to some observations on networks and their impact: I had observed at Quarré-les-Tombes that political representation is a more complex phenomenon that it may seem. Whereas some people appear predestined to obtain a local mandate easily, others fail in the early stages. Not only do they fail to obtain a mandate; they never even reach the decisive threshold of eligibility. I therefore drew a clear distinction between the elected and the eligible. I meant by the eligible those individuals whom the members of a local society can recognise as legitimate representers, a recognition not based solely on qualities or abilities attributed to the individual, but resting mainly on the affiliation, real or supposed, of these individuals to one of the networks that structure local life. I stressed that the affiliation may be only supposed, for the network is not in any sense a fixed reality. It is the result of a number of concrete actions, and it can grow larger or smaller over time, in line with its real effectiveness. But there is another factor which must be taken into account. The network cannot be reduced to its intrinsic qualities: it takes part of its power from the way people see it. The important thing is that the surrounding society should be able to establish a relationship between the candidate and one of the dominant networks, either through the operation of memory or by inference from his entourage. In other words, the network exists potentially and is brought into being by the actions of its members and by symbolic operations effected from outside, consisting in the attribution of affiliations.

Hence the 'realist's' questions: What is the extent of the networks? What are their limits? have no real sense, strictly speaking, since the networks' potential is never fully realised. Nevertheless, one can distinguish different contexts in which the operation of the networks can be observed. Hitherto, I have looked at three types of public figure: the first relies on a network of relationships extending over the communes belonging to a canton and links several families occupying local positions. This kind of network has its origins in the early years of the Third Republic: the situation described at Quarré-les-Tombes can be considered typical of many others of this kind. We have also encountered a second type of link, whose territorial extension is greater: here what we have are bonds forged over a long period between families who play a prominent role at departmental level and more modest lineages, for example, the Flandins and the Devoirs.

The third type of relationship brings together dominant political families, like the Flandins and the Ribières: the workings of their alliances do not abolish the differences between them, particularly political differences. Yet patterns forged over a long period make these families into partners or adversaries who are more or less indispensable to anyone aiming at a career in public life. It is a world of tacit pacts, where people recognise each other with no need of speeches or formal statements; where each observes the other closely, weighing up his chances, while preserving outside the periods of electoral excitement a serene and friendly neutrality. Only a few personalities have stamped their imprint on these privileged spheres. Thus Pierre-Etienne Flandin left as his inheritance a characteristic political style: the Yonne remains the paradise of the moderate stance, which does not mean that political divisions are entirely blurred. But network politics predominate over the activities of parties, in the sense of highly structured organisations. Here confrontation rhymes with cohabitation . . .

3

Ups and downs in politics

So far, we have an image of the world of local politics which emphasises stability and continuity: the stability of public figures secure and at ease in their family strongholds, and continuity in the shape of systems of transmission of political office like an inheritance from one generation to the next, on condition that they tend it and make it bear fruit. This image does indeed correspond in great measure to the stability of French provincial life. It is a world where the long-term view prevails: dramatic events are few, though this very fact increases the impact when one occurs, to the point where certain periods, like the break between Church and State, and later the Resistance, take on the status of myth. But the prevailing mood can be perceived as one of cosy cohabitation, with everyone in the kitchen, helping to prepare a delicious republican banquet. This image is not entirely unrealistic; historians and political scientists have drawn our attention to the contrast between the political stability of the rural heartland of France and the agitation which prevails in the capital and certain other large urban centres. Some writers have found pleasure in contrasting the harsh confrontations of national politics with the more tranquil delights of local politics. I myself felt the attraction of this image of a timeless provincial world, but close daily observation of people's activity forced me to qualify this image, and I would like now to examine the rather more chequered careers of certain individuals, which suggest that the landscape is less peaceful than one might imagine.

As we all know, professional politicians are rarely contemplatives: what they have they have had to fight for, and they know its price. Alongside our local dynasties, who in the words of Figaro 'merely put themselves to the trouble of being born', there are many who have had to struggle for a place on the stage. It is a long climb to the top, and the man who decides to invest his energies in that direction may be confronted by many obstacles, and may be forced to change direction many times. In the race for legitimisation, a man must be ready to take on the most varied roles: there is the lucky winner, of course, or, at the other extreme, the eternal loser, but there are also a number of supporting roles, such as the challenger, the newcomer who disturbs the reigning order, and so on. The list is by no means exhaustive, but I have not the space here to devote to a complete taxonomy of contenders, which would weary the reader, in any case. Instead I shall give some real examples which demonstrate the hazards of political life. The inner dynamics of political action, and the specific weight of circumstance, can be clearly seen at the point where these destinies cross those of the winners.

Scenes from political life

The setting was Auxerre, shortly after the municipal elections in 1983. Sitting in a café, I overheard a heated conversation about the Socialists' defeat. 'Hammered again; let's face it, they're hopeless', said one man. 'I'd like to see you try; have you any idea what it's like trying to get the other lot out, with Soisson as mayor?' 'That's what I mean, they've got no chance; no one is going to budge Soisson; so why bother? And they always put up the same people . . .' 'Just a minute, look at the results elsewhere; the Socialists have collapsed all over the place – you have to remember that, before you start blaming individuals!' The conversation went on for some time, and it reflected a more general feeling. The collapse of the left was being greeted with fatalism. For years they had been battling to take over the town hall at Auxerre: every time, they came up against the same obstacles. In 1983, the verdict was clear: 60.8 per cent for the list of the outgoing mayor, Jean-Pierre Soisson, and 36 per cent for the list headed by his Socialist rival. These results should obviously be seen against the background of a drop in popularity after two years of a left-wing government. Six years earlier, in 1977, the left had won 46.8 per cent of the votes in the municipal elections, as against 53.18 per cent for the right. That had represented a real advance for the coalition formed by Socialists and Communists in the quest for votes. That was the year when in many towns 'new mayors' emerged who in many cases were to play an important role in the life of the community. That same year a new generation of local councillors, aged under forty, came in. Auxerre, however, was untouched by this phenomenon; granted, it had already elected a young mayor in 1971, and the right had been established there for many years. So the vote was stable, and there was a charismatic figure already in place. This explanation for the lack of change in Auxerre would, I believe, satisfy most political commentators; they tend to look at the balance of forces, then at how the votes are distributed, and once the result is announced, they tend to concentrate on the winner.

As for the loser, all we note is his disappearance. If he was a significant figure, he is eclipsed for the moment and perhaps one day we will see him back in the corridors of power. If he never managed to make his mark, he is now no more than a shadow. Those are the two extremes. In the middle are all those who manage to get elected, but can never carve out a role for themselves, other than as leaders of the opposition, or implementers of strategies which fail in the end. In the tribe of politicians, the losers occupy a particular place. The very word has a contemptuous ring: journalists single out 'losers' and 'winners', as though the latter were destined to triumph no matter what. This method of classifying politicians is obviously open to question, though it probably finds an echo with the general public. It is too superficial, and encourages a black-and-white view of the world, and an image of political competition as a sort of wrestling match between the wimp and the tough guy, or the goodie and the baddie.

It may, therefore, be rewarding to take a closer look at the way political life works, but without giving undue attention, as even so-called objective approaches generally do, to those who emerge as winners from the electoral combat. Instead of asking who won, why not try a different question: Why did the other man lose? It is perfectly understandable that up to now no one has taken much interest in what happens to the losers. Our concept of political science seems to hold firmly to a few simple ideas, amongst them the notion that defeat is an arithmetical concept, and all we need to understand it is a list of 'reasons', essentially a number of objective facts, with maybe just a dash of subjectivity. This is reassuring, but it is not much use as an explanation. Anthropologists, on the other hand, working in the different sort of societies they usually study, have produced some very detailed work on lack of power, on the inability of certain individuals to impose themselves as leaders. Studies like those by Marc Augé on witchcraft among the lagoon-dwellers of the Ivory Coast[1] demonstrate clearly the great importance given in both public and private life to those situations in which the individual does not realise his ambition to be recognised by others. How should we interpret situations in which one can observe the erosion of the powers of the individual? How conceive of political activity in the negative?

The theme of defeat often cropped up in my conversations with informants, and I felt I must pay close attention to it. After all, the anthropologist works on the principle of accepting everything he is told. Hence the great importance I attached to what I might call, echoing Nathan Wachtel, 'the vision of the vanquished'. But let there be no misunderstanding: the individuals I invited to speak on this subject are all in their own way 'winners'.

The heights of Auxerre

I had an appointment on this particular morning with Michel Bonhenry in one of the buildings of the lycée Fourier, where he was conducting an oral examination. After some initial difficulty, I located his classroom. The lycée Fourier stands on the heights of Auxerre, in a district which was built after the war for office and industrial workers, at a time when Auxerre was expanding rapidly. It is a predominantly 'technical' institution: this fact, and its location in the town, differentiate it from the lycée Jacques-Myot, which is right in the centre of Auxerre, between the prefecture and the Abbey of Saint-Germain. It is quite obvious that the lycée Fourier does not attract the same sort of pupils as the Jacques-Amyot, an establishment founded in 1858 to which the local bourgeoisie traditionally send their offspring. In the entrance-hall of the lycée Fourier, I notice an impressive display of precision tools made by the pupils.

Michel Bonhenry is a friendly, jovial man; one can easily imagine him in his role as teacher. He took me to a café not far from the school, on the ground floor of one of the large blocks of flats which dominate the city. Here we held our conversation, to the muffled sound of an old juke-box which would start up from time to time in the depths of the bar.

What did I learn that morning about Jean-Pierre Soisson's challenger? I asked him about his political career, and also about his family background. He was born in 1939 in Auxerre, and went to school there. His father worked at the prefecture. 'He was well known in Auxerre; my mother was from a very humble background – she worked at Soisson's [a draper's shop belonging to the forebears of the present-day deputy and mayor].' He had several brothers and sisters, but none of them was active in politics. 'I'm the only one in the family who has ever stood in an election.' His interest in politics was not a new thing. He was a militant 'from way back' in the Socialist Party, which he joined in 1969. 'It was after the events of '68', he told me, 'that I realised I had to make a commitment. But even when I was very young, I went to a lot of meetings of the municipal council and the General Council. I was curious about these matters: they interested me. One day Claude Estier came and held a meeting in Auxerre, and it was after that meeting that several friends and I decided to join what was then called the "new" Socialist Party.'[2]

The cantonal elections of 1970 came round. 'Soisson was considered to be very strongly established; no one wanted to stand against him. I agreed to be the candidate.' The canton of Auxerre-ouest, where Bonhenry stood on this first occasion, takes in nearly the whole of the town, together with the surrounding areas from which people travel to work in Auxerre. A difficult canton for a young candidate with no previous experience.

Moreover, the 'new' Socialist Party had a poor image, for it was still dragging along the reputation of the moribund SFIO, which had been getting very poor results. Its worst score had been in the preceding elections in 1964, when the Socialist candidate was clearly outstripped by his Communist rival, winning only 5 per cent of the votes. The party's fortunes were therefore at their lowest ebb. Jean-Pierre Soisson, the young man who had been elected deputy at the general election in 1968, was also actively preparing for the municipal elections which were to take place in 1971, a year after the cantonal elections. It was going to be a hard fight, so the appearance of a new man on the left was welcomed; for Michel Bonhenry, it was an opportunity to embark on a political career by taking on a serious opponent right from the beginning. Moreover, the party's situation was so precarious that the candidate was for a time spared the internecine squabbles in which the leadership of the SFIO had so often indulged.

The result – 25 per cent of the vote – was more than encouraging. Although beaten this time, Bonhenry was seen as a serious challenger for the forthcoming municipal elections. Within his own party, he was seen as a man with new ideas.

Just to give you an idea, in 1969 I worked quite a bit with François Mitterrand; I used to see him a lot at Avallon. It was the time when the Convention of Republican Institutions was thinking of joining the Socialist Party. In fact, I was criticised by some people because I had links with François Mitterrand. He wanted to make the party more dynamic. I used to see him every two or three weeks or so. The man I wasn't keen on was Guy Mollet. To me, the SFIO were fossils. The fact is, there was nobody in Auxerre who could put up a real fight against the right.

After the cantonal elections, the name of Bonhenry was better known in Auxerre. So when the Socialists had to present a list at the municipal elections a year later, they called on him once more. 'I was chosen to head the list, and got some other people together, but I could not manage to form a list with the Communists – they refused point blank.' So on the one hand there was a 'Popular Union' list, from the Auxerre branch of the Socialist Party and the Parti socialiste unifié, and on the other a 'Unified List for Modern, Social and Democratic Municipal Government', presented by the Communist Party. In 1965 there had been only one list on the left, led by the Communists. This time the situation was reversed; the Socialists had their own lists, and were stronger than their left-wing rivals. Once again Jean-Pierre Soisson beat them both, and became mayor. However, it was an honourable defeat for Bonhenry, who now became, as it were, Soisson's 'official' rival. He now had to decide how to use that position.

Until the 1983 elections, minority parties did not have the right to any seat in towns of more than 30,000 inhabitants: the victor's list took all the seats, and the victor therefore enjoyed not only effective power, but also the advantages of the privileged platform for his views offered by the municipal council. His unlucky opponent could make no headway unless he was in a position to capture a mandate and figure amongst those who 'serve the community'. Once he was a bona fide elected representative, the opposition leader could increase his credibility by participating in committees, and keeping himself informed on issues he knew something about. After the 1971 elections, therefore, Michel Bonhenry cast around for an elective position which would enable him to promote his ideas. A favourable circumstance came to his aid, which was the redrawing of cantonal boundaries in the Auxerre region. The town had expanded, so in order to keep a certain balance in the size of the different cantons, what was in effect a new canton was created, covering the north-west part of Auxerre and four adjoining communes.

The election took place here in 1973, and the main rivals were Bonhenry and one of the mayor's assistants. The Socialist candidate won by a comfortable margin (53.99 per cent of the vote). 'I have taken an interest for many years in the public life of this canton and I have always lived here, so I knew its needs', he stated in his election address.

> I am also aware of the financial difficulties involved in trying to meet those needs. For a Socialist member of the General Council, the solution can never be simply to increase local taxes like the party in power: instead we will fight to change the direction of political, financial and economic decisions taken at national level.

This speech was addressed to the working population of Les Hauts d'Auxerre, which Michel Bonhenry was to represent from that time on in the General Council. Incidentally, note the candidate's insistence on his local roots: he was born in the district, and had spent his life there. We also see the appearance of a criticism not only of government policy, as embodied in the mayor of Auxerre, but also of the council's record of management.

The candidate was thus addressing the ratepayers' pockets, blaming the problems of local finance on unwise spending by his rivals in the town hall. This was, by the way, one of the themes being pursued by the Socialists at that time: 'When Soisson was elected, he embarked on a number of developments', Bonhenry told me,

> some reasonable, others less so. He announced *urbi et orbi* that Auxerre would have 65,000 inhabitants by 1965, and that we could expect 100,000 inhabitants by the year 2000. I questioned his figures, tentatively, because I didn't have a research team behind me, at a commission of a planning body set up at the time, saying they were unrealistic, because the town was in fact hardly expanding at all. But I was the only one to say it, and Soisson can be extremely plausible. He embarked on some very ambitious plans, but he was counting on the number of ratepayers growing steadily, which did not happen. Despite subsidies, Auxerre piled up major debts, which showed up in the local budget and therefore in the local rates-demands. Soisson was soon called to account.

Bonhenry was referring to 1976, a difficult year for the mayor, who until this point had always been assured of the votes of the residents of Auxerre: at the cantonal elections he was beaten by Etienne Louis, a young Socialist graduate of the National School of Administration, and a native of Auxerre. The latter had attacked in particular a development which had by no means met with universal approval among the voters, and the attack had struck home. Perhaps the voters were tired of Soisson; perhaps they wanted to punish him. Whatever the reason, the left seemed to be on the point of overcoming its traditional handicap.

The year after, the municipal elections came round:

I was to head a list. But Auxerre was the only town of more than 30,000 inhabitants where no agreement was reached with the Communists. That is to say, an agreement was always in the process of being negotiated. At one point it looked as if we were going to make it, but I decided to break off talks because with just three weeks to go before the election the Communists were making crazy demands. For example, they wanted me to sign a paper promising never to increase local rates. I refused. So with three weeks to go before the election, there was still no agreement. That fact had to be announced. It was awful: it lost me the municipal elections, because there were quite a large number of abstentions on the left, and that was enough to make all the difference. It was such a sensitive subject that although the campaign lasted two weeks, we did not put up any posters for the first week, because we were still not sure what might happen. Finally Soisson got in with a very small margin. I might add that if I had been enough of a cynic to pretend that there was an agreement with the Communists, I would have got in.

So Bonhenry failed for the second time to become mayor of Auxerre in what proved to be the crucial year 1977. According to the Socialist candidate, victory was within the grasp of the left. If we look at the figures, however, this is not so clear: the total of votes going to the two lists, Socialist and Communist, is only 46.8 per cent. There was no need even for a second round. It is true that the mayor's list won by a smaller margin than in 1971, but his victory was unquestioned. 'Whoever runs Auxerre needs a clear head', Jean-Pierre Soisson had written, some time before the elections, in an article answering the criticisms of his rivals, but alluding also to the disputes between the factions on the left.[3] These certainly constituted a serious handicap: they hindered the possibilities of advance that had been glimpsed in the success of Etienne Louis in the cantonal elections. Bonhenry had managed to attract 33 per cent of the vote, there was an abstention rate of 23 per cent, and no doubt some of those could have been attracted to the left. That was Bonhenry's theory, at any rate. One thing is certain: the advance of the left was halted in 1977. In 1982 Jean-Pierre Soisson recovered his seat on the General Council and was re-elected mayor in 1983 with seven extra points. The figures speak for themselves.

In the period after the 1977 election, Bonhenry manned the outposts: he was twice re-elected to the General Council and headed the opposition list in 1983. He was a candidate in the general election in 1981, but was beaten in the second round: on that occasion, Soisson's margin may have been tiny (he won only 50.07 per cent of the vote), but there was no gainsaying the fact that he had held fast, even in the middle of the wave of Socialist victories. The rivalry between the two men had now existed for more than a quarter of a century; it was an unequal contest, which reflected not only the unchanging face of larger political circumstances, but also the difficulty experienced by one side in 'gaining credibility'. Like most elected representatives describing their struggle and the obstacles they have encountered, Michel Bonhenry rationalised these when he spoke to me. He explained the reasons for the left's defeats. At the same time he 'explained himself', that is, he justified his choices of strategy. However, this kind of explanation is by its very nature ambiguous, and more complex than it appears, because the person concerned, even when concentrating on the external circumstances of the event and the presence of others, whether allies or rivals, is in fact talking about himself all the time.

Let us return, for example, to the disagreements of 1977. At that time Bonhenry found himself standing against the local PCF leader, Guy Fernandez:

> Fernandez is not from around here; he was sent by the national party. He's an apparatchik, not somebody with a local following, like Lavrat [the mayor of Migennes]. Lavrat has got a lot of ex-pupils; he's a good teacher and a nice man, and that counts. It's the same with me – I know thousands of people in the constituency because I used to be their teacher. The CP is particularly sectarian here. In 1977 I had the feeling things were turning nasty. Fernandez wouldn't discuss any common programme with me. All the Communists cared about was the number of places on the list. I tried to warn the Socialist party leadership, but they didn't realise what was going on. They only reacted after the breakdown of the talks was made public. The leadership did everything to get the talks started again. They sent Joxe down here for twenty-four hours to order me to make it up with the CP. I told him: 'What's done is done; I'll look like a puppet of the CP if I go back to discuss a common programme with them now.' Joxe told me: 'This is going to lose you the election.' He was right.

Bonhenry had thus come up against duplicity in his allies and a lack of understanding from the leadership of his own party in Paris. He was just a provincial candidate bound by injunctions emanating from higher spheres. Although nominated by a party apparatus and surrounded by supposed friends, the candidate was isolated, in a sense. To some extent, his sincerity conflicted with the realpolitik. He refused to countenance cynicism and false promises. By the way he told this story, Bonhenry was inviting me to judge between the two protagonists in the debate: who was right, he himself or Joxe? Now, the answer to the question as posed is obvious: who would not prefer honesty in politics to a hollow façade destined to ensure victory at all costs? What we have here, clearly, is an instance of special pleading, which incidentally I have noticed in many conversations with politicians. No matter who they are talking to, they always make a speech. Recounting an episode in their political career is like narrating a historical epic.

Naturally, the narrator places great emphasis on the vigour with which he struggled, and exalts his triumphs; however, he cannot neglect his setbacks. To explain is to bring out the complete significance of defeat – to learn from your own mistakes. The analysis of this defeat brings out a lesson the application of which goes well beyond Auxerre; it says something about a given state of the Socialist Party and two different ways of relating to the PCF. Subtly, the listener's complicity is invited; naturally, you have your own ideas, and you're not to take sides, but surely anyone in his right mind can see . . .

However, I must make it clear that I do not see this kind of analysis as a deliberate attempt to influence the listener. It is simply one of the modes of discourse used by a public figure, and there are two reasons for that. One relates to the very nature of the discourse: politics involves judgement. The other relates to the role of the politician in public life: he must in a very real sense of the word capture his audience.

The situation recounted to me by Bonhenry attracted my attention for yet another reason. In talking to Joxe, the candidate mentioned his image in Auxerre; in fact that was a primordial issue so far as his local strategy was concerned. He could not afford to look like a puppet of the PCF, even if it cost him the election. Remember that all this was taking place in the town where he was born, whereas the other two main actors represented, each in his own way, the interests of a party. Fernandez was described as an outsider sent in by the party. As for Joxe, he was merely a messenger bringing instructions from Paris. His job was to see that a certain political line was followed, but he came up against the intransigence of a militant looking at it from the local point of view. It seems to me a vain endeavour to try to decide between the weight of the arguments advanced by the two sides, but I do think the role of Auxerre is revealing. This is where Bonhenry's personal and political history come in – assuming the two can be separated. Bonhenry emerged at a difficult time for the Socialist Party, that is, the end of the sixties. At the time he was one of the few people possessing the qualities necessary to be elected: he was a new man, a native of the place, not compromised by the internecine quarrels within the party.

Thanks to his profession as a teacher, as we saw, Bonhenry already had a local foothold, a factor not to be sneezed at. These assets allowed him to get ahead in politics, despite the fact that he never made any attempt to rise within the party apparatus. He himself underlined his independent spirit, and did not hesitate to criticise the attitudes of some of the leadership, particularly after the victory in 1981:

I have no official position now in the Federation. At the moment I support Rocard, but I'm not a blind follower of anyone. It's the same with the party leadership. I haven't always been popular, because I say what I think. When we were in government, I made it known I couldn't take some of the Ministers seriously, because not one of them, except Rocard, ever asked for my reaction, as a local politician, to decisions taken at national level. Then when I saw Mitterrand giving a medal to an extreme right-winger . . . it's hardly surprising if people don't know what to think. We've never been consulted; the Ministers are scared to consult the local branches. I put it to Quilès when he came: 'Was it a good idea to amnesty the generals?' And I advised him to ask the members what they thought at the meeting.

A free spirit, or an isolated individual? Apart from the particular case of Bonhenry, we seem here to be touching on a more fundamental issue, that of the complicated relationship between an elected representative and the party to which he belongs. For the local politician in an urban context, whether he likes it or not, is a party member. As one of the Federation leadership was later to put it crudely, speaking of another local politician: 'Without the Socialist Party, he's nothing.' This was an exaggeration, for belonging to a party is not in itself an assurance of electability; when Bonhenry halted the advance of the right in the municipal elections, and got himself elected for a canton, he succeeded where others had failed, and that was due in no small part to his local roots. Yet the argument between Joxe and Bonhenry demonstrates the strong tension between those local roots and the duties which come from belonging to a party. The secret is to combine the two registers harmoniously. What went wrong for Bonhenry? At a certain point he had to resign himself to choosing between what he saw as his local image and the demands of national strategy; events forced a sort of telescoping of his commitment to his party and the nature of his support in his locality. His margin for manoeuvre became extremely narrow, since an individual wins votes by demonstrating his allegiance to the town rather than as a spokesman for the party. The historical circumstances were the cause of the discordance here: one can easily imagine a different situation, in which a local politician might more readily reconcile the two aspects.

During these years of political struggle, Bonhenry was facing a formidable opponent: apart from his personal qualities, and the fact that he could count on the moderate vote, Soisson had had a ministerial career. But for Bonhenry there was a more important factor at work:

Soisson has had luck on his side; all his political life, he has been lucky. First of all, there was the Ben Barka affair in 1967: that ruined Lemarchand's career as a deputy in the National Assembly; Soisson did not get in that year, but the events of 1968 brought about fresh elections, and Soisson took the seat from the Socialists. In '70 the outgoing member of the General Council decided not to stand again, which left a vacant seat; then the same thing happened in '71 – the mayor was old and decided to retire.

Soisson was just lucky; this began at an early age: 'Soisson is from a wealthy family; mine is very humble.' Bonhenry's analysis emphasised the gap between two men. One was born lucky and was carried along on the wave of his own success. The other never enjoyed the same advantages and had to face difficulties in life and politics. To some extent the mayor's behaviour reflected his privileged position; he was very sure of himself and reacted badly to criticism: 'When I said in 1977 that the population of Auxerre had not grown, that it had fewer than 40,000 inhabitants, he attacked me and said I was against the town. Yet I had the figures . . .'

The view of events offered by Bonhenry is revealing: it emphasises inequality between victor and vanquished, a social inequality originating in the backgrounds of the two men, and exacerbated during the whole course of their political career. Setting aside for a moment the individual circumstances and the political aspects of the polemic between the two men, it is clear that quite apart from this particular instance in Auxerre, any political rivalry which opposes the same two individuals over a long period of time – as often happens in French towns – will give rise to a relationship between the two antagonists. This relationship undoubtedly affects their behaviour. Each thinks and acts in anticipation of the other's reaction, and in addressing the voters, he bases his argument on what the other has to say. Legitimacy is thus built on the negation of its political opposite, so that Bonhenry's emphasis on the social gap between himself and Soisson was revealing. We have already seen how election to political office is inseparable from a world of affiliations and networks which allow someone to emerge as eligible, but a politician has to foster his own credibility: in defeat he has to ensure that he remains the 'special adversary'. He must continue to be in the eyes of others the victor's 'natural' counterpart, and he must embody the alternative; political interplay is so arranged that anyone seeking election has to agree to be seen as the negation of what the opponent is supposed to embody: 'I am everything you are not' could be seen as the motto here.

It is sometimes said that the losers find it hard to recover from their defeat. This is particularly so in cases where the usual balance of power is suddenly reversed and victor and vanquished swap places. If we take into account that a political struggle creates a relationship, a subtle form of partnership between the two protagonists, then we can see that an event of this kind does constitute a real jolt, in that it brings about a complete reversal of something that has come to be almost a tradition. The most spectacular example was François Mitterrand's victory in 1981. Where we have the opposite case, as in Auxerre, where the relationship remains steady, it acquires, for the loser as much as for the winner, considerable powers of legitimisation. Thus the loser's discourse is ambiguous by its very nature; while consecrating the stability of this relationship, it is also full of thoughts of revenge. In 'explaining things', the loser is not only pleading his defence; he is also advancing slowly towards a possible reversal of the situation. If we keep in mind this very specific characteristic of politics, that winning votes is a continual effort, we will understand why political discourse can never be couched in the present tense: defeat is represented as a moment – which may admittedly be quite long – of a process orientated towards the future. However, in the short term 'explaining things' is also a way of ensuring that the cards are shuffled and dealt out again: 'Here I am [I represent everything my opponent is not] and here I stay [you recognise yourself in me, because you know you are not like him].' Every politician is potentially a loser: victorious on one level, he turns into a loser again when he climbs to the next rung on the ladder. Bonhenry was both things at once: elected to the General Council, he failed to become mayor, just as on the national stage not every deputy will become President. Bonhenry's conversation that morning summed up all the paradoxes of his precarious profession.

Friends of friends . . .

On 4 July, the leadership of the Union pour la démocratie française met to select their candidate for the elections to Senate due to be held in the autumn of the same year. It was an important decision, in that the candidate chosen had every likelihood of being elected because of the strength of the UDF in the department. There were several contenders, but the outcome was particularly vital for two of them: Henry de Raincourt and Daniel Dollfus. The former was chosen to form a joint list with the outgoing senator for the Rassemblement pour la République, Jean Chamant. Henri de Raincourt was young, still under forty, but he already had experience of local politics. The de Raincourt family were prominent in the Sénonnais, where they had a large farm. Henri's father and grandfather had held office in the Chamber of Agriculture; they were members of the General Council and mayors of the commune in which the family mansion is situated. His great-great-grandfather was a Legitimist, secretary to the Count of Chambord during the latter's exile. Henri's father was a senator, but was killed in a car accident. His successor was Paul Guillaumot, a farmer of humble origin, but Guillaumot was keen to groom young Raincourt to replace him.

After studying agricultural science, Henri took over the family farm; he very soon won his first local mandates and gained a reputation as an accepted authority on agricultural issues. He represented Chéroy on the General Council, and was mayor of Saint-Valérien: he was young, but his family was part of the political heritage of the department. The name figures substantially in a study of local history. I would hazard a guess that his rival's name lacked the same resonance. 'De Raincourt was the obvious choice', people told me later, as though his challenger had been doomed to anonymity. The meeting of the selection committee was seen as a relatively insignificant episode in a classic career. But it can also be seen from a different viewpoint, namely that of the man who was eliminated from the competition.

Let me turn, then, to Daniel Dollfus, and his role in the department of the Yonne. There is no great mystery about him. He was a member of the majority on the town council of Auxerre, to which he had been elected in 1965, when Jean Moreau was guiding the destines of the town.[4] But Dollfus was not a native of Auxerre, or even of the Yonne. He was descended from an old Alsace Protestant family, which produced wealthy manufacturers, ministers of religion, doctors and politicians.

My great-uncle was none other than Scheurer-Kestner, who defended Captain Dreyfus. I might add that this scandalised certain Protestant circles, which were pretty anti-Jewish. I am very proud of him. I could also mention my grandfather, who was a deputy under Napoleon III and who after 1870, when Alsace was annexed by Germany, became a dissident deputy in the Reichstag. The Germans ended up expelling him from Alsace.[5]

To the people of the Yonne, Dollfus was a 'Parisian'; he arrived in Auxerre as the results of chance, having had professional contacts with the mayor, Jean Moreau. The latter owned a factory, and called him in as a consultant. Dollfus had previously been involved in Antoine Pinay's factory at Saint-Chamond, and Pinay, a political ally of Jean Moreau, had recommended him.

'After this consultancy, Moreau decided that some of my ideas were worthwhile, and asked me to draw up a report on the treatment of household rubbish – particularly methods, costings and outlets for products and by-products.' Dollfus thus went to work for the town hall at Auxerre, which had commissioned the report. It was very good, and its author won Jean Moreau's esteem. 'He said to me at the time: "Wouldn't you like to come on the council?" I replied that I did not live in Auxerre. "If that is the only problem", was his reply, "come and stay at my house." Shortly afterwards I appeared on his list and got on to the council.' Before this point, Dollfus had had a rather unusual intellectual and professional career. First of all he studied theology, with the aim of becoming a minister. 'I realised that mankind needs not just words, but practical help. I thought about how I could be useful to my fellow-men in different domains.' Dollfus next launched himself into the study of law and became a barrister; he then did a degree in medicine, and would have been found at the Hôtel-Dieu Hospital in the morning and in the afternoon at the law-courts.

When he finished his medical studies, he gave up the law and specialised in endocrinology. Meanwhile, he had taken a degree and a post-graduate diploma in philosophy. He worked at the physiology laboratory in the Faculty of Medicine, and was contacted there by the firm of Bedaux, specialists in ergonomics, who asked him for some help with problems of fatigue amongst industrial workers. 'I did research into how one can reduce fatigue by adopting rhythms of work which are better adapted to the human body and facilitate both industrial and human development. The worker is less tired, and therefore more efficient.' For several years he carried out his medical work and his research for Bedaux in tandem, then the company invited him on to the board. Later there were some changes at the top, and Dollfus, who was one of the leading members of the board, was given the opportunity to set up a limited company with some other directors; thus he became the head of the Institut français de développement économique, which he ran for thirty-odd years. In this capacity he carried out some very important economic consultancy commissions.

His professional competence and encyclopaedic knowledge were recognised by his colleagues on the municipal council, and earned him their admiration and respect. 'Go and see him', I was advised; 'he knows a lot. He is not only an economist, but a doctor as well, and I believe he knows quite a bit about philosophy!' I was not disappointed when I later conversed with the man thus described, for he spoke very lucidly. But it is important to stress that apart from his professional competence, Dollfus is a man of humanitarian ideals, who gives great importance to the betterment of mankind. Unlike many politicians, he spoke to me in the language of philosophy. I therefore asked him if he was really interested in the workings of politics. I had thought that all his activities of this type were restricted to Auxerre, but in fact his passion for politics, both local and national, went back further than that.

I have always been tempted by politics, because one can better the lot of mankind not only by economic, social and psychological measures, but also by political ones. That is why I wanted to get involved in politics. I got to know François Mitterrand towards the end of the Resistance. After the war, we founded the UDSR. I belonged to it for several years, because I liked its level-headed social and economic doctrines. There were people in it like Pleven, Bonnefous and Claudius-Petit, who are very reasonable, thoughtful human beings. So I was treasurer until 1965. In the summer of '65 we rented a property next door to Mitterrand's; as treasurer, I was in constant touch with him, and our two families were very close. Danièle Mitterrand and my wife are still friendly. One morning, Mitterrand came to my house at breakfast time and told me: 'Well, I've just got back from Paris, and I have said yes: Daniel Mayer won't be the candidate [for President of the Republic] – it will be me. We must get to work on it straight away, and I need you as treasurer.' We talked a bit more, and I questioned him about our position in relation to the Communists. He told me he would be the single candidate for the left. So I asked him: 'What are our commitments vis-à-vis the Communists?' He gave a very vague response. I have never been able to find out what exactly had been agreed on this point. I told him: 'I am loyal, and I won't abandon you on the verge of an election, because I know all the ins and outs of the finances. But after I have done my bit and arranged the finance you need, I won't be able to carry on, because I believe like Blum that the Communist Party does not belong to the left, but to the East. I think it is dangerous to get mixed up with them.'

François Mitterrand was not in fact elected in the end, but he stuck to his alliance with the Communists. Under these circumstances, Dollfus left his original allegiance and joined the Centrists, who were regrouping at the time around Jean Lecanuet.

I remained friendly with Mitterrand. I do still sometimes have lunch or dinner with him – in fact I saw him not so long ago, but he knows I no longer share his views. When I saw him he said to me: 'You see how right I was? The CP has less electoral support than ever', which was true. I told him that was neither here nor there, because the CP's strength is in the trade union Conféderation générale du travail and other bodies which still have a great deal of hidden influence.

When the Centre des démocrates sociaux was founded after the 1965 elections, Dollfus joined it, as it shared the ideas he had developed in the UDSR. 'Don't forget that until 1958, François Mitterrand was elected in the Nièvre as the voice of the centre, supported by the votes of the right.'

When Dollfus joined the municipal council in Auxerre, he already had a wide and varied experience of politics. He had rubbed shoulders with Mitterrand, now identified with the Union of the Left. In rejecting this alliance with the Communists, in line with his concept of the centre, Dollfus had taken a decisive step. When he joined Jean Moreau's team, then, Dollfus seemed destined for an outstanding political future in this traditionally moderate municipality. Apart from his knowledge of the world of politics, he had been an adviser to Bénard (a Minister in the Fourth Republic charged with launching the nuclear energy programme) and he had been Principal Private Secretary to Jean Monnet. These brilliant antecedents, and the intimate knowledge of government thinking of which Dollfus could legitimately boast, made him into a rather exceptional character for his colleagues on the council and other political figures in the department. As the mayor of Auxerre was elderly, many were convinced that Dollfus's aim was to succeed him, and it would seem that the intimacy between them favoured this interpretation.

Strangely enough, Dollfus's exceptional qualities turned out to be a disadvantage. His first brush with Jean-Pierre Soisson came in the general election in 1967, when Soisson first stood for deputy. Jean Moreau was unwilling to be brushed aside in this fashion, and decided to stand as well, with Dollfus as his substitute. There was thus a primary election on the right, from which Soisson emerged victorious: at the second round, Moreau refused to stand down in favour of his rival, and Louis Périllier, the candidate for the Fédération de la gauche démocrate et socialiste, won.

At the time, both men knew that what was really at stake was the post of mayor. Both Soisson and Dollfus, each in his own way, represented a possibility of renewal. But the former had an 'objective' advantage over the latter: he was a native of the place. People who remember this episode still insist today on the fact that for them Dollfus was an outsider: 'We all knew Jean-Pierre, whereas the other fellow . . . And then, he organised an American-style campaign. We weren't used to that. Mind you, he seemed very well qualified.' Although Soisson was also breaking with the traditions of Auxerre by challenging the mayor as he did, it is obvious that the voters were not pleased by Jean Moreau sponsoring a newcomer. The 'American' style adopted by Lecanuet's followers has since been imitated by all the parties, but in a provincial town in the sixties, the novelty was not greatly appreciated, as Dollfus learned to his cost. But another factor was decisive in what we must call his defeat, even though he was only standing at a remove. This was the reaction of local political figures.

As Dollfus himself explained:

> In 1966, Senator Guillaumot was president of the CDS in the Yonne. He did everything to prevent me standing as substitute in the general election, because he supported Soisson. He preferred to push him, which I can understand, because he was a good friend of Soisson's father, who was president of the Chamber of Commerce.

One might object that Dollfus equally enjoyed the support of Jean Moreau; but it is important to remember that Guillaumot represented a rural area, and the constituency included a large rural vote. Some of Dollfus's friendships were somewhat unexpected: 'I was very friendly with the FGDS candidate, Louis Périllier; he had also been in the UDSR.' The fact is that Dollfus's career had mainly developed in the context of Paris, where he encountered people who like himself would later try their hand in the provinces. He was now encountering a different system, where local networks came into play. In theory, Dollfus should have been able to count on the leader of his own party, but local ties and local affiliations overrode that. What we are seeing here is precisely the process of production of an eligible candidate. The respective positions of the two rivals in the system of relationships in Auxerre were quite different. Both could be considered competent and effective, and both professed a desire for change; therefore other factors came along to determine the choice. There was the question of political tendency, but there the differences were less significant than one might think at first glance. Soisson may have benefited from being a supporter of Pompidou, but Dollfus belonged to the group in government. The reality is that it was Soisson's integration into local networks which tipped the balance in his favour, even before the voters made their choice.

Let us be clear about this concept of Dollfus's 'non-eligibility'. It will be objected that he had in fact already won an election (to the municipal council). But that took place in a completely different context. In the episode which concerns us, what was at stake was the local party leadership. The rivalry was 'between friends', people in the same camp. This is the reverse of the example of the right/left divide we looked at earlier. In that kind of competition, the loser forges an identity for himself: he embodies one of the two forces facing each other, and therefore he has a clear duty to continue being himself. His defeat serves to reinforce his legitimacy in such circumstances. In a case like that of Dollfus, however, a process of leakage takes place: the losing candidate is deprived of a certain amount of legitimacy, which flows to his rival, as happens with communicating vessels. The system does not have room for two, so one is doomed to disappear. The rivalry between Dollfus and Soisson presents a very clear example of one particular pattern, in which the process of legitimisation is governed from beginning to end by the system of local relationships. For such a situation to arise, the organised structure (party or other form of political organisation) must be very loose; the vertical system of relationships gives way to modes of expression which may appear more individualistic (the personal preferences of one particular leader), but which in fact at a deeper level bring us back to the system of local relationships, traditions and ways of seeing the world.

Can one recover from a defeat within one's own camp? How can one continue to cohabit after an experience of this sort with one's own political allies? Dollfus's subsequent career offers some insights into this question. In 1968, an opportunity arose for the right to regain the constituency after the dissolution of the Assembly which followed the events of May of that year. Dollfus takes up the story:

> Jean-Pierre Soisson came to see me: 'Look', he said, 'on the political level we are not far apart; let's work together. There are two important positions: deputy in the Assembly – you can help me get that – and senator. M. Guillaumot has not got long to go in his present term, and I know he intends to retire at the end of it. You can be senator if I support you.' So I agreed to help him: I liked his ideas and he was open-minded on social issues. He was elected deputy in 1968.

So Dollfus had by no means abandoned the idea of making a career in local politics. After all, it was Moreau and not he who had been beaten; his rival's proposition was not unattractive. Soisson showed political realism in preferring to have Dollfus on his side rather than embarking on a struggle which could ruin his chances against the left; we must remember that at the time he approached Dollfus he had not been elected, but was merely the candidate selected by one side. Dollfus for his part saw an opportunity to win a seat on a prestigious body and enjoy the advantages of a long mandate. So the individual aims of the two former rivals coincided. In the event the agreement was to prove less fruitful for one of the parties. What happened was that M. Guillaumot decided to stand again for Senate, first of all in 1968, and again nine years later. Dollfus was therefore obliged to wait until 1986. Such are the hazards of political life at local level. It would not, I believe, be rewarding to linger solely on the tactical aspect, or to speculate on the hidden intentions of the two protagonists. That would be to ignore the fact that they are both, willy-nilly, part of a larger system, where nothing can be guaranteed. The fact that the seat in the Senate was not left vacant at the planned time only goes to show the sort of objective limitations which lie in wait for any strategy, however well thought out.

The rest of the story, however, reveals that the episode was not just the result of chance. We now move forward to the meeting in July 1986, when a new obstacle on the path to the Senate suddenly loomed in the person of Henri de Raincourt. Paul Guillaumot spoke to the committee in favour of this candidate. As the former substitute for the father, he had always wanted to see a representative of the family back in the Senate. 'Soisson sat there without saying a word to challenge Guillaumot', Dollfus told me.

> There was a clear division in the votes; the political vote, that is the votes of the four parties making up the Union pour la démocratie française went to me, but on the other hand the votes of the members of the General Council who were at the meeting did not. I realised later that they did not in fact belong to the UDF . . .

So that is how the seat in the Senate finally eluded our municipal councillor after a series of episodes spread over a period of about twenty years. In his version of events, Dollfus emphasised the fact that Soisson had not kept his promise. But had there really been a promise? What were its exact terms? One prominent figure, to whom Dollfus had mentioned his situation, told me: 'I warned him that a promise of support was not enough. All the candidates have promises of support; what counts is the number of votes.' The members of the General Council played a decisive role in the decision to reject Dollfus as candidate: like his predecessor, de Raincourt was immediately identified with the rural milieu. In other words the farming vote was decisive, for as we all know, the General Council represents the rural voice. In such a context, Dollfus was the victim of what we might call a chink in his armour. He was a man of the town, and had never managed to develop a rapport with the rural councillors. His chances were reduced for that reason, and not simply because of internecine manoeuvres.

Dollfus was like a player holding cards which were not relevant to the particular game in progress. He had a permanent handicap, not so much in his real personality as in the image other players had of him. They never denied that he had very good qualities, but it was perhaps those very assets which were the cause of the problem. We have seen that because of his economic expertise, Dollfus was seen from the beginning as a supporter of modern ideas, in contrast to an electorate the majority of whom were conservative; similarly, his tendency to see the philosophical aspects of issues, and to take seriously ideas for improving society, contrasted with the discourse of councillors who saw themselves as 'practical men'. His political commitment, and his desire to foster an atmosphere of tolerance, brought Dollfus up against some unexpected problems. Thus, in 1979, he stood in vain for election to the General Council:

I decided to stand at Seignelay. There were several rival candidates: I myself for the UDF, one from the RPR, a Communist, a Socialist, and a PSU candidate. I built my campaign on opposition to the Communist. Unfortunately, the RPR spent its time fighting me, instead of the left. I have always been a man of the centre, but since I could not hope to get the Socialist vote, I needed the RPR votes at the second round. After a campaign centred on opposition to me, their candidate refused to stand down in my favour: he withdrew purely and simply after the first round, I only got 45 per cent of the vote, and the Communist got in. That's where factionalism gets you, when we should be fighting for ideas.

Dollfus thus had difficulty accepting the rather peculiar climate of political competition, the guerrilla wars waged from time to time between individuals from different parties on the same side. As a municipal councillor, it was his practice to lend an ear more readily to criticism voiced by the minority on the left, which he said was often pertinent. He could see no sense in quarrelling about anything other than vital issues. Socialism, State intervention, forms of industrial management: these were the issues on which he felt debate was necessary. This rather high-minded view obviously conflicts with the more mundane reality of actual political life. Yet we saw that Dollfus never gave up his ambition to have a political career. Can one reconcile the irreconcilable, the pragmatism of the strategist with broad philosophical aims?

As we look back over Dollfus's lengthy progress, we see how difficult it is to make one's way in local politics: it is like a race in which one of the competitors is handicapped by the power of influential local networks. Of course, the circle in this instance was much larger than in earlier cases: at this stage we are no longer dealing with the small enclosed world of the rural commune, and party political affiliations are explicit; there is no question at this level of concealing them under a supposedly apolitical stance. In fact, membership of a political party is an indispensable condition for entering the arena: before he can aspire to represent the local community, the candidate must be accepted by his party. At every stage of his political career he must win the status of eligibility anew. Thus Dollfus, who had easily acquired eligibility at successive municipal elections, found himself obliged to fight again for this status amongst his peers when the elections to Senate came along. The stakes had gone up, and a new hand had to be dealt. With the change of electoral context Dollfus had to start again from nothing. However, within the restricted group of the committee charged with selecting the candidates, the choice of eligible candidates adopted forms analogous to those which we have already encountered in respect of village networks. When one is looking at an urban context, or a competition for office at departmental level, political commitment begins to be taken directly into account. However, setting aside the political content of the message which the candidate sets out to impart, his discourse is spoken within a sort of echo-chamber, whose importance we should not underestimate. If the discourse does not find an echo first of all amongst his fellows, his 'friends', as they are called, it is entirely possible that our candidate will find himself wasting his breath. The key figures, the vital links in the system of relationships, are the ones in the front row of the stalls or in the wings. The destiny of the candidate depends to a great extent on whether these people welcome him into the bosom of the political family.

A disruptive element?

I had just been for a pleasant stroll along the banks of the Yonne. As you follow the river, the landscape is soft and luminous on these summer mornings. On my arrival at Coulanges-sur-Yonne, I realised that I had forgotten to bring writing materials (very Freudian!), although I was on my way to interview the member of the General Council for the canton. I immediately rushed into the nearest shop, a sort of general store, only to find it full of holiday-makers examining the fishing-rods, dinghies, lifebelts and other sailing equipment the owner stocked. No doubt about it, my attention was wandering . . . Leaving the shop, I made my way to the town hall, and hurried up the steps to the secretary's office: the cool inside was welcome. Grégoire Direz, who is also the mayor of Coulanges, greeted me and launched straight into the heart of the matter; he was a young man, very keen to see his projects carried out, adapting them to the particular sociological and political characteristics of his canton. First of all he spoke about the history of the canton: he had written a book on this subject. Three main characteristics stood out, according to him: conservatism, Jansenism and patriotism. The Yonne was a community of small peasant proprietors in which there had developed a strong sense of national identity.

For a long time, Coulanges was a 'red' canton. It is close to Clamecy, and was greatly affected by the events of 1851: in that year the workers engaged in transporting timber on the river rebelled against the seizing of power by Louis-Napoléon, and suffered severe repression. Ever since then, the area had been strongly leftist. Grégoire Direz pointed out to me that in

September 1945, the Communist Party got its highest score there, with 38 per cent of the votes. The member elected to the General Council at the time was none other than the president of the Communist Federation, which was then very powerful in the department. Nowadays, it seemed, things were different, since my informant had been elected in 1982 as a member of the RPR. In his view, the change was due to the decline in economic activity, accompanied by a remarkable increase in the number of elderly people: the over-sixties represented no fewer than 40 per cent of the population. It was the highest percentage in the Yonne. This change probably provides at least part of explanation of the 'moderate' majority. Direz felt it was more accurate to speak of a balance between right and left, for the leftist tradition was still very strong. François Mitterrand got 57 per cent of the votes in 1981. Direz's predecessor as member of the General Council was a Socialist. In the two communes abutting Coulanges, the votes generally went to the left: there was a working-class population, employed in the quarry at Andryes and at a charcoal-manufacturing firm in Crain.

So the present member of the General Council could legitimately boast of having overturned a tradition which made Coulanges, situated on the edge of the Nièvre, a sort of political prolongation of that department, and an annex of Socialist Clamecy. How had he got himself accepted in this rural canton? Did he belong to a family with roots in the area?

I do have some links with the Yonne, but my family is really from Bessy-sur-Cure, which is in another canton nearby. How did I come to represent Coulanges? I stood in 1982 with the support of Chamant, the president of the General Council. The only reason I got away with it is that no one thought I had the slightest chance. If anyone had foreseen my success, I would never have been allowed to stand. But that's nothing new . . .[6]

It was not in fact the first time Direz had stood in an election. As he explained, he had entered the field the previous year, in exceptional circumstances:

I stood in the Nièvre in 1981, in François Mitterrand's constituency. Jacques Toubon asked me to do it. Naturally, I hadn't the least hope of success against Bernard Bardin, the Socialist chosen to succeed Mitterrand. But the campaign taught me a lot. The reason I got elected in this canton was the experience I had acquired the previous year: you learn a lot as a candidate.

The least one can say is that Direz's first steps on the political path had a certain panache; in such an unequal contest, the candidate who is bound to lose gains from a certain amount of reflected glory. Another important point: right from the start, Direz presented himself as a party man, and in fact more precisely as a man on a mission entrusted to him by the RPR. It was the General Secretary himself who had chosen him. Therefore, when he later stood on a local election, Direz was a marked man, somebody who was political, unlike other characters who preferred to cloak themselves in a prudently apolitical garb, of as pale a colour as possible. Direz presented a different image, one in which dynamism was inseparable from political affiliation.

Direz's political vocation does not appear to have been sparked off by his family; his father was not particularly interested in such matters:

'Was anyone else in your family ever elected to office?'

'No, no they weren't . . .'

'Anyone belong to any party in particular?'

'I have an uncle who is a Communist. He was the head of the Resistance around here. He has held one or two offices. He is a municipal councillor in Bessy-sur-Cure. But that's not very important, though I used to go to Bessy in the holidays.'

Grégoire Direz was a very bright student: he went into the preparatory classes at school for the entrance exams to study engineering at the Ecole centrale. After the Centrale he went to the State college for the senior civil service, the Ecole nationale d'administration. Not content with the administrative role in the upper reaches of the civil service for which his double qualifications equipped him, he resolved to enter politics. He joined the leadership of the RPR as an adviser on public finance. It was in this capacity that the young man was sent to Nièvre in 1981. Back in a region which he had known since childhood, he decided as the cantonal elections approached to stand in the Yonne.

'Was it the RPR who asked you to stand?'

'No, it was my own decision.'

Direz's idea apparently aroused no great enthusiasm in the local party machine. Nevertheless they did select him. It is true that they did not rate highly his chances of turning the dominant current in his favour. The fact is that in the RPR, as in any other political group, newcomers from Paris, particularly if they are graduates of the civil service college and emanate from the highest spheres of the party, are considered a nuisance. In this case it was his success on the ground which proved decisive. To everyone's surprise, he beat the man whom the outgoing councillor himself had chosen as his successor with just over 50 per cent of the vote. Two factors counted in Direz's favour. Firstly, he was very active during the campaign and went from door to door introducing himself to the voters, in every single commune. His diligence was rewarded. Secondly, the rivalry between communes played a part: we must keep in mind that a member of the General Council is chosen to represent an entire canton, which in the case of Coulanges-sur-Yonne meant a long strip of territory covering about forty kilometres.

At opposite ends stood the communes of Mailly-le-Château and Etais-la-

Sauvin. The outgoing councillor was mayor of Mailly, and his putative successor lived in that same commune. 'People at the other end of the canton, in Etais-la-Sauvin, did not even know him', Direz told me. 'In that respect we were evenly matched.' So although Direz got only 40 per cent of the votes in Mailly, he got 64 per cent at Etais. There can be no doubt that parish-pump politics played their part here, the winner being the man who was relatively less implicated in local affair, and with the advantage that Etais had a larger number of voters. Etais heads the list of communes by number of farms: it has 65 for a total population of 754 inhabitants, as against 501 in Mailly. Such a situation presents a clear advantage to an outsider: the lack of uniformity in the canton favours him. Lack of uniformity, and more importantly, lack of an identity. What we have here is a political unit with no real centre: there is a county town, of course, Coulanges, but with 597 inhabitants Coulanges cannot pretend to any influence as a commune. Moreover, the decline in the economically active population and the disappearance of traditional industries, such as the quarries, have accentuated this loss of local identity. Up to this point, identity had been manifested above all in a particular political tendency. But as the years passed and the same councillors went on and on, that choice had lost all real substance.

Direz thus came along at a crucial moment in the life of the canton. Neither candidate could be assured of victory: it was a time of decay of the fabric of society and segmentation in the political sphere. At such a time, when the communes were withdrawing into themselves, it was important not to be seen as representing one rather than another; non-affiliation to local networks became an advantage, so long as the candidate could boast of belonging to somewhere nearby. 'It's not as though he was a stranger – he has roots not far from here.' Such roots were not, however, a sufficient condition; what finally swayed the voters was the candidate's double stance of having a clear political identity, and ideas for the future of the canton. Paradoxically, Direz's political label was not a handicap in this case, because he campaigned in a way which invited people to define their own political identity. 'This is what I am', he seemed to say, 'right-wing, RPR, opposed to the Socialists, and so on.' His attitude, as it were, challenged the voters, more accustomed to tacit acquiescence in an already weakened leftist tradition, since it implied a second question: 'What are you, exactly?'

The second question Direz posed concerned the future of the canton. He brought forward proposals for the canton as a whole, aimed at the development of certain sectors, particularly tourism, promoting the idea of collaboration between different communes on particular projects. Here again the electors found themselves facing choices, involving a possible change of sociological and economic identity for the area. Direz's campaign succeeded, not only because he was personally involved to a high degree, but also because it came along at a time of uncertainty. The candidate set himself the task of swimming against the prevailing current of pessimism. By taking a definite stance in favour of local development, he made an impact in a situation where it was vital to act and get ideas accepted. The election became a contract between the candidate and the voters: they agreed to elect him, and he promised to work alongside them to restore the canton's lost identity. Afterwards Direz set to work to achieve that goal, with all the political risks it implied.

The strategy can be seen in the new councillor's first steps. He wasted no time in setting to work on his delicate task. There was no association of communes at Coulanges to promote collaboration.

I set up a multi-purpose association, a Syndicat intercommunal à vocation multiple; I was elected in March, and the SIVOM was set up in November, so I hadn't wasted any time. Luckily I knew the General Secretary of the prefecture from our time at the Ecole nationale d'administration. We got along very well, and we drew up some broad statutes which enabled us to get a lot of things done. The General Secretary of the department participated in the meeting and explained to the mayors what we were trying to do. The statutes were adopted. The whole process was made easier by the fact that nothing had been done for the last thirty years. Everything we achieved afterwards was done under the auspices of this association.

It had wide-ranging powers:

To give economic help where likely to bring about job-creation and economic activity in the canton, either through the setting-up of new industries or by agricultural developments; coordinate help for the elderly, within the framework of the joint national and local body envisaged by the circular of 7 April 1982, and in general research and carry out collective tasks of a social nature; set up and run, on demand, and at the expense of each commune, services such as public and school transport; research, set up and, where appropriate, run schemes or facilities aimed at increasing tourism, sport and cultural activities; set up and carry out, in accordance with the wishes of the municipal councils of all the communes in the association, a joint programme of roadworks; group together and put out to tender works required by the communes in the association, buy items of equipment and recruit maintenance workers.[7]

On reading this text, we see that the powers of the SIVOM did not cover just the usual aims of associations of communes, such as school transport and road maintenance. It was also the main instigator of initiatives aimed at exploiting local resources to the full. Direz's activity was targeted at two areas in particular: tourism, and encouraging retired people to move into the area. The rocks of the Saussois area, bordering the Yonne, are a great attraction to rock-climbers, so a leisure complex was developed in this area. The role of the association of communes and its president, Direz, consisted of drawing up a coherent programme for the provision of amenities, and rounding up the necessary finance. Using the intercommunal charters, new procedures aimed at encouraging local development within a regional framework, they were able to obtain financing from the region. The department was another source of funding which enabled them to get off the ground.

'In the case of the charter', Direz told me,

I got the finance because I was the first to ask; but it must be said that before 1984, the region had not spent a single franc on the canton. Tourist amenities contribute to economic development. Let me give you an example: there was not a single shop in Coulanges before. It is seven kilometres from Clamecy, and people had to travel all that way to do their shopping. I got them a Rapid'Marché because I managed to persuade the owner of the chain – he is a graduate of the Ecole centrale [School of Engineering] and I've known him for a long time. Thanks to the tourist amenities, there are enough customers in summer to compensate for the very low turnover in winter. That way we have a supermarket open all year round, which is a boon to elderly people, as they don't have to go all the way to Clamecy.

Policies for the elderly were one of Direz's main concerns. In 1983, an agreement between the State and the SIVOM facilitated the establishment of a coordinating authority, charged with the task of developing specific cultural activities for the elderly and setting up an advice and information bureau specially for retired people. Direz was keen, moreover, to encourage elderly people to move to the canton, by setting up a retirement home at Mailly-le-Château:

We are going to have a big problem around the year 2000, the problem of the elderly: a large number of people who move into this area belong to that category, and we are very anxious that this should continue, for economic reasons. But that means we must respond to the demand for facilities, by building more old people's homes, sheltered accommodation, and so on.

Direz showed me a dossier he had drawn up in connection with his project for Mailly-le-Château: the financial side was somewhat complex, since they were not asking for a subsidy from the department, but for a capital guarantee.

It was obvious that Direz thoroughly enjoyed planning and development work. Every dossier represented a large amount of preparatory work, calling on all his financial skills. He also had to travel around visiting the different bodies which might contribute to the achievement of the project. This is the world of 'joint financing' at which some local councillors are more adept than others. Even Direz's financial wizardry was not enough: he also had to be very persistent, to find out who were the right people to talk to, to be very convincing – in other words, create a favourable impression in many different spheres. At all events, he was a trained lawyer. It was hardly to be expected that he would be content simply to rub along on good terms with his colleagues and official bodies. He was a go-ahead type of person, ready to ring any doorbell if he thought it would help. For better or for worse, he was that sort of man. I was told about one occasion when he approached the prefect during the interval at a concert, and wanted to discuss some local affair before the official had even had time to get up from his seat. The prefect's response was cool, to say the least. The fact remains that from the moment of his election, Direz was highly successful in obtaining finance. For example, when the intercommunal charters procedure was set up, other councillors scarcely reacted at all at first. The Coulanges project was ready long before any other association of communes had taken any interest at all in the matter. So Direz had every right to be pleased with himself: in terms of subsidies, whether from the department, the region or the State, Coulanges is today one of the better-off cantons.

It must be said that this is a view of local political activity far removed from the well-known prudence of local councillors. Direz was a man in a hurry . . . In any case, it is doubtful whether he really had a choice between the traditional policy of sticking to what has always been done, and his own more dynamic approach. We saw that the reason he was elected was that he promised the canton the recovery of its identity; his legitimacy as an elected councillor was to a great extent based on his ability to restore some sort of coherence to the canton by bringing it within the framework of a global project. He had to act and produce visible results. I asked him how he had managed to get communes to collaborate, when they are notoriously jealous of their autonomy and anxious to look after their own interests.

I work with the mayors: we get together often. You've seen the dossiers drawn up by the SIVOM – no canton produces anything remotely like them. I draft them; I'm the General Secretary of my canton. They're proper dossiers, and the mayors can see I'm doing a good job. The association works very well; recently we had a problem with Crain. We wanted to set up a group of craft workshops, and we had a debate on the subject. There was no suitable site for the workshops in Coulanges, and the SIVOM decided to set it up in the neighbouring commune, since there was a site available in Crain next to the silo. Their municipal council refused at first. Then when they saw that the rest of the association was voting for it, they agreed to accept it. Crain and Coulanges are old rivals, and Crain has always been haunted by the fear of absorption by Coulanges.

I should add that there is also political enmity between the two communes, and Direz scored his lowest poll in Crain, in 1982. The following year he supported an RPR candidate, who ousted the mayor of Crain, but shortly afterwards the new mayor also adopted a hostile attitude towards Direz. Obviously, all these mini-tensions affected the workings of the association of communes, but in general Direz kept a steady hand on the tiller. His language, as a highly educated graduate of one of the best colleagues, may have grated at times, but he also impressed his partners in the SIVOM, who were farmers, craftsmen or retired people. Each had an interest in playing the game and obtaining for his own commune the fruits of cooperation, to which they were all gradually growing accustomed. It was not only a question of supporting tourism and retirement homes; Direz put a large amount of emphasis on other tangible achievements, such as improvements, renovations and the building of new facilities. This was not merely a way of fulfilling needs – in fact one could argue that these initiatives were aimed rather at stimulating demand. The facilities were the outward sign of a positive approach. The canton began to feel there was a coherent programme for the future; things were being built with an eye to the long term. Direz encouraged people to think that his plan could rouse the area from its traditional apathy.

What we have here is also an image of the elected councillor's role; here he is rather like a demiurge, someone who makes plans, who is prepared to meet the challenge of the future. Within this perspective, the intercommunal charter was treated as a development plan, and that met with a favourable response from the officials involved in drawing it up. The head of the research and planning section of the departmental planning authority told me that the Coulanges charter was like a complete town plan, with designated areas for craft workshops, and leisure activities. Of course, some people complained that Direz had delusions of grandeur, that he was a technocrat and was confusing a rural canton with a large town. He came close to being considered a Paris-educated megalomaniac. Direz made an eloquent plea for departmental planning in his paper, *L'Yonne-sud*, immediately after his election. However, we must not forget that decentralisation was just taking its first faltering steps, and the exact role of the department was not clearly defined until 1983.

'Everything points to the need for planning at departmental level', Direz wrote. 'As half the General Council is renewed every three years, a three-year plan, if debated and adopted in the first months after the cantonal elections, could be both the charter for the party in power in the department and a framework for action for the following three years.'[8]

In the same publication, which came out regularly from 1982 till March 1985, activities undertaken in Coulanges were commented on in detail. The tone of the leaders, written by Direz, was political, a none too subtle expression of his RPR allegiances. As one might expect, neither the government's economic policy nor its concept of decentralisation found much favour in his eyes. The leader for December 1984, for example, uses a broad theatrical metaphor to describe François Mitterrand's position: 'He is like Macbeth, parading his army on the ramparts of his besieged castle, confident in the witches' prediction that he will not be vanquished till

Birnam Wood come to Dunsinane . . . Well, Birnam Wood is on the move, and has been since the summer . . .'[9] Direz denounced both Socialist neglect and the empty rhetoric of the two extremes, the Communists and the National Front, addressing himself to the population of the southern part of the Yonne, which, as we have seen, was not particularly drawn to right-wing ideas. His paper presented a curious mixture of partisan political statements and pages devoted to local achievements; apart from information about Coulanges, there were items about the development of other cantons and pieces detailing the tourist attractions of the region. In each issue there was also an interview with a major political figure; it might be Jacques Chirac, Simone Veil, Alain Poher, or one of the people in charge of regional policy, such as Robert Poujade, or the president of the General Council, Jean Chamant, or the president of the Savoy Regional Council, Michel Barnier.

As a politically partisan paper, *L'Yonne-sud* was an organ of propaganda during the various elections of the period, municipal, regional or European. No other political tendency was expressed in it. Obviously there was no question of its offering a forum to the left-wing councillor representing the cantons in the south of the department. However, there was an attempt to balance political and local coverage, and there was also a food column written by Marc Meaneau, the famous chef from Saint-Père-sous-Vézelay, and the odd cultural item, such as a piece by Jacques Lacarrière on Restif de la Bretonne. Another characteristic of the paper, which was very well presented, was the large number of photographs of Direz. His picture adorned the leader, he usually appeared alongside the personality interviewed, and there would nearly always be a third photograph showing him at an official ceremony or a meeting.

The large number of photographs is no surprise in a political publication of this sort. Firstly, one of the purposes of this kind of bulletin is to remind the voters that their representative is active on their behalf and has taken part in a large number of public acts: politicians, whether of the left or of the right, are always anxious to reaffirm their existence in this way. But there is a second explanation: we must remember that the aim of Direz's action was to create a sense of local identity. The reproduction of his photograph seems to have been part of this task, helping the local inhabitants to see beyond the narrow horizons of their commune to a wider view of development involving faith in the effectiveness of the association of communes and the policy of creation of facilities. In this sense, it was absolutely indispensable that the councillor should not deny his political identity: in the strategy which he was pursuing, there was no room for ambiguity, and claims to an apolitical stance were no longer appropriate.

A contrast has often been drawn between the elected representative who is 'political' and the one who is 'technically competent'; but it must be said that Direz – and not only Direz, because one can easily think of a number of 'new men' like him – though priding himself on his administrative competence, which he acquired at an excellent school, greatly enjoyed the hurly-burly of political life. This is a rather strange mixture: on the one hand he claimed to be looking after the interests of the whole community, but on the other he clung to a staunchly partisan viewpoint. It could be said that the mixture facilitates peaceful cohabitation with political adversaries, and we can see that this was the case with Direz, so long as the adversaries were not involved in his actual constituency. 'Take the example of the problems with the Nivernais canal: there I saw eye to eye with my counterpart in Clamecy – Bardin, the Socialist member of the General Council', Direz told me, referring to his intervention in a discussion about the upkeep of the canal in a meeting of the General Council. It seemed like a fairly technical issue: the department, the region and the State were each in some measure responsible for the upkeep of navigable waters, and the actual point under discussion was how much the department should contribute to the fund. However, the real issue was the relationship between the three entitities. Another canal, in Burgundy, had been allocated a larger sum of money from the fund, and Direz's complaint was that the matter had not been properly negotiated, so that the department was being called upon to contribute financially without being adequately consulted. He therefore put forward an amendment aimed at making the attribution of departmental credits conditional on a minimum amount of discussion between the department and its partners. When a vote was taken, it was obvious that only the left-wing councillors were in favour of the amendment. As a matter of fact, in other circumstances, I heard certain Socialists who were critical of Direz's political views praise his pugnacity when it came to local affairs; some of them even admitted that he had been quicker than they to realise the potential of decentralisation and the intercommunal charters policy.

Paradoxically, those who were upset by Direz's voluntarism as a politician and administrator were people on his own side. His relationship with the local RPR party machine quickly deteriorated, and their regular skirmishes ended in his expulsion. *L'Yonne républicaine* published some of Direz's comments on the affair:

> You saw fit to report this 'fact' in your columns in June 1985. Yet the matter has never been laid before the Central Committee of the RPR, which is the only body competent to decide. I have no intention of engaging in polemics with anyone. I would simply like to observe that I am not responsible for what I might charitably call the misunderstandings within the local party apparatus.[10]

Let us examine the overt, or explicit, causes of this situation. Public comment was evasive, but in private, people who knew the circumstances made no secret of the bad feeling that existed between the mayor of Joigny, who was elected to the National Assembly in 1986, and Direz. This may be the principal explanation, or Direz may have had other enemies. I do not wish to linger on the anecdotal aspect of the thing, because I tend to give more importance to another major factor, one which was decisive for his political future, and that is that Direz was a disruptive element. He could not be integrated into the dominant categories in the department. This can be seen quite clearly if we cast an eye over his activities from the time of his election. His entry into politics took him a little bit by surprise: at the time, what impressed him most was that he had been singled out by the president of the General Council. His membership of a political party, and the ideological commitment which that implied, formed part of an identity strategy which also included a development project. Unlike other eligible candidates, who benefit from the start from their position in the local party apparatus, or from membership of a systematic network linking several communes, Direz had to create the conditions for his own political longevity.

We should not be surprised that the double affirmation of identity expressed both in the candidate's self-promotion and in the large number of projects for which the canton requested financial support from the department provoked an ambitious reaction amongst Direz's colleagues. The reaction made itself felt, not only at the meetings where the canton presented its projects, but also behind the scenes. Yet Direz was only doing what any councillor does, that is, using every available opportunity to promote his projects. There was nothing unusual in his behaviour: he was on the winning side, the right, which had a majority in the department, and all he wanted was to be as effective as he could as a councillor. Perhaps he just tried too hard, and began to be seen as a nuisance who was upsetting old routines. We must not lose sight of the fact that after decentralisation, some councillors felt they had their backs to the wall, and had to accept much more clearly defined responsibilities in the running of their community. I will return to this point later; for the moment, suffice it to say that waving the flag of local development and bringing forward a large number of projects can make it seem that you are trying to show other people how it should be done. Direz was the youngest member of the General Council, and it was his first elected position, whereas the majority of councillors had already been returned several times.

In the reactions to Direz's behaviour, we see the importance of the unspoken, but inflexible, rule: 'Know your place.' Behaviour which might be helpful at the level of the canton, such as showing initiative and being at the centre of activities, is not necessarily so welcome in the larger sphere of the department, amongst one's peers. I do not mean to imply that the best tactic at that level is to be resolutely discreet and keep a low profile – only that if you do not, you must make sure you have some solid allies within the General Council. On this point, only time will tell if Direz can manage to make his way into the unspoken hierarchy of local figures.

Direz was impatient, someone who was disruptive through excessive diligence, so he had to run the risk of being isolated or even rejected by his peers. But his excess was in fact the reverse side of the lack, or at the very least the absence, of a local network of legitimising support. 'I had no family roots in the area. There are some councillors whose families have been in this business for a long time', Direz told me. There was no bitterness in his remark; on the contrary, it seemed that the fact made him all the more determined to press ahead. He stood for election as mayor of Coulanges in order to increase his local involvement, rather than because he had any interest in running a small commune. But he was aiming higher. The question arose quite naturally: 'What about the general election?' I asked him. 'Yes, I'll be standing', he replied, with a smile of anticipation which as good as announced the start of his campaign.[11]

Before leaving me, Direz fished a number of copies of *L'Yonne-sud* out of the attic of the town hall. The topic of his family was mentioned again, and he suddenly returned to the story of his uncle, the Communist from Bessy-sur-Cure. 'Do you know', he began, 'that he led the Resistance group which liberated Auxerre?' He pointed to an old photograph which had been reproduced in *L'Yonne-sud* of a group with his uncle and his grandfather in the middle. The man who was now mayor of Etais-la-Sauvin was in the photograph too, so it was no coincidence that Etais was one of the communes that gave most support to Direz. Again we have the paradox here of the right-wing politician whose imagination is captured by the exploits of the bold young Communist who led the Resistance. As I left the town hall, I pondered the various paradoxes in the destiny of my informant. He had turned his back on his uncle's political beliefs and joined a party which later let him down. He was now a supporter of Barre in the Union pour la Démocratie française. Some time earlier, *L'Yonne républicaine* had called him a renegade, and the journalist ended his piece with the words:

> Direz makes no bones about his ambitions vis-à-vis the second constituency. But he needs a party behind him. As the RPR has slammed the door in his face, he's knocking at the door of the UDF. But he should not count his chickens. J.-P. Soisson, the real master of the UDF in the Yonne, has made it quite clear that Direz is welcome to join the party, but with no promises so far as the next general election is concerned.[12]

This account is interesting: it tells us almost as much about the way journalists approach politics as about the actual situation described. If you read between the lines, the writers is suggesting that what makes Direz, just like every other politician, run is ambition, and that everything else is just tactics of varying degrees of subtlety, designed to assure his success. In a sense, one can hardly quarrel with this analysis, and its extension to politicians in general, but there precisely is where it falls down as an explanation. The journalist is offering a key to the behaviour of an individual, but the same key opens every door. An anthropologist, on the contrary, would be inclined to give much less importance to the motives, conscious or unconscious, of the individual elected representative; his personality and his intrinsic qualities, such as ambition, skill, experience, and so on, are much less interesting to the anthropologist than his position and his changing role in the community he represents. The struggles of someone like Bonhenry, Dollfus or Direz, and the obstacles placed in their way, can tell us a great deal about the inner workings of local politics.

In examining the importance of networks, we discovered a universe in which certain landmarks enabled the voter to take his bearings and make the right choice. In such circumstances, there was an advantage in reproducing well-established positions, and passing them down the line without too many changes. Hence the overall image of a fixed order. Yet this is not the whole story. In the case of the three men we have just looked at, we see a different dimension of political action, where the candidate's future is not mapped out in advance. What all three stories have in common is that the candidate had a hard struggle just to survive. The permanent quest for representative office here takes on a particular character, in that it involves not only the relationship of the candidate to the voters whose support he is soliciting, but also his relationship with local political circles. To exist, in politics, one must first of all to come to term with a norm which is imposed on all applicants; those best prepared to comply with this norm are obviously individuals who already have the advantage from the start of an element of legitimacy. Others, less integrated, are doomed to isolation: they either do too much or too little. In their anxiety to make a name for themselves, they strike a false note: too American in one case, too much imagination in another. Observing these incompatibilities is like looking at a negative of regulations or rules which are never articulated because they have been totally interiorised by the masters of the game: 'Keep to your place; stick to your last; demonstrate by appropriate ritual the nature of your relationship with your peers.'

It is obvious that the norm cannot be simply imposed: the game also demands a series of sanctions which can run from isolation to expulsion.[13] It is this element of instability or even disorder which accounts for the instability of political relationships. Thus new figures can emerge from time to time, and they in turn can bring about alterations of varying degrees of importance in local practice.

In order to exist in politics, a candidate has to climb into the ring and take part in the struggle between parties; he also has to survive the process. The experience of defeat can be very revealing. Let us leave to one side for a moment internecine quarrels, where a candidate has the bitter experience of being beaten by his friends rather than his enemies, for as we have seen, achieving eligibility often involves a bitter struggle within the party, though it is not always visible on the surface. When two heavyweight parties are involved, we no longer have just the two main contenders in the ring, but a much more complex set-up, with messengers bringing orders from the top. From the local point of view, the position of the loser cannot be considered as a given reality: it is a relationship which he builds up over time. His continued political existence may depend on knowing how to negotiate from a position of defeat, not simply settling down in a situation which is after all uncomfortable, but using it as a launching-pad, a position giving him an advantage not only vis-à-vis the enemy, but also vis-à-vis his friends.

What have we learned from these different cases? The following, at any rate: that politics involves a complex interplay between the individual, networks, circumstances and the voters, i.e. the public, who in the end, we must suppose, decide the winner. Our tradition of political analysis talks and thinks obsessively about power; yet perhaps those involved in fact have very little power over the factors that really count. There is always a card which slips from their grasp, perhaps because public life is by its nature precarious, or perhaps because the world of politics is a contingent world, a world of becoming rather than being. We should at least realise that political representation is created as it goes along. There are certain parameters which constrain, but politics also has a random dimension; it has to come to terms with the reality of events in the present, while it manipulates relics of traditions which have sometimes ceased to have any meaning in themselves. At the end of this alchemical process, it is possible for certain individual figures to emerge and take up a prominent position in local political life. Some go on to greater things, others run out of steam; the random part is what makes the politician run, and that is what he is always trying to control with words. Words addressed to the voters, to the imagination of others: necessary ingredients of representation. There is a need to speak about himself, to explain his actions, justify them, prophesy for the future, go over past events, if necessary. No one escapes unhurt from the political arena.

4

The new deal: decentralisation

A little commune in the Avallonnais, on a rainy afternoon. Yet spring had come, for this was May 1982. On my way to the town hall, I ran into several people I knew. The mayor of a nearby village, for example, with his assistant mayor: 'Coming to the meeting?', he asked me. I scarcely had time to reply before an official car drew up near us, and out stepped the sub-prefect. There were numerous councillors going into the town hall. The mayor was on the first-floor landing to welcome us, then we all went into the council chamber. The meeting of the association of communes was declared open in the presence of the sub-prefect, his secretaries and the official in charge of local works.

For some time the meeting was taken up with routine matters: road repairs, and the organisation of the school bus service. What about the footbridge over the Trinquelin, which was damaged the previous year? Not to worry, the first instalment of the subsidy had not been forgotten. The president of the association then presented the budget, followed by a breakdown of the figures into capital and running costs – nothing very technical, for the papers had been drawn up in advance by the secretary of the association. The sub-prefect then became involved in a discussion with the representative from the Ministry of Works, to which my neighbours listened with varying degrees of attention. They were commenting on the budget, and the scheduling of future projects. Outside, the rain had stopped; from where I was sitting I had a good view of the surrounding forest. My attention wandered as I recalled a recent stroll through the copses of hornbeam and beech.

Suddenly things changed and the councillors looked tense. The sub-prefect was the only person talking. Certain expressions kept recurring: 'decentralisation', 'transfer of executive powers', '*a posteriori* checks'. He was outlining the basis of the reform of local government enacted by the law of the previous 2 March. This reform represented a big step, for it meant that councillors were no longer under the complete control of the central government. The sub-prefect quoted from the text of the law, under which 'the decisions of the communal authorities are fully operative once they have been published or notified to interested parties, and communicated to the representative of the State in the department, or his deputy in the *arrondissement*'. For example, if the auditor of a commune decided not to authorise payment on an item of expenditure, he must justify his refusal and notify the mayor. The latter could require that the payment be made, but in that case, as the sub-prefect emphasised, the mayor accepted responsibility.

The key word had been spoken: mayors and municipal councillors were to have 'increased responsibility'. People glanced round at each other (those present were all mayors or assistant mayors). Some short questions revealed the general anxiety. For example, the sub-prefect had explained that the prefect – henceforth to be known as the Commissaire de la République – could inform the regional auditing body if a commune's budget did not balance or in cases of revenue deficit. The delegates were worried: would they have access to advice from government officials, or would they at least be warned before such action was taken? The prefect reassured them, though stressing the need for care. At the end of the meeting, people were not too sure what they thought of the reforms. 'I was not particularly keen to be mayor', one man told me, somewhat nonplussed by all the changes, 'but people know who they can rely on to get the work done.' Most people opted to wait and see. The meeting was followed by a reception at which the sub-prefect was able to inform himself about local matters in a more relaxed atmosphere. I asked him whether he himself was optimistic about the way the new law would work. He admitted that it would perhaps create some problems for the mayors of rural communes, and he felt the government officials should continue to help these people. But overall the system should benefit from the transfer of powers and responsibilities. Evening was falling as I left. The rain was almost gone, and I had the feeling that I had witnessed an important event.

Something irreversible had taken place that day. The State had come to the village like a prince 'restoring' power to peasants who had never aimed so high. Everyone looked uncomfortable in their new role.

The reactions I observed on the ground might seem rather strange. One might have expected more enthusiasm. Under this reform, the State devolved to other bodies a certain number of powers which up to then it had monopolised, thus increasing the power of elected councillors. François Mitterrand, recently elected President, referred to it as the most important act of his presidency, thus underlining the importance which Paris attributed to the decentralisation. On all sides, the first reaction was astonishment that it had been so briskly dispatched. Was it not a kind of coup by the State against itself? One could understand that an opposition which had some strength at local level should seek an extension of local power: it was a good way to harass the government, and no doubt worth a few votes. But that the same opposition, no sooner in power, should actually undertake a vast programme of reform was rather more surprising, especially since the French, as we all know, have a tendency to worship the State. It is expected to provide welfare and prosperity, though of course it is also an excellent target for complaints and individual paranoia, as we see, for example, in the image of the policeman or the taxman. A job in the civil service is seen as the safest refuge from the rigours of the economic crisis. Everyone curses the Leviathan, but who would be bold enough to seek freedom from it?

Decentralisation interrupted a state of affairs which was stable, to say the least. The modern administrative system of France was set up in 1789; since then, each piece of the puzzle (commune, department, external services of the State) had become more firmly fixed. The left, faithful to its Jacobin ideology, continued to venerate the results of the great Revolution. Some fringe groups in the centre and even on the right exalted the regionalist ideal, but they were isolated within a compact ensemble strongly attached to the notion of the unity and uniformity of the Republic. For many people, of the most diverse political tendencies, a serious application of the plans for decentralisation was tantamount to destroying an edifice that had stood for two centuries. The system set up by the Constituent Assembly had not essentially changed during the whole of that time. There is abundant archive material showing the reasoning behind the system, and how communities reacted to its establishment.

Origins of the departments: dividing to unite

And lo, they made the departments . . . It began with the redrawing of the administrative map of France, which was carried out by a committee of the Constituent Assembly and submitted to the Assembly in 1789. The division of France into departments is still an important factor in political life.[1] It came about because an elected assembly decided one fine day that the administrative divisions hitherto used must be completely reorganised. It was not a new idea: enlightened spirits like Turgot and Letrosne had previously proposed substantial reform of local administration. The former, in his *Mémoire sur les municipalités*, suggested the creation of three levels of administration: town or village, district, and *arrondissement*. The latter proposed that the country should be divided into 25 *généralités*, 250 districts and 4,500 *arrondissements*. On the eve of the Revolution, a then unknown priest, the Abbé Sieyès, wrote his *Etude sur la division de la*

France, in which he advocated the creation of 50 provinces, each composed of 40 *arrondissements*, divided in turn into 20 parishes. None of these different projects was ever carried out, but the members of the committee followed the same basic principles and were thus able to carry out the reform quickly.

Why the haste to undertake such an enormous project? Just imagine for a moment the tangle of administrative divisions under the *ancien régime* in what constitutes the present-day department of the Yonne.[2] The earliest were the ecclesiastical divisions, such as the diocese of Sens in the north, with its five archdeaconries of Sens, Gatinais, Melun, Provins and Etampes, which copied exactly the five *pagi* of Roman times. In the south, on the other side of the river Serein, lay the diocese of Auxerre. To the east of the Serein were parishes belonging to the diocese of Langres; to the west, the diocese of Autun. If we turn to administrative divisions under the monarchy, first of all we have judiciary divisions. In the north of the present-day department was the bailiwick of Sens. The bailiwick of Auxerre was created in 1371 and corresponded to the earldom of the same name together with the area situated between the rivers Loire, Yonne and Cure. The south-western part of the department came under the bailiwicks of Avallon and Semur. The situation had changed over the course of preceding centuries. In the north certain parishes coming under the jurisdiction of the bailiwick of Sens had found themselves annexed by the neighbouring bailiwicks of Provins, Nemours and Moret. Sometimes the boundaries between them grew blurred. In 1789, when each parish had to send delegates to the chief town of its bailiwick, many were unsure where to go: for example, the delegates from the parishes of Donziois went to Nevers, whereas they actually came under the jurisdication of Auxerre.

The same territory was divided for tax purposes into areas which did not correspond to the diocese or to the bailiwicks. On the one hand there were the *élections* of Nogent-sur-Seine, Montereau, Sens and Joigny in the north, Vézelay in the south, Saint-Florentin and Tonnerre in the east, and Gien, Clamecy and Montargis in the west. Auxerre and Avallon, since they were Burgundian towns, were *pays d'état* and therefore organised differently. Here the tax division, the *recette*, did not have legal jurisdication in fiscal matters, whereas the *élection* did. In the *pays d'état*, fiscal disputes were settled by the bailiwick tribunals. If we add that the divisions in the north and east came under the jurisdication of the *généralité* of Paris, whereas those in the west came under the *généralité* of Orleans and the three *recettes* under that of Dijon, we have some idea of the complexity of local administrative divisions. This was not irrelevant to the daily life of the peasants, particularly in those parishes which because of the vagaries of the boundaries found themselves straddling two different divisions. For example, at Chitry, the village street was the boundary between the *généralité* of Paris and the *généralité* of Dijon.

A kind of warfare broke out. Residents in the *généralité* of Paris stored their wines in cellars opposite their houses, on the other side of the road, to avoid taxation; in 1759, residents in the *généralité* of Dijon had to pay a one-off tax of 100 *livres*, to which they thought their neighbours should contribute, on the grounds that they stored their wine in Burgundy; there followed a number of law-suits, which gave rise to fierce enmities and sometimes turned parents against their own children and vice versa.[3]

If we further add that there still existed a strong sense of loyalty to the 'provinces', which were former fiefs which had been gradually incorporated into the royal domain, though still retaining their separate customs and certain of their privileges, we have a clear idea of the motley nature of the body, far removed from our modern concept of a nation. The territories which were later brought together to form the department of the Yonne belonged to several of these provinces: Burgundy, of course, Champagne in the case of the earldom of Joigny, Ile de France in the north and Orléanais and Nivernais in the case of the *élection* of Vézelay. The latter, incidentally, belonged to the Burgundian diocese of Autun.

The difficulties caused by the overlapping of several types of division hampered the work of administrators in every field, from tax-collection to road maintenance. Administrators had proposed on several occasions that the parishes be redistributed amongst the *généralités*, but without success. Shortly before the Revolution, the assembly of the department of Tonnerre and Vézelay was asking 'that the department be defined, as far as possible, by fixed, immutable boundaries, based on natural divisions'.[4] This same jumble of administrative divisions was to be found almost everywhere in France. The members of the Constituent Assembly, strongly influenced by the rationalist spirit of the Enlightenment, could hardly accept such a situation, redolent as it was of irrationality, and a relic of a crumbling regime. Radical reorganisation of the kingdom was called for. There must be an end to the local anomalies and privileges created by this state of affairs. The redrawing of the administrative map of the country was done therefore with the aim of making the general interest prevail over local privileges. Hence the remark of Thouret, the spokesman of the committee, to his colleagues: 'What would be the gain, if the provinces were to take the place of the orders?' He underlined the idea of the unity and indivisibility of the body politic when he added: 'There is no such thing as the representative of a bailiwick or a province – only representatives of the nation.'[5]

Aiming to create a system of homogeneous divisions, the committee called for a geometric division of the country into '80 large divisions, which would be known as departments'. Each department was to measure 324 square leagues and to consist of nine districts, each divided in turn into 9 cantons. There were two advantages to this system: it would get rid of former anomalies by creating new, equal and uniform units, and the confusion caused by the old overlapping of categories would disappear. These abstract principles of uniformity and equality initially prevailed in the debate. However, the cold geometry of Thouret's report soon came up against the more localist attitudes of delegates from the provinces, who represented precise interests. Mirabeau came to general attention in this debate by taking the opposite stance to Thouret: 'I would favour', he said on 3 November in the tribune of the Assembly, 'a realistic division, one which would take account of each region and its circumstances, rather than a mathematical division, which I consider Utopian and scarcely feasible.'[6]

Not one centre, but many: the real meaning of boundaries

Following a lively debate, it was decided that there should be between 75 and 85 departments. Each department would be divided into districts and there would be a council in every town, parish or rural community. It was left to the provincial delegates and commissioners to arrange the details. As soon as the new division of the country into departments was announced, the different towns went into action, sending delegates on special missions to Paris. The archives are full of the petitions which flooded in. Some towns were anxious to preserve their traditional pre-eminence, while others hoped to achieve the envied status of chief town of a department.

Auxerre, for example, hoped to be the chief town of the future department; its delegates pointed not only to the demographic weight of the town, with its 12,000 inhabitants, but also its age-old role as diocesan centre and chief town of the bailiwick. Moreover, it was an important commercial crossroads and a natural entrepôt, through which all the timber and wine of the region passed as it was carried down the Yonne to Paris by horse-drawn barge. However, the location of Auxerre, on the edge of three *généralités*, four dioceses and six bailiwicks, presented an obstacle to such an ambition. Auxerre could not carve out a department for itself without encroaching on neighbouring divisions. Other towns nursed similar ambitions. Sens as the centre of an archbishopric, a bailiwick, one of the oldest in the kingdom, and an *élection*, also had a good claim to be chief town of the department. The town had a clear economic function, as the grain store for a prosperous agricultural region, but it too had its rivals: Provins, capital of Brie in Champagne, and Montereau, which stood at the confluence of the Seine and the Yonne, also wanted to be the chief town of a department. Meanwhile the delegates from the bailiwick of Auxerre had got together in Paris with their colleagues from Burgundy, and had come up against a problem: Burgundy measured 798 square leagues, and the extent of a department was to be 342 square leagues, so there was no question of

Burgundy being split into any more than two departments. This division was made, and it was decided that Chalon should be the chief town of one department, and Dijon the chief town of the other, which would take in the surrounding towns, among them Autun. However, this left an area in the north of Burgundy, and it was decided to form a third department by adding to this area the bailiwicks of Auxerre, Avallon, Semur-en-Auxois and Saulieu, the earldom of Joigny and the part of the Tonnerrois which belonged to Champagne. In exchange, the marquisate of Arc-en-Barrois was ceded to the department of Langres and the earldom of Bar-sur-Seine to the department of Troyes. There was an objection from Châtillon-sur-Seine, which would have preferred to be the chief town of a department embracing Avallon, Semur and Tonnerre, but the Burgundy delegates rejected this claim.

Auxerre was thus fitted into the new map, but Sens encountered a major obstacle. It was originally to have been the chief town of a department bordering on the department of Paris, but in view of the size of Paris, it was decided that it should have a smaller surrounding department, whereupon Sens found itself relegated to the edge of the departments of Meulun and Troyes, and Auxerre. As it was no longer in the centre of a department, it could no longer aspire to the role of chief town, and asked to be joined to the department of Auxerre. In the south, Autun was attached in the end to Chalon, and Dijon was given Semur and Saulieu in compensation. However, the inhabitants of Auxerre were no more prepared to lose these towns than they were to accept Sen's offers.

> We cannot countenance the loss of Semur, Saulieu and their dependancies. Their inhabitants are in daily contact with us; Sens and Auxerre, on the other hand, have no commerce between them. How can it be natural to separate towns which depend on their mutual commerce, and join together others which are completely independent of each other?[7]

The Auxerre delegates were suspicious of the sudden desire manifested by Sens to belong to their department, suspecting correctly that Sens had not given up its claim to be chief town. Until such time as the matter was decided, Auxerre arranged to send two extra delegates to Paris. The department was finally delineated on 15 January 1790 and Sens was merely the chief town of a district. The question was hotly debated right up to the last day, as can be seen from the successive alterations to the southern boundaries of the department. On 13 January, the little town of Courtenay was shown on a map of the department of Auxerrois presented to the committee by the Marquis of Maubec, the delegate for Sens. But at the last moment there was an agreement with the delegates from Orléanais, and Courtenay was attached to the department of Orleans.

Such was the birth of the department of the Yonne, aptly named, since the only thing Auxerre and Sens have in common is the river which flows through both. Like other departments, it is essentially an artificial creation. Each of its micro-regions has a strong identity of its own, a fact which has had an effect on subsequent local political life. Looking back over the debates which preceded the establishment of the department, one is struck by the extraordinary fervour it aroused. Every last town and village stirred itself to send petitions and delegations. Theoretically, the impulse behind the redrawing of the map was a centralising one, since the aim of the committee was to sweep away local privileges and form a unified nation around a strong central power. But the task was soon in the hands of local representatives, and what was heard in the debates was the voice of strong local interests. For this reason, the department ended up as a sort of compromise between the egalitarian and universalist spirit which found favour in the autumn of 1789, and the deeply rooted traditional customs and practices of the real France. It was a pragmatic compromise, the end result of a process of bargaining between the representatives of different local interests.

One thing is particularly noticeable: all the delegates fought hard to make their town the centre of the new division. It was not simply a question of administrative pre-eminence, but of safeguarding the economic future, and being the administrative centre was seen by all as a guarantee of prosperity. This is true not only of large towns like Auxerre and Sens: the sub-division of departments into districts and cantons aroused the same ambitions and rivalries. In January 1790, there were no fewer than 1,800 delegates extraordinary in Paris, and fresh emissaries were constantly being dispatched with urgent instruction from every town and village. On 16 January 1789, we find a certain M. Chauchon, a former tax-collector from Vézelay, arriving in Paris on a mission entrusted to him by his fellow-citizens. Vézelay was not keen to see its district dominated by the little town of Avallon – indeed Vézelay felt it should be the centre. Chauchon got to work the next day to plead the cause of Vézelay, but to no avail, for in the end it was attached to the district of Avallon. When the municipal officers heard the bad news, they swiftly contacted one of their number in Paris, a M. Resnier, urging him to intervene afresh: 'All will be lost. Our best citizens will move away; labourers and artisans will not find work; what little commerce there was will disappear and soon our town will be a desert.' Vézelay continued to try to swing the committee in its favour right up to 27 January, the date of the vote on the bill concerning the department of Auxerre.

However, Avallon had not been idle either, as can be seen in the following petition from its aldermen:

Avallon offers many advantages which merit consideration. It is pleasantly situated, attracting the attention of travellers; it is on a road intended for stage- and post-coaches, under a plan presently being discussed between the administration of the province and the Avallon delegates in Dijon; it is an entrepôt for the commerce of the regions of Auxois and Morvan. Such are Avallon's claims, which surely must lead to its being considered one of the principal towns of the province.

The arguments of both towns were heard, but Avallon's more central position geographically, and its population, which was three times the size of Vézelay's, gave it a decided advantage. Vézelay only pressed its claims the harder:

Avallon is the centre of a bailiwick, Vézelay of an *élection*. Avallon has a salt warehouse, and Vézelay has one too; Avallon has no commerce, but Vézelay does a considerable trade in wood . . . Vézelay has a large and spacious abbey church, and many convents and monasteries. In the environs there are extensive Church properties. All these will be of no value to the State, for our degradation and lack of resources must lead to a poverty-stricken population, and if private houses are deserted, chapter properties will not find tenants.[8]

Vézelay's pleas fell on deaf ears, however, and it ended up the chief town of a canton.

In the end the department was divided into seven districts: Auxerre, Avallon, Joigny, Saint-Fargeau, Saint-Florentin, Sens and Tonnerre, a division which corresponded in the main to different geographical characteristics. The fertile, undulating plateau of the Champagne area of the Sénonnais is quite different from the damp, wooded region around Saint-Fargeau, or the granite lands of the Morvan, adjoining the town of Avallon. Naturally, the divisions approved on 26 January 1790 could not please everyone. Some people even suggested, in a conciliatory move, that the administrative centre should be distinct from the judicial centre, which would have allowed the courts to be situated in those towns which were complaining of having been overlooked for no good reason. Such a plan, however, contradicted the expressed aim of the committee, which was to create a simple and unified administrative structure; the issue was decided by the decree of 23 August, which established that the chief towns of districts were to have the law-courts.

This decision inflamed discontent. For example, the village of Avrolles, situated between Saint-Florentin and Brienon, was the scene of confrontation between inhabitants of those two towns; Brienon was dissatisfied that it had failed to be achieve the status of chief town of the district and had therefore lost the law-courts to its rival. 'The whole population of Saint-Florentin rose up. They overcame the forces of order in Avrolles and swore they would murder all the inhabitants of Brienon . . .'[9] The agitation later died down, but Brienon swiftly persuaded 39 of the 57 communes belonging to the district of Saint-Florentin to sign a petition, asking to be attached to a different district. The departmental authorities proposed in a speech to the National Assembly on 5 October 1790 to reduce the number of districts by suppressing those of Saint-Florentin and Saint-Fargeau, but the suggestion was not put into practice.

The simultaneous sub-division into cantons gave rise to the same kind of disagreements. 'To our astonishment', the municipal council of Courson reported, 'we find practically every parish claiming to be the chief town of the canton.'[10] So there were fierce arguments between parishes, which in many cases flared up again a few months later when magistrates were chosen. The meeting held at Ouanne for this purpose saw the rival village of Leugny put up its own candidate against the one selected by the chief town of the canton. The meeting turned into a pitched battle, and the mayor of Ouanne received a blow and had to withdraw.[11] In the original version, the department consisted of 69 cantons; the law of 28 Pluviose, Year 8 of the Revolutionary Calendar, creating the *arrondissement*, and that of 8 Pluviose of the same year, reducing the number of magistrates, modified the original plan: the districts disappeared, to be shared among the four *arrondissements* of Auxerre, Avallon, Sens and Tonnerre. However, the 40 cantons created at that time have lasted with no great changes down to the present day.

The debates occasioned by the creation of the department of the Yonne demonstrate, then, the tensions between a universalist ideal and the local interests which are the product of history, but they can also tell us a great deal about our traditional concepts of political divisions. During those months when everything was in the melting-pot, we see a real obsession manifest itself on the part of local representatives: their parish must be the centre of an administrative territory. An outside observer might be surprised at the bitterness of the struggle to be the centre, which even pitted village against village. After all, was it such an advantage to be the administrative centre? So far as the district and cantonal divisions are concerned, it would seem to be a case of ancient rivalries between parishes. Yet beneath these expressions of local identity, an idea was being formed which was to have a constant influence on political relations in the country. It was essentially the notion of centrality.

A great deal has been written about centralism as the defining characteristic of the French system: usually the term refers to the domination of the capital and the central administration over the rest of the country, known dismissively as 'the provinces', with all the unfortunate connotations of that term. On the one hand we have the central government, and on the other a series of marginal bodies: the imbalance between them has been demonstrated a hundred times. There is, however, another factor which deserves consideration, and which becomes very apparent from a scrutiny of the process of creation of the departments, and that is that the high value accorded to the notion of the centre operates at every level, from the capital down to the tiniest parish. Deep in the provincial heart of France, there were fierce struggles over which locality was to be recognised as the chief town of a district or canton. It was this obsession with centrality which finally decided the shape of the departments. We saw that the map of the Yonne was redrawn several times, in line with the separate claims of towns like Auxerre, Tonnerre or Sens to be departmental chief town. The bargaining between the representatives of adjoining territories, eager to swap one group of parishes for another, was similarly driven by the desire to see their towns become the centre.

From this time onwards, local politics would be organised around two relatively important types of centre: the chief towns of *arrondissements*, where the sub-prefecture was located, and the chief towns of cantons where the magistrate sat, and the post office, the police station and the main shops were located. The rivalries which came to the surface at the time the divisions were made continued to manifest themselves for a long time afterwards, mainly because the decision to limit the number of cantons meant that a large number of parishes disappeared from the administrative map. In some cases the trauma has remained till the present day. It is no secret that the inhabitants of Mailly-le-Château resent the presence at the cantonal elections of a candidate who already holds office in Coulanges-sur-Yonne.[12] Their displeasure is not unconnected to the fact that on 8 Pluviose of Year 8 of the Revolutionary Calendar, Mailly-le-Château lost its status of chief town of the canton, which was transferred to Coulanges. Numerous examples could be given of this phenomenon, which is in no way peculiar to the Yonne – on the contrary, it is more marked in certain other departments: take the case of the long-standing rivalry between Toulon and Draguignan, where the prefecture has moved back and forth from one to the other without ever really achieving a solution satisfactory to both parties.

First steps towards reform

The division of France into departments and communes with uniform institutions marks the emergence of the system of political representation of the modern nation-state. But it contained the seed of a confusion. The architects and adherents of the Republic insisted that it must be conceived as a pyramid of powers, with each local division receiving identical treatment from the central administration, while enjoying a measure of authority. This identification of national unity with the notions of the centralised State and the Republic meant that subsequent critics of centralism were suspected of being indifferent to the unity of the nation and of being anti-republican.

In practice, however, over the course of the nineteenth century the principle of centralisation grew somewhat more flexible. As early as Year 8 of the Revolutionary Calendar, the Directorate abandoned the system of cantonal councils, adopted five years earlier, under which the communes were grouped together and supervised by commissars nominated by the executive power.[13] This system was quickly seen to be unpopular and ineffective, as the decision-making centre was too far removed from the population concerned. The failure of the cantonal councils marked the furthest limits of the process of centralisation. Subsequent regimes limited themselves to adapting the administrative arrangements inherited from the committee.

Nineteenth-century liberals were very keen to establish the legitimacy of local institutions: municipal councils were made elective as early as 1831, but it was not until the laws of 12 August 1872 and, more particularly, 5 April 1884, that the principle of election of mayors and assistant mayors by councils was recognised. At departmental level, a similar process led to the General Councils being elective. The law of 10 August 1871 gave members of General Councils the right to elect their president and agree internal rules, and enlarged the scope of their financial and managerial powers. The main innovation was the creation of the departmental committee, the executive organ of the General Council and the real executive body of the department, though its powers were limited. The prefect was still charged with the prior investigation of all matters concerning the department, and ensuring that the decisions of the council and the departmental committee were carried out.

It must be recognised that there was a great debate, over a period of about half a century, for and against decentralisation. However, we can distinguish two very different aspects of this debate, and two different sets of aims. On the one hand, there was a technical approach to the issue, which was mainly concerned with reducing the financial tutelage exercised over local councils and widening the scope of their remit. The decentralisation issue was also part, however, of a larger critique of authoritarian government, particularly during the Second Empire. The tutelage exercised by the prefect, 'the poor man's Napoleon', as he was dubbed by Aulard, was attacked by republicans and Orléanists opposed to the absolutism of Napoleon III.

The theme of decentralisation therefore found an echo in the last century amongst parliamentarians and pamphleteers. However, the enemies of centralism sought not so much a redistribution of power as a more flexible application of the regulations in force, a more representative system of local government, an extension of freedoms, or in some cases the overthrow of the particular regime in power. But even Tocqueville and his friends, the most anti-centralist of the authors of the Constitution of the Second

Republic, who incidentally were outvoted in committee in the National Assembly, never dreamed or proposed that France should have a federalist or regionalist structure.[14]

Throughout this period, one observes a strengthening of the administration at departmental level. Whereas the commune remained in a condition of financial dependence on the State, which enjoyed extremely strict powers of control over local spending and taxation, the department grew progressively stronger, to the point where it was recognised that it could have private interests (properties and so on), and later, in 1892, financial autonomy. As for the municipal councils, the law of 1884 defined more clearly the scope of these bodies and their mayors. The choice of mayor and assistant mayors, for so long the prerogative of the State, now fell to the municipal council, which was also given general powers of decision. The prefect's discretionary power of annulment for reasons of illegality disappeared, though the financial tutelage exercised by this official continued to weigh heavily on basic areas such as the budget. The 1884 arrangements did not question the pre-eminence of State tutelage, but they did open the way to a subsequent reduction of the direct control exercised by the prefects, who thus ceased to be seen as 'petty provincial Napoleons'.

From that date until 1982, evolution in local politics was marked by two tendencies: on the one hand the relationship between the central administration and local bodies took on a more technical aspect, and on the other, the system of control was lightened, especially after 1945. The practice of the prefect annulling decisions taken by the municipal councils had certainly fallen into disuse well before 1982. The central authority asserted itself not by repressive methods, but through its technical services. There was an increase in regulations of all sorts; the State set up structures which were more and more complex, to which local bodies had to adapt, so that their dependence continually grew.

The State kept its control over local initiatives by means of subsidies and a multiplicity of financial incentives. Indirect tutelage was also exercised over the implementation of decisions, most communes being obliged to call on the technical services of the State for building works, agriculture, and so on. The technical services thus gradually increased their influence over local affairs. At the same time, the fiscal system, from municipal tax-collectors up to departmental paymaster, controlled local finances. So there was an increase, excessive perhaps, in regulations, subsidies, services and the government bodies set up to provide the services. There was a growing ambiguity and confusion between representatives of the State, such as prefects, and the law itself, between subsidies and regulation, service and control: such were the characteristics of the Provider State in the decades after the Second World War.

It must be said that local representatives soon learned to adapt to this system. Complicity between the prefect and 'his' councillors enabled the former to consolidate his power locally by arbitrating in the distribution of the manna from the State. At the same time, mayors and members of the General Council derived their authority from their privileged access to the representatives of the government. Yet if tensions arose, the prefect could be made the scapegoat, and the local representatives could hide behind the financial tutelage exercised over them. This was the traditional way 'decentralised power' worked, and as Pierre Grémion has shown,[15] it was a system well suited to a strongly agricultural society. Certainly the drift of the population away from the country and the growth of industry changed the rules of the game. 'Tame Jacobinism' and its Third Republic-style local politicians gave way to the 'new mayors', people in charge of large urban centres, who were less inclined to bow down to the financial tutelage of the prefect.

From the point of view of the State, the huge increase in technical responsibilities and the increasing gap between central government and its provincial services began to put a question mark over the effectiveness of the entire centralised system. The abnormal enlargement of the State was leading to an ever-increasing number of regulations and a huge bureaucracy. In short, as the General Director of Local Councils admitted in 1978: 'Nowadays the State does too many things. Its omnipotence is fast becoming impotence.'[16] It was at this time that the first effects of the economic crisis and the slowing-down of growth led experts to propose a decrease in the State's responsibilities.

The State was, as I have said, strong, but it was also vulnerable, not only to a financial deficit due to the increase in the burden it bore, but also to a loss of legitimacy. The citizen had increasingly come to feel excluded from a game conducted in code between local elected representatives and officials, both groups cultivating an opaque and ambiguous language. Various studies and proposals appeared during the presidency of Giscard, which suggests that his government recognised the problem, though it never really tackled it. Reports prepared by Alain Peyrefitte and Olivier Guichard proposed a technical solution, aimed at simplifying administrative procedures and making them more accessible to the public. The law of March 1982 had the same purpose, but it also emphasised the need for an increase in local democracy. 'Transfer of power to elected representatives': this, significantly, was Gaston Deferre's slogan when he launched himself on the enterprise. Decentralisation was about reinforcing the initiative of local politicians, more than changing the relationship between the citizen and his institutions, which was the principle of the 'new citizenship' exalted at the time by Pierre Mauroy.

The reform can be defined as the transfer of responsibilities and human and financial resources from the State to three different levels of local body: the commune, the department and the region. The law of 2 March 1982, which was followed by a considerable number of other legislative and regulatory texts, either abolished or reduced, according to circumstances, the legal, technical, administrative and financial tutelage of the State, and at the same time transferred executive power in the departments and regions from the prefects to the presidents of elected assemblies. This was an important point, for it ensured that even before their responsibilities were clearly defined, it was clear that local politicians would be central to the process.

Their respective powers were defined less than a year later by the law of 7 January 1983, which concerned the division of responsibilities between the State and local bodies. Whole areas were handed over to the latter; the idea was to distribute homogeneous blocks to each type of assembly, as far as possible. Basically, the communes were given responsibility for town-planning, the departments for social welfare, health, inter-city transport, school buses and rural works, and the region for vocational training, planning and economic development. We should notice, however, that there was one clear exception to the rule of transfer by homogeneous blocks: this was education, where all three levels of body were involved, the region being in charge of *lycées*, the department of *collèges* (secondary modern schools) and the communes of *écoles* (primary schools).

Decentralisation had named the players and dealt the cards; now it could not avoid the question of means. What human and material resources would be made available to the elected representatives to enable them to carry out their new responsibilities? There were fears that decentralisation was a first step towards austerity. The idea was that the services corresponding to the transferred responsibilities should gradually be attached to the administration of the department. Moreover, specific grants would be made to the department to cover its new responsibilities. Apart from the grant for running costs already in place, the State instituted an allocation for public works to communes and departments; the amount was fixed in relation to real capital expenditure by these bodies. In the case of the departments, account was also taken of subsidies to rural works. Other financial transfers concerned particular taxes: the region received the money from the car-registration tax, while the department received the road tax and a large part of the property transfer tax. To compensate for the shortfall even with these transfers of tax-revenue, there was also a global allocation for decentralisation linked to the running grant.

Such were the broad lines of the new State policy towards local authorities. It represented the complete overthrow of some very deep-rooted customs, in that executive power changed hands, the prefect being relieved of the majority of his prerogatives. It was a good deal for the elected councillors, whose major weapon up to that point had been their ability to pull strings with the prefect or members of the government. The effects of this string-pulling might be felt in the way the prefect drew up the budget, or in the various subsidies that could be gleaned here and there. But essentially an office like president of the General Council was an honorary position, something to put on one's visiting-card, which was probably rather impressive even without it, rather than a position of real power. It often went to someone well known outside the department, mainly because the council felt it expedient to offer it to whoever was felt to have most leverage at national level.

In the Yonne, for example, we notice that Pierre-Etienne Flandin never sought to become president of the General Council. The honour fell instead to his contemporary, Bienvenu Martin, a senator who had also achieved a ministerial portfolio, though without ever advancing to the front rank of politicians like his illustrious colleague. After the war, Moreau, the mayor of Auxerre, who headed the list in the general elections, and was a Minister under the Fourth Republic, was president of the General Council until his electoral defeat in 1958, but it was his role as mayor and member of the National Assembly which won him local fame, rather than the fact that he was president of the General Council. After 1982, however, things were quite different. It was then worth while to become president of the General Council, not only because of the transfer of executive power, but because of the predominant role given to the department under the new arrangements. For we must not lose sight of an important point: decentralisation did not alter the divisions invented by the committee in 1789 in any way. It is true that a new factor was introduced by the creation of a new administrative entity, the region. But those who had advocated a regional or regionalist updating of the divisions of France were disappointed. Just as earlier attempts to restructure the commune, by linking or joining several communes together to rationalise management, had failed, so now the department continued to be the cornerstone of the French system.

Representing and administering: guardians and messengers

So now the departments had at their disposal the means to manage directly those matters which came within their remit. Previously, it was true, road-maintenance and social welfare, the two largest items in the budget, had been decided on at departmental level, but the initiative in these matters had rested with the State, since it was the prefect who drew up the budget and put it into effect, as well as having authority over the departmental services, so that the role of the General Council was purely consultative. That did not mean, of course, that the councillors were entirely without influence.

On the one hand, the law of 1874 had created the Departmental

Committee, a body emanating from the General Council, and given it certain rights: the committee was given information about reports before they were communicated to the Council, and it controlled the management of departmental funds. It distributed subsidies which had been voted globally, and determined the order of priority of building works to be carried out. Moreover, councillors could address themselves directly to the officials in charge of departmental services; at meetings of committees, these officials had to provide any details requested. Moreover, the General Council could speak directly to the government, in that it could address complaints to the relevant Minister, through the intermediary of its president, and express an opinion on the condition and requirements of the different public services. The Council could formally express a wish on economic issues and questions of general administration. The wish could be proposed by one or more councillors, the relevant committee would be advised of the wish, and it would be debated in a public session. This practice was only moderately successful, in that the usual outcome was a lengthy debate, followed by the adoption of a motion which tended to be symbolic and ritual in nature, though it at least expressed the concerns of local groups.

Christian Pineau, a Socialist Minister under the Fourth Republic, has given us an interesting account of one of these debates:

> The autumn meeting was mainly devoted to the discussion of the Council's wishes. Everyone knew these debates were pointless, but in public life there are certain traditions and nobody is willing to stand up and propose their abolition. There again, why give up the pleasure of seeing one's name in a prominent place in the local papers after a speech expressing the hopes and aspirations of the community?
>
> 'May I ask you to be brief, gentlemen?', the president of the Council, Gérard Fricot, requested jovially, in a probably fruitless attempt to shorten the debate. 'I would like to finish before dinner, and we do have a record one hundred items to get through.'
>
> The discussion opened with a regular feature from previous years, a demand from two veterinary surgeons for curbs on the activities of blacksmith farriers. Two other councillors who were farriers riposted in no uncertain terms . . . The proposal was finally passed on to the working group on miscellaneous matters, which is another way of saying that it was shelved until the following year.
>
> Next came the issue of home distillers, in all its multifarious aspects. There was no question of any member being caught unprepared on this particular issue; doctors, for example, had one view of the question, and wine-growers, another. On this occasion, the champions of home distilling made certain critical remarks about aperitifs and wines, to which the wine-growers responded with a number of highly familiar quotations from famous authors who have written in praise of the grape.
>
> Troncin, the Communist deputy, said it was 'the same old story: the little man sacrificed for the benefit of large concerns'.
>
> Nobody bothered to ask what he meant, exactly, because he always said the same thing. Dolivon then brought the debate to a close with a statement which brooked no disagreement: 'I don't care what anyone says, alcohol is not to blame for alcoholism.'[17]

This brief extract gives a humorous but essentially accurate view of the old-style meetings of the General Council, so far as I can judge from what I was told in the Yonne. They were assemblies representing a predominantly rural electorate, which did not demand miracles, but wanted its interests looked after. One of the main tasks of a member of the General Council was to respond to requests emanating from his canton. Sometimes these would take the form of demands for intervention with the authorities about problems with a pension, or obtaining a job in the civil service for a family member. These requests came via some public institution such as a school, hospital or old people's home on whose board of governors the councillor for the canton sat. Other demands came from communities, such as hamlets or villages, anxious not to be left out of the provision of amenities. We must remember that priorities for road-maintenance were debated in the General Council, so it was worth having the best possible spokesman.

So, the task of the councillor was to act as a skilled intermediary between the population and the supra-communal authorities, traditionally represented by the prefecture. Strictly speaking it was not his job to administer his territory. A member of the General Council did not necessarily have to be the mayor of one of the communes in his canton. The French system originally distinguished clearly between the two functions: locally, the mayor administered, and the member of the General Council was a representative. As we saw earlier, the division of the country in 1789 consecrated, as it were, the triumph of polycentrism, hence the multiplication of small centres in the form of rural communes, which have not been substantially altered by any of the reforms. In an attempt to increase efficiency and tighten political control over the countryside, cantonal authorities were set up in Year 2 of the Revolutionary Calendar, but the enterprise soon proved a failure and the Constitution of Year 8 drew the appropriate conclusions: the canton was never an administrative entity afterwards.

If a member of the General Council could be said to administer anything, it was not his canton, but the department as a whole. In practice this did not prevent the simultaneous exercise of more than one function; for example, the member of the General Council might also be mayor of one of the communes, or even of the chief town of the department. In the case of the Yonne, out of 40 members of the General Council, there was only 1 who was not also on a municipal council. Five were ordinary councillors, and the rest were mayors of one of the communes in their canton. Should one see this simultaneous exercise as diluting the difference between the municipal and the departmental function? In practice the distinction remained, and most councillors followed the basic recipe of never putting forward as members of the General Council the same sort of arguments they would employ as mayors. People had internalised this idea to a very great degree, as I can illustrate from my own experience. In conversation with members of the General Council, I would sometimes begin with the words, 'M. X, you are the councillor for the canton of . . .'. Several councillors interrupted me there to remind me that they were not councillors for a particular canton, but for the department.

It seems that the member of the General Council had to avoid playing the role of super-mayor. Under the particular conception of representation which prevailed here, the individual was defined by the role of intermediary to which I referred earlier. I was re-encountering here a view of the political function which is widespread and shared by many societies far removed from our own: in Ochollo, for example, dignitaries are defined as 'messengers'. This was exactly the role of the member of the General Council, to be the bearer of demands emanating from his canton. That meant, of course, that he must be open to all the demands. That was the very essence of his function, to take in at a glance the composite whole, whereas the mayor's point of view was by definition partial, confined within the limits of his commune. No matter what size of community he managed, the mayor did not enjoy the ubiquity of the councillor. He could be defined rather as the guardian of his territory, and in fact, he had a peace-keeping role by virtue of his office. However, the main point is that the mayor, unlike his circulating counterpart, had the task of guarding the inheritance handed down from his ancestors. The true mayor, in the French tradition, was essentially sedentary; there was no call for him to go beyond the borders of his little empire. He was to maintain law and order, and take action, from time to time, perhaps, but basically he had to resist the siren call of politics – in short, be a moderate, which as we have seen is not the same thing as having no opinions: such was the ideal patriarchal image of the traditional mayor.

By contrast, the figure of the member of the General Council was more politically partisan right from the start; this again was an aspect of his function of representation. The mayor had the virtues of the man who brings everyone together, whereas the councillor emerged as the expression of the political preferences of the moment. The cantonal elections offered an opportunity to take the pulse of political opinion at regular intervals. Overt politicisation was the name of the game here, whereas in municipal elections the exacerbation of conflict would be considered dangerous. The member of the General Council had to have a political label, even though he might be just a quiet local notable, willing to take a few trips to the chief town of the department. Others were active politicians, more committed than one might expect to a particular party. There was an ambiguity here, which was the result not only of the dual nature of the councillor, but also of the mode of election. Within his canton, once the election and its aftermath were over, his duty was to show by his actions that he served as faithfully the concerns of those who supported his rival as he did those of his own supporters. At departmental level, however, he was now a member, for better or worse, of a faction, be it in the majority or a minority, and he must therefore vote on certain issues which might have a precise political significance, such as a response to the policies of the particular government in power. Under the traditional procedure of the expression of wishes, the councillor might be the spokesman for local pressure groups, or on the contrary an adversary of some such lobby.

As a member of the departmental assembly, however, whatever his degree of overt political commitment, the councillor had to take sides – that was the second part of his nature. I am referring now only to the concept and practices prevailing before the law on decentralisation. To sum up, the function of the member of the General Council took its meaning from this perpetual movement from A to B, from the local to the global, from rural apoliticism to the game of party politics, from the world of elected representatives to the world of civil servants. That is why the members of the General Council, however settled they might be, however much they were local notables, all to a greater or less degree caught the virus of mobility. The reader may feel that I am too quick to generalise. It may be objected that urban and rural councillors did not play the same role in their communities. In town, the population would spontaneously turn to the mayor, rather than to the member of the General Council, who might very well represent only a limited area, if the town, as was usually the case, had been divided into several cantons. Obviously there we would have an example of exactly the opposite pattern to the one prevailing in rural milieux. It is undoubtedly true that the General Council was an institution intended to protect the interests of rural France. However, the practice of simultaneous exercise of more than one function allowed urban representatives to lay siege to the General Councils, often to good effect. Moreover, the councillor for a town embodied the function of representation in exactly the same way as the councillor for a country area; but in the case of the former, the political function tended to override the role of intermediary, though the inhabitants of an urban canton would nevertheless still turn to their councillor for certain things.

One of the questions frequently explored by specialists in local politics was the real extent of the power exercised by members of the General Council under the old system. The answer usually swung to one of two extremes: some writers insisted that in comparison with the omnipotence of central government, embodied in the person of the prefect, the General Council and its president never counted for very much. Let us look, for example, at a speech to the Legislative Assembly in which Chaptal described the Napoleonic system of administration:

The prefect knows only the Minister, the Minister only the prefect . . . the prefect does not question the orders he is given, but puts them into effect, guarantees and supervises their execution, and transmits orders to the sub-prefect; the latter transmits them to the mayors of cities, towns and villages, so that there is an unbroken chain of command from the Minister to the administered, which permits the transmission of the law and government orders to the smallest ramifications of the social order with the speed of electrical fluid.

Not much room in this outline for the kind of deliberative body represented by the General Council. We find a more recent echo of the same thought in some remarks made in 1973 by a councillor, Robert de Caumont:

Members of the General Council can only comment in response to a report from the prefect. This report exerts an undeniable pressure on the decision of the assembly, whether by the delay in producing it, the arguments it presents, the conclusions it suggests or the recommendations it carries. Often the majority of councillors will be loath to go against the report of the prefect, so that rapporteurs do no more than paraphrase its terms (it is not unknown for the officials to actually draw up the final document).[18]

Some other authors present a quite different view of the General Council. Pierre Grémion, in his study of 'power on the periphery', sees the department as 'the meeting-place of a centralist rationale and a localist rationale'. In this sense it is not merely a territorial division, but rather a 'system of power and action able to neutralise the State precisely at the point where the State attempts to embody its will. The administrative system of the State is thus subject to a severe check at the periphery'.[19] In this analysis of centralism, which it sees as in practice a tame form of Jacobinism, Grémion demonstrates that local councillors constituted in their way a counterweight to the central power and that the relationship between officials of the State and elected politicians was governed by ideas of negotiation and compromise. This view, of course, goes against well-known theories about the derisory, even rather quaint, function of local political figures, but it has the merit of taking into account the real activities of elected representatives and the permanence of departmental structures throughout the ups and downs of history.

These two different views, though they may disagree in their diagnosis, have one thing in common. Both 'measure' to some extent the power of local dignitaries by the same criteria as those of prefects and other representatives of the State. Such a procedure may seem acceptable, since it is based on the existence of a constant balance of power between elected representatives and officials of the State. Yet I believe that, however accurate their critique of French centralism, however pertinent their conclusions about power at local level, something escapes all these observers. Perhaps it is because in this particular case, the question of power is not the central issue. Like it or not, until 1982, the General Council had very little power compared to the prefect. At the same time, as Grémion correctly realised, the councillors had other advantages. This explains why, at the time when the prefectural ideology was at its height, elected representatives could nevertheless make their voice heard. These advantages can be summed up in one word: position. This means not only the special position of the councillor vis-à-vis his territory, but also his position in the strictly hierarchical sense, the elected representative as dignitary in the eyes of his fellow-citizens.

We are therefore thinking, not about the problem of the distribution of roles between the central administration and local powers, but about the place of the individual in civil society. One of my informants who had a long experience of office made some interesting observations. 'I was elected for the first time in 1959', he told me.

> At that time, the General Council bore no resemblance to what it has become today. When I first became a councillor, it was marvellous, a sort of club to which the taxpayers paid one's subscription. The club met twice a year, one session lasting for two days, the other just one day. The prefect drew up the reports, and one voted on them. It was very nice.

The comparison between the Council and a good club is revealing, for it has two connotations: that the member has been recognised as belonging to a select brotherhood, and that he personally has been awarded a mark of distinction. He might have little opportunity for significant activity, but at least his fellow-citizens had not skimped: they had paid – note the telling metaphor – for his seat. In other words, they recognised him as worthy to sit. For surely that was the supreme activity of the Council? From this angle, there was no attribution of power, simply the assignation of a distinguished position, above the common herd, signalled by enrolment in the club.

In other words, electing an individual meant recognising in him certain qualities which might give access to other advantages: from that point onwards he was to engage on a centripetal movement. It was expected that he would develop a capacity for making contacts to the benefit of his electors. It was at that point that the notion of power on the part of the elected representative began to arise in people's minds, though in a purely hypothetical fashion, expressed in speculation. We have all heard a dialogue like the following: 'Do you think the councillor can help?' 'Well, he said he would try, and you can generally trust him.' 'Yes, but I wonder if he really knows the right people?' There are two classic questions in the petitioner's mind: 'Will he agree to help?' and 'Does he know the people who really matter?' In any department, there are a few really important people: then a mass of others, recognised and distinguished by the community, but no one can be sure how effective they are. Power begins in people's expectations: 'I may as well try him – it's better than nothing.' Here we have in one simple sentence a summary of the specific situation of the member of the General Council.

The General Council as a meeting of notables

It will therefore come as no surprise to learn that members of the General Council were often chosen from amongst local notables. This can readily be demonstrated by glancing at a list of members of the General Council of the Yonne, choosing a year at random, say 1925.[20] The majority were from the liberal professions: five doctors, a dentist, a vet, six lawyers and a bailiff, and one ex-Minister (P.-E. Flandin). There were also several high-ranking civil servants, a member of the Council of State, a Treasury official, a deputy in the National Assembly, a journalist, a headmaster, two teachers, two merchants and two manufacturers. The others, ten in all, were landowners and farmers. So although it was a rural department, categories directly related to the land were far from being in the majority; our list, like others relating to different periods of the Third and later the Fourth Republic, demonstrates the influence of doctors and lawyers in country districts, and also the trust accorded to natives of the department who succeeded in the highest spheres of Parisian life.

Is the situation any different sixty-odd years later? The first thing that strikes one about the social composition of the General Council of 1985 is of course the predominance of civil servants. Representatives of the liberal professions still attract the votes of their fellow-citizens: there are two doctors, a surgeon, a chemist, two vets and two solicitors. However, out of a total of 40 councillors, 16 are civil servants, including an emeritus senior member of the Council of State, a Treasury official, an auditor at the public revenue office, a high-ranking lawyer and 7 teachers. It is true that there is nothing new about teachers having an influential role in local life, but they are no longer content with their traditional role of secretary at the town hall. In the Yonne, as in many other departments of France, primary and secondary school teachers are more and more frequently becoming fully fledged politicians. As far as the high-ranking civil servants are concerned, it is still the case now, as it was in the past, that being voted on to the General Council is equivalent to recognition of merit. For some, it is also the first step in a possible political career. If we take the Council as a whole, farmers, with only 7 representatives, are in a very reduced minority. Finally, we should note the presence of 4 company managers and 3 shopkeepers or artisans.

If we compare the average age of councillors now and then, we see that in

1925 it was 46, whereas in 1985 it goes up to 55. Obviously this can be tied to the phenomenon of overall ageing of the population in France, but what is more interesting, to my mind, is the fact that the Council now attracts people who in an earlier period might have felt they were too old to contest a seat and win. I know of one mayor who waited until he had retired to stand for election, after a lifetime in the civil service: 'I know all about handling reports; I felt it made more sense to place my skill at the service of others, rather than retiring to cultivate my garden.' He told me this as he was about to stand for the third time, aged seventy. Joining the council is seen as a good way of remaining active, especially for someone who has led a very busy professional life. It is this same motive which leads others to remain in seats they won several years earlier, and which they believe they can continue to fill, probably even more effectively once they can devote more time to Council business.

An example is M. Janot, a former senior member of the Council of State, who retired several years ago. He has been a member of the General Council for three decades, representing a rural canton in the north of the department; he was also mayor of a small commune in his canton for years. M. Janot was a high-ranking civil servant who held many important posts over a period of about fifty years. He was first of all legal adviser to President Auriol, then economic adviser to General de Lattre in Indo-China, Principal Private Secretary to M. Letourneau, governor of Indo-China, and General Secretary of the Council of State. He was invited by General de Gaulle to join his cabinet when he returned to power in 1958. Janot was put in charge of constitutional issues, as the government representative on the Constituent Committee, in which role he was influential in the drafting of the Constitution. Later he had many other important positions: General Secretary of the African Community, and Director General of French Radio and Television. Although he retired in 1986, M. Janot kept up several activities in Paris, as member of a committee on banking, member of the board of governors of the French Red Cross and President of the General Assembly of the Assurances générales de France (AGF). M. Janot was chairman of the Departmental Committee for a long period; he took an early interest in the setting-up of regional authorities, and was a member from the beginning of the Comité départemental et régional and of the economic and social committee for Burgundy. Today he is vice-president of the Regional Council, in charge of cultural issues and social development. Though keenly interested in regional questions, M. Janot does not neglect the department: he is the general *rapporteur* for the Yonne budget, a key post since decentralisation. Hence he has a very full timetable. He told me:

I spend two days a week in Dijon, one day a fortnight at Auxerre, and every weekend in my canton. This week, for example, I spent the whole of Monday in Auxerre, and on Tuesday and Wednesday I was in Dijon. I came back to Paris yesterday evening and I'm off again this evening to Auxerre, as I have an important meeting there tomorrow morning; after that I go to see the rector of the *lycée technique* (technical school) in Sens in the early afternoon, and go back to my commune in the evening. On Saturday I'll have to return to Paris on some other business. I have been interested in local politics for a long time, and I'm happy, because since I retired I have been just as active as when I was working.[21]

At seventy-one, M. Janot is indeed still a very active and busy man: perhaps local politics is a fount of perpetual youth.

The relatively advanced age, then, of the members of the General Council is a clear indication of the role played by the elderly in community affairs. This phenomenon, however, also demonstrates another characteristic of French life – that politicians stay in office for very long periods. Many writers have pointed to the simultaneous exercise of more than one function as the essential characteristic of local politics, but to a great extent continuity in office is the other face of the process of becoming a local notable. 'An elected councillor is like a good wine', I have been told. 'He must be allowed to mature slowly.' The comparison is apt, to judge by some statistics which I have calculated quickly: if we take the total number of members of the General Council for the Yonne, the majority have held office at least twice, 7 are in their third year of office, 6 in their fourth and 3 have been re-elected for the fifth time in succession. These figures point to a deeper reality: the first vote is the recognition of a particular position – it opens the doors of the club – but it does not guarantee that magic quality which is the sign of the true representative, his *mana*. From the point of view of the voters, the first election is speculation on the future; taking a cue from given signals (family, network, social position, political affiliation), they assume a certain potential on the part of the candidate. He is not required to confirm that assumption immediately, if particular signs suggest that he will pass muster. Continued re-election will allow the potential to bloom, and 'power' to appear. Then, and only then, does the representative become a notable, that is, in the proper sense of the word, one worthy of note.

'Power to elected representatives'

These, then, were our notables. I feel that the word 'notable' is just right for these people who are recognised by others as being like them, but with a certain mystique as well. For a long time the General Council was little more than a gathering of personalities who had these mysterious qualities in common, though the influence exerted by individuals might vary. Faced with such an assembly, the prefect only had to demonstrate a minimum of authority, coherence and realism to impose a general policy acceptable to the great majority. However, prefects came and went, but the councillor stayed. Let us not forget that mobility is the rule for civil servants; they might administer, but they could not, by their very nature, aspire to the symbolic quality of continuity. The prefect and the councillor belonged to two different orders, which did not, incidentally, prevent each of them from taking advantage in his own way of the situation – the prefect by establishing his own position as the indispensable organiser, and the councillors by slowly building up their role as notables.

When the Socialist government decided to give 'power to elected representatives', this cosy cohabitation was disturbed. In concrete terms, the reform meant that the councillors became fully fledged administrators of their department. The General Council ceased to be a purely deliberative body. The prefect's former powers were transferred to the president of the General Council. The prefect retained his primacy, it is true, but only, and here we have a vital nuance, in the formal sense, as representative of the State. Thus, by a curious reversal, he was now the notable, but with this difference, that no one had elected him, and he represented no one except his Minister. It was therefore with no great enthusiasm that the Commissaire de la République, as the prefect was now called, signed the various agreements under which the president of the General Council obtained the means to exercise his authority, such as staff, vehicles, premises, and so on. The fact is that until this point, in the Yonne, the General Council had practically no staff or equipment. In some of the larger departments, the president had a secretary and a few employees, but this was not the case in the Yonne. The first task of the new executive was to set up its own services, which it did by taking over the majority of staff working at the prefecture: there were about forty people, to whom were added the staff of the departmental Social Services Authority, and part of the staff of the Building and Works Authority. Today about 700 people draw their salaries from the department: 250–300 belong to the general departmental administration and the rest are employed by the Social Services Authority, except for about 30 people formerly employed by the Building and Works Authority, who now come under Planning and Transport.

Simply quoting these figures gives some idea of the significance of the change. By taking over the services of the prefecture, the departmental authority has become a reality. The Council, however, has been cautious about increasing the number of new posts. It was found necessary to recruit people such as chauffeurs and typists, but the only large-scale new creation is the general departmental administration, the head of which is a key person, responsible for the operation and coordination of the whole. The president chose for this post an exceptional sub-prefect, who knew the Yonne very well, since he had been general secretary of the prefecture from

1971 to 1974. He had then gone to Paris to work for one of the councillors who had been made a Minister. I asked him how he saw his role: 'I am an expert at the service of the elected councillors', Jean Pélissier told me. 'When I was general secretary of the prefecture, I used to draw up the budget. I still do, but now I do it in a different spirit . . . My task is to translate into administrative terms the political decisions of the General Council, not to impose my own views.'[22]

Pelissier does not conceal the fact that he left the prefectoral service because he disagreed with the government of the time; he soon developed an interest in decentralisation, and now prefers to work for the president of the General Council. It is also true that the big decisions are now taken in the offices housing services which until 1986 were in the prefecture. These offices will have to be enlarged in order to accommodate the 'transfer'. All this reorganisation was done in stages, without too much upset. There was a little bit of friction, just as there was elsewhere, between a prefect understandably reluctant to commit hara-kiri, and a president resolved to see the will of elected councillors prevail on certain issues. The choice of someone familiar with prefectoral practice as head of administration proved sound. There remain a few logistical problems, of course: the councillors have no offices, and the president is still accommodated in an office in the prefecture, but these are not of the essence, for everyone is aware that things have changed.

This feeling was summed up ironically by one councillor: 'If I wanted to be nasty about decentralisation, I could say that what the prefect used to do in a quarter of an hour, fifteen councillors now accomplish in two hours.' Certainly, one need only glance at people's diaries to note the proliferation of meetings. First of all there are the plenary sessions of the Council, which are held once every three months. The work of the Council is prepared by the president and the board, who meet every month and whose main task is to distribute subsidies among the different bodies once the main lines of the original budget have been voted on and accepted. There are five parallel organic committees to look after important matters and prepare reports which are submitted to the board or to the whole Council as appropriate. Apart from these standing bodies, working groups may be set up to consider particular problems.

Although the previously existing structure of committees, board and president has not changed, the transfer of responsibilities nevertheless implies a clear assumption of power by the elected councillors. There is a change of attitude, in that the councillor is no longer the representative of a particular territory, or the pillar of a club, but a member of a governing body. He has to adopt a managerial point of view and tailor his moves to the global policy for the department as a whole, at least in theory. This is a big change from his traditional role, since it forces him to move away from an individualist towards a more holistic approach. If the truth be told, at the time the new system was being set up, not all councillors were equally capable of adapting to the change. Many of them had some administrative experience as mayors, but it was usually confined to the modest bounds of a smallish rural commune.

In the Yonne, the system therefore relied initially on a few men: the president, his director-general, the general *rapporteur* on the budget, the chairman of the finance committee and the chairman of the public works committee, a retired building contractor. The key figures are actually few in number: apart from those already cited, there are two vice-presidents, both deputies and mayors, one at Auxerre, the other at Joigny. It is surely no coincidence, then, that we find among these key figures ex-Ministers, high-ranking civil servants, such as Chamant, Soisson, Auberger and Janot, an experienced politician, Paul Flandin, and a highway engineer, André Marie. Politics is not irrelevant to the choice of these men: the balance between the UDF and the RPR within the majority must be respected, though the majority has chosen to govern alone, its Socialist and Communist rivals being confined to membership of the committees.

In word and deed

In practice every councillor has to join one of the five committees, and it is within these committees that political differences are aired, and the necessary compromises hammered out. The plenary sessions of the General Council are public: thus one can attend the debates preceding the vote on the budget, which has been drawn up by the president and discussed in committee and by the board. The occasion is formal: the president and the first five vice-presidents are seated on a raised platform, and the councillors around a large semicircular table. The president's speech, outlining his general policy, is followed by a breakdown of the budget by the *rapporteurs* of the different committees, such as road maintenance, social services, culture, and so on. To the layman sitting in the public gallery it can sound like an endless litany, interrupted at regular intervals by ritual question and answer: 'No objections? Carried.' Occasionally, however, the litany is interrupted by a councillor demanding to speak; he raises an objection, and generally follows it up with some remarks of a fairly political nature.

At one session I attended, which was mainly soporific, a diversion of this kind arose after about an hour. The issue under discussion was the decommissioning of one of the roads in the department, the reason being that this road ran straight through a site in one of the communes of the Puisaye, in the western part of the department, which had been acquired by the Club Méditerranée for development as a huge tourist complex. One of the Communist councillors immediately attacked this plan, complaining that they would be giving an indirect subsidy to the Club Méditerranée and to the Lyonnaise water company if they made them a present of the road, the CD 207. He went on to denounce the policy of the department, saying it was just like the government of the day. It would be happy to provide facilities in France for the whole of Europe to come and sun its bum, rather than promote real industrial recovery. Needless to say, several councillors from the majority party riposted in similarly colourful terms, until finally the president intervened to restore calm by pointing out the opportunities for local employment in the scheme and stating categorically that the department would not be contributing financially.

I noticed during these exchanges that several speakers turned to face the public gallery, even though on this hot July afternoon there were only two of us present. I had no difficulty in guessing the identity of my companion, as he was taking notes and was obviously covering the event for the local paper. After the president's intervention, the report was accepted, with only the three Communists voting against it, and the litany continued, with only one further argument, less animated this time, over the maintenance of the Nivernais canal. The problem was that the department was not even represented on the relevant body, even though it contributed jointly with the central government and the region. This gave the Socialists an opportunity to vote in favour of an amendment presented by a member of the majority, in defiance of his friends' advice. These internal disagreements emerge from time to time on both sides. They are not so serious as to disturb the balance of power; they simply allow the more 'unruly' elements to express their feelings, and occasionally form tactical alliances. Someone remarked to me that it was a good idea for someone occasionally to throw a little spanner into the works, even inadvertently, otherwise they would just be sitting opposite each other all day long like china dogs.

The next day *L'Yonne républicaine* published its account of the meeting: 'The General Council and the Club Méditerranée: no direct subsidies'.[23] It quoted the intervention by the Communist deputy and the president's response, adding that the Socialists were broadly in favour of the proposal. So as well as the vote on the budget, the session had given the minority party a chance to state its position publicly. The attitude of the speakers, turning to the public gallery, showed clearly enough the purpose of their speeches; and as it turned out, their efforts paid off. Here we see an illustration of the real meaning of these meetings of the Council: they do not significantly change the decisions taken by the president and the board, but they provide the councillors with a platform on which to display their talents as representatives.

For the opposition, being very much in the minority, there is hardly any difference between this mode of expression and the old system of expressing a wish. Now, however, the participants must show greater competence. It is no longer a member of the administration who has the most important role, but a politician, a 'colleague'. It is not so easy for him to gloss over the implications of a report, or grossly oversimplify its contents, as used to happen when the prefect displayed his omnipotence. Councillors now have much easier access to departmental services and can improve their knowledge of matters once considered too technical for them: as the director general of departmental affairs remarked to me, councillors are now administrators, and need to possess at least the rudiments of administrative science. This remark shows the extent of the change that has taken place.

It must be admitted that the General Council was changing, even before centralisation. The commune as a unit was proving ill suited to the administration of rural areas with a declining population, and in practice there was a great deal of cooperation between communes within the framework of the canton. Both in the Yonne and in its neighbouring department of the Nièvre, the General Council had the task of distributing, with the agreement of mayors, the departmental subsidies for maintenance, and the creation of various types of facilities. The Nièvre had created a departmental fund for the latter purpose, and in 1977 the Yonne adopted the procedure of joint contracting, to which they later added the procedure of intercommunal charters. Each year, a certain sum was allotted by the General Council to the cantons, to permit them to build certain facilities; the councillor had the task of arbitrating locally between the demands of the different communes. He also had the task of finding further subsidies from the State or the region to carry out more ambitious projects. Joint contracting could involve up to 1.7 million francs over a period of three years. For about twelve years, then, the councillors had been in the habit of drawing up reports, often with the help of the sub-prefect; nowadays they are more inclined to turn to the departmental administrators, who now hold the purse-strings.

Despite the transfer of powers, which has been considerable, the General Council in the Yonne remains subject to certain constraints: the two sectors which swallow up the most money, road-maintenance and social services, are items which are very difficult to reduce. Out of a total budget of 874 million francs in 1987, obligatory and discretional outgoings on social services amounted to 340 million; another 129 million had to be spent on road repairs. These figures show quite clearly how narrow is the margin of manoeuvrability open to the council. However, councillors now aspire to a more active role in the local economy. Like everywhere else, the area has an unemployment problem: it is a daily preoccupation for constituents and cannot be ignored. Hence the temptation to take a more active part in economic affairs, though in theory economic planning is the job of the region, and the department has no call to encroach on its territory. Apart from the contracting arrangements outlined earlier, there is the device of cross-financing, which gives the department a role in certain financial operations. The simple fact that the administrative services now give some consideration to local development projects is a novelty in itself.

The president of the General Council admits that one of his aims is to see the department becoming a fully fledged partner in the social and economic life of the area. Right from the first year of decentralisation, he allowed a substantial rise in grants to the communes, for he considers it essential that the General Council should back the initiatives of the mayors. Ideally, he feels, there should be two-tier system of management: at the centre, the president and the council deciding the political and budgetary policies at departmental level; and all around them, in each canton, the member of the General Council and the mayors administering and running things. This is a very different model from the earlier system, which essentially promoted a *polycentric* base. Under this system, the most important division was the canton. The member of the General Council was a representative. The purpose of the council was to bring these representatives together periodically, and it was the prefect who in a sense guaranteed the coherence of the whole. The reformed system, on the other hand, promotes concentricity rather than polycentricity. Under the new structure, the unity of the department, embodied in the figure of the president of the Council, takes precedence over the division into cantons. Administration becomes the councillors' essential function; their legitimacy comes from their competence rather than their abilities as representatives.

Let me try to explain this a little more clearly. Of course, the model I have sketched is to some extent an idealised one. The function of the member of the General Council remains ambiguous, and great play is sometimes made of this fact. Where the change can be most clearly seen is in the figure of the president of the General Council, the master of the game, the super-mayor of what we might call the whole community, as distinct from the small scattered communes. Now, there is no relationship of this kind between the department and the region – in fact such a relationship would be unthinkable. The engineers of decentralisation were content simply to arrange for co-existence between the new territorial division and previously existing ones. The departmental authorities have not advanced beyond a cautious wait-and-see policy so far as the region is concerned. 'I hardly know what to think of the Regional Council', confesses the president of the General Council, although he himself was once president of a body known at the time as a Regional Public Establishment.

It is an institution which has not yet reached a state of equilibrium. We have not yet found a terrain on which to establish contacts, although I have a very good relationship on a personal level with the president, who is a senator, like me. The region has to find its cruising-speed: it is early days. The idea of the region is not clear. I do not wish to pass judgement, because it would be premature. For the moment we are trying to achieve something which can be helped along by personal friendships: a good *modus vivendi.*

This absence of links between the Regional Council and the General Council, despite the fact that some members belong to both bodies, reflects a deeper reality: the Burgundy region is essentially an artificial entity, at least to the north of the Côte-d'Or. Although they may think of themselves as Burgundians in relation to wine and culture, the Yonne councillors find it difficult to accept that their affairs should be decided in Dijon. They do not mind so much in relation to planning, which can be regarded as something speculative. Serious issues, they feel, should continue to be the prerogative of the department.

King Jean

The right-wing majority on the General Council form a single group, the Union for the Future of the Yonne, headed by the leader of the UDF, Jean-Pierre Soisson. The RPR has fewer councillors, although it is the party of the president, Jean Chamant. Chamant has been president since 1970, but as he pointed out to me: 'The position has changed, since decentralisation. Before the reform, the president's role was essentially a formal one; he was there to chair the meetings of the council and represent it on public occasions.'[24] Jean Chamant is a popular and respected figure in the department. He is a cultured and affable man, a superb speaker – I was told that as a child he had received a prize for public speaking – quite the opposite of a technocrat, someone whose authority is recognised by all when he chairs the debates in the Council. Even his adversaries recognise that he is a master of the art. Like other politicians who served their apprenticeship under the Fourth Republic, such as his friend Edgar Faure and his former colleague from the neighbouring department, François Mitterrand, Jean Chamant can be diplomatic and flexible if required, while still obstinately pursuing his own ends. He is a grass-roots politician: not a week goes by but the local press carries a report and a photograph of the president of the General Council at an inauguration or some other public event.

He has been a representative of the department for more than forty years, having first been elected deputy to the National Assembly just after the Liberation. His career is revealing:

My family is from the Yonne, and I went to primary and secondary school in the department – I was at the Ecole Saint-Jacques in Joigny. Afterwards I studied law and worked at the court of appeal in Paris. However, as you can imagine, I had built up a strong network of friends and contacts after six years at school here.

From his carpeted office in the Senate, Chamant looks back over an active career in politics. The war years decimated the ranks of politicians. We saw earlier how even formerly highly regarded figures such as Flandin disappeared from public life after the war. A new generation then emerged:

It was the spring of 1946, and the draft Constitution had been rejected. Friends of mine in the department approached me; I knew they were looking for a young person to conduct public meetings. I contacted people who were already active in the Constituent body, and that is how it all began. I stood in the election in November, held on the basis of proportional representation.

Chamant was elected as an Independent together with the mayor of Auxerre, Jean Moreau; the two men sat together in the Assembly throughout the Fourth Republic. He was invited to enter the government for the first time in 1955 as Secretary of State for Foreign Affairs in a Ministry headed by Edgar Faure, who was a friend, as was the Minister for Foreign Affairs at the time, Antoine Pinay. At the 1956 election, he was beaten by a Poujadist, but the latter's election was declared invalid. Jean Chamant replaced him, but preferred to clarify the issues by resigning and forcing a by-election in July of the same year, at which he was massively supported by the voters, and won the respect of his adversaries for his sense of fair play. The elections in 1958, following the return of de Gaulle, marked a turning-point: 335 outgoing deputies failed to win re-election; Chamant, however, survived the storm, and shortly afterwards became vice-president of the National Assembly.

This promotion brought me closer to Jacques Chaban-Delmas, whom I already knew because he had been a member of the Assembly since 1946. I also saw rather more of the Prime Minister, Georges Pompidou. These factors probably explain why after the 1967 elections, I found myself on the list of deputies who had a chance of being invited to join the government.

In fact Chamant became the Minister for Transport, a post which he retained for four years. As a lawyer, he had no previous inclination towards such a technical Ministry: 'When the Prime Minister told me of my nomination, I said I knew nothing about transport. But he replied: "All the more reason to believe you will be successful, as you will have no prejudices." And in the event that proved to be so.' Today Chamant can boast of having conducted the negotiations for the European Airbus and launched the initial studies on the High Speed Train. He was a Minister under the successive presidencies of de Gaulle and Pompidou, but in 1962 he broke with the Centre national des indépendants et paysans, to which he had belonged for a long time, disapproving of its extreme position with regard to Algeria, and formed the Independent Republicans with Giscard d'Estaing. He supported Giscard in 1974, then after the defeat of the right in 1981 he rallied the RPR.

For a long time Chamant was best known locally as a deputy and a Minister. Only after de Gaulle introduced the system of election by a simple majority vote in single membership constituencies did he turn his attention to one particular area. He chose the Avallonnais because its 'Flandinist' tradition accorded well with his own beliefs. He was also a native of the area. A few years later, Chamant was elected to the General Council as member for the rural canton of Quarré-les-Tombes:

The councillor had died, and the other councillors came to see me to urge me to stand. I was fairly sure it would not cause resentment vis-à-vis the other cantons in my constituency, and that no one would reproach me for standing there rather than elsewhere, because it is the smallest canton in the Yonne. Until then I had been quite happy not to be involved in local politics, as it left me free to devote myself equally to all the communities in my constituency. But in the end my decision did not adversely affect my relations with the voters.

Chamant seems to have developed a taste for local politics, for he first of all became president of the General Council, and then was elected mayor of Avallon when his predecessor, weary of the responsibility after twenty years, retired. 'I had no reason to want to be mayor until then. Nor had I ever made any attempt at it. The mayor was a man I knew, and I had no reason to jostle him. You know, if you have friends in office, the wise thing is to leave them alone...' Chamant served only one term as mayor, from 1977 to 1983, when he left the post to his first assistant mayor. During the previous year, decentralisation had turned him into the key figure in the department, and he took a very keen interest in his new role. He had become a senator some years before; so after several decades in which his activity had centred on political life in Paris, he made a fresh start, and turned his attention entirely to local affairs.

The change is significant; should we interpret it as a gradual abandonment of active politics in favour of a more honorary position? Certainly the Senate offers public figures a less exposed but still attractive status. In the lift and the corridors which led to Chamant's office, I had noticed several former politicians, who were greeted by colleagues with a respectful 'Good morning, Minister', in recognition of their past services to the nation. In the case of Chamant, however, the simultaneous exercise of the functions of Senator and member of the General Council gives quite a different impression. Through decentralisation, which neither he nor his friends voted for, he has reached a highly prominent position. His diary made this clear: two days a week in Auxerre, and a large number of meetings, not only with voters and mayors, but also with people vital to the local economy. He is keenly interested in the workings of decentralisation, and he is not the man to delegate. 'The General Council and the Regional Council are quite different', I was told, by someone who sits on both bodies. 'In the Regional Council in Dijon, there are three vice-presidents, who can sign documents and enjoy a measure of independence, whereas with the General Council in Auxerre, the president has a board around him, but he does not delegate any powers to its members, only to the head of services.'

It is as though Chamant, at the head of the General Council, was once more a member of government. He is anxious to assume to the full the powers devolved to him by the new legislation. Not that this concentration of powers is a synonym for authoritarian rule: members of the council in charge of sectors like the budget and public works have plenty of room to exercise their initiative. However, it is clear that the two-man team of the president and his director-general (like the Minister and the sub-prefect) are the cornerstone of the whole edifice. When Jean Chamant speaks of his department, one can sense a sort of identification between the man and the institution. As president of the Council, he behaves a little like a schoolmaster, restoring order from time to time when oratory threatens to turn into an uproar. He is pleased with progress to date:

> The councillors participate in the life of the department in a way which goes far beyond their canton. Perhaps I am spoiled in that regard here in the Yonne, for I have some very good people: I am not referring only to very distinguished people, such as the councillor who is a graduate of the Ecole Polytechnique, another who is from the School of Engineering, our retired senior member of the Council of State, or the councillor who was an auditor at the public revenue office. We are very lucky to have people of that calibre, but we also have people from the professions, small businessmen and farmers. They are all excellent individuals, as I think I am competent to judge after seventeen years as president: there is absolutely no comparison between the General Council as it used to be and as it is today.

A large part of his activity revolves around his identification with the General Council. His aim is to make the Council a recognised voice in the workings of the local economy. Apart from the political activity which that implies within the Council itself, he has another ineluctable task, which can be summed up in three words: 'selling the product'. For one of the weaknesses of the General Council as an institution is that to most people the department is a purely bureaucratic concept, just one more cog in the political machine. Chamant's ambition is to improve communication, in other words, build up a good image of the department, just as some mayors have tried to do for their communes – sometimes to the point of making a spectacle of themselves. Without going to those lengths, Chamant would like to create a more attractive image of the department. However, this demands a great deal of investment, and a change in the role of the members of the Council. For the moment he contents himself with spreading the good word by means of frequent meetings with local industrialists. 'It gives me a chance to say a few words about the new role of the General Council.' So the president has both an administrative function and a public relations function; however, his work also has another, more directly political side. With his long experience, Chamant has close personal knowledge of people on the political scene: at the cantonal elections, newcomers, that is, people who are standing for the first time, will seek his support. It is not unusual for him to travel around and appear at their rallies. It is no small advantage to a candidate to be able to count on his support, for all the mayors around here know the man affectionately nicknamed 'King Jean'.

Nor is his role limited to supporting existing candidates. Several councillors told me that he had encouraged them to stand. 'I prefer to have good people round me', Chamant explained,

> so when the opportunity arises, I take it . . . But it depends also on the circumstances. I leave it to the candidates to decide if they want me at their rallies. Mistakes can happen: in 1982, we failed to take back a canton from the Communists because our candidate, after doing very well in the first ballot, turned down my offer to chair an important rally before the second ballot, saying: "There's no need". He managed things very badly, and got beaten.

The president intervenes with the aim of ensuring continuity, meaning the continued undisputed predominance of the 'moderates', who more or less correspond to the Independents, who have consistently remained in power, though at times under different labels. This is no doubt part of the secret of the remarkable political longevity of 'King Jean' and the respect he enjoys among colleagues on the local political scene.

The end of a tradition

We have come a long way since the members of the committee decided to divide France into its roughly hewn units. The entire edifice of departments, communes and cantons has stood firm through the different regimes the country has known. The fact is that French centralism is quite different from the caricature people have drawn of it: certainly one of the pillars of the system was the army of civil servants sent out from Paris, but we should not underestimate the polycentric system of elected bodies which informed the whole and rounded it out. On the one hand we can see a strong opposition between Paris and the provinces, but on the other hand we can see also in the chief towns of departments another France which quietly developed its own hierarchies of power under the auspices of the prefect. The specific form of representation embodied in the member of the General Council grew in the shade of this tradition. By definition, the power of these notables could never be comparable to that of the representatives of the central power. In being chosen, in being accorded a position in public life, they were being designated messengers. In exchange, the meeting at a central place of all these figures, in assemblies whose purpose was purely deliberative, gave the department public existence.

It was precisely because it overturned these arrangements that decentralisation was in fact the 'great issue' that its instigator claimed. The response of the councillors of the Yonne was significant. They realised there was a great deal at stake, for the whole concept of political space was altered. The reigning polycentrism was giving way to a concentric system: since decentralisation, the president of the Council occupies the whole of the centre, surrounded by an assembly which is no longer the long-winded, somnolent body seen in the recent past. Everything indicates that in future the councillor will cease to be a representative and a messenger. He will have to take account of the overall interests of the department, and become in short a fully fledged member of local government. In other words, the councillors have returned, two hundred years later, to their original vocation, at least as the committee saw it, which was to be the administrators of the department. Is this an enrichment of their role? It can hardly be denied that it is, so long as the huge volume of information that must be digested does not overwhelm local democracy. The president has to be in the front line of the transition, leading the collective education in practices which are undeniably novel. It is not the least of the paradoxes of French political life – and the Yonne is no exception in this respect – that this figure should so often be an elderly person, skilled in the art, amongst others, of representation.

5

Parachuting in

A republican banquet

Tonnerre, 10 May 1987

The first thing one sees is a magnificent thirteenth-century building. It is a handsome timbered hospital, the pride of the inhabitants of the little town. Not far away flows the Armançon. There is a feeling of tranquillity on this ordinary Sunday morning; the church bells are ringing, and people are strolling down the main street or loitering at shop windows. I was listening to a satirical programme in the car. The special guest, Jean-Pierre Cot, was doing his best to keep up with the wit of the professional comedians. The things politicians have to do to polish their image and get their party's 'message' through! Today is 10 May, the Socialists' big day: it is the anniversary of their victory six years ago, yet here they are, struggling to regain lost ground.

Behind the old hospital of Tonnerre, there is an unusual excitement in the air; there are masses of people, streamers, badges and a table set up in the open air with piles of the sort of pamphlets you get at political rallies. 'Yes, I have an invitation. Look, here comes Geneviève P., she'll confirm . . .' 'Good morning, yes, that's right. Henri Nallet said it would be all right.' 'Excuse me, could you stand a little to one side? They'll be here at any moment.' I step aside, and just have time to say hello to André Fourcade, the mayor of Dannemoine and one of the organisers of today's event. 'Stand back! Back! They're here!' No, it's a police car – they can't have arrived yet. Yes, here they are! There is some jostling; one or two people step back, but others press forward. The Renault 25 stops right in front of me. 'He' steps out of the car, 'he' being Laurent Fabius, come to visit the Socialists of the Yonne who have turned up in their hundreds to meet him. I find myself directly facing the former Prime Minister. He shakes my hand spontaneously: 'How are you?' I have no time to answer, for already he has turned to other people. The photographers are busy snapping him. A few words with mayors and leaders of the Socialist Federation. They are on a tight schedule, and behind Fabius the deputy, Henri Nallet, who is the host and master of ceremonies today, keeps an eye on the clock.

The detailed itinerary for the visit reads as follows:

09.30 Arrive river embankment, Pont-sur-Yonne. Welcome by Roger Lassale (former Socialist deputy for the constituency), Jean-Paul Rousseau (First Secretary, Federation) and Henry Nallet (present deputy and former Minister of Agriculture). Proceed on foot through market to reception rooms.

10.00 Arrive reception rooms, meeting with elderly residents and presidents of clubs and societies.

10.30 Depart Pont-sur-Yonne.

11.30 Arrive Tonnerre, hall in Priory (facing Old Hospital). Welcome by Tonnerre branch. Meeting with approx. forty young people (press only at this).

12.30 Proceed to town hall. Meet M. Roze, mayor of Tonnerre (finish 12.50).

13.00 Arrive banquet room Old Hospital.

The republican banquet is to be the highlight of the day. It is now 11.30, and up to now, Fabius has adhered to the timetable; he did not linger in the north of the department, for it was still early in the day, and Pont-sur-Yonne was just one stop on a crowded tour. Time now for the meeting with the youngsters. 'Hurry, please.' 'Where have the young people got to?' 'There are not going to be enough of them.' 'This way, quickly.' There is a surge of movement. I am allowed in with the local press. Timidly, the youth representatives file in and sit down. There are about fifteen of them altogether. Fabius invites them to move closer, they sit round in a circle and the introductions are made. There are several young people in their last year at school. Nallet opens the proceedings: 'Here you are, chatting to an ex-Prime Minister. Now is your chance to ask some questions . . .' Silence in the room, then one of the participants breaks the ice. 'I'm here from a local radio station. In your view, what is the best way of solving the present crisis?' Fabius speaks quietly, almost confidentially. He is very relaxed, and has his hands in his pockets; as far as he is concerned education and training are vital, and he expands a bit on that. The next question is also about education, then they turn to current affairs, the wave of privatisations, the television channel TFI, and problems in the media in general. One questioner mentions the anxieties of young people over nuclear energy. Some are worried about the percentage of the budget spent on defence: is there any real difference between the left and right on this?

From time to time a few more young people join us. Gradually everyone relaxes; the speaker is deploying all his didactic skill. This is the Fabius we all recognise from the television chat-shows, and for a moment it feels as if we're in front of the box. This feeling is in fact a product of the nature of the ritual. Roles have been clearly assigned from the start: the young people are to be the journalists. They may sometimes express concern, but there is no debate, and no one really argues. In fact, the tone is not political at all: Fabius presents himself as an expert, facing people looking for 'solutions'. The hour is over, and we leave the Priory in a calm frame of mind.

On to the town hall: the guest of honour is accompanied by a select group of people chosen by Nallet, and local journalists. We walk along the main street; the traffic has been diverted, and the pedestrians have also disappeared, either because it is getting on for lunch-time or because of the police presence. The town hall is a bit further down, on the right. When we get there, we follow Nallet and his guest to the mayor's office. The schedule allowed for a brief conversation, and brief it certainly is. M. Roze does not share his visitors' political convictions. However, both sides are anxious to be polite; I am told that if Fabius had had more time, they would have organised a small reception. Never mind, the main thing is to receive the visitor politely. The mayor accompanies his guests on their way out, and they all linger for a moment on the steps of the town hall to shake hands for the photographer of *L'Yonne républicaine*, so that it can publish a nice spread the next day.

Back to the Old Hospital: huge tables have been set up inside the magnificent building. At one end of the room there is a raised dais with the flag of the Republic behind it and a banner saying 'Happy birthday to the left'. People have gathered from Auxerre, Avallon and the north of the department, to celebrate this 10 May which saw the return to power of the left after such a long gap. There are more than five hundred people present, and there is a little confusion. 'Do you happen to know which is the Auxerre table?' A bit further on, someone from a village in the south can't find where they've sat him. All the old faces are there, of course, the militants from way back; but there are also new faces, sympathisers whom everyone is glad to welcome. Now that we have all found a place at table, hunger begins to make itself felt, and people stare longingly at the menus. But there is some business we have to get through first. The mayor of Dannemoine, André Fourcade, welcomes his guests in a brief speech. Even now it is not time to eat, for next we have Jean-Paul Rousseau, the First Secretary of the Federation. A political speech this time, criticism of the right, and exaltation of the achievements and innovations of the left. 'I would give anything for a glass of wine!' My neighbours' attention is wandering as the speech continues, but the speaker shows no sign of flagging; luckily, a troop of waiters bring us drinks. A buzz of conversation begins to be heard; the speaker is on his summing-up . . .

The atmosphere warms up as the meal advances; at the main table, in the centre in front of the dais, are seated key men with their wives. Nallet sits on Fabius's right, Rousseau on his left. But the style is different from old-fashioned banquets where the wine flowed like water, in imitation of the inevitable floods of rhetoric; our modern-day Socialists would not dream of surrendering to pleasure in this way. After the cheese has been brought round, it is the deputy's turn to speak. He congratulates everyone on the fact that the Socialists have brought together five hundred people, a record in the Yonne. He mentions François Mitterrand, who 'rescued us from despair', and reminds us that Fabius has visited Auxerre before, supporting him during the election campaign, a year ago. With a final word about Socialist unity, he surrenders the microphone to the former Prime Minister. Fabius's speech deals entirely with the prospect of a return to power of the left. He underlines the divisions on the right, the government's economic and social failures, and their lack of understanding of the problems of youth. He raises his voice at regular intervals, triggering the audience's applause. The climax is reached when François Mitterrand is once more evoked as the man on whom all the Socialists' hopes are pinned. There are great waves of clapping as the speech ends. Up on the dais, Fabius, Nallet and the other leaders congratulate each other to the sound of applause.

The day is not over, however. After this successful event, the itinerary directs:

15.00 Book-signing and contact with party militants (finish 15.30).
16.00 Depart for Noyers with journalists and small group of guests.
16.15 En route Noyers, stop at lay fête, Les Brions leisure centre Tonnerre (finish 16.30).
17.00 Arrive Noyers. Welcome by M. Pellerin, mayor of Noyers. Visit Noyers on foot, meet press.
17.45 Depart for Tonnerre Hospital. Meet M. Migigniac, hospital director (finish 18.30).
18.45 Return to Priory, reception for party militants involved in organisation of visit.

By now it is half past three; we leave the table rapidly, and a number of people surround Fabius, asking him to sign their menu. Professional as always, he asks their names, exchanges a few words and passes on to the next person. At the same time we all make our way to the exit, which is at the other end of the large hall. The organisers keep an eye on their watches, run off to attend to some detail and rejoin their guests. He briefly inspects some paintings exhibited on one of the walls of the room, but it is now time to leave for Noyers. On this visit, tourism and politics are combined. Noyers is a very pretty village, with houses going right back to the fourteenth and fifteenth centuries. There is a brief stop on the way at a fête organised by the lay youth club, then on to the main square in Noyers. Just before the arrival of the official cars, I hear the owner of a nearby café wondering if they will actually turn up: 'It is very unusual', he remarks, 'for people like that to come here, people you see on the telly.'

A small crowd forms round the car. The tour begins, guided by the president of the local archaeological society. Fabius and Nallet walk through the narrow streets, admiring the buildings. Behind them come the group of party militants and guests who followed them from Tonnerre. Fabius is shown a toyshop: immediately, the owner comes out and offers a package to the former Prime Minister, 'for the children'. She supports the left and wants to pay homage to one of its leaders. He thanks her, and with a slightly embarrassed air hands the package to his driver. Nallet and Fabius go into some more shops: a well-known second-hand bookshop, and a local craft gallery. At one point, a man comes out of his house and calls jovially: 'Come and have a glass of wine with me!' He repeats the invitation, and jokes with them, but they cannot stop, for they must press on to the town hall. There the atmosphere is relaxed and there are no long speeches; the main business is meeting some elderly residents who want to shake the hand of one of the 'stars' of the left. Before getting back into his car, Fabius records an interview in the street. Again the same old question: does he think Mitterrand will stand in 1988? The former Prime Minister responds patiently. The radio people are happy: with Fabius one take is enough, even with all the noise. This has only lasted a few moments; now it is off back to Tonnerre, where they still have to visit the hospital before the reception.

The day has been a success from every point of view, according to the party militants I overhear. Fabius may not be a particularly outgoing sort, but he certainly knows how to put his message over. He was 'just like on the telly, except that he was actually here'. The party strategists feel things are moving at last in the Yonne. Last year Mitterrand came to Auxerre, and there was a meeting at Avallon with Jospin and Lang present. Now Fabius. This is the big advantage of having an ex-Minister of Agriculture as deputy. As André Fourcade put it, waxing lyrical; 'Henri Nallet chose Tonnerre. He is a bright star in the skies of the Yonne.' The deputy and his friend showed their organising mettle in setting up this republican banquet. Yet there is still a question to be asked. Nallet is a newly elected deputy, recently descended from the upper echelons of power. Was Fabius's visit aimed at putting the department on the map, or was it perhaps a piece of self-promotion by Nallet, designed to strengthen his position locally, as suggested by a headline in *L'Yonne républicaine*? This read:

10 MAY, FABIUS HELPS NALLET TO MOVE IN[1].

What exactly was Nallet after?

Grey spring
Flogny-la-Chapelle, 31 March 1987
Imagine a cold, grey, rainy morning. Mud and more mud; this sinister landscape irresistibly recalls stories which marked my childhood, tales of Verdun told to me by my grandfather with the help of old copies of *L'Illustration* fished out of the attic. As I enter the village, I catch site of the war memorial. It is cold, and I hurry on to the town hall, happy to escape for a moment from this landscape, and also a little anxious. Henri Nallet has told me I can see him at his surgery for constituents in Flogny, but he may have cancelled it, for few people are going to be tempted out of doors in weather like this. The town hall looks empty, but I knock timidly, and a voice answers. That's a relief! The door opens with a creak, and I peer in. A man is seated at a table in the huge room. For a few seconds I feel like a student turning up for an oral exam. Nallet gathers up the papers on the table, then he stands up, shakes my hand and asks for a few details about my research. I explain briefly, and give him some off-prints with the first fruits of my work. He is familiar with the world of research, he tells me, having belonged some years earlier to the National Agricultural Research Institute. He is therefore quite willing to answer my questions.

What made me want to see him? Quite simply, something that I had been told over and over again on my travels through the Yonne: 'Nallet is not from here – he parachuted in. We don't really know what brought him here.' His arrival in the department coincided with the big electoral shake-up in 1986. Ever since de Gaulle's return to power, deputies had been elected by a majority vote in single member constituencies, with two ballots. Each constituency grouped together several cantons; there were regular boundary-changes in the run-up to elections, which gave rise to great arguments between the Ministry of the Interior and the Opposition, and accusations of gerrymandering by the party in power, but everyone had grown used to the system. Ever since the beginning of the Third Republic, France had swung between two main models: election on a majority basis, with the unit before the war being the *arrondissement*, and the list system of proportional representation, which had been favoured by the Fourth Republic.

Fabius's government decided to return to the list system of proportional representation, which according to its supporters more faithfully reflects the wishes of the electorate. I do not wish to rehearse here all the arguments and criticisms which this initiative sparked off at the time: more interesting from my point of view is how the change was experienced at local level. Under the list system, the notion of the constituency within a department disappears, and it is the share of the vote won by a political party which is most important. Each party is given a share of the seats in exact proportion to its share of the votes in the election. Under the system of election on a majority basis, the relationship between the votes and seats is less straightforward. There is the first round, and everyone counts their votes, then within each political camp there are agreements to stand down, in order to favour the candidate with most votes. If no agreement is reached, we have the problem of 'triangular' contests, fratricidal combats where two candidates on the left (or on the right) face an adversary who can count on all the votes on his side. In cases like this, electoral calculations may be thwarted by internal quarrels: a candidate who gets the majority of votes at the first round may still find himself beaten as the result of dissensions within his own camp.

Another characteristic of the single-member constituency system is the importance of personalities. In each constituency, voters are choosing not just a party but an individual: in order to win, the candidate has to make himself known to the largest possible number of potential voters. He has to take very close account of local geographical and sociological factors, such as the presence or absence of a large-sized town, or, in a rural constituency, the existence of different sectors, with different ways of life and traditions, such as wine-growers and stock-breeders. The system of election on a majority basis reflects the importance of territory in political life. It is not enough to have a political majority; the relationship between the voters and the candidate is much more subtle than that, and it is a relationship which deepens over the years if the candidate proves to have the required qualities. With a system of proportional representation by department, the situation is quite different. The decisive criterion for election is the candidate's place on the list. If he is lower than the top two places, that will mean his elimination in most cases, however popular he may be with the voters. Another important constraint: under proportional representation, the candidate's message must be addressed to the department as a whole. He must therefore keep the references to particular local circumstances to a minimum, and emphasise political ideas.

We see, then, that the choice of a new voting system, just one year before the general election, was bound to have a very direct effect on political life in the Yonne. In the previous elections, the tide of Socialist victories had carried two local Socialists to the National Assembly. Of the three outgoing right-wing deputies, only Jean-Pierre Soisson had managed to get himself re-elected. However, the big shake-up that began in the course of 1985 was based on developments over the intervening five years. It became clear that the Socialist score in May 1981 had been exceptional, the result of euphoria. In the mean time, the elections to the General and municipal councils had shown the limits of the Socialist advance. Whereas out of 3 deputies two had been Socialists, out of 40 members of the General Council, only four were Socialists, so the gap was enormous. Taking into account also the results of the European elections the previous year in the Yonne, the left knew that the most it could hope for at the next general election was one deputy. During the term which was drawing to a close, neither the Communists nor the Socialists had made any advances, even in their respective strongholds. The Socialists would find it easier to get their one and only left-wing deputy for the Yonne to the National Assembly with a system of proportional representation.

This was the prevailing view among the strategists of the Socialist Party, having regard to the figures and the general atmosphere: as elsewhere, their main aim was to 'limit the damage', to try at least to maintain their basic position, but with no illusions about the ability of the deputies and the party militants to make up for lost ground. This was the stage matters had reached when the summer recess came along and temporarily interrupted the excitement which had reigned for the last couple of months. In the Yonne, people in general had taken very little interest in the technical debate between professionals on the comparative advantages of the simple majority vote in single-member constituencies as compared with the list system of proportional representation. So far as the man in the street was concerned, that was better left to specialists who enjoyed arguing about these obscure points . . . with the result that when they came back in the autumn to find that the Socialists had placed at the head of their list a man who was a stranger to the department, people were totally bemused. Hearing the name Henri Nallet for the first time, the voters began to realise the significance of the new method of voting. The two sitting Socialist deputies were each well known in their respective constituencies: Roger Lassale in Sens-Joigny, in the north, was mayor of a commune and a member of the General Council; in the south, Léo Grézard, the deputy for Avallon–Tonnerre, was also a member of the General Council for Avallon and a member of the town council. Yet here they were standing down in favour of a man apparently selected in Paris, for the local Socialist Party militants were as surprised as everyone else.

In the end, the Socialist list consisted of Nallet, Jean-René Poillot, another 'Parisian', who was close to the Minister Paul Quilès and had been trying for some time to find a seat in the north of the department, where he had a home, and Guy Ferez, a young municipal councillor in Auxerre. On the right, the RPR and the UDF had formed a common list, with Jean-Pierre Soisson as the obvious choice for head of the list, and behind him Philippe Auberger, who was standing for deputy for the first time. Auberger was no novice: he had served his apprenticeship as mayor and member of the General Council for Joigny, and his family belonged to the area. He was a tax inspector who had been an adviser to Jacques Chirac at the beginning of Giscard d'Estaing's presidency and rose to become the key figure in the RPR in the department. After a campaign in which there were no big surprises and all the candidates showed great professionalism, the result confirmed the forecasts: each party had one deputy. The people of the Yonne knew Soisson very well, and Auberger a little; as for Nallet, he had a long way to go to assure his legitimacy.

Hence my curiosity that morning in Flogny-la-Chapelle: I wanted to know how he viewed his own situation as someone who had 'parachuted in'. Did he intend to stay on in the Yonne? Or was this just fall-back position until better days and a more welcoming constituency should beckon? Until now, I had been dealing with people who could all boast of being true natives. However, although local roots are important, we all know that some of the people in the front line of national politics must at some time have landed in areas they hardly knew in search of a seat. Mitterrand, Edgar Faure, and more recently Bérégovoy and some others have all had that experience. Forget local roots and land of my fathers. All that these people have going for them in that situation is their status in political circles in Paris, their persistence and their ability to overcome the many obstacles in their path. Their only hope of consolidating their precarious position is by the demonstration of practical abilities on the ground.

'I came here by sheer chance', Nallet himself told me.[2] It was in fact the party machine that decided to send him to the Yonne. 'This department was seen as missionary country in some ways: the Socialist Federation was not strong, and the number of deputies and councillors was small.' But what future did he see in that situation for himself? What did the department mean to him?

I wanted to stand in the general election. I could have stood elsewhere, particularly in the Manche, where I have a good network of contacts. But the PS had made certain promises to Olivier Stirn, who wanted to move from Calvados to the Manche. That made sense; so I did not stand in the Manche, and instead they sent me here to the Yonne. I only knew Joigny and Vézelay, as a tourist: I had never set foot in Auxerre.

However random the choice may have seemed to the candidate, the selection of this department did respond to a certain rationale. Henri Nallet was at that time Minister of Agriculture under Fabius: he had taken over the previous spring from Michel Rocard, who had suddenly resigned to demonstrate his disagreement with the change in voting methods. Nallet was someone who up to that point had played a technical rather than a directly political role in the government, and he was now to be 'launched' into public life. It was feasible on two conditions: one was to find a vacant seat, and the other was to find a predominantly rural seat where he could exercise his talents as an agricultural specialist. At the time, the Socialists were facing a difficult problem. It was clear that some of the deputies elected in June 1981 would not be returned this time round; as there was a reduced number of seats, the selection of newcomers aroused reactions of distrust and non-cooperation. Nallet could not be sent just anywhere.

'I was sent here because to a great extent the seat was "free" and because my network of contacts at national level, Ministers like Joxe in Saône-et-Loire and Bérégovoy in the Nièvre, wanted me to come down to Burgundy.' Seen from Paris, the thing was relatively simple; the idea was to strengthen the political structure of the area by giving a newcomer the chance to show on the ground the qualities of leadership he had demonstrated in government. But 200 kilometres from the capital, in the seat itself, things were seen differently. 'I arrived in November and I had to integrate into the group composed of the deputies and the Socialist militants. It was not particularly easy, but the campaign throughout the winter of '85–'86 went rather well.' In the event, the Socialist list in the department as a whole got more votes than Mitterrand in the first round of the presidential election. In Avallon the results were better than those obtained five years earlier by the retiring candidate.

In short, a successful entry into public life for the man who a year earlier had been working behind the scenes as adviser on agricultural matters to the President. However, it had not been 'particularly easy', as people other than Nallet himself also admitted.

Local objections

'Not everyone was happy at first with Nallet's selection. The Federation had already picked Grézard to head the list, almost unanimously. His majority was the larger because there were rumours of somebody being brought in from outside. Better close ranks, we thought, even if we have to force things a bit.' I am speaking to one of the members of the Federation's executive committee. A year has gone by since the election, but memories still linger of the tensions that shook the little world of the local militants and leaders. The Socialist Party in the Yonne consists of fewer than five hundred people; nevertheless, here as elsewhere it is divided into currents of thought which are represented on the executive committee according to the results of votes taken at the national congress. There are periodical readjustments, and militants are sometimes seen to change tendencies in the hope of improving their chances of getting on to the executive body or being selected to stand in local elections. Imagine for a moment – this a purely hypothetical case – that on the one hand we have a number of militants who are pro-Chevènement, and on the other, a number who are pro-Mitterrand:

in that case a newcomer would do well to be a follower of Rocard, since his chances of advancement will be higher, each tendency being represented in line with its weight nationally. Some of the internal problems of the Socialist Party at national level are mirrored in a slightly caricatural way within the small Federation of the Yonne, but on the whole there has been a real attempt in the last few years to remedy a situation which had grown confused, to say the least, by the time François Mitterrand led the Socialists to victory throughout the country.

The present-day secretary of the Federation told me that his predecessor resigned in 1982 and became the leader of the Radicals in the department.[3] The Federation in the Yonne had a poor reputation with the national executive, going back to the time of the municipal elections in 1977 when Bonhenry refused to back down over the disagreement with the Communists. The following year there was a second clash, when Etienne Louis was selected as candidate for the general election, since he did not fulfill the condition of having been a party member for three years, and refused even to ask for the necessary dispensation. When Jean-Paul Rousseau became secretary in 1982, he set himself the aim of restoring some order to the organisation, which from the outside looked more like a casual gathering of individuals, not very willing to abide by difficult collective decisions. The majority of present-day leaders are teachers, attracted by public life and hoping to win some kind of elected office, if they do not already hold any. Rousseau is a teacher himself. He is from Burgundy, but not from the Yonne, though married into the department, as he put it. He settled there in 1969. At the time of the Algerian war he was an active member of the French National Students' Union. He was one of the leaders of the Fédération générale des étudiants en lettres (FGEL), and was close to Kravetz and Pénichou. An extreme left-winger in 1968, he later changed direction, and joined the Socialist Party as an activist in 1973.

Rousseau thus has long experience as an activist; he belongs to a generation which aimed to break with the old social-democratic and bureaucratic party machine. There are other leaders with a similar history, all of whom have learned to adopt without too much difficulty the managerial vocabulary that has come to predominate since the political turning-point of 1983. The simultaneous presence of contradictory elements in the party no doubt explains why the outside observer gains the strange impression of an organisation bereft of memory. The French Socialist Party, like any other party, likes to remember its great heroes, such as Jaurès, Blum, and so on. But here in the Yonne there is very little talk of the local history of Socialism. In the period just before the war, the Yonne experienced the triumph of the Popular Front and the takeover by the left of the majority of municipalities. Since then, however, it is as though one layer of activists was piled straight on top of another, the present completely obliterating even the recent past, so that no trace of it can be seen. This stacking seems to be an attempt to cover up the variety of stances local Socialism has adopted, even in the last twenty-five years, in line with the evolution of the party nationally.

The activists themselves constitute a living record of these mutations. The old guard are from the French Section of the Workers' International, the SFIO, and lived through the great epoch of Guy Mollet, later pinning their hopes on the possibility of a large federation which would appeal to the centre; next there are those who aimed to 'change things' by following the joint programme of the left; we must not forget the ecologists, with their desire to preserve a certain quality of life and landscape, and finally we have the 'modern tendency', the children of the Mitterrand generation, over whom the shadow of revolution or revolt has never fallen. All these people rub along together, but because of their different allegiances, there is only one name capable of uniting them, that of François Mitterrand, who symbolises for everyone the potential achievement of all these superimposed and apparently contradictory aims. So the Socialist Party in the Yonne lives in the present: we saw it mobilise its forces very effectively to celebrate an anniversary, but it was the anniversary of Mitterrand's victory, and the whole thing was clearly envisaged in the context of the approaching end of his presidential term. The aim of the exercise was to mobilise local activists. The aim of the local Socialist Federation was to make itself indispensable at election time, in selecting the candidates and ensuring their success.

This ambition could not, however, conceal a reality that was even more complex than public statements by the leadership might suggest, though they made no attempt to conceal the variety of different tendencies and groups existing within their organisation, or the differences of opinion which might lead to a split. The task of the secretary is precisely to avoid loss of votes by arranging the necessary compromises before it is too late. But if we are to understand the nature of the local Socialist Party fully, we must take account of another factor which we have not so far estimated. We have looked at the leadership and the activists in the Federation, but not the people who, as it were, ensure the party's public visibility: the elected councillors and deputies. The most representative amongst them are on the executive body, for example, Bonhenry, Grézard and de Lassale. But there is a world of difference between the behaviour of these people and that of the 'party apparatus'. The elected representatives consider themselves first and foremost grass-roots politicians: their first loyalty is to the population of their commune or canton. Some of them pointed out to me the contrast between the stability of their own position locally and the upheavals which have shaken the leadership of the Federation during the past fifteen years.

Rousseau, on the other hand, and this is probably the last remnant of his far left origins, dislikes this 'local notable' side of being a local politician. 'I loathe and detest the system whereby one man exercises several offices.' He was elected to the General Council in 1986 and emphasises that he deliberately decided 'not to take on too much'. He is on the cultural affairs committee of the Council, but refuses to spread himself over other elected offices, or to sit on many boards of clubs and associations as other councillors seek to do. This may be due to the fact that he is from a different generation, or that he is a newcomer to public life. Possibly it has something to do with his position in the organisation. Sitting talking to him in a committee-room in Auxerre, I felt I was a million miles away from the issues that concern most of the people I had been meeting up to now.

'We could do with a few local notables!'

Roland Enès is a very active political figure. At present he is a municipal councillor in Avallon. The right has had the majority here for many years. Two mayors have come from one of the best-known families in town, the Schievers, owners of a very successful large grocery store, which expanded to a chain of supermarkets with branches all over the region. Georges Schiever was the mayor of Avallon in the days of Pierre-Etienne Flandin, whose moderate stance he shared. His son Jacques took over, after a short gap, in 1953. Jacques retired in 1977 and was replaced by Jean Chamant, who in 1983 was replaced by his first assistant mayor, Léon Laurent. Unlike the Schievers, the latter is a self-made man; he tells how he started with nothing, then had the happy idea of remoulding first bicycle, then car tyres. He thus built up a business which is one of the economic mainstays of the town, employing over a thousand workers. The firm is attached to the Michelin group, and is the only factory which has weathered the effects of the economic crisis without too much trouble. His success in business, together with Chamant's sponsorship, carried him to the town hall, despite the fact that he did not belong to the traditional local bourgeoisie.

Roland Enès, from the opposite side of the political spectrum, has been struggling for years to enlarge the support for the left in this town, which he knows inside out. He is careful to point out that he was not born in Avallon, but in a commune some thirty kilometres away, though he has been settled here for a long time. He was appointed schoolmaster in 1962. At teacher training college he was in the Communist youth organisation, but he left at the time of Hungary, and joined the Socialists in 1959. His left-wing beliefs date back to his childhood, when he noticed the gap between his own family, who owned a small grocer's shop, and 'Monsieur le Comte', the local aristocrat. After taking part in several election campaigns, Enès really entered public life at the time of the municipal elections in 1971.[4] On that occasion, Jacques Schiever, the outgoing mayor, decided to present a coalition list, and he invited the young schoolteacher to be on it. Enès agreed, and that is how he was elected to the municipal council. Whatever his differences with the mayor, he reasoned, getting involved in local affairs was a good springboard from which to launch an effort to strengthen the Socialist presence.

A second event confirmed this strategy: the cantonal election of 1973, in which Schiever was defeated by a surgeon from the hospital, Léo Grézard, who stood without a party label. The campaign was rough, as we can judge from the mayor's attacks on his rival; 'Well, doctor', he wrote in the interval between rounds, 'you have never held any elective office in the department, but we all know the sort of unhealthy climate you have managed to create and maintain at the hospital, and that is enough for us.' This slur on the surgeon's professional activity by a man who set himself up to be 'an enemy of class struggle and a lover of order in every sphere of life'[5] did not meet with the expected response. As one local commentator wrote after the election: 'M. Schiever's election committee were very active, perhaps excessively so . . . Many voters, particularly in the rural areas, did not greatly appreciate their zeal, especially when they smeared an important local institution like the Avallon hospital, by questioning the reputation of an experienced surgeon.'[6] The Socialist Party supported Grézard at the second ballot, and he later joined the party. He was re-elected in 1979, with a larger share of the vote; his rival on that occasion was Léon Laurent. Enès stood that same year in the canton of Quarré-les-Tombes, where he had the satisfaction of forcing Chamant to a second ballot, though he did not manage to beat him.

But let us go back two years, to when Jacques Schiever decided to retire as mayor of Avallon. On that occasion Enès headed a Union of the Left list, in opposition to Chamant. Grézard's was the second name on that list, which had the slogan 'change, but in an atmosphere of confidence, calm and security'. The political nature of the contest was clear, the left aiming to beat a well-known personality identified with the government in power. Enès and his friends won only five seats, a rather disappointing result considering that they had taken as much as 40 per cent of the votes at the first ballot. So Grézard was now a member of the municipal council as well, but the numerical weight and influence of the Socialists was limited. Enès continued to take a strong interest in the running of the municipality, and accepted certain appointments from the mayor. He sat on certain cultural bodies and on the committee of the Senior Citizens' Association. Grézard, on the other hand, took little to do with the commune, and concentrated instead on the canton, anxious not to appear to the inhabitants of the rural commune as a man too attached to the town. Such a strategy was likely to win him votes in the countryside, whereas if he presented himself as the representative of Avallon he might arouse the suspicion that he would be inclined to favour the town, particularly in the distribution of facilities and subsidies, to the detriment of the villages which were also part of the canton.

It would appear that this strategy paid off, for at the cantonal election, where Grézard was originally in a more precarious position than his rival, Léon Laurent, he managed to turn circumstances to his advantage. Although he was beaten in Avallon, the size of his majority in the other communes won him the election with a margin of fewer than two hundred votes. The surgeon's personality was an important factor in his success, much more so than in the case of Enès. Relations between Grézard and the Avallon bourgeoisie had never been easy. As a well-known surgeon, the doctor was automatically a member of local 'society'. He was a cultivated man who had all the bearing of a local notable. His prestige as a surgeon was not irrelevant to his political success, for he enjoyed the confidence and even the gratitude of many fellow-citizens who had at one time or another had need of his expertise. Yet although he had practised in Avallon for a long time, he was still considered an outsider, at least by the traditional local elite.

I heard a telling anecdote about the surgeon. It seems that when he first arrived in Avallon, he offered his services to a clinic owned by an old local family, only to have it intimated to him that he was attempting to rise above his station. The doctor in charge of the establishment at the time was in fact the brother of Jacques Schiever, the mayor of Avallon. Years later, when Grézard had become an important figure, he had the satisfaction of buying the property which had housed the clinic, and making it his home. As people said, 'He had an insult to avenge'. Was that his motive for joining the Socialists, in an area where local notables tend to belong to the other side? Or was it simply a refusal to bow to the conformist culture of this little provincial world? Whatever the answer may be, Grézard was never very keen on getting involved in the running of the town. He felt he was part of a very small minority, facing first Chamant and then his successor, Laurent. Both Laurent and Grézard were strong personalities, in their own way, but too different to get on well: quite apart from political divergences, they were a world apart in values – Laurent was a somewhat paternalistic factory-owner who valued economic success above all else, Grézard a hospital consultant with a passionate interest in literature. They had a few memorable clashes at the first meetings of the municipal council, but then each kept to his own territory. Laurent took a keen interest in municipal affairs: 'He runs the town as if it were one of his factories', people joked. He could be found daily at building-sites, or supervising roadworks or the cleaning and restoration of the war-memorial. Grézard, on the other hand, looked after his canton, getting his mayors together and trying to encourage inter-communal initiatives. It was noticeable that all the mayors turned up to these meetings, except, of courses, the mayor of Avallon, the main town in the canton. Similarly, Grézard was absent from the meetings of the municipal council. Such is the nature of local politics . . .

Although he held the same political views as Grézard, Enès took a completely different stance vis-à-vis Avallon: 'I have always been very involved in the affairs of the town, although I have been criticised by the left for backing up the team in power, and by the right for getting in the way.' Like the mayor, the Socialist schoolteacher is a visible presence in the town. He learned his job, to some extent, under Schiever, as he explains: 'I got to where I am because my family used to shop at Schiever's. He had known me since I was a kid, and he knew I was no extremist.' It was more or less thanks to Schiever that Enès took his first steps in politics, even though the two men were on opposite sides. He therefore feels no need to rebel against the conformist tendencies of the local bourgeoisie. The schoolmaster has been adopted by the town, and he is keen to get involved in its affairs and leave his mark. Even though the left was beaten again in the 1983 municipal elections, its leader, who on that occasion presented a programme of improvements to the infrastructure and detailed plans for social welfare, was not discouraged.

At first he was unceremoniously brushed aside by the new mayor, who relieved all the left-wingers of their responsibilities. Enès, however, continued to sit on the council, and be the voice of protest. At the same time, he refused to play the game of knee-jerk opposition; instead he read the dossiers seriously and turned up twice a week at the town hall. Gradually a relationship of mutual respect developed between Laurent and his rival.

> Laurent is very authoritarian, and somewhat isolated. He does not accept the advice of his assistant mayors. I am the only one who will speak up, and I am often better informed than his assistants. In a lot of areas there is not much room for manoeuvre; I am not sure my budget would be very different if I were mayor: you can play around with about 1 per cent, not much more . . . I do object to some things, of course: for example, I spoke up against the subsidy to private schools. The left is now being given some responsibilities again; for example, I was unanimously elected to look after the schools' budget.

The situation has changed, and the old anathemas have gone out of style. The Socialist councillor wants to hear 'a new political vocabulary' and admits he is happy with the open-minded approach adopted by his party. Speaking of the party, how is the Avallon branch these days? 'There are about forty members, but only two or three of them turn out to put up posters.'

For Enès, this is not the main issue; he is more interested in strengthening his position as a responsible and constructive councillor. He feels that being acknowledged by his adversaries as a man open to reason strengthens his position locally: 'I have a coffee every Saturday morning with the mayor: people see us together.' The cohabitation works, and is apparently fully accepted by both men. Unlike Grézard, Enès seems keen to become even more involved in municipal affairs. Is he not in danger of placing too much emphasis on the 'local notable' side of the job? His answer is unambiguous: 'We could do with a few local notables on the Socialist side!' So, each in his own way, both men have given prime importance to their work as councillors; in a sense, they have split up the territory, Grézard cultivating the rural voters of the Avallonnais and Enès looking after the town. But the principle is the same in both cases; their first duty is to the local population, and only afterwards to the party leadership. This attitude is shared by the majority of councillors. For example, Roger Lassale, in the north of the department, who before he became a deputy joined the General Council the same year as Grézard and is also the mayor of Pont-sur-Yonne, says exactly the same. The priority is to increase the left's zone of influence by taking over local political functions, letting the leadership deal with the Byzantine controversies and debates between the various tendencies in the party.

Reconciling party and local interests

If you were looking for a metaphor for the situation of the Socialists in the Yonne, you might decide to say that there is a stable pole, the 'councillors with their feet on the ground', and a series of shifting spheres reflecting the changes which periodically affect the leadership of the Federation. The gap between a localist conception of politics and the vertical representation in which the constraints of the party prevail can be seen clearly when the time comes to select candidates for the general election. In these circumstances, whatever the voting system, national political considerations used to take precedence over everything else. If we look at the candidates selected by the Socialist Federation since 1958, we see a certain fluctuation. In the constituency of Sens–Joigny, a new candidate appeared at every election until 1978, when Lassale was selected as candidate and re-elected easily three years later. A similar situation arose in the second constituency, Avallon–Tonnerre, where Jean Chamant faced a different Socialist opponent every time, each one doomed to failure. For example, one of the leaders of the Federation, Jean-Marcel Bichat, was beaten in 1973, and was dropped at the next election in favour of Calliope Beaud, who had made a name for herself several years earlier by leading the opposition to the siting of a fluorine plant near Vézelay.[7] Like Bichat, Calliope Beaud was not really a local candidate, though she had a second home in Vézelay. A graduate of the Institute of Political Studies, she worked as a public relations adviser in Paris. Her ecological concerns (she was a member of

Friends of the Earth) marked her out as a new kind of candidate, very different from the classic local notables. Although she got a good result – losing by a narrow margin to the candidate chosen by Chamant to succeed him – she was dropped in 1981 in favour of Grézard. Throughout this period, the constituency of Auxerre was the most stable: the FGDS candidate was elected in 1967, then beaten by Soisson the next year. Then came Bonhenry and Etienne Louis; Bonhenry was selected again in 1981.

This rapid turnaround of candidates was a sign of the tensions within the party machine at the time. With the exception of Bonhenry, who from the first time he ran for the General Council set himself up as a challenger to the deputy and mayor of Avallon, there was no sign that the Socialists thought it worth while to combine local and national politics. The only Socialist deputy for Yonne in the National Assembly during the ten years preceding the election of Périllier and the initiation of a Union of the Left strategy in 1967 was Jacques Piette. He was parachuted into the department in 1956 on the orders of the national leadership of the SFIO. The system of proportional representation then in operation helped him: he was at the head of the list, for he was a figure close to Guy Mollet and had made a name for himself as a leader of the OCR during the Resistance. After the return to power of General de Gaulle, the change to a system of election on a majority basis proved fatal to his ambitions. He was beaten in 1958 and 1962, and never managed to establish his position as a leading politician in the department.

The Socialists increased their support during the fifties and carved a niche for themselves by attracting a decent percentage of the vote, thanks in some measure to the system of grouping electoral lists, but they seem to have been completely disorientated when the voting method changed in 1958 to a majority system. Unlike their right-wing rivals, who chose as candidates in the general election people already well known in the municipal and the General Council, the SFIO, just like the Socialist Party later, preferred to keep the two categories separate: this implied that the gap between 'local notables' and real politicians was to have serious consequences, for until 1981, the only left-wing success was when Périllier, again a candidate imposed by the leadership, by François Mitterrand as it happened, won the constituency of Auxerre in 1967. Now, that particular election was characterised by a great deal of wavering on the right, with the concurrent candidatures of Soisson and Moreau, and by a high level of politicisation of the issues. Moreover, Périllier's success did not last long, since the ebb in the fortunes of the left carried him off at the next election. It was not until the 1978 election that the distinction between local notables and national politicians began to be called into question, and this was probably not the result of chance. It had been noticed that the left-wingers who had been successful nearly everywhere in France at the Municipal elections, the 'new mayors of 1977', as they were called, had all put in years of patient work, particularly in local clubs and associations, and had participated fully in local life.

In the Yonne, the mayor of Pont-sur-Yonne, Roger Lassale, was a good example of this kind of candidate. His claims were based on a very active career in local associations. He came to the little town to take up a post as a teacher in a local school, and very quickly took over the running of a sports club, La persévérante pontoise, which he turned into a first-class organisation by greatly increasing the number of different sections. His main enthusiasm was for football, and people were very aware of his dedication. He also took an interest in other areas, such as activities for senior citizens. In this way Lassale achieved tremendous popularity, not only in the town, but in the canton as a whole, and in fact in the whole north of the department. In choosing Lassale as their candidate, therefore, the Socialist Federation were attempting to reconcile local influence with political aims. They had learned the lessons of 1977. This seemed to be the end of a divorce which had existed for too long between those who embodied a local territory, with all the weight of its particular history, and others who claimed to be the bearers of political values.

This new tendency was accentuated at the early general election of 1981. As we saw, the candidates chosen as the standard-bearers of Socialism were all three well-known local councillors: Lassale, Bonhenry and Grézard. For the strategists of the time, Etienne Louis's failure at the last election had also signalled the failure of what was known at the time as the 'technocratic' approach. Although he was born in Auxerre, there was a great gap between the candidate, a graduate of one of the most prestigious educational institutions in France, the ENA, and the population whose votes he set out to attract. In the constituency of Avallon, the selection was rather more difficult. Calliope Beaud was in many ways similar to the new candidates who had begun their public activities in clubs and associations. Her commitment to the ecology movement, and the fact that the Socialist Party was anxious to raise women to their rightful place in French political life, were weighty arguments in favour of selecting her a second time. Her political activities and her position as assistant mayor in Vézelay made her a credible choice.

And yet in the end the member of the General Council for Avallon was chosen. In opting for Grézard, the selectors were taking his widespread appeal into account. He was respected by the rural population of the Avallonnais, and by the non-Communist left in Tonnerre, he had been on the General Council for a long time, and he had a thorough knowledge of local issues. His attitude to the bourgeoisie of Avallon was a guarantee of his Socialist convictions. At the same time, his position in local society seemed likely to prove reassuring to a moderate electorate, some of whom had voted for Mitterrand more because of the dissensions among his rivals than because they hankered after any kind of radical change. The selection of Grézard marked the triumph of a certain realism: the idea was to suit the candidate to the terrain, respecting the traditions of Flandin's former stronghold. The tactic proved successful against the retiring deputy Delprat, who belonged to the Centre national des indépendants et paysans (CNIP): Grézard won. He benefited both from the wave of enthusiasm for Mitterrand's victory as President, and from his own patient work among his fellow-citizens. Similarly the election of Lassale seemed to indicate a profound change in the political make-up of the department. It was the first time in the north of the Yonne that the Socialist candidate had beaten the Communist in the first ballot and gone on to win at the second. The success of the Socialists against the right may have proved ephemeral, but the fact remains that this readjustment within the left temporarily revived the electoral health of the Socialist Party in all three constituencies.

It must be admitted that this reconciliation of the local and the national initiated by the Socialists of the Yonne at the beginning of the eighties was fairly fragile. At party headquarters in Auxerre, the leadership were often irritated by the lack of interest shown by the new deputies in the sort of issues which continued to divide the party at its congresses and make the front pages of the newspapers. The two deputies were more keen to be involved in local issues; they were learning their trade. They went to all the agricultural fairs and other public events; Grézard questioned the Minister in the Assembly on particular agricultural issues; they were not idle. This was the form their militancy took, and they maintained their independence from the local party machine. Although the gulf between the professional political men and these local notables did not entirely disappear, the former nevertheless came to recognise the quality of the latter's work. Slowly a more constructive compromise began to be reached between ideological aims and everyday realities. Naturally, the municipal elections of 1983, which were a sort of warning-shot fired across the bows of the government, were a rude shock to the left in the Yonne. There were negative results in towns like Sens, Auxerre and Avallon, with no compensatory gains elsewhere, except in Migennes, which remained faithful to the Union of the Left team, headed by a Communist.

This episode did not, however, call into question a strategy which promises in the long term to increase the strength of the Socialist Party. What it did was to raise questions again about the ability of the Socialists to put down deep political roots in the area. The new wave of activists after 1981, and the distrust of ideology, favoured a more pragmatic vision. There were now many people willing to devote themselves to obtaining a municipal or cantonal mandate. The process of reconciliation of the political and the local was thus well advanced when the sudden announcement of the new system of proportional representation in 1985 caught the movement for strengthening local roots unawares. The first shock for the deputies was the very disappearance of the constituencies. Each deputy had always been very careful not to interfere with the activities of his colleagues in other constituencies. As one of them remarked to me: 'We behaved rather like super-members of the General Council. Even with Soisson, we respected the status quo and the limits of each deputy's constituency.' Such a division of territories might work very well under a majority system of voting, as it confirms the local legitimacy of the deputy, and makes each candidate his own ideal successor. But all that changes if the voters have to elect their deputy by departments. A deputy who has taken a great deal of trouble over his constituency can find it has become a handicap. He has spent all his time in the north of the department, so nobody knows him in the south, or vice versa, in which case his desire to stand again may meet with objections, even from within his own camp.

A second trauma overlaid this one: it soon became clear that people at party headquarters were giving a great deal of thought to the preparations for the general election. In 1981, they had been carried along by the impetus of Mitterrand's victory; they had to work quickly, and the best-known candidates locally were the ones selected. Five years later, the situation had changed drastically: the Socialist party knew it could not take victory for granted on this occasion; in order to limit the damage, and avoid disappointments, it had to choose the candidates very carefully. An idea going the rounds was that candidates elected in the wave of the enthusiasm of May 1981 would be unlikely to meet with success in the present troubled circumstances. Also, the system of proportional representation, it was believed, would enable a solid group to be built up at the National Assemblies of personalities who had proved their worth even if they had never been elected to office before. Henri Nallet was one such figure, and the announcement of his arrival in the Yonne was a shock not only to the department's Socialist deputies, but also to the local party leadership, who had never demonstrated a great commitment to discipline, and who resented what they considered interference from Paris in their internal affairs.

From the top down: chronicle of a parachute landing

Pierre Joxe was the man chosen to announce the candidature of the Minister for Agriculture to the militants in the Yonne. We have met him already, back in 1977, when he tried without success to persuade Bonhenry of the need for an agreement with the Communists in Auxerre. Joxe had had oversight of the internal affairs of the party in Burgundy for a long time, and knew that his mission was not an easy one, since the Yonne Federation had already selected Grézard to head their list. Grézard had accepted, and now he must be persuaded as diplomatically as possible to move aside. Lassale, on the other hand, had showed little inclination to stand again as deputy, but had agreed to figure on the list of candidates in the regional elections, which were to take place at the same time as the general election. Pierre Joxe showed great tact: he first went to see Grézard and asked him what his attitude would be if the possibility of bringing in Nallet were put to the local leadership. If Grézard objected, Joxe would let the matter rest and Grézard could probably head the list. Some time later, there was a meeting between Joxe and the local leadership to which Grézard was invited. One of those present told me what happened:

Grézard said nothing. Joxe implied that he would be amply compensated. The meeting went off quite well. Joxe argued along political lines: he was there to represent the party machine. Really, the main friction arose right at the beginning, when the idea was first floated. Some people said if we invited Joxe to come, we could hardly send him away empty-handed, and so it proved.

In the end the Socialist Federation of the Yonne announced in a rather terse communiqué that Nallet was the candidate. The organisation was torn apart once more, but it must be said that though the majority protested against the procedures employed by the party leadership, there were many who were not displeased by this sudden but beneficial change. Bonhenry, for example, published a long piece in *L'Yonne républicaine* wishing Nallet every success. All that remained now was for the main actor to make his entry . . . 'I went on a senatorial-type campaign', he told me. 'I visited each and every mayor. I was Minister for Agriculture at the time, so the prefecture and local officials took me seriously. You never know how an election will go, but so far as they were concerned, I was the Minister.' In other words, he did not come to the Yonne as a politician or a party militant, but as a statesman anxious to win recognition for his expertise from a local elite going well beyond Socialist circles.

I concentrated on my field of expertise, agricultural problems; in my discussions with mayors, officials and trade union leaders, I dealt with local and national farming issues. My aim was to be seen by important figures in the rural milieu as an expert in these questions. I played my two trump cards, which were my position as Minister and my expertise. I believe it worked.

The idea soon got around among significant local figures that Nallet knew his stuff, even if he did not belong to the Yonne. The distrust remained, but it was gradually counterbalanced by this impression of professional competence. 'I spent a lot more time with mayors and going round farms than I did on platforms in town.' The Minister was not a particularly experienced public speaker, and he was a novice at politics, but this relative innocence proved to be an asset locally. 'Nallet is a man who knows how to listen', people would say. 'He is less outgoing than Soisson, but you get the impression he is not playing to the gallery.' The man who made this remark to me was a councillor on what he called 'the other side', so the comment is revealing. I mentioned it in my discussions with Nallet about his campaign, and he told me that he had 'deliberately adopted that strategy'. He saw himself as a competent professional. People who know him seem to have been seduced rather by a sort of inability they sensed in him to 'play at politics'. The expression is significant: I heard it used in a village where people were complaining about certain other political figures shooting their mouths off. The newcomer's success was due to this paradoxical mixture of expertise and obvious lack of experience. It cannot be denied that his imposition from above was resented. But on the one hand he was not a star, having only recently emerged from the shadows; and on the other, he did not give the impression of being a demagogue or a wheeler-dealer, and both these facts helped to defuse suspicion and prejudice.

Nallet chose his company wisely; if the truth be told, he did not initially seek to win the favour of the Socialists. The situation was too tense for them to accept him without baulking. Knocking at the doors of mayors was to turn out to be more effective, for it gave him an entry into local political circles, and got him recognised by his peers. In many ways the campaign must have been like an obstacle course. The effort the candidate put into it may seem surprising, for the system of proportional representation tends to place more importance on the party political aspect of the list and less on the personal charisma of the candidates. Nallet could have saved energy by simply standing as the official candidate for his party. Yet we see that by going round his obstacle course of the local elites, he was emphasising his personal qualities rather than imparting a message laden with ideology. There was a great deal at stake, in the sense that Nallet had no wish to suffer the fate of a shooting star in the Yonne. He had to think of the future. He was therefore not content simply to be the man who spread the good word, his party's missionary. His aim was to legitimise his own position locally, by making a large number of contacts throughout the department.

The method chosen by Nallet, his 'senatorial-type campaign', as he called it, seems to me to demonstrate a very realistic approach to the problem. I have tried to show the importance of local networks. Here once again, the hypothesis is confirmed, though in circumstances very different from those described in earlier chapters. From the point of view of confirming his position locally, Nallet's problem was this: there was a group of Socialist voters, sufficient, in one way or another, for him to be assured of success, particularly in view of the record of his predecessors and the advantages offered by the system of proportional representation. However, he wanted to go beyond this partisan base and win the votes of a rural electorate, who are usually attracted to moderate parties. If he were to appeal to a larger segment of the electorate, and maintain his position over the long term, he had to be something more than just the Minister who had come along to head the Socialist list. He had to become an influential figure at departmental level, that is, he had to integrate fully into the world of local politics. As it happens, his strategy was not so different from that of Jean Chamant, another Minister in the Fifth Republic, except that the Socialist candidate could not boast of local roots or benefit from a deep-rooted political tradition in the department. He had no political 'godfather' in the Yonne, and his adversaries had no hesitation in polarising the debate by pointing to him as the embodiment of 'five years of Socialism'.

However, not all the right-wing candidates took up these entrenched positions. Jean-Pierre Soisson extended a courteous welcome to the outsider, and it was in Auxerre that Nallet chose to install his headquarters. Some people describe the two men as in some sense accomplices, and contrast this with a certain coolness between Soisson and the other right-wing candidate, Philippe Auberger, the mayor of Joigny. However, it was unlikely in any case that Soisson would adopt a sectarian attitude towards the left. He was a convinced Barrite, and seems to have been anxious above all to preserve some political diversity in the department and hinder the expansionist policies of the RPR. Naturally, Soisson did not make any concessions to the left during the election campaign, and he stood as a resolute adversary of their list, but his initial attitude did facilitate Nallet's entry into local political circles. The reward for Nallet's industry was a precious asset: he acquired the quality of eligibility which had been lacking when he first appeared in the Yonne. It is no doubt true that his position at the head of the list allowed him to be quietly confident of being elected. But what works on paper does not always work on the ground. His future was mortgaged in two ways: one, he was unfamiliar with local political circles, and two, he was not welcome to the activists in his own party.

It is certainly clear that at first the welcome from the Socialists was cool. André Fourcade, one of the most active party members in the Tonnerrois, told me the story:

> We were all devastated when we heard a candidate was being brought in from outside. Rousseau rang me up: 'You are in a strategic position', he told me; 'you are the only Socialist mayor in the area. I've heard Nallet wants to meet you.' I told him I had not the slightest interest in meeting Nallet. In the end he came to Dannemoine; I remember he got here at three o'clock on the dot. It was all very formal: 'How are you, Minister?' 'Very well, thank you, mayor', and he explained that the party had

sent him so that he could join the other Socialist deputies in the Assembly as a specialist in farming issues, I kept insisting that it would have to be made up to Grézard, and he gave me his word it would.[8]

Later relations between Fourcade and Nallet grew more cordial, fortunately. But this first contact shows the mixture of distrust and irritation experienced by the Socialists in the area, obliged to welcome a guest they had never invited. Henri Nallet had set his sights on the long term; therefore he did not make a great effort at first to find acceptance among his own kind. Instead he concentrated on confirming his acceptability by speaking in a non-sectarian fashion to political circles as a whole: 'That way I also won over, indirectly, the Socialist network in the department. They heard what I was doing, how I was going about things, and gradually relaxed. In the end they thought to themselves: "Well, he's going the right way about it; that's fine by us." Then there were the results on 16 March.'

These were indeed encouraging: the Socialist Party got close to 30 per cent of the vote. It was less than in 1981, when it took 33.68 per cent, but circumstances were much less favourable this time round, and the share was in line with the national average, which implied a very good performance. From this point onwards, both the Socialists and the other political groupings had to reckon with the newcomer. This was even more the case since Nallet had lost his ministerial post when his government lost its majority, and was going to be able to devote much of his time to the department. The new deputy was not the sort of man to harbour any illusions; he now had to transform this early success, and have himself recognised as a true leader by his own troops. He had come into politics treading carefully, for at forty-seven years of age he was still an unknown, unlike certain big names the party had put in elsewhere, like Bérégovoy in Nevers or Jospin in Toulouse. Of course the insistence with which he had been recommended, when he did not even have a party card in his pocket, indicated that his future was being planned at the very highest levels. Yet no matter how lofty one's sponsors, acquiring acceptability at local level is a long-term affair. This the new deputy realised. However, there grew up a sort of osmosis between himself and his adopted department, with the result that although a novice in politics, and a stranger to the area, Nallet slipped very happily into his new role of representing an electorate he had only just met. A glance back at his career may help to clarify this strange partnership between a man and a place.

How the seed was sown . . .

Paris, National Assembly, 26 January 1987

Many comings and goings in the corridor, as I wait for the deputy for the Yonne. I have just spotted Henri Fizbin, deep in conversation with one of his colleagues. Further on, a door opens, it is Huguette Bouchardeau, looking very busy trying to sort out her day's appointments with one of her assistants. An elderly deputy steps out of the lift opposite me; I try hard to put a name to the face, but my memory lets me down. Here comes Nallet now, showing a visitor out of his office. He ushers me into a bright, airy room. We are far removed from the mists of the Yonne and interviews in town halls riddled with damp. But the man himself has not changed – he is still the same attentive listener, responding precisely and with growing animation to my questions about his past, for which he seems to feel a great affection.

Many people who have been in contact with the former Minister have told me how much they appreciated his modesty and level-headedness: 'He is a left-winger, we realise that, but he does not make it too obvious.' I passed on the remark to Nallet, together with my surprise at the fact that I had just heard him describe his early years as a time of strong political commitment. He interrupted me to confirm that he had become active politically at an early age. He joined the Catholic Youth Movement, the JEC, at thirteen, and rose to occupy important positions in the leadership. At the beginnings of the sixties he was its national president. He supported peace and independence for Algeria, and was active in the French National Students' Union, where he met all the people who would later play an active role in the events of May 1968. His brother Jean-François was general secretary of the Students' Union. He has other friendships dating from this period, for example his friendship with the architect Roland Castro. Many of his associates joined the PSU and later the Socialist Party. He himself refused for a long time to join any party: 'There were two reasons', he explained.

> First of all, I am suspicious of any party apparatus. Secondly, towards the end of my time in the JEC [Jeunesse étudiante catholique], in 1964–5, a major crisis blew up. I found myself at the centre of the crisis, confronting the apparatus of the Church, and my distrust of organisations and hierarchies dates from that time. From '65 to '81 I saw myself as a committed intellectual, attempting to reflect on the society in which I lived. I worked with the Farmers' Union and at the National Agricultural Research Institute, and I took part in conflicts, debates, and the whole growing movement of awareness of issues in the farming world.

Nallet got to know the world of farming when he moved on from his activity in the Catholic Student Movement. In 1964, several former leaders of that organisation got together:

> They organised meetings with all sorts of people, from Jean Boissonnat to René Rémond, including people like Edmond Michelet and Michel Debatisse. Some time later, Debatisse asked me to come and join his team from the JEC, which was about to take power in the Farmers' Union, the FNSEA. It was part of the new left; there were people in it like Serge Mallet, the sociologist.

In 1965, Nallet, who had a degree in public law and politics – he had studied at the Institute of Political Science in Bordeaux – was put in charge of the institute for the training of young farmers. A year later, Debatisse made him his main adviser. This was when the future Minister for Agriculture learned his job, tramping the length and breadth of rural France, and getting to know all the key figures in the farming world. However, Nallet was considered too left-wing by his boss, and was dismissed from his job in the late sixties. He went to the National Agricultural Research Institute, where he remained for eleven years.

Although he had been penalised for his political views, he remained allergic to party activism. He participated in acts of solidarity, like helping the Chileans exiled by Pinochet in 1973; he was also involved in founding the magazine *Politique Hebdo*, which gathered together representatives of the progressive and pro-Third World intelligentsia. But he remained on the edges of the world of politics until the presidential campaign of 1981, when he became one of François Mitterrand's expert advisers. After his election, the President offered him the job of adviser on agricultural matters, and this was the turning-point. Through working with Mitterrand on papers which the latter understood very well, having himself been deputy for a rural department, Nallet won the prince's favour. In April 1985 he succeeded Michel Rocard, who had resigned in protest against the introduction of proportional representation. 'So that is how I became a Minister . . .' As told by Henri Nallet, things were very simple: one has the impression that he just left himself be carried along by favourable circumstances. Certainly, fate was kind to the future statesman: his arrival at the presidential palace and the sudden resignation of the acting Minister were lucky breaks in a career hitherto condemned to anonymity. When he was invited to replace Rocard at a moment's notice, Nallet was seen by most people as a 'technician'. This image was in fact a help, because at the time everyone was tired of the type of ideologically committed Socialist, so he built his campaign in the Yonne around his image as a 'capable and efficient' Minister.

It is understandable, therefore, that the rural electorate and local public figures were doubly pleased to see a candidate disinclined to revive the old ideological debates (we should not forget that barely a year had passed since the arguments about education had turned the whole country upside down), and likely to be useful in the future because of his close contacts with the President. Even if Socialism was not exactly popular, it was still better to be represented by a former, and possibly future Minister, than by someone whose aura did not reach beyond the department. In welcoming Nallet, the people of the Yonne thus felt they were adopting an expert, an open-minded sort of chap, and a man of influence. Nallet, for his part, found he now had the opportunity to play a political role, and strangely enough it seems to have been his enjoyment of the daily round of political life that was mainly responsible for his success in the Yonne. There was in fact no contradiction between the young Catholic activist of the sixties and the outsider who launched himself a quarter of a century later into local political networks. Both felt the same passion for politics as action; for although Nallet was a man of strong convictions, his behaviour was very different from that of the militant resolved to convert others to his ideas. Political action in this case meant something quite different – it meant persuading people of many diverse tendencies and backgrounds to work together on tasks conducive to the common good. How to define such tasks? How to convince people of the worth of projects that demand new forms of cooperation? More than the pleasures of the notable role, it seems to have been questions like these which motivated Nallet's actions.

This was a new and previously virtually unknown way of looking at things, for this was a world where people's ideas ran very much along lines predetermined by local traditions and the networks underlying them, in a way which had come to seem 'natural'. It appealed to a much larger electorate than just the left. Nallet himself seems to have got caught up in the game; chasing votes may have looked at first like rather dreary obligation, but he got down to the job – I heard this particular expression used by several of the people around him – of finding new ways of bringing together the important figures in the social, political and economic life of the department. The time had long gone when he had any need to set off on the campaign trail and win his political spurs. If the truth be told, it was mainly his loyalty to Mitterrand that made him do it originally: 'When Mitterrand appointed me Minister', he told me, 'I realised within the first two days that the very least I could do was face the general election. When you are given such a responsible position, there is no point in saying, "I'm only an expert, not a politician". Mind you, I can't say I leaped at the idea of coming down to the Morvan to campaign, right in the middle of winter . . .'

It appears that the President had intervened to ensure a department was found where his adviser would have a decent chance of success. Two indications of this, amongst many, are firstly, the reward which finally came for the retiring deputy sacrificed to the cause. A few days before the election, it was learned that Léo Grézard had been appointed from outside the civil service Counsellor to the Public Revenue Office, which drew a barbed comment from the satirical weekly, the *Canard enchainé*. Secondly, the following year, when voting on a majority basis was restored and Nallet decided to settle on a constituency in the south of the department, Mitterrand, who happened to be in the Yonne, made a special trip to Avallon, to demonstrate his desire to see his former Minister re-elected.

Nallet, meanwhile, had not been idle. The return to the previous method of voting meant the reappearance in the Yonne of the three former constituencies, with one minor alteration: Migennes, formerly attached to the constituency of Sens–Joigny, was now part of Avallon–Tonnerre. So it became important again to put down local roots, which was no problem for the two right-wing deputies, one of whom had a solid base in Auxerre, the other, in the north. The south was perfect for Nallet: it had voted Socialist in 1981, and had a predominantly rural electorate.

The choice of constituency was thus easy, but another problem remained to be solved. If he intended to settle here, he had to find a suitable place as his headquarters. He chose the town of Tonnerre: from the political angle, it would have been awkward to settle in Migennes, which is in some ways the Communist stronghold in the department, and in Avallon, the presence of Grézard, who still kept his mandate as member of the General Council, might have reopened old wounds. Moreover, there is a mutual distrust between the people of Migennes and those of the Morvan; the choice of Tonnerre, the geographical centre of the constituency, and a place with less polarised traditions than the other two, seemed the prudent option. Finally, it had the not inconsiderable advantage of a direct train link to Paris.

> I therefore took what everyone in the department knew to be a highly symbolic step. I bought a house in Tonnerre. I let it be known that I had bought it, how much I had paid, and how much I had needed to borrow. It is a large house, and I have set up my offices there and stay there when I am in the Yonne; my wife comes down at weekends.

Spadework

Tonnerre is a small town which has been badly affected by the economic recession. Previously, a small number of factories between them employed most of the workers: one was the Petit Bateau factory, and another Steli, who make television sets. It seems they are under threat of closure, which would affect not only the population of Tonnerre, but also that of the surrounding cantons. The town itself tends to vote conservative, but the small wine-growers who live all round it, many of whom now work in the factories, form a left-wing electorate, the 'red belt', as it is known locally. The mayor of Tonnerre had stood as an apolitical moderate, but the member of the General Council was a Communist who was very popular in the area. This man decided not to stand in the elections in the autumn of 1988, because of his age. The circumstances therefore favoured Nallet's candidature. Nallet, however, who refused to enter into polemics with the Communists and who enjoyed excellent relations with the Communist councillor, decided to take his time. He was careful not to rush in and announce his candidature, but simply to demonstrate by his presence and his efficiency that he was the best man available to fill the former councillor's shoes.

This method, eschewing polemics and thundering declarations, demands a large amount of grass-roots work to compensate. Obviously, Nallet did not do everything himself: apart from his parliamentary assistant, and a secretary paid from his parliamentary secretarial allowance, he also had the right as a former Minister to a second secretary. Moreover, his former colleagues in Paris continued to work for him voluntarily, on the grounds that he was the Socialist Party's spokesman in big debates on agriculture. He led the two big debates of the parliamentary session, one on the finance law and the other on the privatisation of the National Agricultural Savings and Credit Bank. He also had certain international responsibilities as president of the World Food Council. While remaining the uncontested Socialist expert on agriculture, and at the same time making frequent journeys abroad, Nallet set up a strong network of helpers in the Yonne. In the front line, of course, were his secretary and his parliamentary assistant: in Auxerre, at first, and later in Tonnerre, these two helpers would always arrange his appointments, and deal with briefings sent to him. He held surgeries at weekends, going round the different communes in his constituency. For example, in the last two weeks of May 1987, his diary mentions five surgeries, each lasting a whole morning: Tonnerre on the 15th, Cruzy-le-Chatel on the 16th, Chablis on the 22nd, Avallon on the 23rd and Saint-Florentin on the 29th.

Judging by his diary, he had a very full timetable from October to December of that same year, attending all sorts of events: he met a group of women farmers doing a training course at the school in La Brosse, and attended the AGMs of the agricultural cooperative of les Plateaux de Bourgogne in Tonnerre, the judo club and the sports club in Tonnerre, the committee twinning Tonnerre with Monabaur in Germany, the Union of Socialist and Republican Councillors in Appoigny, and the Agricultural Mutual Aid Society in Auxerre. He visited the Laurent tyre factory in Avallon, the police station in Tonnerre, the Aléonard Tuilerie factory in Pontigny, and the inauguration of the Hôtel des Postes and a school in Chailly. There was a meeting with an association of farm workers in Tonnerre, another with the wine-growers of Molosmes, and another with the mayor and council of Andryes. He attended the celebrations of the sixtieth anniversary of the Fédération des oeuvres complémentaires de l'école publique de l'Yonne (FOCEPY) in Auxerre, the Chablis wine festival in the presence of the Chinese Ambassador, a fête organised by a hostel for young workers in Tonnerre, the wine festival of Saint Bris-le-Vineux, and a public debate on the topic Psychoanalysis and Politics with

J.-P. Soisson and the sociologist E. Enriquez in Auxerre, and chaired the presentation of diplomas to blood-donors in Tonnerre.[9]

This list of activities clearly demonstrates the efforts made by Nallet to enlarge his following. I took it from a copy of the *Letter from Henri Nallet*, which he sent out every three months to a number of people. His aim was not simply to be seen at all these events: by mingling with representatives of all the varied sectors of the population, he was likely to encounter people who could be helpful to him by acting as messengers between himself and the particular professional or cultural community they represented. Nallet's behaviour was constantly dictated by this desire to enlarge his circle of acquaintances. In this he was unlike his predecessors, who were more anxious to ensure the good will of their supporters, although they realised that the position of the left in the department was weak. Nallet told me at our interview: 'The Socialists are active, but they do not control any networks in the department.' Whereas the right still reaps the benefit of the painstaking work of politicians like Flandin at every level of society, the Socialists have all too often spent all their energy in internecine quarrels. Nallet set himself two complementary objectives, aimed at remedying this defect: one was to create a network of elected councillors at departmental level, and the other was to establish strong links with all the key figures in the local economy.

In the Yonne, as in other departments, there is an Association of Socialist and Republican Councillors, but it was not very active. One of Nallet's first acts was to organise a series of one-day conferences on current topics, such as schooling, employment and peripheral housing estates. He invited experts and professional people directly concerned with these issues in the department to come along and share their experiences. An effort was made to attract not only Socialist councillors, but also the Independents; he welcomed people from the whole political spectrum, in other words. The aim was to create a spirit of cooperation amongst people who had perhaps rubbed shoulders with each other for a long time, yet whose worlds were in many cases far apart. That is why, apart from the association of councillors, Nallet set up groups to study issues directly relevant to the Yonne, such as food and farming issues, or tourism, and liaise with his team of collaborators in Paris. 'There are about sixty people altogether, between the various teams. That is a functioning network, to which I alone have the key, and I intend to keep it. All this has not gone unnoticed in local political circles; they realise that I can count on the support of some very good people.'

Another network which greatly interests Nallet is that of local industrialists. He decided to visit all the manufacturing industries in the department, one by one. 'I write to the head of the firm and ask for a guided tour. I am always given a very good welcome, even by businessmen who are well-known right-wingers. I get around a lot: I usually spend three days a week in Paris, and four out and about.' As we saw, Nallet's contacts go far beyond the limits of his constituency. Compared with traditional practice, his strategy is more global, as he tries to take in all aspects of the economic and political life of the department. I can well imagine that the idea of cultivating the bosses was not too popular with Socialist activists, but then people's ideas have changed a great deal since 1983. Nallet gave the task of coordinating contacts with the business world to a young man, Paul Girard, who is the mayor of a small commune near Auxerre. Girard is rather different from his fellow-Socialists: he is not a teacher (most of them are), but works at the Auxerre Chamber of Commerce and Industry; also, he came over from the PSU. The Socialist Party even put up a candidate against him in the cantonal elections of 1985.

Nallet has managed to involve all the leaders of the local party in his strategy of broadening the basis of support, starting with J. P. Rousseau. He works closely with a group of Socialist councillors whom he sees regularly. The party has recognised him as the legitimate leader; the parachute landing and the rows are all behind him now. Proof of this is the striking change in the attitude of André Fourcade, who made no effort to hide his displeasure at his first meeting with the Minister for Agriculture. In the space of a few months, he became an enthusiastic supporter of Nallet, and one of his trusted collaborators in the Tonnerrois. 'I learned more in a year with Nallet', he told me, 'then in ten years with the Socialist Party. Nallet asked me to work closely with him, and to go over certain dossiers. We meet often and talk over problems.' In short, Fourcade never tires of praising his new boss. His proudest moment was the organisation of the anniversary of 10 May, when Laurent Fabius came. However, there is a bond of another sort between the two men: 'I am from the south-west, from Auch in the Gers. I'm a Gascon, and so is Nallet: we are like d'Artagnan and Cyrano', Fourcade jokes. They both have a slight regional accent, and they share a certain nostalgia for their home territory. Both arrived in the Yonne as the result of sheer chance: one was appointed a schoolmaster, and the other sought election.

This reference to his roots is also a clue to Nallet's great interest in local affairs, to the point where one wonders if he really needs to expend quite so much energy to secure his position. Nallet's tone changes when he refers to his native town, Bergerac, or to his father, who was an optician, or his grandfather, a watchmaker. 'They were people with a highly skilled trade, who never made much money, and were never businessmen.' We were talking in his office at the National Assembly, and up to this point I had been dealing with a conscientious professional, a political activist who demanded a great deal of himself. Suddenly I felt it was the man himself speaking. I understood far better than I would have done from a long speech why he had such a passion for politics.

My father was a political fanatic. He got involved very young, joining the Croix de feu, like many others of the same background and generation. Then, during the war, he was in the Resistance, and after the Liberation he joined the Radical Party. He was a follower of Poujade, mainly to protect the interests of his trade, but he left in 1958. He was an important figure in the Chamber of Commerce – I think he was President of the Commercial Tribunal. He was a very active man, very interested in social questions, a defender of widows and orphans. Anyone who had any problems went to see old man Nallet, and I always saw him take the causes he defended very much to heart. I had long and sometimes violent political arguments with him, particularly over Algeria. They were dreadful, but in some ways I think we both enjoyed them . . . I often talked politics with my father, and we always disagreed violently, but it never caused a real split between us.

In my companion's eyes there is a trace of the intensity with which these arguments with his father must have been pursued. They disagreed violently, but at a deeper level they remained friends. In some ways father and son were poles apart. Young Nallet was close to the centre of power from an early age; and later, when he returned to politics after his time in the National Agricultural Research Institute, he shot straight up to the highest levels. He chose the 'right side', and he had the benefit of a very influential sponsor when he entered public life. Yet he remains fascinated by the figure of his father, a generous man, a fighter, wandering from one political group to another, with no thought of recognition. It is in his relationship with his father that one must seek the origin of the strong desire for commitment visible even in the young Catholic activist. Hence his nostalgia for his youth in Bergerac, for life in the provinces, where relationships are more straightforward, and public figures more personally involved in managing affairs. Nallet's decision to settle in Tonnerre perhaps marks a return to his origins, a way of rejoining the past despite the passage of the years. In his declared intention of putting down roots in his adopted department, in his strong desire to be accepted, one can see the end of a long quest, the possibility of satisfying a long-repressed desire at last. It seems as though this irresistible attraction has been noticed by the inhabitants of the place: where they had expected a technocrat, they found a true lover of provincial life.

Lessons to be learned

The metaphor of the politician 'parachuted in from outside' seems to suggest a situation in which local connections play no part whatsoever: yet paradoxically, the case we have just examined only serves to confirm the extraordinary importance of local connections at all levels of French political life. In France, a politician is above all the representative of a territory with all its traditions, a territory as it has been shaped by the presence of man. In this context, François Mitterrand's poster for the presidential campaign of 1981 is extremely significant. It showed the candidate's face, against a background of the Nivernais countryside, with a village and its church tower. A politician's power is sustained by the serenity of the native heath to which he or she returns. The President has continued to make constant references ever since to his provincial roots.

France's European neighbours are often surprised at the importance given in France to local mandates by people who have important positions in national politics. In many countries, the two types of political activity are clearly separated: local government on the one hand, parliamentary on the other. In France it is more or less obligatory to occupy local and national office simultaneously. There are many cases of politicians who get into the government because of their professional ability, and manage to win a parliamentary seat. However, they cannot then just sit back if they want to continue in politics. If the occasion presents itself, even government Ministers will stand at municipal or cantonal elections. To take just two examples amongst many, we have Pierre Bérégovoy starting a career in local politics in the Nièvre, and Jacques Delors standing for mayor in Clichy-sous-Bois.

Someone who has been elected to represent a territory must be able to produce proof of local connections to acquire real legitimacy. The whole vocabulary of politics is full of allusions to this: people are always talking about 'roots', a politician will refer to his constituency as his 'patch', he will call his constituency duties 'putting in the spadework', and so on. These metaphors reveal the double connotations of the word 'territory', in that it refers to the constituency, but it carries also a semi-agricultural sense, the implication that the political environment is subject to the same hazards as the physical environment. For example, there is a whole political vocabulary of 'storms', and 'spring' is used to refer to a time of innovation and reform.

The unwillingness to accept politicians 'parachuted in' shows us that in the French system the deputy is supposed to belong to his constituency and identify with it. The two key metaphors are radically opposed, since someone who lands by parachute has fallen from the skies, as opposed to someone who has been nourished on the soil of his ancestors. An opposition is thus set up here between the native son and the man who is sent down from higher spheres to the grass roots, to use another significant metaphor. The idea of falling from the skies implies that the candidate is an outsider, or perhaps something even more alien, and it carries a notion of disruption. In contrast to the person with local roots, the one 'with both feet on the ground', like a peasant on his plot, the person who parachutes in occupies an unstable position and is therefore a potential source of disorder: I remember we were taught at school that our ancestors, the Gauls, feared one thing above all else, which was that the sky would fall on their heads.

The practice of dropping candidates by parachute is not new: yet it is interesting to note that the fact of not belonging to an area one hopes to represent politically continues to be a handicap, in fact and in people's imagination. The newcomer will have to think in terms of gradually 'cultivating' local opinion (yet another agricultural metaphor). Everyone knows that in France a political career is impossible without some kind of local roots. Only when a politician has managed to keep the same mandate for several years in succession can he be said to have succeeded. By the end of a successful career, a politician should have 'founded a line', that is, he should be in a position to designate his successor, who will follow the same path in turn. Many candidates who parachute in are rejected by the voters: proximity to the seat of power does not always impress the man in the street. There is no point in listing the people who have seen their hopes dashed in that way. Suffice it to say that newcomers from Paris are not always a great success in the provinces. Even in Paris, there have been some stinging defeats: Couve de Murville, for example, in the 16th *arrondissement*, or Michel Ornano when he stood for mayor of Paris.

Even those who win a seat in the wake of a successful campaign by their party, or under the list system, are not assured of re-election. The Yonne has known one outsider who made little impact on the department, though he was one of the famous figures of the Third Republic. Paul Doumer, the future President whose assassination was to hit the headlines in 1931, lost his seat in the constituency of Laon at the 1889 elections. Two years later, the deputy for Auxerre died, thus giving him the opportunity to return to the Chamber. However, the new deputy was not welcome locally: the purchase of a house right by the railway station made a very bad impression, as did Doumer's reluctance to savour the local Chablis at official functions. Doumer abandoned the Yonne definitively when he was appointed Governor General of Indo-China; later he was re-elected in Laon. Here we have a perfect example of an outsider unable to build on one isolated and precarious success. In Auxerre there is only the name of a single avenue to mark this inauspicious encounter between one of the key figures of the Republic and the town he failed to win over.

No doubt one should distinguish between two types of parachute landing. One, which is to some extent the product of the system, takes a purely pragmatic approach to local matters. Put simply, it recognises that a political career is only possible if the candidate is willing to stand at the coalface, and not always where he would wish. This could be called a rational landing. However, there is a second approach, where the politician sees the parachute landing merely as a first step into local public life, after which he gets down to work. Nallet is a good example of the second case. He had to tackle a sort of assault course, which demonstrates the extraordinary significance of local connections in the French political system, and tells us a great deal about the persistence of traditions and values inherited from the past. Does this mean that the candidate must take on the mantle of a local notable if he is to ensure his political survival? As we saw, Nallet's efforts to find acceptance were more complicated than that. He was not simply chasing votes: his repeated visits and journeys through the Yonne led him to formulate an overall view of the future of the department. His ideas of collective effort and building up teams to develop soundly based economic projects should be seen in that context.

Nallet's personality and methods favoured these initiatives, but he also encountered a population that was becoming more and more convinced of the need for action in the face of the economic crisis, an electorate which was not satisfied with being courted only at election time, but wanted a more rigorous approach to economic problems. A dialectical process thus began which tended to reconcile the local with the political, overcoming ideological oppositions now considered a dead heritage from the past. As a consequence, the role of the party with its internal disputes was minimised. The main thing now was the setting up of teams capable of responding to social needs, analysing complex issues and running things in a more dynamic fashion. One wonders if this tendency will prevail amongst Nallet and his friends, and whether it really spells the end of old-style Socialism in the Yonne. One thing is certain: the parachute landing has had unexpected results, for it has disturbed old habits and called into question certain entrenched attitudes. However undemocratic the practice may have appeared at first from a strictly local viewpoint, in some ways it has proved salutary: it has offered a means of overcoming the strange division between the two worlds of the local notable on the one hand and the party activist or militant on the other which used to be typical of the Socialist Party. The presence of the newcomer was bound to shake up local political circles, but they could hardly remain indifferent to Nallet's popularity. There is one last question, which I propose quite deliberately not to answer: is this the beginning of a gradual change, here in the Yonne also, in the whole composition of the political landscape?

6

The Communist Party and real life

'You seem to be forgetting the capture of the Bastille, Your Grace!'
The owner of a prominent château in the Yonne will never forget the above pained response to one of his suggestions. The secretary of the town hall must have been in a bad mood that day . . . The aristocracy is not what it was, obviously; it has long since ceased to be a leading force in society. Yet two centuries after the Revolution, the old wounds have not healed.

One morning in January 1988, I was at a meeting of the board of the General Council: the board members were all drawn from the right-wing group which held the majority, and the purpose of the meeting was to allocate departmental subsidies. There were a large number of applications to be considered. However, they had already been looked at in committee, so few required much further discussion. Several points were thus quickly dispatched, ranging from subsidies for new developments to the allocation of education grants. Suddenly one item, anodyne in appearance, provoked a heated discussion. It was about the price of a publication from the departmental archives. This leaflet was going to be distributed free to educational establishments, and any remaining copies sold off at 25 francs a copy. The problem lay in the topic the leaflet dealt with: The Yonne during the Revolution of 1789. One of the vice-presidents spoke up: 'The way the Revolution is presented nowadays is frankly disgraceful. We are told it brought us out of darkness into the light of day, as Jack Lang put it.' He went on to suggest that it might not be a bad idea to look at the content of the leaflet before sending it out to schools. The president proposed that a committee should be set up to look at the issue. The obvious person to chair the committee was a particular individual well known for his balanced approach. The man promptly declined, on the grounds that he had no wish to get involved in the question of the Revolution: one of his wife's ancestors had fallen victim to the guillotine, and he did not approve of murder. There was now some animation in the chamber, hitherto engaged on more mundane matters. I heard one voice say that now might be the time to ask a few questions about the way property confiscated under the Revolution had been sold off. There were a few more remarks here and there, the idea of appointing a committee was approved, and we moved on to the next item on the agenda.

I was not entirely surprised that 1789 and its various consequences should still provoke arguments. In the Yonne, as in many other rural areas, the Revolution is certainly not over. It has continued in two guises, one the long dispute between supporters of clerical and anti-clerical ideas and the other, closer to our time, the events of the Resistance. The latter event, in particular, has had a profound influence on the department, though it was seldom mentioned in most of the villages I visited. Yet suddenly, in the midst of an anecdote, I would realise that it had not been forgotten. Certain allusions were not clear to me, since I had not lived through the events described, and some episodes were shrouded in mystery. I was often advised to consult one of the few authoritative sources, former members of the Resistance who have become the guardians of the memory of those dark years. They are the voice of the people, the living memory of a heroic past. They see themselves as the inheritors of 1789, artisans of a national insurrection which freed their country, thought it may not have radically changed the system.

In the Yonne the Communists were the main driving-force in the local Resistance, leading the very first groups of underground Maquis in 1942. Many militants were taken to concentration camps or executed in those dreadful years. By the time of the Liberation, they had won great respect for the sacrifices they had made, so that in the first post-war elections they took almost a quarter of the votes, in a department where they had previously been insignificant. For several years afterwards, the Communist Party was the only properly organised group on the left in the department. As time passed, however, it grew more and more isolated. The rest of the story is well known, and follows developments in the country as a whole up to the 1970s: the acceptance of the joint programme of the left and its relaunch, but at the expense of the Communist Party, which quickly ran out of steam while its Socialist partner steadily grew in strength. There is no need to rehearse here the reasons for the decline of the Communists. We can leave to specialists the task of analysing this issue and deciding whether the problem for the Communist Party was the decline of the traditional working class, or its pro-Soviet image, or the strategy adopted by the Socialists towards the Communists, or possibly a mixture of all three.

My interest lies rather in the extraordinary bond I observed on my travels between the population and the Communists, even though their overt political stance provoked hostility, derision, and at times sheer hilarity. One mayor who made no attempt to hide his dislike of the left nevertheless told me: 'We are very fond of our Commies!' Driven, no doubt, by my professional training as an anthropologist, I decided to centre my research on this ambiguous relationship between the Communists and others, this strange mixture of rabid antagonism and barely disguised respect. The task of political analysis is to discriminate and distinguish: in this it simply mirrors the explicit rules of political competition. Both sides have their specialists who devote themselves to minute analysis of parties and electorates. Their work is an invaluable source of information for anyone who wishes to be initiated into the mysteries of these modern institutions.

Analysis discriminates . . . but what happens in real life? This was the question towards which I was led by people's opinions of the Communists. I was also moved by the rather pathetic spectacle of a species perhaps on the verge of extinction, which has suddenly become aware of its own fragility. No one is afraid of the Communists any longer – in fact a vague feeling of compassion surrounds the few remaining active militants. Already they inspire a sort of nostalgia. To whom will history now entrust the task? This is the question I heard implied in a vague anonymous murmur. Political habits are beginning to crumble, for it is clear that the Communist party no longer fills the role conferred on it by decades of struggle. I am not interested here in the old issue of the electoral weight of the PCF, but rather its influence in public life, which, looking back, seems to have been absolutely extraordinary. What particularly attracts my attention is the social bond of which this influence is the product.

At first glance, the Yonne would seem to offer a poor illustration of Communist influence. The department has a tradition of moderate politics, and it lacks the huge industrial centres which spearheaded political struggles, so it is hardly surprising that the Communist Federation has never been very large. There is, of course, Migennes, with its railway-workers, the only town to elect a Communist mayor, and Sens, where the PCF was for a long time the dominant force on the left. After all, the town belongs to the outskirts of Paris rather than to provincial Burgundy. But what about the rest, the countryside, for example? Contrary to appearances, the Communists have a decided presence there, and not only in the most obvious places. In the eastern part of the department, all along the Paris–Dijon railway-line, from Tonnerre to Ravière by way of Ancy-le-Franc, there are traces of that 'rural Communism' which is a stable feature of the party. But even in the more remote areas, on the edge of the Morvan forest, the Communists have their place in the local political landscape.

This Communism of the soil is remembered by commentators whenever a figure emanating from it becomes prominent. Waldeck-Rochet, and more recently André Lajoinie, are representatives of this Communism in peasant clogs. We know very little about the degree of attraction (or repulsion) it exercises in the villages. I wanted to find out who these people were whose history or whose political activity identified them in the minds of their fellow-citizens with the Communist Party. I felt they must represent the exact opposite of the 'urban' Communists in Sens and Migennes. These were all interesting issues I felt should not be sidestepped, so the Yonne offered an interesting area of inquiry precisely because it was not a Communist stronghold.

Théo

The village of Saint-Léger-Vauban is proud to be the birthplace of the strategist whose name it bears. Yet the majority of visitors do not linger in Saint-Léger, but hurry through it to their real goal, the Abbey of La-Pierre-qui-Vire. I took the same route through a thick copse, but turned off to the left before the end. There was a group of houses on the edge of the wood, with a man digging his garden. He noticed me, and called out. He was a tall, resolute-looking man: yes, this must be the chap, Armand Simonnot, otherwise known as 'Commander Théo', the man who symbolises the Resistance around here. There were numerous books in his house: there were party leaflets, and pride of place was given to the special editions of books at reasonable prices for the worker; there were also many biographies; some time later, when we knew each other better, my companion would show me some items which he particularly prized, such as some very old numbers of the anarchist magazine *Le Libertaire* and a copy of *Fils du peuple* signed by Maurice Thorez.

Théo is from one of the poor peasant families which for generations have cultivated plots of mediocre land in these hamlets ringed by the forest.[1] Like many another young peasant, his father took himself off at the end of the last century to Paris, where he worked as a chauffeur and his wife as a housekeeper. Young Armand was brought up by his grandparents. His grandfather, François Simonnot, had fought in the Franco-Prussian War of 1870, and one of his great-uncles had made a name for himself as a cavalryman in the Imperial Guard in the Crimea and Mexico. Now the grandfather was back on the land, but he was old, and Armand took over the farm on his death. Armand's father came home, having spent the best part of his life in Paris, but he died a year later, in 1925, as the result of wounds received in the war. In 1928 Armand was called up, and when he returned eighteen months later it was to find that his seventy-year-old grandmother, unable to carry on by herself, had sold the animals. He gave up the land, and worked for several years in the forest as a woodcutter and by stripping the bark of oaks for use in leather-making in the Avallon tanneries.

From 1934, he worked in one of the local sawmills, specialising in producing construction timbers until the outbreak of war. He was recalled to the navy, where he had done his National Service, and sent first to Toulon and then Brest. We can skip the detail of the events of these months, when confusion was at its height, and simply note that the young sailor decided to volunteer for transfer to the army. Simonnot was in the last line of defence before Paris. In the general débâcle, he managed to make his way back to Bordeaux, where he learned of the armistice. In August 1940, back in Saint-Léger, he returned to his job as a carpenter. He then began a double life: by day he was a conscientious worker, and by night, a leader of the armed Resistance.

Simonnot had already been fighting Fascism for some time; he was attracted by the extreme left from an early age, and from 1928 he was a subscriber to *L'Avant-garde*. However, the internal dissensions which were rocking the Communist Party at the time, and which ended in the dismantling of the Barbé–Célor leadership, rather dampened the young man's enthusiasm. He joined the League of Combatants for Peace in 1932, but he remained convinced that the PCF was at the forefront of the anti-Fascist struggle, and took out his party card on 1 January 1935. On the eve of war, the Saint-Léger cell consisted of twenty-one members. The linchpin of the local party was a woman, Maria Valtat, who was, according to Simonnot, his 'spiritual mother' and who inspired the first resistance group in the Avallonnais. She had been in the leadership in the Yonne since before the war. The party's influence had grown in the pre-war period, particularly among the railway-workers of Laroche–Migennes, but it had been considerably weakened by the German–Soviet pact and the ban to which it gave rise. The main leader in the Yonne, René Roulot, a native of Auxerre, set himself the task of rebuilding contacts, with the help of a small team of activists representing the different regions of the department. In September 1940, the first underground meeting of leaders took place.

Le Travailleur de l'Yonne, organ of the Communist Party, reappeared clandestinely in 1941. Russia's entry into the war in June had marked a decisive turning-point. However, 1942 was to be a black year for the Communist Party in the department: René Roulot and the majority of the underground leadership were arrested one after the other, and nearly all were shot or died under torture.

They had to begin again from scratch, and a new man, Marcel Mugnier, was sent down from Paris, where he was under sentence of death in his absence. His task was to energise the Resistance and set up the Communist-led FTP partisans in the Yonne. Simonnot, Maria Valtat and their friends began the task of recovering a large amount of arms and ammunition which had been dumped in the forests of the Morvan in June 1940: in the débâcle, a regiment of French troops had abandoned lorries loaded to the roof with arms. Mugnier describes the situation:

> Maria Valtat provided a contact with the Sylvère family, who had a business growing wood for the production of gas. They helped us to hide several young people who were on the run from the forced labour service, and wanted to join the partisans. The family were from Paris and no doubt came here on the orders of the party. They helped us considerably. We were engaged in recovering arms and ammunition dumped in the forests of the Morvan in June 1940. The father rented a whole floor of a hotel in Quarré so that we could put up people on the run. We stockpiled the arms, then sent them to Paris via a chain we had set up. They were used by the Paris partisans.

Maria Valtat and Théo, as he was to be called from then on, were in charge of a group of Spanish anti-Fascists in Saint-Léger-Vauban. 'We used to go out with this group at night to recover the ammunition, following the directions of a forest warden who was in contact with Sylvère.'[2] One can imagine that to carry out this kind of underground work, the members of the Resistance must have been highly integrated with the local population. Théo recalls the generous attitude of the mayor of Saint-Léger: 'He was anti-Communist, but above all else a patriot.' This mayor was in fact re-elected in 1945, and Théo was one of the members of his council. Théo's popularity went well beyond the boundaries of the canton. He could boast of having been the first man in the Yonne to join the partisans. 'I was enrolled by François Grillot, the departmental commander of the FTPs, at the end of September 1942. He asked if I had a weapon, and since I did not, he lent me his own gun, an automatic.'

A few months went by after his initiation, then the Vauban Maquis was set up in spring 1943. Its area of activity was around Ravières, on the borders of the Yonne and the Côte-d'Or. There were twelve members of the group, which operated in a strategic area, along the Paris–Dijon railway line and the Burgundy Canal. They carried out continual acts of sabotage, hunted by the Germans, but always managing to escape because of their mobility. The forest offered an almost impregnable refuge, but there were always informers. Théo recalls one couple, collaborators who had frequent German visitors to the mill where they lived. The men from the Vauban Maquis hid not far from there, in Armand's home, and they had a party for Christmas. It was surely no coincidence that the Germans came to carry out a search on New Year's Eve. Some weeks earlier, the Abbey of La-Pierre-qui-Vire, which played its part in the Resistance by sheltering English pilots and concealing deserters from the forced labour service, had been searched from top to bottom.

Théo and his men managed to flee before the arrival of the Germans, and hid in a disused chapel in the middle of a pine forest. Simonnot told me the story of those difficult days:

It was gloomy: we lived in semi-darkness. You could see a bit better in the mornings, because of the white covering on our threadbare blankets. The tiles on the roof were loose, and all night long the wind would blow snow in on us. It was hard to sleep. Somebody would get up and wind up the gramophone: 'The barge sails past . . .' We'd all start dreaming. One of the more religious men would maybe put on the 'Hymn to the Virgin'. In would come Bébert from guard duty, frozen to the marrow, covered in snow and grumbling: 'Turn that off – you'll have me in tears', and on would go his favourite record: 'The Young Guard'. Not that he was a revolutionary, but he found that tune inspired him, and so did all of us.[3]

The Maquis never consisted of more than twenty people until 1944: after the Allied landings, it grew rapidly, and by the end of the war, Théo had enrolled 182 individuals. He became the real head of the Vauban operation. The leadership of the FTP had placed political figures at the head of the Maquis, but they were not universally accepted. On 14 August 1944, the appointed leader, Jean, was deposed, and in a vote the men chose the leader who would go down in history as 'Commander Théo'. This was undoubtedly the only example, certainly the only example in this area, of the democratic choice of a leader. The Vauban Maquis took part in the liberation of Auxerre, and then was integrated into the French army with the creation of the 1st Regiment of the Morvan. Armand Simonnot took part in the German campaign with the rank of lieutenant.

The Communists enjoyed tremendous respect after the war: we have seen how Simonnot was elected councillor in his village. On that occasion even the monks voted Communist: the Resistance had formed bonds of respect and complicity between the brothers of La-Pierre-qui-Vire and the carpenter from La Provenchère. Maria Valtat joined the municipal council of Auxerre, and some time later she moved to the outskirts of Paris and became deputy mayor of Blancmesnil. Simonnot also moved to Paris, having been asked to join the party's security section. The historical head of the FTP, Charles Tillon, made him his bodyguard. Then the euphoria died down, Thorez and the Communist ministers left the government, and at 44 rue Le Peletier, party headquarters, the mood was sombre: the time had come to settle old scores. 'I remember the meetings of the executive, because I was on security duty every Thursday. They began at half past eight, and it was often well after midnight when they came out of the room.'

One day Simonnot's boss Tillon emerged shattered from one of these sessions: his trial was over, and he had been relieved of his responsibilities and removed from the party leadership.

Almost immediately, we left Aubervilliers, where Tillon was deputy and mayor, and I went with the family to the Basses-Alpes. We found a house in ruins – in fact the whole village was in ruins. We set to work, and as a carpenter I was able to make myself useful. I stayed with them for ten years, coming back to Saint-Léger in the summers. When they moved to Aix in 1962, I came back again to La Provenchère. I continued working as a carpenter and also sold Christmas trees.

I asked him whether he still took part in municipal affairs. 'I've voted for a long time now in Aubervilliers; the right is in charge here . . .' The truth is that Simonnot is no longer a party member, but although there have been some petty-minded reactions from the party apparatus, local Communists cannot deny him his due. The bonds between former members of the Resistance are too strong; and in any case, Théo is a symbol through the area of the predominant role played by the party in the Resistance.

The Morvan forest has not changed to the present day: it still stands guard around the edge of the villages. Local people know a thousand and one paths through the forest, guiding themselves by small strips of cultivated land on which stand a few houses, a tiny hamlet, or sometimes just the remains of abandoned homes. There is protection from the ruling society and the police in the semi-darkness of its thickets. Since time immemorial, these forests have been an area outside the law: they were a paradise for poachers, and a place of refuge for all those who clashed with the authority of the lord of the manor, or with the police or gamekeepers. In the course of the nineteenth century, republican propaganda found its way into the hamlets in the clearings, where there were members of secret societies struggling against the reigning powers.

The forest is propitious to resistance of every sort: the established order finds obstacles to its imposition, and so rebellion has been a constant in the history of these woods. At the end of the last century there was a highly organised movement of social protest amongst the woodcutters. Another thing which has always annoyed the guardians of the established order is the fact that the forest of the Morvan touches the edge of four different departments. Rebels could brazenly slip out of one department into another, under cover of the woods, so escaping the jurisdiction of any particular authority.[4] The members of the Resistance did exactly the same: the 'elusive' Vauban Maquis, as the Germans dubbed it, could slip out of the Yonne or the Côte-d'Or and take refuge in the woods on the edge of the Nièvre; like many Maquis, it covered a territory which broke completely with the standard political and administrative divisions in the country. This was the only period in French history in which two completely different types of territorial division co-existed. On the one hand, there was the traditional system of division as set up after 1789, with its designated centres, its prefectures and the same officials as before, all backed up by the 'occupying authority', the *Kommandatur*; there had been no major upsetting of arrangements, and routines had survived the shock of the invasion. On the other hand, a new kind of division had come into being, forged by the activity of Resistance networks. Vauban, Camille, Verneuil in the north: the different areas of activity were gradually delineated.

However, these areas were by their very nature fluid, which affected the nature of command within the Resistance; strictly speaking, it was not exercised over a territory. After the Liberation, certain Resistance leaders, who had been in charge of forces in perpetual motion, were appointed prefects overnight. This meant a return to traditional territorial demarcations, and the recognition of traditional hierarchies, and the process was not entirely easy, as can be seen nearly everywhere in the troubled period of the purge of collaborators, where the debate on the moral acceptability of certain acts was followed by debate on the issue of who was best placed to administer punishment: those who had themselves been combatants, or the newly restored authorities. The former could plausibly claim the advantage of proximity; they had seen what their enemies had done, and had in some ways observed the behaviour of both sides from the inside. Official authority could claim a more global view, but everyone knew they were doing so with the aim of reimposing the authority of officials and ensuring the continuation of an order which the generation of the Resistance – a young, sometimes very young group – knew to be flawed and weak.

Even ignoring for a moment the many attacks on freedom, the repression and the persecutions, many young people had been deeply disillusioned by the fact that the French administration collaborated with the occupying forces in setting up the forced labour service, under which French workers were sent to Germany. These were the young people who, as we saw, went to join the Maquis. These new recruits found an echo of their own feelings in the Communist criticisms of the wealthy and all those social groups in general which had readily accepted collaboration and believed they had found a providential saviour in the figure of the aged Marshal Pétain. The fascination exercised by a figure like Théo cannot be overemphasised. The very fact that he was elected commander of the Maquis by his own men is significant: emerging from the lower echelons of society, like many other Maquis leaders, Théo had no previous vocation as a leader. In fact, this modest woodcutter does not challenge established hierarchies even today. In the course of our conversations, he made a point on several occasions of mentioning his exact rank in the regular army at the end of the war: lieutenant, not captain. Similarly, he was careful to distinguish the different levels of responsibility of the Communist leaders he mixed with after the war. Yet in less than three years, he had become a leader and a historic figure.

Although Simonnot returned after the war to the modest place he occupied in society and in the party, he remained a legendary figure locally.

Rural Communism is founded in large part on the symbolism of the Resistance. Many young people attracted to the party immediately after the war by their memory of its sacrifices may have left it by the late forties, but the flame of remembrance was still burning. The Communist presence was not limited to participation in the peasant trade unions of the Mouvement pour la co-ordination et la défense de l'exploitation familial, for even in a department like the Yonne, where the MODEF's role was limited, party militants kept alive the memory of their historic activity within the National Association of ex-Combatants and Members of the Resistance. The heroic deeds of the Resistance are commemorated every year on the anniversary of the Liberation. The dedication of war memorials offers another opportunity to bring together ex-combatants and highlight the major role of the Communist partisans. All this serves to maintain a particular image of the party. One of the people I talked to, someone who could scarcely be suspected of Communist sympathies, told me: 'At least they were not afraid of risking their lives: they didn't stand on the sidelines.' Everyone readily admits that Socialists and people on the right also played a part, often a heroic one, in the underground struggle. However, no other party as such was as clearly committed to the Resistance. The Communists may not have succeeded in convincing the surrounding population that their ideological message was correct, but certainly the villagers were given daily demonstrations of the link between a political ideal and the struggle against the invader.

Such, it would seem, are the origins of the respect accorded to the Communists. People's reactions are sometimes tinged with ambiguity, for in the very moment that someone is emphasising the tenacity with which the partisans fought, he may be expressing relief that the PCF did not take advantage of the circumstances of the time to strengthen its hold on the community. The word 'red' is often applied to quite small areas where the percentage of party members or sympathisers is higher than usual. For example, the commune of Saint-Brancher has its 'red zone', composed of two hamlets which always vote further to the left than other places. One particular family was prominent in the local Resistance. One of the sons was amongst the founders of the Vauban Maquis. From that time until his death in 1981, he remained one of the party's accredited propagandists, standing in the cantonal elections if so required, though always without success. Another former member of the Vauban group lives in the same commune; he was also among the first to join Armand Simonnot. He has subsequently shown the same loyalty to the party as his colleague from Saint-Brancher.

One, two or three families are enough to constitute a nucleus and assure the continuing vitality of the Communist option for many years. In view of the small population of the communes, nuclei of this type are enough to ensure the continuity of the party. It cannot, of course, be considered a driving force under these conditions; but the important thing is that the Communist identity is kept alive more or less everywhere. In the case of Saint-Brancher, the origins of the nucleus are easily discerned: from 1935 to 1938, the schoolteacher was a Communist party militant, André Durand. His wife was also a schoolteacher in one of the commune's hamlets. The two future members of the Maquis and their schoolfellows were strongly marked by their teacher's ideas. Outside the classroom, he managed to inspire a debate on French society and communicate his left-wing ideas to the young people around him. In three years, he turned the commune into one of the key places for the PCF in the Avallonnais. The example of Saint-Brancher is typical, for as we saw earlier, its mayor, Boijard, had been one of the pillars of Radicalism in the area. A son who shared his political views succeeded him, and remained mayor throughout the war. When one of the young Communists was harassed at the beginning of hostilities, the mayor intervened personally and managed to have him placed under house-arrest rather than sent to prison. Boijard's solidarity stood firm throughout, though he was never actively involved in the Resistance movement.

Epineuil wine

During those difficult years, then, one can see the emergence of a line of continuity from anti-clericalism through to Communism. Through its role in the Resistance, the party achieved a legitimacy amongst the peasants which it had previously lacked. Before the war, Communists were seen mainly as agitators, and their internationalism, particularly their links with the Soviet Union, rendered them suspect. Yet even then, the patient work of some militants had borne some fruit. We have noted, for example, the influence of André Durand, the Saint-Brancher schoolmaster. He has never left the department; he taught there all his life, and today, at the age of seventy, he is the member of the General Council for the canton of Tonnerre, M. Durand's career is interesting from several points of view, and we shall be spending some time in his company. Whereas Théo is a striking character, the embodiment of the popular and patriotic rebellion against Nazi oppression, in M. Durand we have more of a Communist anti-hero. Unlike Simonnot, who never felt any real interest in local politics, M. Durand is the classic example of a born councillor, though he has experienced rejection at the ballot-box. His case prompts a query: does eligibility reside in exactly the same circumstances for Communists as for members of other parties? What sort of relationship exists between a councillor and his party when the party is ruled, as we know the Communists are, by a system of democratic centralism?

André Durand belonged originally to the Puisaye, and is the eldest son of a poor peasant family. In the normal course of events, he would have taken over his parents' farm, but the First World War altered his destiny, as his father was killed when André was still too young to take over. He was a clever child at school, and his schoolmaster encouraged him to go on to take his leaving certificate. The master's friendship and help made him decide to follow the same career. In 1930, he went to teacher training college, where he joined the Communist Youth Organisation. The party's influence was strong in the teaching profession, but André's choice of party was also the result of his family background. Like the Morvan, the Puisaye is a wooded region inhabited by poor peasants. It was one of the historic centres of Socialist activity; the woodcutters' movement was particularly strong at one period.

In 1885, there was a major strike by the woodcutters of Saint-Fargeau. It was aimed at an increase in wages, which the timber-merchants were resisting. The prefect of the Yonne wrote to the Minister of the Interior:

> They live in extreme poverty, but there is also a political intention behind the strike. I have been impressed by their firm conviction that the social revolution is imminent. They are in touch with people in Paris such as MM. Vallès, J. Guesde, Chabert, and Vaillant. They receive some financial assistance.[5]

The woodcutters' attachment to Socialist principles was nothing new; these ideas were already the inspiration for certain secret societies such as the Cousins of the Black Snout or the Friendly Cousins set up by these workers. The movement would eventually culminate in the formation of a powerful woodcutters' union.

Agricultural labourers, small peasants and woodcutters had participated earlier in an uprising which has become famous in the annals of the Republic: it took place the day after the coup d'état by Louis-Napoléon Bonaparte, on 2 December 1851. The uprising broke out simultaneously in Clamecy in the Nièvre, in the neighbouring communes of the canton of Coulanges-sur-Yonne, in the Auxerrois and above all in the Puisaye, where the rebels seized the town hall of Saint-Sauveur on 6 December, then marched on Toucy. A second group got as far as Chavannes, eight kilometres from Auxerre. The two bands 'sowed fear and terror in their path, looting, sounding the tocsin and forcing peaceful citizens to join their march', as reported a year later in the *Annuaire de l'Yonne*.[6] Gendarmes and lancers were called in as reinforcements, and soon put down the revolt. The repression was harsh: many prisoners were deported to Algeria, among them an ancestor of M. Durand. 'All my relatives on my mother's side were extreme republicans', he explained.[7] His ancestor's example was not lost on the young man. Then there was a second relative whose influence also affected Durand's political commitment: this was an uncle on his mother's side, an engine-driver on the railway-line between Clamecy and the Puisaye. He was originally an active trade unionist, then he joined the Communist Party, and he exerted a strong political influence within the family, accentuated in Armand's case by the early loss of his father. He was later to become one of the local Resistance leaders, and was mayor of Clamecy for two years after the Liberation.

André Durand himself joined the Communist Party in 1933; at that time he was a member of the Amsterdam–Pleyel Committees. There were 144 of these in the Yonne, a result of the mobilisation against Fascism. The young schoolteacher and his wife were appointed to the school in Saint-Brancher, where they faced a difficult task, for the number of pupils was very high because of the large numbers of children supported by public assistance in the region: there were several village schools, in one of which there were no fewer than 145 pupils. This situation, as we know, did not diminish the political ardour of the young schoolmaster. He was a member of the same cell as Simonnot and Maria Valtat. Durand left the area in 1938: his wife was in poor health, so they moved to Epineuil, a village on the outskirts of Tonnerre.

In Epineuil, the schoolmaster was also by custom the secretary to the town hall. Durand therefore learned all about the day-to-day running of the affairs of the commune. At the same time, he won a reputation as a conscientious secretary. 'I used to spend a lot of time at the town hall: I would sometimes stay there working for thirteen hours at a stretch.' Durand remained fond of his home territory, the Puisaye, but he gradually got to know the wine-growing area in which he had settled. The Tonnerrois was quite different from the woods and forests that he had known until then. There was no point in expecting the same tradition of rebellion against the established order. Small-scale wine-growers constitute a different kind of peasantry, more individualist and, though influenced by anti-clerical ideas, little drawn to the Socialist creed. The political scene was dominated locally by the local notables, headed by Perreau-Pradier; the rise of the left in the thirties was not translated into electoral victory in 1936, when Pierre-Etienne Flandin's companion kept his seat.

On the outbreak of war, André Durand was called up: though he did not know it at the time, many years were to pass before he saw Epineuil again. It was the time of the 'phoney war', and the schoolteacher found himself in Alsace; when the Germans swept into France, his regiment withdrew to Picardy. It suffered great losses, and the survivors ended up in Etampes in Loiret, where they were taken prisoner. Durand was in prison in Germany throughout the war. He resisted as best he could in the camp: he wrote pamphlets inciting the prisoners not to work for the Germans and attempting to communicate his progressive ideas to his fellow-inmates. He made one attempt to escape, which failed when he was arrested at a railway station. He was freed by the Allied troops: 'When the Americans came, I stayed on for a fortnight longer than the others, to tell them which guards had been brutal to us.' Durand than returned to Epineuil. He was not surprised to learn that he had been put forward as a candidate in the cantonal elections: 'People remembered that I was a decent sort. The party comrades put my name forward even before I got back. There were five candidates, all committed to the programme of the National Council of the Resistance: one from the Mouvement républicain populaire, one from the SFIO, one Independent Socialist, a Radical and myself, Communist.' Durand had to plunge straight into his electoral campaign. This was the first time he had stood in an election: 'A lot of the people from around here were in the Resistance. The day I arrived, they were celebrating victory in Epineuil. Some people from Tonnerre came to fetch me to make a speech there. I had a rabid anti-Communist as my opponent, but in the end I was elected.' Durand was a member of the General Council for seven years. What happened was that after a year they drew lots and half of the councillors had to stand for re-election at the end of three years, the other half remaining in office for six. André Durand was one of the lucky ones, but he was to see his party's fortunes gradually ebb and feel the effects of the break between the Communists and their Socialist and MRP Christian-Democrat allies.

'When I stood again in 1952, we had a Socialist prefect; I would have stood a chance with two opponents, one from the SFIO and one from the MRP, but the prefect advised the Socialist not to stand, to ensure that I was beaten. He therefore withdrew, and my opponent got in: he stayed there until 1976.' In the mean time, Durand, who had gone back to teaching, took an active part in the affairs of the National Union of Teachers: the union was dominated by the Socialists, but Durand was so well respected by his colleagues that he became assistant secretary at departmental level, specialising in educational methods. He was also on the municipal council for his commune, and got himself elected mayor with ease: 'They weren't Communists, they were Republicans, but they trusted me because of my experience as secretary to the town hall.' This situation was typical of what became known as Tonnerre's 'red belt' in the immediate post-war years. Several Communist mayors were elected by voters who did not necessarily share their political principles. To some extent, the phenomenon was the result of sociological factors: many of the inhabitants of villages in the Tonnerrois were forced to seek work in factories in town because farming and wine-production did not earn them a living. Also, the memory of the Resistance and the Communist partisans was still very much alive. One of the teachers from the Tonnerre college, Abel Minard, had been shot by the Germans in April 1942, and it was the partisans who liberated the town.

The Communists profited from this symbolic capital. They could also rely on their expertise in running local affairs. Durand was on the finance committee of the General Council: 'One day I even chaired a session of the Council. Jean Moreau, the President of the Council, was often held up in Paris because at the time he was the Minister for the Budget. On this particular occasion, as it happened, he arrived in the nick of time, for I was finding it difficult to keep order. But usually the atmosphere was pleasanter then than it is now', he told me. He recalled that when he became mayor of Epineuil, local wine-production was in a dreadful state. Many of the wine-growers had been taken prisoner at the beginning of the war, and the vines had slowly become overgrown. Seeing this, Durand and his councillors launched a campaign to improve the fields: 'I went to a rural development agency, the SAFER, and they provided me with a very active agent who helped me to buy up the land; we had it cleared, then sold back to the wine-producers. We cleared 100 hectares, of which 70 now produce wine. About twenty wine-producers benefited from the scheme, most of them raising a loan to buy the land.'

Epineuil wine went on sale again, and Durand is very pleased with himself for having rescued the label. He himself bought about 4,000 square metres of vine, a purchase that naturally set plenty of tongues wagging: 'When I was buying up land for the SAFER, some said I was putting it on the register in my own name. Later the gossips said I had bought forty hectares!' But for the majority of the population of Epineuil, the operation was a success. Apart from the direct economic benefits, it has contributed to the prestige of the commune. One reason for Durand's popularity in Tonnerre and the surrounding area is that he is the man who brought back Epineuil wine. Looking at his background in a farming and woodcutting family, there seems to be nothing to suggest he would later become an expert wine-producer.

Paradoxically, it was almost certainly M. Durand's political commitment which turned him first of all into a competent local administrator and then into the sponsor of a viable economic enterprise. When I asked him whether the revival of wine-growing had led to the creation of a cooperative, he replied that it had not; there could be no question here of any form of collectivisation, even a capitalist one. In this the Communist had to admit defeat, as he recognised: 'Around here, you would lose customers if you said your wine was from a cooperative.'

Durand himself cannot be said to have lost any 'customers'. With his reputation as teacher, trade unionist and efficient mayor and councillor, he is very much in the forefront of the political scene. For many years he was regularly beaten at the cantonal elections; then in 1976 his old adversary, an auctioneer from Tonnerre, decided not to stand again. The local economy was in serious trouble, with the biggest employer, a factory making washing-machines, on the point of shutting down. The mayor of Epineuil led the workers in a fight against such a drastic solution. 'The prefect at the time', he told me,

> was in favour of the closure. When the cantonal elections came up, he encouraged the mayor of Tonnerre to stand: this was a right-wing doctor, whose personality was such that he was not much liked even by his colleagues. I was on the board of governors of the hospital myself, as a trade union representative from the CGT. The retiring councillor warned the prefect: 'If you insist on sponsoring the doctor, you'll end up with Durand.' A week before the election, he was so sure I would get in, he offered to pass over all his files relating to the General Council. I was elected, and that saved me a bit of time. I had been nibbling away at my opponent's majority at every election, but I had worked out that at the rate I was going it would be the year 2021 before I got in.

So, perseverance got its reward, and Durand regained his seat twenty years after his first victory. He was retired by this time, and could devote the greater part of his time to politics and to his many public activities. He is a member of practically every local association, from blood donors to the republican brass band. What about the party? M. Durand has many years of activism under his belt, and he has always remained loyal to the 'party line'. That is one of the reasons why he has so often been selected as a candidate, though some of the elections were lost in advance, like the elections to Senate. However, Durand is not the creation of the party. He staunchly defends the cause of his party, and takes an active part in the struggle, but he has become a local notable in his own right. His voters make no bones about it – they vote for Durand, not for the PCF. The image of the popular figure overlays that of the party representative. No doubt Durand has also adapted to local conditions, taking intelligent account of the evolution of local society, whether it be the ageing profile of the population in the rural communes of the canton, or the decreasing interest amongst workers in what the Communist Party has to say. This explains why in his role as member of the General Council Durand has concentrated on local activity, without deluding himself as to the political significance of the voters' behaviour.

Durand stood in the 1982 cantonal elections, which saw an ebb in the fortunes of the left after one year of Socialist government. Yet he was re-elected to what was to be his third and last term. He had already stood down as mayor at the previous municipal elections, being replaced by a Communist. As far as the General Council was concerned, he was well aware that his probable successor would be the Minister Henri Nallet, who was already deputy for the constituency. Durand saw no reason for bitterness in this fact, and even showed a certain amount of sympathy for the newcomer. He was not the sort of man to sit around and bemoan the decline of his party: experience had shown him that even a long succession of electoral defeats, such as he himself had known, can be overturned. As there was no sufficiently convincing Communist candidate, the best thing was at least to support the election of a left-wing candidate. Durand has always been a firm supporter of unity: the alliance with the Socialist Party might have broken down at the top, but what mattered was the situation on the ground. Durand had not changed since the days when he was active in the Amsterdam–Pleyel Committees: he felt there was a demand for unity coming up from the grass roots, and that the role of politicians was to turn that collective will into the driving force behind positive actions.

I spoke earlier of Durand as an 'anti-hero', because he was not one of the glorious band of underground fighters in the Resistance. Circumstances willed otherwise, but in any case after the war the time of the hero had passed. The treatment meted out to the bravest Communist fighters by the party leadership reveals only too clearly the results of the sudden return to reality. Heroes had their place, certainly but that was in the history books and on monuments. The same thing could be said of the whole society that survived those dark years. No one wanted to keep harking back to the exploits of the past; the country had to be rebuilt, and what was needed was men of good will. Durand was absolutely typical in this respect of the generation which at that point took charge of local affairs and set about building the future. He had been profoundly affected by the war, and had paid his debts: he represented the experiences that many others had lived through. There can be no doubt that this conformity to the norm favoured his political career. He assumed the symbolic mantle of a prestigious party, yet retained his links with the common man. This nicely judged mixture of symbolism and normality went a long way to determining Durand's acceptability as a candidate.

At first, in the immediate post-war period, he was seen above all as a representative of the PCF, but later the positions were reversed, and when he returned to the General Council, it was because he had carved out a personal vote for himself over the years. One might be tempted to think he had no further need of the Party, that indeed it was the party that could not afford to lose such a popular candidate. Yet this would be misleading, for in fact Durand's loyalty to the party was one of the mainsprings of his success, even amongst voters who did not share his views. His identity was bound up with the party, and his unswerving loyalty over decades to the same cause was seen by the voters as a virtue. In this context, the association Durand/PCF was a symbol of reassurance. At one point the PCF went to a great deal of trouble to convince people that the Communists were democrats like everyone else, not revolutionaries ready to devour their partners. Durand was a classic example of this normality proper to a party that had mellowed, and was no longer the cradle of subversives but a source of efficient Ministers.

One might then wonder what distinguished Durand from any other local notable, either in his political stance or in the day-to-day running of local affairs. The question is not an idle one, for the Communists take the demand for local democracy very seriously. Durand behaved in the first instance like any other councillor. He 'cultivated his patch', and devoted himself to responding satisfactorily to the demands of the population, by frequent representations to the authorities. Durand was an expert in this role of mediator between the population and the bureaucracy, for over the years he had built up vast experience. While I was speaking to him in his little office at home, we were interrupted several times by the phone. He held frequent surgeries, but people had no hesitation about ringing him to inquire about the progress of such-and-such an affair in which they had sought his help. Durand replied patiently; like his fellow-councillors, he considered it important to listen to the demands of his fellow-citizens.

'A respected member of the General Council': this is how I heard him described in Auxerre. He was on the committee for agricultural matters. Durand was no orator: he did not often speak in the plenary sessions of the council, but he was very effective in committee. His political opponents appreciated his expertise in wine-production, and his open-minded approach to problems, free of party prejudice. He was strongly attached to the notion of co-existence, and regretted the virulently anti-Communist tone that some leading lights in the Council saw fit to employ in the plenary sessions.

Not that this behaviour greatly surprised him, for he remained convinced that there are clear battle-lines in politics. He had chosen his side. It is perhaps this conviction that they are on the side of the people, with the consequences it has for the daily conduct of their affairs, that distinguishes Communist councillors. Having announced that they are on the side of the workers, they cannot devote themselves exclusively to the classic role of mediator. Durand, for example, was always present at moments of social conflict, going to see the workers in their factory, joining their demonstrations, giving out leaflets, and so on. His prestige as an elected councillor was to some extent placed at the service of the cause. Yet even in the most politically significant situations, there was a symbolic distance between the councillor and his comrades. He was not exactly an activist like the rest; he must always be seen as a representative of the people as a whole, not simply of a minority. This distinction is rendered visible in the tricoloured sash which is worn to identify elected politicians in street demonstrations. In other words, the gap between representative and represented is a structural constraint on the Communists, just as it is on the other political parties.

If we think in terms of the old Leninist opposition, between formal democracy and real democracy, then we see that here it is the form which has come to the fore: the symbol represented by the elected politician is instrumentalised by the process of underlining the attributes of his function to the masses. To adopt another term familiar to Marxists, we see that this kind of political activity makes use of the 'fetishism' involved in the very notion of election. Understanding this, we can appreciate the ambiguous position of a Communist councillor. He sees himself as different from other councillors, more in touch with 'real life', in the shape of the concerns and struggles of the working class: in that sense, he is a 'true democrat', as they say in the party. Yet he must also safeguard his position in the world of electoral politics; he must dress, to paraphrase Marx, in the rags of the republican tradition. For this reason, the Communist councillor cannot be a local worthy in exactly the same way as his colleagues from other parties. Durand is a classic case. He had to keep a subtle balance between an ideal of direct democracy and the constraints of electoral politics in our tradition. However, the path that leads from Communist militant to Communist notable is sometimes more of a slippery slope than it seems, and the risk of sliding imperceptibly from one extreme to the other is a real one. Moreover, even the most convinced materialists end up playing the game of symbols, valuing fetishes above reality. Durand seems to represent a middle way: he managed to keep his direct contact with his voters, while using the political resources offered by his election, and his knowledge of the workings of the administration, to achieve his cherished aim of reviving the local wine industry. Perhaps we should now consider whether it is possible to go beyond this, and divert the fetish to more politically committed ends. To find our answer, we must travel on.

Laroche–Migennes

Certain place-names are highly evocative: Laroche–Migennes is one. It summons up memories of journeys to the South of France, evoking not a town but a railway station, an obligatory halt, the last stop before we leave the Paris region. Laroche–Migennes is synonymous with the railway. Auxerre, Sens or Joigny: these names call up visions of a town, a cathedral, the banks of the Yonne. Laroche–Migennes just says 'railway', and in a way this is appropriate, for at the outset the town was a mere abstraction. It is true that there was a village at the confluence of the Yonne and the Burgundy Canal; but the town really only began with the advent of the railway. When it was decided to build a line between Paris and Lyons in the 1830s, two men fought to have the line follow the valley of the Yonne: one was Viscount Taillepied de Bondy, prefect of the department from 1833 to 1841, and the other was Marie Denis Larabit, a graduate of the Ecole Polytechnique, a former officer in the Engineers and deputy for Auxerre under the July Monarchy. He summarised the issues as follows: 'Remember that if the railway does not go through here, it will certainly go through either the Loire Valley or the valley of the Seine, and in either case we will lose the majority of our present advantages.'[8] After several years of debate and consideration, the route proposed by the two men prevailed and was accepted by parliament in 1844. This route, which linked Dijon and Paris via Tonnerre and Sens, did not touch the town of Auxerre, which at the time was not eager to see the new engines cross it: hence the choice of a country spot, and its subsequent growth as Laroche-Migennes.

Laroche and Migennes are in fact two neighbouring communes. The station is situated in Migennes, and the place owed its growth to the locomotive depot which was built there. Migennes was an obligatory halt for steam trains on the Paris–Lyons line: the trains 'took on water' there before continuing on to the South. One hundred years after the opening of the Tonnerre–Dijon line in 1849, the Migennes depot employed more than 1,500 railwaymen.

Nowadays the urban district created in 1963 by linking Migennes and the surrounding communes has a total of 13,000 inhabitants, 8,000 of them in the town. Activities tied to the railways are not so important now as they were in the past. The death-knell sounded for steam at the beginning of the 1950s, when the Paris–Lyons line was electrified. Suddenly jobs at the railway depot vanished: the number of people employed by the railway was practically halved. The railway was the big local employer, and redeployment was not easy. Nowadays steel manufacture, furniture-making and the food industry have rescued the local economy, which was nevertheless greatly weakened by the decline of the railways. The council had to fight hard to prevent the transfer to Montluçon of a furniture factory employing forty workers.

Unlike the nearest towns, Joigny and Auxerre, Migennes gives the impression of a town without a past. There are no monuments, no old churches, houses or other remnants of times past. Everything is organised around the railway. The wanderer will find no pleasant views of the Burgundy Canal or the river Yonne, none of that tranquil unspoiled landscape glimpsed in other parts from the river bank. This is a world criss-crossed by lines of steel, with the railway line and the locomotive depots, though these already belong to the realm of industrial archaeology and are no doubt doomed to be demolished. On 25 June and again on 31 July 1944, Migennes was the target of Allied bombings aimed at the total disruption of the movement of German trains. Nearly half of the town was destroyed, and the railway installations almost totally flattened. Nowadays, two great parallel axes, the railway line and the main street, enclose an area filled with traditional working-class houses. On the outskirts are the council blocks of the neighbouring commune of Cheny, which were built later, and estates of detached houses, which testify to the residents' marked preference for individual suburban dwellings.

The visitor cannot fail to be surprised at the way the surrounding countryside with its villages imperceptibly gives way to this environment, which could easily be a suburb of Paris if it had a few bus stops and Métro stations. Strangely, the town hall does not stand in the centre of the town, but at the end of the main street. The real centre of the town is the railway station and its surrounding area, where the shops and bars are to be found. The part of town where the town hall stands is always described by the people of the town as a 'nice idea', which seems to imply that they are not too convinced by the judgement of the former mayor who had the town hall built there. It would perhaps be an exaggeration to say that the town hall stands in the middle of a no man's land, but it is nevertheless interesting to note the remote location of a building which one would expect to find closer to the centre of the town's activity. Not that its situation prevents people visiting the place. Whenever I went there, I observed the presence of a large and determined public. On the ground floor they have gone in for an open-plan system, with no real walls between offices – just transparent glass panels, or removable partitions. This layout is not without significance, as it appears to facilitate contact between the people and the local administration. People come and go, and they even come back . . .

The mayor, Guy Lavrat, seems to be much sought after: in fact he seems to be something of a one-man-band. From morning to night, he devotes his considerable energy to solving local problems. Lavrat is an efficient manager, yet, as many people told me, 'he makes no secret of his party label'. Migennes is in fact the only large council in the department to be led by a Communist. After many years of activism, during which he stood several times for different elective offices, Guy Lavrat was elected member of the General Council for the canton of Migennes in 1976, the same year André Durand got elected in Tonnerre. In the aftermath of this victory he became mayor in 1977, and the Union of the Left list which he headed won again in 1983. This Communist majority in Migennes is no historical aberration. As far back as 1935, the town elected a Union of the Left council. However, the Socialists had the majority then, and the mayor, a schoolteacher named Masson, was a member of the SFIO. During the war, one of the principal Communist leaders in the Yonne was a railwayman from the Migennes depot, Louis Riglet; he led the Pierre Sémard Resistance group which was responsible for dozens of derailments. He was also responsible for the destruction of the giant five-ton crane from the Paris depot, used in cases of serious derailment, and for many other acts of sabotage. Arrested in 1944, he died under torture at the age of thirty-four. Throughout the war, the Communists strengthened their hold on the railwaymen, and gradually displaced the Socialists in public opinion.

After the war, however, when the situation was most favourable to them, the Communists failed to take the town hall of Migennes. The problem was that their ranks had been decimated, and the death of Riglet had left a vacuum. In 1947, they decided to put up Prosper Moquet, a railwayman from the Paris region who had also made a name for himself in the Resistance, and who had already been brought in as an outside candidate for deputy in 1945, and succeeded without difficulty under the system of proportional representation. Victory therefore seemed to be assured in 1947, but Moquet was soon disillusioned. There were three rival lists: his own, a right-wing list and an SFIO list headed by the former mayor, Masson. At the second ballot, the right-wing list stood down and let its votes go the Socialists. It was a classic 'third force' device, and it worked: Masson's Socialist successors won in the same way, though this time by means of a frank and open agreement with the right, and they remained in power until 1977. It was only the local application in Migennes of the Union of the Left strategy which enabled the Communists finally to win.

A militant mayor

Politics seemed to be lagging behind sociology in the case of Migennes. By the time the Communists got into power, the railwaymen who were the mainstay of their electorate were a reduced group. Even so, they were the dominant force in local politics. The very history of Migennes is bound up with that of the railways: one of its proudest boasts is its major role in the wartime battle for the railways. During the years when conversion to a different type of economy was taking place, the council was of a 'Socialo-Centrist' tendency, and one might logically have thought that as Communism lost its traditional social base, it would suffer a loss of support. That did happen initially; as in the rest of the department, there was a fall-off in the Communist vote, particularly at the beginning of the seventies. But from the end of the preceeding decade, and notwithstanding the national defeat of the left in 1968, the Union of the Left strategy seems to have paid off: Lavrat's election is an obvious illustration. I have no intention of analysing voting patterns in Migennes, however. What interests me are local perceptions of the Communist Party and its candidates, and what I would like to investigate is why Lavrat suddenly became the favourite when he did, and why he has been able to retain his position for such a relatively long period – he has been mayor and councillor for over ten years now. How did he come to represent, if not a consensus, at least a viable option, and in the event the best available? It is an important question, for Lavrat has gradually increased his personal standing in Migennes, though there is apparently nothing in his background to predispose him to such a triumph.

In connection with this last observation, one might add that in the 1983 election, Migennes was voting for him on his record, or perhaps one might say more broadly on his behaviour in the role of elected representative. The mayor had become an accepted part of the local political landscape; yet the relative lateness of his success is indicative of the relationship between public figures, whatever their electoral fortunes, and ordinary society. Here we are dealing with a very different situation from that experienced by our rural Communists in the Tonnerrois and the Avallonnais. Lavrat was interested in politics long before he ever knew Migennes and its surrounding area. He was not born in the Yonne, incidentally, but in a neighbouring department to the west, the Cher. Here we find another type of peasantry, who lived by loading timber. 'They were half-way between peasants and workers', Lavrat explains. One of his grandfathers was a wagoner in his village. The Loire Valley, where the future mayor of Migennes spent his childhood, is an area of traditional industry. For a long time, Fourchambault was an important centre of the French metallurgical industry; the last smelting furnaces were closed down in 1883, but other activities had taken over by then, and the area had an organised working class, strongly influenced by the Socialist movement and later by the Communists.

Such was the atmosphere in which Lavrat, born in 1926, grew up. His father worked in a hosiery factory in La-Charité-sur-Loire. 'My family all voted as far left as possible', he told me.

> My father was an activist in the Popular Front. A relative of his, Celestin Lamy, was the member of the General Council for Sancergues. One of my mother's cousins became mayor of Nevers after the Liberation. It was a hotbed of reds. Even before the war, there were people who voted Communist, and in the canton where I was born, the member of the General Council is always a Communist. My grandfather was a member of the woodcutters' union, and my father belonged to the Amsterdam–Pleyel Committee.[9]

Lavrat went to teacher-training college; he sat the examination in Auxerre, and it was there he joined the FUJP, a patriotic Communist Youth movement, in 1944. After the war, he was appointed schoolmaster in Perreuse, Puisaye. He lived in Saint-Sauveur, where his wife, the daughter of a Communist activist from the Yonne, was also a teacher. At that time, the party was highly influential throughout the region; Lavrat quickly rose to be a member of the committee and then in 1952 of the secretariat of the

Yonne Federation. Around the same time, he was appointed to a post in Sézy, not far from Migennes, where he was a teacher first of all in a primary and later in a secondary school.

'I stood in several elections during this period', Lavrat told me. In 1951 he stood in the cantonal elections in Saint-Julien-du-Sault, in 1958 in the canton of Joigny, which at the time included Migennes and its surrounding area, and then in 1967 in one of the cantons of Auxerre. Subsequently he became better known by standing in the constituency of Auxerre in the general elections of 1962, 1967 and 1968. He was ahead of the other left-wing candidates in the 1967 election: it was a close-run election, but he was in a good position to win. However, following a national agreement with the FGDS, he had to stand down in favour of their candidate, Périllier, who got in. For the mayor of Migennes, this was a significant date, as it set the seal on a balance of forces which would henceforth favour the Socialists. As he related to me:

> That was when we let ourselves be caught up in the system . . . I had a chance of being elected, though it was a close-run contest, but we agreed to make the sacrifice, and I stood down. I am convinced that is one of the reasons people say: 'Voting for anybody other than the Socialists is wasting your vote.' In '68 people were saying to me: 'We like you, but if we vote for you, you'll only stand down in favour of Périllier . . .' From that point on, no Communist candidate has ever overtaken a Socialist, whereas in the Sénonnais the Communist was always ahead of the Socialist until 1981.

Lavrat's political activity came to be concentrated more and more on the Migennes region. On the one hand, the party sent down a full-time activist to run the Yonne Federation, and from then on that individual would be the candidate in the general election in the Auxerrois, though he never managed to turn the tide in his favour. Then, the creation of an autonomous canton enabled Migennes to split away from Joigny, which traditionally votes for the right. Meanwhile, Lavrat had become one of the most respected voices in the town. The voters were increasingly dissatisfied with the electoral strategy that enabled a candidate to stand down and pass his votes to someone else in order to keep out a common adversary. However, the double success of the Communist candidate, in the cantonal and the mayoral elections, was not just the result of a change of strategy by the parties, but was also the fruit of patient labour. Lavrat's job as a teacher helped him, as it helped his colleague André Durand in Tonnerre. But Lavrat had also been careful not to neglect the traditional left-wing groups in the town, beginning with the railwaymen. Their numbers might be greatly reduced, but their influence was still predominant.

One reason for this was the number of retired railwaymen living in Migennes, but one must also recognise the role of the 'railway culture' which permeated the whole town. Many residents whose job or profession was in a different sector had grown up in families in which the majority of the men worked at the railway depot. The physical presence of the locomotives, the smell, the noises, the station at the very heart of the city – all these things shaped their daily lives. Within this railway culture, everyday life is suffused with myth. The two are inextricably bound together, and even today, coming into contact with locomotives and seeing the convoys passing through Migennes, one is irresistibly reminded of the old steam trains, and the epic encounter between man and the iron monster immortalised in the pages of Zola. Nearer our own time, we have the heroic acts of the men who sabotaged rails and buildings under the most dangerous conditions, men who paid the price of the victory they did not live to see. Migennes is a community where the glory of an industrial age now gone for ever lives on into a present which is desperately trying to find a way out of its difficulties. It is clear now that nothing will replace the railway; in this town, as in others which grew in the shade of a single large industry, all that can be hoped for now are piecemeal solutions. The town has had to learn to juggle the service sector and small businesses in an attempt to rebuild the local economy, though without ever burying its railway past, even symbolically.

Seen in this context, Lavrat's election takes on its full significance. The Communist is seen as the 'natural' representative of the railwaymen, if only because of the links between the party and the CGT trade union confederation. Lavrat had the good sense to respect the role of railway culture in the town, as the presence of nine active or retired railwaymen on the town council amply attests. At the same time, he is happy to represent the middle classes: his position as a teacher makes him a suitable representative of those employed in the tertiary sector and in small businesses. But what about all the others, particularly the unemployed, who form quite a large group amongst young people here? (The unemployment figures are a little higher than elsewhere in the department.) The mayor is conscious of the limited role the town council can play in economic matters, but he has a clear stance on his responsibilities in the face of the economic crisis. He participates actively in any movement aimed at defending jobs. When there was talk of moving a furniture factory to Montluçon in the name of rationalisation, he was in the front line of the campaign against the move. With the support of the prefect of the Yonne, the council managed to stop the transfer, which would have had a disastrous effect on local employment.

Another area of militancy is housing. He fights evictions from council housing, and has been present on several occasions physically blocking the bailiffs:

We prevented the eviction of an unmarried mother; the prefect took me to court for obstructing the bailiffs in the execution of an eviction order. A petition was got up in the block of flats, and we came to an arrangement with the council housing office. We managed to have the tenant placed under court supervision, and the court paid half the sum owed.

The mayor pointed out that another Communist member of the General Council had been taken to court recently: this time it was because in a newspaper article he had referred in not very flattering terms to a company that was laying off workers, and was found guilty of libel. Guy Lavrat seemed to be suggesting that the Communists are more militant than their colleagues from other parties.

He makes no attempt to disguise his dislike of the welfare approach to unemployment and similar problems adopted by the Socialist government. He fought long and hard against the Community Work system, unlike certain other mayors, who while repeating the party line of opposition to the government's social welfare policies, retain some of them in practice. The people of Migennes have had ample opportunity to consider Lavrat's profound conviction that Community Work is just a way of concealing reality from young people, and something which simply permits increasingly sophisticated forms of exploitation of the available labour force. A pamphlet distributed during the last election campaign denounced 'modern forms of slavery such as Community Work, training schemes, short term contracts and other casual employment'.

It is clear that in many situations, Lavrat has been a militant mayor. This image is confirmed by his interventions during the public sessions of the General Council. His behaviour offers a strong contrast with that of the rural Communist councillors. It is important to be clear about this: Migennes is only a small town, but it has a sizable working class, and the weight of a deep-rooted tradition. Lavrat can boast that he runs the town efficiently, and that numerous new facilities have been provided during his term of office, but the popularity he enjoys is essentially related to his prompt reaction to examples of injustice, whether in the form of evictions, or a threat to the jobs of a group of workers. He is perceived locally as someone heavily committed to the struggle, much more so than his Tonnerre colleague, who is seen more as the representative of a particular place.

When people describe Durand as 'the man who revived Epineuil wine', they are defining and appreciating him in relation to a rural society in which industrial activity is perhaps indispensable to the local economy, but older values have not disappeared. In such a situation, the elected representative must recognise and accept that there is no clear dividing-line between the peasant and the proletarian elements of local society, and strike a balance between direct action in relation to areas of social conflict, and a more universal approach which takes in the population of the area as a whole. Hence, perhaps, a certain blurring of the image of the party man, since what is wanted is an assurance of balance; and, as we saw, people vote for Durand rather than for the party, doubtless because he represents a possibility of reconciliation between the past and the present, or at least the gradual evolution of local society.

In the Tonnerrois, heterogeneity is the outstanding characteristic, and the problem is to link together activities and ways of life which are very different from each other, with wine-producers on the one hand and industrial workers on the other, and somewhere in between, agricultural workers who also engage in other occupations. In Migennes, one starts from a strongly homogeneous population: they have had the same historical experience, tied to a single industry, so the problem for today is to create diversity and encourage redeployment by bringing in as many new jobs as possible, without, however, betraying the past or abandoning the ex-railwaymen who live and work in the town to an uncertain future.

Tonnerre, Avallon and their surrounding area provide an example of a rural context with some degree of industrialisation: Migennes is a typical case of the modern urban problem of modernisation of the structures of production, therefore the elected representative here has to demonstrate his capacity for action. There are two possible attitudes. One is to try to solve the problem by attracting industries to the area. However, as we all know, offers are thin on the ground, and this type of 'managerial' solution soon comes up against the economic realities of the country as a whole. The other possibility is to keep the spirit of protest alive, and lead a movement whose target is the welfare services of the State. This is the stance adopted by the mayor of Migennes. It is in no way incompatible with efficient management, as can be seen from the excellent facilities, particularly sporting and educational ones, enjoyed by the commune. But everyone knows that Lavrat is more than just a good manager, and the secret of his legitimacy is his permanent commitment to protest action and his questioning of the managerial and consensus seeking values of the government. Durand and Lavrat fall, to my mind, on either side of the dividing-line between a Communist approach appropriate to a rural society and the form of militancy required in an urban situation. Not that Migennes and Tonnerre are very different in size: the difference lies in their history and economy. One could of course amuse oneself by contrasting the personalities of the two men, noting that at the meetings of the General Council Lavrat is more outspoken than his older colleague, or that Durand is readier to fraternise with people whose views diverge widely from his own. We might suggest also that the difference in their ages is of some relevance, and that Durand, who is ten years older than Lavrat, has mellowed with the years and lost some of the edge of his militancy. These considerations, apart from being highly subjective, merely state the obvious. It is true that the two men have very different personalities, but that is not enough to explain the consistency of each of their political styles. Durand's behaviour strongly resembles that of the majority of rural Communist councillors, whose style of local politics exploits the resources of republican symbolism, in contrast to the tendency of urban representatives to play the card of 'protest' against a government which is seen as attempting to conceal reality under a cloak of consensus, modernisation and welfare provision.

In contrasting political styles and attitudes to the role of the local elected representative in this way, one runs the risk of giving a reductionist view of reality. I have sketched a rapid portrait of the mayor of Migennes, emphasising the interest he shows in the running of his council. After his election, he took leave of absence from his job, in order to devote all his time to his new function. When he retired from teaching, he nevertheless remained fully active, and as we saw, he was at the town hall every day. His political role has not diminished his managerial role, and it would be wrong to see him as a sectarian figure. At the meetings of the General Council, he performs the function of a critical member of a minority tendency, calmly expressing a radical opposition view. Unlike the Socialists, he refuses to compromise with the right-wing majority. The press regularly publishes his arguments and criticisms. Yet he has no feeling of being discriminated against by his colleagues in the majority. His canton is not treated worse than any other when it comes to subsidies: 'Speaking objectively, Chamant doesn't do me any favours, but he does me no disservice, either. We get what we are entitled to, and nobody pushes us around.' Lavrat is an active committee member, and that context, while not abolishing all disagreements, does leave room for dialogue. Human relationships are formed:

> One of the members of my committee is Sadon: he's an adviser to Chalandon, the Minister for Justice. We often chat, and we see eye to eye on a number of practical problems. I wouldn't go so far as to say we're friends, but on the odd occasion . . . For example, we were intending to ask for a grant from the National Council on Delinquency, which depends on the Ministry of Justice, in order to turn an old laundry into a sports centre. He told me to send him a dossier on the project. I sent it, and I have the feeling he passed it on. Or to take another case, we had no solicitor in Migennes for the canton. One day I said to Sadon: 'You might see if you could speed things up at the Ministry', and he took the necessary steps. That shows I'm not ostracised. I also have a good relationship on a personal level with the Secretary General for departmental affairs.

One must therefore distinguish between the Communist councillor's public stance, which he demonstrates together with his colleagues at every meeting of the General Council by opposing the majority's proposals, and this practice of 'co-existence' imposed on him by circumstances and from which he tries to obtain as much advantage as possible for his town and his canton. What we see here is exactly what we see at national level: events on stage are important, but so is what goes on in the wings. By juggling the two modes, Lavrat can be seen as a 'good' mayor, both pragmatic and militant. The first of these qualities is, as it were, subsumed under the second, and it is this fact that distinguishes the urban Communist councillor from his colleagues, whether of the right or the left. To a certain extent, while the Communist strategy has undoubtedly been subject to all sorts of variations, there has nevertheless been a continuity in its expression, and in the image the Communists offer to the inhabitants of the towns they run, for half a century. The militancy is designed to carry on the tradition of the Resistance in local mythology. The heroic acts of wartime are matched, as it were, by a stubborn adherence to a line in everyday struggles. Local Communism draws its legitimacy from this continuity.

In the shadow of the council blocks

Until the most recent redrawing of constituency boundaries, Migennes was in the same constituency as Sens and Joigny. For a long time the Communists were the most influential group on the left, with their stronghold in Migennes and the advantage of a very strong position also in Sens, at the other end of the constituency. It is often said that the main political figure in Sens, apart from the mayor, is the Communist member of the General Council, Jean Cordillot. He does not deny this. Some of his opponents have admitted they would have been happy to see him as mayor: 'Just a pity you're a Communist!'

I met the councillor at his home, in an area of small detached houses next to the new hospital in Sens. As soon as one leaves the town centre with its four famous buildings, the Cathedral and the Archbishop's Palace, the Baltard Market and the town hall, one is in a suburb dominated by blocks of council flats and shops, separated by patches of waste ground. It was very warm that August afternoon, and it was with a feeling of relief that I went into Jean Cordillot's office. It was lined with books published by the Editions Sociales. Cordillot was about sixty. He welcomed me warmly, with just a trace of an accent which I recognised at once. As I had suspected, he was from the Morvan, from a village in the Nièvre. His family were peasants who worked loading timber in winter, and as a child he spoke the local patois, only really beginning to speak French when he went to do his last year at school in the chief town. No, his family were not very interested in politics, though it must be said that the village tended to support the Popular Front.

Because he did well at school, Cordillot was encouraged by his schoolmasters to become a teacher himself. But his whole world was turned upside down in June 1940. 'One Sunday in June, somebody came into the farm-yard: 'The Germans are in Clamecy', he said; 'I've got to get away.' I was seized with despair that June.'[10] After months of uncertainty, defeat... Cordillot was teaching in Nevers at the time, and although he did not actually belong to a Resistance group, he would sometimes 'give a hand' to comrades more deeply involved than himself. He became a Communist in 1944: after the Liberation, he went back to teacher-training college in Auxerre to finish the last year of his course, and it was there he met his wife. Her father was a schoolteacher and Communist militant in Irancy before the war: in December 1940, he was dismissed from his post, and the following year arrested and sent to Auschwitz, from which he never returned. Between 1947 and 1950, Cordillot had a job as a tutor in Vierzon in the department of the Cher, and he followed a course of study at the same time which qualified him to teach in a technical school. The Communists were very powerful at the time in the Cher, so this was where Cordillot won his spurs as a party leader. A little later he returned to the Yonne, where his wife's family lived, and where there was a vacancy in the local technical school. He soon became secretary to the Communist Federation in the Yonne, but he did not become a full-time activist, preferring to combine his teaching with political activity. He ceased to be secretary in 1972, though he remained a highly influential local leader.

Cordillot was elected deputy for the Yonne in 1956, under the system of proportional representation, but lost his seat two years later to the Gaullist mayor of Sens, Gaston Perrot, though he continued to pose the major challenge to the right in the north of the department. In 1967, he obtained 47.5 per cent of the votes in the constituency as a whole, and a majority of the votes in Sens. Standing that same year in the cantonal elections, he became the member of the General Council for one of the cantons of that city, and so he has remained ever since. 'At that time my career was watched with a great deal of interest; the party's fortunes were at their lowest ebb, and I was the only Communist on the General Council. By the time of the following election the situation had changed: we won the cantons of Migennes, Vermenton, Tonnerre, Ancy-le-Franc and Seignelay.' Jean Cordillot was always the party's candidate in the general elections: he generally came out top of the left in the constituency, though he was overtaken by the Socialist candidate in 1981. When the boundaries were redrawn in the 1986 election, Migennes was cut out of the constituency. That explains partly why the Communists were unable to recover their lost ground, vis-à-vis the Socialists at least, in the 1988 election.

Seated in my comfortable chair, facing Jean Cordillot, I listened as he reeled off the long list of election results marking the various stages of his political career. Beyond the figures, beyond the now muffled echo of past electoral battles, I was astounded by his extraordinary persistence. I tried to imagine the intellectual development of the man who sat opposite me. Like many others, he must have been pro-Stalin; then came the Twentieth Congress, Hungary, Prague, May 1968, the joint programme of the left, its collapse, the Communists in government, Afghanistan and then most recently the party's turning inwards on itself, just when its Soviet elder brother was experimenting with glasnost. That must be the story of any militant's life: all the tireless explanations he has had to furnish to others, while himself searching for a coherent stance, the 'concrete response to a concrete situation' so beloved of the Leninist tradition. Cordillot must sometimes have found it a bumpy ride, yet he clung to his beliefs. It is this steadfastness which has won him the respect of the voters, and even of other politicians from totally opposed parties. In the local political landscape, he functions as a valuable landmark, one of those fixed points from which one takes one's bearings. Stability in this context is perceived as a virtue, and it is no coincidence that the Communist Party was represented by the same individuals for so long.

Curiously, it was in fact the full-time activist sent in by the party who had the shorter career. Regularly defeated in the Auxerrois, he was the member of the European parliament for a time, but he never really managed to gain a foothold in the department. The party in the Yonne rests on two pillars: Jean Cordillot and Guy Lavrat. 'My old-time comrade': that is how the Communist councillor refers to the mayor of Migennes, for the two men are bound by an ancient friendship. They have a great deal in common, after all: their childhood in the Nièvre, their peasant background, similar professional lives. They were both influenced by a strong tradition of working-class struggle in the old industrial and mining centres of the Nièvre and the Cher: Lavrat is from the border area of the two departments, while Cordillot learned his militant politics in Vierzon. Neither of the two men belonged originally to the Yonne: they settled in the department because they were linked to it by their marriages. The similarity in the two stories is revealing, in that their legitimacy is not founded on any ancestral link with the places where they forged their political career. It is rather the result of tremendous perseverance on the spot: Cordillot plays a great part in local life and gets involved in conflicts in the Sénonnais with the same ardour as his colleague in Migennes; in Sens, in other words, we find those forms of action typical of urban Communism. To sum up, if the two Communist leaders have a trait in common, it is their unshakeable fidelity to the party they have never ceased to serve.

The friendship between Lavrat and Cordillot must take some of the credit for the image of consistency presented by the Communists in the department. The party itself and its structures contribute, but once again what really matters in practice is the informal links which ensure the smooth daily running of the party machine. Both leaders occupy a prominent place within the party, not merely ensuring the coordination of local political activities, but also managing people. The two leaders are highly experienced in this role. Grooming new leaders and future elected representatives demands a very good knowledge of local circumstances and a great deal of tact. Some choices are obvious; for example, when the time came to select a Communist candidate in the canton of Ancy-le-Franc for the 1976 elections, one name stood out, that of the secretary of the local branch, a man who had received his political education from a former leader of the quarrymen. In this area, where stoneworking and quarrying have shaped local history, being the spiritual heir of a quarryman was an undeniable asset; the candidate was elected, and had his mandate renewed in the cantonal elections of 1982.

Usually, however, finding a new generation of leaders is a delicate matter, for the Communist Party as much as any other party. Older leaders regard themselves as indispensable on the grounds of experience. They tend to emphasise the difficulties of finding suitable heirs. In Migennes, Guy Lavrat had brought on to the council at the last elections a teacher who had been secretary of the Migennes branch until the events of 1968, when he left the party. Later he rejoined, and agreed to form part of the mayor's team, so that the mayor looked upon him as a possible successor. His hopes were soon dashed, for the new councillor abandoned the party again for a group on the far left. Lavrat makes no attempt to conceal the fact that he was deeply hurt by this unexpected desertion. For the moment he appears to have given up the search for a successor. At the last election, he and Cordillot were again the Communist candidates. In Auxerre, the party put up its present secretary, a literature teacher who is a native of the Yonne, aged thirty-nine and already a member of the Regional Council. Another teacher, like the four members of the General Council: consciously or unconsciously, this choice reveals a didactic vision of political militancy, and the influence of a generation of schoolmasters on the local party organisation. The main Communist leaders, like Riglet, Roulot and many others, who perished during the Occupation, were workers. Their successors began a new tradition. We should note also that the teacher-training colleges have been the breeding-grounds for the two fraternal enemies of the left. The Socialist Party has made great inroads amongst teachers, some of whom were originally attracted to the PCF, then rejected its democratic centralism.

The social and cultural role of the party

Looking at the results obtained by the Communist candidate at the last presidential election, many commentators concluded that we were witnessing the irremediable collapse of the party. Just a few weeks later, it won a respectable number of seats in the National Assembly. Not only that, but the very same voters who had rejected André Lajoinie turned round and voted for the outgoing Communist deputy, or the Communist candidate, in their constituency – they were apparently 'frozen in the past', as Bernard Kouchner, one of the victims of the Communist advance under the Socialist policy of reconciliation, bitterly complained. Once again everyone had underestimated the strength of French local politics, in which the Communists are a traditional ingredient. The different personalities I have sketched give a clear enough picture of how deeply rooted the party is in French society. By closely observing certain local situations, and listening to the protagonists, we have glimpsed some of the reasons for this deep-seated influence. The political survival of Communist representatives was not simply the result of a fortunate historical accident, as one might have thought from the astonishment betrayed even by party leaders on the night of the last general election.

No, it was not a 'wonderful surprise'. My wanderings through the Yonne had shown up two sorts of factor: one concerned with the individual actions of the party's political representatives, their ability to animate political life in their cantons and towns; the other belonging less to the realm of what we usually call 'politics', and more to the realm of culture, in the sense given to this term by anthropologists. Culture embraces all the beliefs and customs of a community. This ensemble of beliefs and customs is shaped by history, but it also interprets history in the light of its own codes, selecting certain episodes, and certain personalities, to build up a more or less coherent image of society. In France, Communism is a cultural fact: not only because it is a doctrine or a militant organisation, but because it occupies a special place in the memory of French people. It represents a tradition of resistance, culminating in the rebirth of the national spirit and the generous sacrifices made during the Occupation years, and that is what is celebrated in the loyal vote for the party. The party cultivates that memory, so that long before any questions arise about the validity of its ideas, or the effectiveness of its actions, it can count on a certain basic support in many cantons. In one place, the collective memory will see an association between the woodcutters' uprisings in the last century and the heroism of the Communist partisans; in another, it is the railwaymen's struggle that is celebrated; in a third, there is a reverence for the exact spot where party leaders were shot, and so on.

If the expression 'roots' has any meaning in such a context, it must surely take account of this cultural compost, on which the values of the party, above all loyalty, continuity and militancy, can flower. Party militants and elected representatives affirm the continuity of a people attached to their earth, and the continuity of an ideal cherished under even the most difficult conditions; they display loyalty to their original reasoned choice; they are the heirs to a tradition of struggle, fighting on the side of the oppressed. That is, broadly speaking, the cultural hand of cards held by the Communist Party in France. Of course, the party does not have a monopoly on these values; after all, any individual could claim to be responding to similar imperatives. The important point is the association between these values, a particular territory and a particular historical tradition. When that association works, the Communist Party emerges as one of the major factors in political life. We have observed that the phenomenon presents itself differently in urban and rural contexts, hence significant variations in the behaviour of elected representatives. This is where local factors come into play: sometimes militancy will come to the fore, and sometimes it will be more important to stress continuity. Some councillors will consider it important to be involved in social conflicts, and others will be more interested in creating a sense of territory and local identity. The task of the politician is to shape his strategy in line with a political culture which he shares with his fellow-citizens, but in which neither he nor they have a monopoly.

Not very long ago, one could always raise a smile with a reference to 'champagne revolutionaries'; now the idea surprises no one. What about the term 'revolutionary notables' in relation to the party's councillors? I have already stated my reservations on this point: the term 'notable' is ambiguous and does not seem to express the double sense of the activities of the people I interviewed. Their representative status is dependent on their having a direct relation with those they represent, yet it also comes from that distance which in republican symbolism characterises the relationship between the representative and those he represents. The representative's militancy, his involvement in the struggle, testify to a form of direct democracy. In other ways, the Communists are little different, as we have seen, from their mayoral or councillor colleagues. Like the councillors, they belong to networks; vis-à-vis the voters, they take on the status of intermediaries in relation to administrative authorities perceived as distant. They defend the territories in their care as much as they can. Within the General Council they dutifully take on the role of opposition, and one sees the growth within committees of good personal relationships between such and such a Communist councillor and someone from the opposite camp. The highest praise of the RPR president of the General Council came from the lips of a Communist: 'He's someone with a natural authority', this Communist told me; 'he has the ability to synthesise ideas, and he has a certain moral elegance'.

Curiously, it was the Communists I interviewed who were most pessimistic about the party's electoral future. Perhaps they underestimate the cultural factors I have just outlined, and their own almost instinctive ability to reap advantage from it. The new policies presented in François Mitterrand's second term may rouse the Communist vote as a reaction, and give the party its second wind. Rather than indulge in any further speculation, I prefer to end with a question I consider vital for the future. I have noted the cultural context within which the Communist Party operates, a context in which memory and the values of loyalty and continuity take priority, and I have stressed the remarkable longevity of Communist elected personnel. I am therefore driven to wonder if the party is not doomed more and more to play the role of witness, or cultural object, through its inability to recover hegemony within its own camp, the left, whether the left is in a majority or not. These are undoubtedly the alternative options: either continue as the embodiment of a political culture which shows no signs of disappearing yet, or become one of the real protagonists on the political stage again. Either a symbol, or a party properly engaged with real life. 'But the two are one and the same', my informants would chorus, in true dialectical style. But what if one were to reject that view?

7

Deputy and mayor

About forty years ago, a group of sociologists decided to examine a medium-sized French town, one whose population was 'neither too large nor too small', a town 'both industrial and commercial, not dominated by any one economic or industrial activity', and reasonably 'separate from neighbouring villages or towns'. The choice fell on Auxerre, which with its 25,000 inhabitants was the perfect example of a provincial seat of a prefecture, a town still redolent of the nineteenth century, with its ancient districts, its rather sleepy industries and the old-fashioned elegance of some of its historic buildings. Forty years on, Charles Bettelheim and Suzanne Frère's work is clearly a classic account of provincial life in France in the immediate post-war years.[1] I have recently reread the description of a stroll around Auxerre with which the book opens, and I must say it held no great surprises: the town centre, rising in tiers like an acropolis on the left bank of the Yonne, has not changed. It is still a labyrinth of old houses, and narrow streets which impede the traffic: as we wander around we come across the two medieval monuments which are the pride of Auxerre, the Cathedral of Saint-Etienne and the Abbey of Saint-Germain. A little higher up, we find the shop-filled streets around the town hall and some typical buildings from the last century, such as the Central Post Office, the Crédit Lyonnais Bank, the Savings Bank and the law-courts. The covered market has been demolished to make way for a large car-park, but that is the only obvious change in the inner-city environment since its protrayal in the book at the beginning of the 1950s.

The big alterations have happened on the outskirts. Wandering round the slopes of the right-hand bank of the Yonne, one sees that the old town is now surrounded by modern suburbs. This landscape, with its clusters of flats and detached houses, offers a striking contrast to the traditional world which still held sway at the time the sociological study was published. Since then, the population of the town has vastly increased; Auxerre and its surroundings now have more than 42,000 inhabitants, though the description 'medium-sized town' still holds good. The town has not developed economically in a way which would have turned it into a magnet for the rest of the region. Its radius of influence is limited, and it is not a leading industrial centre, nor has it benefited as other cities have done from the founding of a university, which would have given it a privileged status in the area. Auxerre is still a medium-sized town and it has now become a middle-class town, thanks to the development of the 'tertiary' sector. In 1975, industry and the building trade employed only 31 per cent of the active population, whereas back in 1950 industrial occupations outnumbered all the rest. But these changes do not alter the essential fact that Auxerre, like many chief towns of departments, gives the impression of being a typical peaceful, provincial French town. It carries on its outskirts the scars of Thirty Glorious Years of Architecture (1945–75), and it has certainly suffered from the economic downturn following the petrol crisis. Yet at first glance, none of this has affected the calm atmosphere emanating from the place.

All roads lead to the chief town of the department, and I have already referred to Auxerre in several contexts: when I spoke about the division of the country into departments, in following the political destinies of certain leading personalities, and in relating certain episodes of local life. These repeated trips have not been the work of chance: the majority of the administrative offices for the Yonne are concentrated in Auxerre, so that the town has always been fiercely proud of its pre-eminence over other chief towns of *arrondissements*. There is nothing surprising in the fact that the town where the prefecture is located and where the General Council sits should attract political representatives from all over the department. However, Auxerre's influence is not solely due to its strategic position within the administrative area. Auxerre also gains prestige from the people with whom it is associated. The mayor of Auxerre is a very important figure in the life of the department. This may be why its mayors seem to be awarded what we might call a long-term contract, for in seventy years the town has known only three mayors: the last but one held office for thirty years, and the present mayor is getting ready to stand for the fourth time, after eighteen years of loyal and devoted service.

This important figure is Jean-Pierre Soisson, whom we have already encountered in his roles as deputy and member of the General Council: he enjoys uncontested legitimacy here, and his fame has tended to eclipse that of his predecessors. The present mayor of Auxerre pursues two careers simultaneously, one in national and the other in local politics. So far as the Yonne is concerned, he is the classic case of a councillor with deep roots in his area, faithful to his town and to his electorate. In his Paris life, he is a politician who does not hesitate to take risks and stray off the beaten track. For example, he recently accepted a post in a Socialist-dominated government, though he is a founder-member of one of the leading right-wing parties, the Republican Party. This step did not go unremarked, and many commentators went to town on the 'Soisson case'. The episode demonstrates quite clearly the discrepancy that may exist between the activities of a politician at national level and his behaviour as a local representative.

One of the characteristics of the French system is that it produces these 'two-headed' figures: there can be no career in national politics without a strong local base, and vice versa. Many of our elected representatives are in the same position as Soisson, that is to say they are both deputies and mayors. For example, the mayors of the chief towns of the neighbouring departments are none other than Pierre Bérégovoy in Nevers, who is also Minister for the Economy and Finance, and Robert Poujade in Dijon, who was a Minister under Pompidou. For the purposes of my study I have not ventured beyond the boundaries of the Yonne, but the two cases I am about to examine in this part of the book, and which involve Auxerre, would also, I believe, be valid for many other similar towns. The first highlights the extraordinary longevity in office of Auxerre's mayors. The second concerns the embodiment in one man of two different forms of legitimacy, two types of discourse and two modes of political behaviour: the local and the national. For the first case, we must go back to the recent history of Auxerre, which will provide us with a striking example of loyalty on the part of the town towards one man, expressed during some very particular historical circumstances. It will perhaps tell us something about the nature of political longevity in the town, and about the circumstances in which such stability is produced.

An embarrassing situation

Spring 1945

Just one year before, the Germans were still parading in the streets of Auxerre. The liberation of the town on 24 July 1944 ended the domination and the exactions of the occupying force. The prisoners were brought home from Germany, and it was time to reckon the final toll: 181 people shot in the Yonne, and 541 taken away to concentration camps, 251 of them never to return. Those individuals most deeply involved in collaboration were tried, and certain zealous Nazi helpers, such as the prefect Bourgeois, were executed. The Free French authorities set up a temporary town council composed in the main of Socialists and Communists linked with the Resistance. The mayor was a respected doctor, Moutarde. His term was short, for in May 1945, in Auxerre as elsewhere, there was a return to universal suffrage and proper municipal elections, the first for ten years. Three lists were presented: one was the list for Municipal Administration and the Defence of the Republic, composed mainly of those who had run the town under the Occupation, and headed by the former mayor, Jean Moreau; the second was a Patriotic, Republican and Anti-Fascist Union list; and the third a Republican and Democratic Union list. Jean Moreau and his friends won every seat; the situation was all the more embarrassing in view of the fact that Moreau was ineligible for elective office, having been stripped of his civil rights for accepting a seat on the departmental council, a new entity created by the Vichy government to replace the General Council.

The prefect outlined the difficulty in his correspondence with the Minister of the Interior:

> It would be a mistake to pretend that all the problems have disappeared. One type of situation which must engage our attention is where a commune has elected a person deemed ineligible, who has therefore been prevented from taking office. A clear example of such a case is Auxerre, where the former mayor was appointed departmental councillor under Vichy, and has now been elected with a large majority. Despite the prohibition on taking office which has been notified to him by the prefecture committee, he has been unanimously chosen for mayor. This illustrates the drawbacks of interim arrangements, for we do not know what the result of his appeal will be, and in the mean time the lack of an effective mayor is hindering the smooth running of municipal affairs, since we are having to rely on the assistant mayors, who lack the necessary authority and responsibility.[2]

The case of Jean Moreau was submitted to an Honour Jury, which finally met on 6 June 1945 and confirmed his ineligibility, arguing that 'he was nominated mayor at the suggestion of the German authorities, and the acts of resistance which he cites came too late to imply participation in the struggle against the enemy . . . moreover, M. Moreau adhered without reservations to the policy of the de facto entity calling itself the "French State" [the Vichy regime]'.[3] Moreau was therefore obliged to withdraw, and his assistant mayor, Martineau, ran the town until 1947. In that year the former mayor, who had recovered his eligibility, won back his office without difficulty, and retained it until his death. That seemingly paradoxical vote of May 1945 tells us a great deal about the links between a town and its mayor.

Let us return to the prefect's letters; here we learn to our surprise that the mayor was reluctant to withdraw even after his ineligibility was confirmed by the jury. 'The most delicate situation', we read in a letter dated 25 June 1945,

> is still that of Auxerre. M. Jean Moreau, the municipal councillor, elected with a very large majority, and chosen unanimously as mayor, has not been rehabilitated by the jury.
>
> The municipal council, which was mainly elected on account of the strong

personality of M. Moreau, is thus bereft, though the last I heard was that it has no intention of resigning. The work of this body, deprived of its leader and criticised by certain political parties and resistance movements, will certainly not be easy.

Moreover, public opinion is passionately divided on the issue of M. Moreau's loss of office; his opponents applaud the move, but the 6,000 voters who supported the former Vichy mayor nevertheless represent a large mass of people, who are not slow to express their displeasure. They draw strength from their number, and also because they lean on the supreme republican principle of universal suffrage, complaining that a law which allows a three-member jury to overturn the will of 6,000 voters is arbitrary. In those circles most favourable to Moreau, it is being suggested that this is a politically motivated act, in which the interests of the town of Auxerre have been relegated to second place.

More objective critics are content to observe that it would have been infinitely better to have had the jury's decision before the election, rather than now. This would have deprived the malcontents of their most persuasive argument, namely that democratic institutions have not been fully restored.

The position of the administration has been helped by the decision taken by the Prefecture Council, at my suggestion, to suspend the right to sit of all those in the department declared ineligible. We have thus avoided the demonstrations which might have accompanied a spectacular departure from the town hall.

No demonstration has taken place; nor do M. Moreau's supporters have any newspaper, so that all they can do is express their displeasure at the official action in conversation: nevertheless, the population of Auxerre is very divided on the issue.[4]

From the point of view of the prefect, obviously, it would be best if the former mayor just quietly disappeared from the political scene, as a collaborator. Moreau, on the other hand, was determined to achieve rehabilitation; as for the majority of voters who had supported Moreau, they resented being brushed aside in favour of a Paris jury. What was the verdict of a few individuals, compared to the views of a population who had been able to observe the behaviour of their mayor every day? It was the same old story, Paris dictating to the provinces, and Auxerre was disinclined to accept the authority of the capital in relation to its choice of councillors. It was indeed a 'delicate situation', as the prefect wrote, and one not made any easier by Jean Moreau's stubbornness.

Moreau considered that he was a truly legitimate representative; by voting for him, the people of Auxerre had recognised the correctness of his past behaviour, and shown their confidence in his ability to run the town. His duty, therefore, was to persevere, even after he was turned out of the town hall, in his role of representative of local interests. In pursuit of this aim, he remained in contact with his team and had no hesitation in turning up on certain public occasions, trying the patience of the prefect, as the latter indicates in another letter:

The council appears to have retained some links with its leader, and certain incidents have occurred which have forced me to make my feelings clear. For example, on the occasion of a visit to the town hall of Auxerre by the Normandie–

Niémen air squadron, Jean Moreau turned up at the town hall claiming to have been invited as a military representative. The General Secretary, who was standing in for me, expressed to the assistant mayors, and to M. Moreau himself, his astonishment that an individual removed from office on government orders should see fit to present himself at an official function. Out of respect for the feelings of the visiting officers, the general secretary did not withdraw from the ceremony, but to mark his disapproval he declined to speak; the president of the liberation committee did likewise.[5]

Seen from this angle, the ex-mayor's attitude looks like provocation: here we have a Pétainist turning up at a reception in honour of the Free French pilots, sheltering behind his army uniform. But from Moreau's point of view, it would have been wrong to behave in any other way. He was convinced within himself that he had acted for the good of the town vis-à-vis the occupying forces. The voters had confirmed that view. To withdraw from public life would be to admit he had been mistaken, that he was in the wrong. Thus, rather than stepping down, Moreau advanced further into the limelight: first he became the member of the General Council, and then deputy, even before he had regained his seat as mayor. A possible explanation might be that in comparison with the whole career of the mayor of Auxerre, thirty years of political life which were part of the history of the inhabitants of the town, the Occupation years were simply a more or less unfortunate interlude. Yet it seems to me that the story has a more profound inner meaning. I would like to consider what Moreau meant to the inhabitants of Auxerre, who did not originally choose him, yet who subsequently showed great loyalty towards him, renewing his mandate at every municipal election.

Industrialists and Radicals

We must first of all note that before his nomination in 1940, the future mayor was already well known to his fellow-citizens. Jean Moreau's father worked in Paris as a foreman in a chocolate and confectionery factory; then in 1890 he decided to set up his own business in Auxerre, where he had done his military service. His shop was in the rue du Temple, in the centre of town. Born in Paris in 1887, Jean Moreau went to school first in Auxerre, then transferred to the primary school of Saint-Fargeau, where he took his school leaving certificate and his higher leaving certificate. His intention was to take over the family business, and he served two years' apprenticeship in Provins. By the age of twenty-one, he was a fully fledged journeyman confectioner. He did his military service in an armoured cavalry regiment, and on his return he married and became his father's partner in the business. At the time, Moreau's factory occupied only a modest place amongst the town's businesses. We must not forget that the economic expansion of Auxerre is recent, dating from the end of the nineteenth century. Up to that point, the transportation by river of timber and other goods constituted one of the town's main resources: even today, the existence of the 'docks area' attests to the importance of these river-port activities. These were gradually to diminish because of the decline in the traditional practice of floating logs down the first stretch of the river, and competition from the railways. The other great resource was wine-production: in 1848, there were 1,800 families of wine-growers in the commune. Then came the Phylloxera plague in the 1880s: a whole traditional industry suddenly disappeared with the collapse of Auxerre wine. On the eve of the First World War, the vines had all but vanished from the slopes surrounding the town.

During the same period, however, new types of industry emerged. In 1847 François Guilliet, a cabinet-maker from a peasant family from the Puisaye, set himself up in business in Auxerre as a manufacturer of specialised wood-turning equipment. His success was remarkable. In 1872, Guilliet was employing 30 workers. By 1886 his factory had expanded to produce a wide variety of wood-turning machinery and had moved to new premises on the Bétardeau Quay by the river Yonne; it now employed 220 people. The firm of Guilliet Sons and Company, set up in 1905, was run by two sons of the founder, Paul and Georges Guilliet, and their brother-in-law Ambroise Commergnat: the latter brought as capital his own wheelwright's business, which he continued to run. The eldest Guilliet brother was a sleeping partner, and a fourth son split from his brothers and set up a new factory in Fourchambault. Later, in the inter-war years, it was Georges who became the real head of the business, and he was succeeded by his son, Robert. The firm continued to expand, with an increase in turnover as high as 145 per cent per annum between 1905 and 1914 and a workforce that grew from 250 to 800 people.[6]

For more than half a century, Auxerre lived in the shade of this great enterprise. Traditional industries, particularly the production of ochre, had declined. Other sectors continued and even prospered, such as the manufacture of furniture and other wooden objects, and food production. During the First World War, Guilliet won some very big contracts; the factory produced 75 mm shells, then lathes for turning shells for Renault. The business expanded and increased its work force: in 1925, 2,100 people were employed at Guilliet's, at a time when the majority of firms in Auxerre employed no more than 100. These figures provide an idea of the importance of the firm to the local economy and to the daily life of the inhabitants of Auxerre. We should note, however, that unlike other great provincial industrialists, the Guilliet brothers never attempted to win political office in the town. Their influence was no less real for all that, but it was exercised through members of their management team being on the council, and above all through links of friendship between all the local notables. For example, Paul Guilliet was a close friend of senator Marcel Ribière; it was Ribière who helped the industrialist to win the big government contract during the war for 75 mm shells.

The Guilliets, however, refrained from direct intervention in the arena of local politics, dominated at the beginning of the century by the anti-clerical movement. We have already encountered the Radical Gallot, whose newspaper *L'Yonne* was a staunch defender of the anti-clerical crusade. Another personality from the same political tendency was also to make his mark on the town: Charles Surugue, elected mayor in 1900, quickly acquired an excellent reputation, not only for the vigour with which he served the republican ideology, but also for the urban transformations he brought about. Unlike Ribière, Surugue was not the offspring of a wealthy family; he had risen through the ranks of the Department of Civil Engineering, reaching the grade of borough surveyor. The new mayor of Auxerre saw himself as a great town-planner, and right from the start he proposed a programme of major projects, including a covered market, primary schools, a 'People's Palace', a theatre, a cemetery and improvements to the water supply. The erection of these various buildings helped to alter the face of the town centre: Surugue was particularly proud of his covered market, built along the lines of Les Halles in Paris. The market dominated the Cathedral, even overshadowing its tower; it will come as no surprise to learn that Surugue invited the Prime Minister, Emile Combes, to inaugurate this monument to the secular. Surugue was a Radical and a freemason, and the banquet for 2,000 guests to mark the opening of the market was the high point of his career. The speaker launched a violent attack on the Vatican and 'the enemies of our country' and toasted the democratic traditions of the Yonne, 'a department whose sturdy wine-growers have always shown a proud independence of character and an ardent love of Liberty'. The market is no longer there today, but other public buildings such as the Central Post Office and the Savings Bank are a testimony to the council's interest in planning during the period in question. However, Surugue attracted criticism, and not only from the local bourgeoisie, who resented his rather excessive anti-clericalism. The building works were costly, and that affected local taxes. Criticised by his own council, Surugue was obliged to resign in 1912 after ten years in office.

His successor, Félix Milliaux, was a native of Auxerre, who had risen through the ranks of the prefectoral system. He was a moderate, and for a long time was vice-president of the Prefecture Council. He had already beaten Surugue in a by-election in 1905. He was selected as mayor after a promise not to do any more building, and he stuck to this excessively cautious policy. In any case, the political life of Auxerre continued to be dominated by the figure of the former mayor: Surugue reached the peak of his popularity when he enlisted in 1915 at the age of seventy-six. The 'oldest recruit' was famous all over the country: on his return he won the municipal elections of 1919 with a list composed of Socialists and Radical-Socialists and ran the town until his death two years later. We should note that in the same year Jean Moreau, the chocolate-maker, became a member of the municipal council, forming part of the moderate opposition led by the lawyer Achille Ribain. The prefect of Auxerre remarked that there was a

> total split between the seventeen supporters of M. Surugue and the rest of the councillors, who are his adversaries. Such a situation would be unworthy of remark were it not for the fact that the opposition contains the better type of person among the councillors. Yet M. Surugue may be forced to rely on these adversaries, for his supporters have neither the experience nor the ability to manage a town.[7]

This antagonism must have lessened with time, for on Surugue's death he was succeeded by his adversary Ribain; the majority of the council had therefore rallied to a figure who represented precisely that 'better type of person', who was irresistibly drawn to the right-wing political tendencies represented in the Assembly by the National Bloc.

Ribain and his list got themselves re-elected with no difficulty in 1925. As one of his opponents sadly remarked: 'Auxerre is the only major town in the region to offer the melancholy spectacle of leftist republicans contributing to the formation of a National Bloc.'[8] I wonder whether it is really so astonishing. Ribain's team, like those which came after it, followed moderate policies, and the constant swing from left to right in the political life of Auxerre between the two wars did not greatly affect the situation. I am not referring now to the opinions expressed by the voters, but to the dominant ideology within the ruling elite, as expressed within the municipal council. For in order to understand the evolution of political events in a medium-sized town like Auxerre, one must distinguish, just as I have done for a rural milieu, between political allegiances as evidenced by votes and the existence of a layer of eligible figures which splits into rival networks potentially capable of imposing their candidates in the context of an election. These networks may represent a strong ideological split, in which case the triumph of one tendency represents a real turning-point in the way the town is run. Equally, however, one may be looking at a case of 'antagonism at a remove', as in the present example, where we have on the one hand the local anti-clerical left, the heirs of Surugue, and on the other the heirs of his opponents. The two rival networks in such a case are defined as the respective guardians of the memory of an individual rather than as protagonists in a real conflict. Hence the possibility of some shifts within each camp, the existence of some room for compromise: in these manoeuvres, the personal qualities of the leaders become important. Thus in the 1929 election, Ribain, the outgoing mayor, found himself accused of lacking charisma, of being cold, even of being uninterested in the people whose welfare was in his charge. It was the man who was being criticised, rather than a political strategy or a team. His team was in fact a prolongation of the mixture of Radicals and moderates presided over by Ribain ever since the death of his predecessor. Amongst the newcomers we find Jean Moreau. He succeeded his father, as it were, by joining the municipal council in 1925.

The chocolate manufacturer was now a very changed man. We left him on his return from military service in 1911. His life as a civilian was short, however, for he was called up in 1914, and a year later went into the air force, attached to Farman 14 squadron based in the Vosges, where he carried out numerous reconaissance missions as a pilot. In 1917 he was wounded by three bullets in the arm during combat in the air. He was promoted to Captain, received the Légion d'honneur, and in November of that same year took command of fighter squadron Spa 93, which he led until the end of the war. Moreau performed a number of heroic acts, and even figures in the Epinal prints, popular pictures of the time depicting traditional or inspirational scenes; one of these shows how Moreau and his navigator decided one Sunday in 1916 to fly over Strasbourg and leave a souvenir of their visit. They sent down a tailor's dummy dressed as a French officer and wearing the tricolour sash, which provoked the fury of the German officers occupying the town. After the war, Moreau's reputation was very high. He went back to the family business, which rapidly prospered under his management and expanded to employ over one hundred workers. So he was already an influential figure when Ribain approached him with an offer to sit on the municipal council. At the time, Moreau seems to have been more preoccupied with developing his business.

I had enough to do. But my father and my father-in-law had been councillors under Charles Surugue. As far as they were concerned, it was my duty to follow their example. Ribain kept on at me. The 'siege' lasted a good two months. 'My list is ready', Ribain said to me one day. 'There is just one space left . . . yours.' I gave in, and that was that . . . As I did not want to be assistant mayor, I was appointed delegate at the town hall: I conducted wedding ceremonies and chaired committees for the award of contracts.[9]

Is this just retrospective modesty, or was he really not interested in politics, at least at the time? We might feel that between his business commitments and his passion for flying, Jean Moreau had precious little time left to devote to politics. Nevertheless, the ceremonial role entrusted to the new councillor gave him a splendid opportunity to get to know his fellow-citizens: conducting the wedding-ceremonies has always been a strategic activity in any town hall. If we add that Moreau was appointed chairman of the committee in charge of erecting a monument to Surugue, under the patronage of the President of the Republic and with the sponsorship of personalities such as Poincaré, Herriot, Painlevé, and Bienvenu Martin, we shall have some idea of the position occupied by the chocolate manufacturer in Auxerre society at this time.

These were the years of maximum prosperity for Guilliet's: between 1923 and 1929, exports in constant francs doubled. The end of the war had seen a short period of social confrontation, with a series of strikes and the emergence of a proper trade union movement. The movement faded away after some of the trade union leaders were prosecuted, but the bosses also made certain concessions, foremost amongst them Georges Guilliet, who was running the firm at this time. He set up a welfare programme, opening a hardship fund, workers' allotments for the use of factory employees, and a pension fund. On the cultural side, a brass band was formed, and a concert and dance were arranged every year on the feast-day of Saint Cecilia. Finally, the firm assisted its workers in buying their own homes. Guilliet's decision aroused great interest among other factory-owners in Auxerre: Moreau's set up a hardship fund in 1920, and a system of family allowances a year later; it provided houses for its workers in 1925, allotments in the following year, and a pension fund in 1928. Jean Moreau was thus in his way a representative of an industrial elite whose paternalistic management produced a high degree of social cohesion, banishing the spectre of class conflict. The ideas which prevailed among local entrepreneurs can be glimpsed in a speech made by Monseigneur Deschamps on the occasion of the centenary of the founding of Guilliet's in 1948:

> The head gives the orders, and the limbs obey. Yet there must always be a bond of benevolent authority which presupposes the notion of justice on one side and active gratitude on the other. An industrial worker is not a machine; he is a partner in the common task and in the common achievement. He will be a willing artisan if he feels he is understood and regarded with affection. The boss must be the boss, but not an autocrat, or an anonymous figure with no sense of his responsibilities.[10]

The middle way: from the Popular Front to Vichy

When Ribain sought a fresh mandate in 1929, Jean Moreau, who seems to have acquired a taste for municipal affairs, was on his list. But this time they found themselves facing a formidable rival. This was in fact an outsider who had been elected as member of the General Council in 1926, and deputy two years later: Jean-Michel Renaitour, a Parisian who owned a house in his canton of Seignelay. Like Jean Moreau, he had made a name for himself in the air force during the war. He was a professional journalist and writer who in 1923 won the national prize for literature with his novel *L'Enfant chaste*. He was thus a prominent figure, with a brilliant and attractive personality which captivated the voters. He had the support of the opponents of the outgoing mayor, though he was standing as an Independent Socialist. On first arriving in the department, he had stood in the general election of 1924 as an SFIO candidate. Beaten on that occasion, he thereafter plumped for the more anodyne Independent Socialist label. Following a campaign based around criticism of the mundane figure presented by the outgoing mayor, the newcomer won with ease. 'Predictably, the list opposing the majority on the outgoing council benefited from the undoubted personal popularity of the man at its head, M. Renaitour, and though composed of the most varied elements, it won by a larger margin than even the most optimistic estimates had forecast . . . The municipal council of Auxerre, formerly in the hands of leftist republicans, has thus gone to the Socialist Republicans', the prefect noted.[11] We may wonder whether the nuance implied any great changes in policy. Certainly Renaitour, unlike Surugue, refrained from any ambitious programme of public works. Like his immediate predecessors, the new mayor remained cautious in matters of spending. Of course, the 1929 crash had damaged several firms, particularly Guilliet's: not only did it lose a large number of its foreign customers, but it suffered from competition because it was slow to modernise, whereas other manufacturers of machine-tools had been gradually replacing steam power with electricity.

As its losses grew, from 1930 onwards, Guilliet's began to lay off large numbers of workers. The council showed its solidarity with the unemployed by a series of measures. A municipal unemployment fund and a food distribution office were set up in 1931, and in 1934 the mayor took out a loan in order to meet the ever-growing demand for welfare services. This policy of solidarity was welcomed by the population, and in the 1935 municipal elections, the outgoing team was returned to power; Renaitour wore the colours of the Popular Front this time, and Jean Moreau headed the opposing list. At the first ballot, the results for the outgoing mayor were less good than predicted. 'In Auxerre, M. Renaitour, the deputy and mayor, whose opponents have long feared to stand against him, had difficulty getting his list elected. The moderates were only beaten by forty votes. M. Renaitour benefited from the withdrawal of the Communist list, and therefore only kept his office thanks to the common front.'[12]

This support from the left was very useful, for at the second ballot, in defiance of the forecasts, the opposition candidates failed to take a single seat. 'I believed like everyone else', wrote the prefect,

> that four or five candidates from Moreau's list would be elected last Sunday, but it did not happen. The Moreau list, which started out well, two weeks ago, made the mistake of letting Renaitour patch up a joint list; M. Moreau was also wrong to hold only one public meeting, and he was beaten in all the hamlets of Auxerre, where Renaitour made a big effort and Moreau did not stir himself at all.[13]

At the second ballot, the Unified Antifascist Action list had withdrawn in favour of the Renaitour list, which won by a narrow margin (2,206 votes to Moreau's 2,166). The latter registered a protest with the prefecture immediately after the election, complaining of a last-minute trick on the eve of the election: 'The Renaitour list pasted over their billboards a notice reading: *Members of the Associations Camelots du Roy and Croix de Feu of Auxerre, vote for the Jean Moreau list! Signed: The Candidates.*' Moreau complained that this had created a false impression, 'deliberately reinforced the next morning by an article in the *Petit régional* [organ of the Renaitour list], with the headline: *Electoral incidents in Auxerre* and published on the very day of the vote'.[14] The Interdepartmental Prefectural Council in Dijon, to whom the affair was submitted, finally annulled the ballot: a new vote was taken in July, but again none of the Moreau list candidates was returned.

Renaitour's authority was reinforced by the incident. The Communists' gesture of support did not lead to any real 'leftist turn' in council policy. When the big strikes started in June 1936, the council showed its solidarity with the strikers in several ways: provision of meals, a canteen for schoolchildren, and material help in the form of bread and other foodstuffs. The strikes had wide support in the Guilliet factories. Renaitour, however, devoted himself to mediating between the management and the trade union representatives. Work began again at the end of June, after a certain number of concessions had been won from the management, but Guilliet's still continued to lay men off, for the firm had not managed to overcome its problems in the machine-tool market. By 1939, the number of employees had fallen to 650. Politically speaking, the town council, while demonstrating solidarity with the strikers, had been careful not to alienate local manufacturers: Renaitour remained faithful to the middle way he had stood for since his entry into the town hall. On 10 June 1940, he was one of the 569 Socialist deputies and senators to vote plenary powers to Marshal Pétain. A new municipal council was appointed by a ministerial order of 19 March the following year. Renaitour was returned to office, as were 11 members of the former council: 10 new councillors were added, among them Jean Moreau.

The council now consisted in part of yesterday's enemies. Renaitour had kept his main supporters, but Moreau's friends were also strongly represented. At the first session of the council, Renaitour declared that the new assembly, appointed in response to suggestions from the prefect, constituted a 'true coalition, such as the present circumstances demand'. Jean Moreau proposed the following motion:

The municipal council of Auxerre, in this its initial session, in the year 1940, wishes to express its profound respect for Marshal Pétain, head of the French State. It promises to set aside all petty quarrels and devote itself entirely to the service of the town. In tranquillity and endeavour, it believes it is obeying the will of the head of State, and contributing to the recovery of a France united and confident of its future.[15]

The motion was passed unanimously. Unity and reconciliation under the auspices of Marshal Pétain: such were the aspirations of the time. A motion dated 3 July 1941 is worth quoting:

In response to a report from M. Henri Moreau, first assistant mayor, the council unanimously agrees to contribute the sum of forty francs to the proposed gifts for Marshal Pétain and Admiral Darlan, who are soon to visit Auxerre. These souvenirs will be offered as a sign of our great respect for Marshall Pétain and the Admiral as representatives of the government.[16]

Renaitour was absent that day, but the allocation from an item in the budget known as the 'contingency fund' was proposed by one of his faithful followers. The mayor was living in Paris, where he ran a theatre; he had just published a new novel, *Les Compagnons du héros*, in which the main character was no less a personage than Simon Bolivar. The epigraph was a quotation from Marmontel: 'It has too much truth for a novel and not enough for a history.' Meanwhile, however, History was pressing on all sides, and Renaitour decided to resign. Jean Moreau was chosen to replace him, with the approval of the German authorities, and was formally installed in office by the prefect, M. Bourgeois, on 23 August. A prefectoral order dissolved the council on 27 September 1941, on the grounds that the majority of councillors had resigned, and set up a small group of ten people, chaired by Jean Moreau and containing local dignitaries such as Berthier, the President of the Tribunal of Commerce, Martinaud, the President of the Chamber of Commerce, Sarrazin, a doctor, and Bouquigny, a former member of the General Council. This list was extended in 1943 when a new order of the prefect set up a more substantial municipal council, containing not only the individuals already mentioned, but also a retired headmaster and headmistress, one of the managers of an ochre-manufacturing plant in Auxerre and an engineer from the School of Applied Arts and Crafts who was in charge of the workshops at Guilliet's.

'Independence' and legitimacy

The first concern of the mayor was to obtain food and energy supplies for his fellow-citizens. He could often be seen in the market-place at the crack of dawn, trying to prevent the hijacking or excessive requisitioning of food. Moreau's shop in the rue du Temple was well known to local housewives, and he was respected for his past military glory and for his strictness during these times of deprivation. Throughout this whole period, Moreau refused all invitations, however pressing, to participate in any form of collaborationist activity. In 1943, the newspaper *Le Cri du peuple* denounced him for 'sitting on the fence' because he had refused to take the chair at a meeting of the Legion of French Volunteers Against Bolshevism. *Révolution nationale* accused him of having proposed a toast before a statue representing the French Republic, though it admitted there was a photo of Marshal Pétain on the wall above the statue: 'Careless habits', the headline read. More seriously, the mayor, who had offered no objections to a change of name for rue Henri-Barbusse, rue Ferdinand-Buisson and Place Salengro, flatly refused to drop the names rue de la Liberté, rue de la Fraternité and quai de la République. Again, when the Germans declared their intention of melting down the statue of Paul Bert for its metal, Moreau stoutly opposed the move, and was successful in halting it.[17]

Whatever his disagreements with the occupying authorities, the mayor of Auxerre seems never to have entertained the idea of renouncing his functions. His enemies would subsequently claim that he gave his support all those years to the collaborationist policies of the Vichy government. *Le Travailleur*, a paper published by the Communist Party, also denounced at the time the friendly attitude displayed by German officers towards Moreau and his family. It must be admitted that although Moreau insisted he did not mix administration with politics, his acceptance of the post of mayor in the company of the principal candidates rejected by the voters in the 1935 elections looks very like an act of revenge. An electioneering pamphlet published by the Socialists and the Communists for the cantonal elections of 1945 contains extracts from two letters dated 4 and 7 July 1941.[18] The first is from Jean Moreau to the prefect, asking the official, in the event of Moreau's selection as mayor, to 'dissolve the council, for I must have full authority, and form a new council along lines which I will draw up for your agreement. The municipal council will thus be a board of management and will be in a position to respond to the directives of the head of the French State with efficiency and independence.' The second letter is also addressed to the prefect, this time by Richelmann, an adviser to the German *Feldkommandant*: 'According to my observations, the first assistant mayor, M. Henri Moreau, would not be suitable to manage the town of Auxerre for a prolonged period . . . As I mentioned to you in conversation, M. Jean Moreau does seem to me to have all the required qualities for such a post.' It is obvious that Jean Moreau did not wish his former opponents to remain on the council, and the occupying forces were also anxious to be rid of Renaitour and his followers. In any case the notion of turning the municipal council into an 'independent' board of management was one that Moreau had been nursing for some time. Moreover, this idea of an 'apolitical' management policy for the town was one he shared with other manufacturers, who had been his supporters for many years.

From the point of view of the industrialists of Auxerre, Moreau represented an alternative to Renaitour. It is true that they had come to accept the latter's policies, for he had been conciliatory towards the local bourgeoisie and willing to compromise. The 'national union' council, of which both men were members had not displeased them. However, making Moreau sole captain of the ship was not seen as a radical change, but simply as putting a strong hand at the helm in stormy times. In short, Moreau was a reassuring presence. Moreover, the Occupation years, far from tarnishing him in the eyes of his fellow-citizens, were to confirm his image as the real 'leader' of the town. For Auxerre, as a middle-of-the-road town, always sought a consensus; it had known outbreaks of class struggle, but the trade union leadership, always a minority, had been decimated at the end of every episode. Guilliet's welfare policies, the cooperatives, the allotments, the chemist's shop and the brass band had also helped to calm these outbreaks of fever. In 1942–3, members of the Resistance were an isolated group; people were more concerned with the hardship caused by rationing. 'Old man Moreau' could help there; an efficient administrator is exactly what you need in times like that! Later, when the Resistance began to spread and underground Maquis were formed in the area, Moreau was to be found making contact with some of their representatives. Finally, in June 1944, thirty-two inhabitants from several communes of the Yonne were arrested and taken off to Dijon as hostages, amongst them the mayor of Auxerre. He refused any favourable treatment, and in the end obtained the release of all his companions.

The mayor's willingness to die with the other hostages as a point of honour has gone down in the annals of the town, to the point of eclipsing other aspects of his behaviour during those dark years. Significantly, a tribute published by *L'Yonne républicaine* (a paper issuing from the Resistance, as its sub-title reminds readers) summarises this period of Moreau's life in a few lines: 'Jean Moreau replaced [Renaitour] as mayor in '41, which led to his arrest in June '44 and detention as a hostage in the Krier barracks in Dijon.'[19] This cryptic summary accords quite faithfully with the view the people of Auxerre have today of their former mayor. Taken as a whole, and I am including here members of the Resistance who were also his political opponents after the war, people thought Moreau had shown great devotion to his town. Renaitour's resignation in 1941, attributed to personal motives, was not greatly appreciated; after the war he continued to sit on the General Council, representing the canton of Seignelay, but he never tried his luck again at the town hall of Auxerre.

As we saw, the prefect found this situation almost incomprehensible. Logically, the mayor of Auxerre should have disappeared from public life in the political upheaval which followed the Liberation. But that view ignores the weight of local circumstances. Many residents of Auxerre voted for the mayor in 1945 for two reasons: first of all, he had kept his word – he had run things in such a way that no one group suffered more than another; secondly, he had responded to events as they unfolded. Many others had observed the same principles of caution and pragmatism, for we are all capable of a high level of ambivalence: and Moreau had the added bonus that he had acted courageously as the leader of the hostages. Paradoxical as it may seem, Moreau's choice of Pétain helped to consolidate his legitimacy. Before that, his exploits as a pilot had won him fame, and he belonged to the Auxerre elite, yet politically he had not managed to make a name for himself: heading a list in the 1935 elections, he had not even led an effective campaign, though the situation was by no means unfavourable to him. When his room for manoeuvre was severely curtailed, however, he did achieve a certain political solidity by convincing his fellow-citizens of his 'independence'. It was independence vis-à-vis the German authorities first of all: a very relative concept, expressed mainly in symbolic gestures, such as saving the statue of Paul Bert. It was political independence also, and here the key word was 'management', suggesting a rejection of overt political affiliations. This kind of independence was appropriate to a town which still had one foot in the last century, and whose economy was mainly self-sufficient, founded on the success of a few family businesses. The disapproval which greeted the verdict of the Honour Jury was a faithful reflection of a local society jealous of its prerogatives and unwilling to accept that Parisians should set themselves up as judges of its native sons.

It will come as no surprise to learn that Jean Moreau, comforted by the votes of the inhabitants of Auxerre, soon registered as a candidate to the General Council. The edict of 13 September had lifted ineligibility from former members of the departmental councils, and Moreau was thus free to stand. Three weeks later, he was elected to the General Council to represent the canton of Auxerre-Ouest, and there he was to remain until 1958. In October, general elections were held to form a Constituent Assembly: Moreau was again a candidate, heading a Republican and Social Action List in opposition to the SFIO and the PCF. This time he was committed to a political line, whereas hitherto he had always stood as an administrator. It was certainly a turning-point in his career, for until then he had only been involved in the world of local politics. He may have been merely following a personal ambition, or perhaps there was some desire for revenge for his exclusion from the town hall. However, while not underestimating the force of these motives, it is possible to offer a different explanation, one that takes account of Moreau's involvement in the world of local politics.

I have already mentioned that Moreau was a member of the Auxerre bourgeoisie, whose interests he had, as it were, come to represent in the running of local affairs. The economic recovery of Auxerre and the task of reconstruction constituted a formidable challenge for the great manufacturing families who still held the reins of the economy in the town. Jean Moreau shared their concerns; Guilliet and his other friends considered that he was capable of performing a political role in the capital, or at the very least acting as intermediary between the world of Paris and that of Auxerre. A successor to Renaitour had to be found, and Moreau seemed to be the man they were looking for. Moreover, he occupied what was seen as a strategic position within a larger formation. We must take into account the departmental network, the system of friendships linking people from very different social backgrounds which had grown up around the figure of Pierre-Etienne Flandin. We have already examined its wide-ranging influence. Events after 1939 had to some extent upset this network by destroying promising careers, amongst them that of the former Prime Minister. At the end of the war, as we saw, he was declared ineligible for public office. Yet he continued to take a close interest in the political affairs of the Yonne. For example, he tried to ensure continuity by encouraging new right-wing candidates who seemed likely to win votes. Flandin sent a messenger to Moreau, who had been part of his network for many years. His insistence was a major factor in Moreau's decision. Flandin, from the wings, was to some extent the new deputy's godfather.

Such were the initial stages of a successful career, for Moreau was to remain a member of the Assembly until 1958. He sat on the National Defence Committee and was vice-president of the Finance Committee. He obtained his first portfolio in 1947, as Under-Secretary of State for Industry and Commerce in the Robert Schumann cabinet. That government was voted out in autumn 1948, but Schumann's successor, Henri Queuille, made him Secretary of State for the Air Armed Forces. In other words, Moreau returned to his first love: he was 'the right man in the right place', as *L'Eclaireur de l'Yonne* wrote in its profile of Moreau, 'a pilot with three thousand hours of flying under his belt, rapporteur of the budget for Air Defence, founder of the Flying Club of the Yonne'.[20] In 1947 he became mayor of Auxerre again. The town held a great celebration at the centenary of the firm of Guilliet on 17 April 1948. The last of the line, Robert Guilliet, had died six years earlier in an accident, and Jean Commergnat, a grandson of the founder, was now in charge of the business. It seemed to have found its second wind after the Liberation, and now had a thousand workers again. The whole of Auxerre turned out for the centenary celebrations. Nothing was skimped: there was a mass in the Cathedral, with the great organ playing, and fanfares of trumpets. The employees donated two sculpted panels, depicting François and Robert Guilliet. A banquet was laid on for more than a thousand guests, with representatives from all over

France and the principal countries of Europe. The under-Secretary of State for Industry and Commerce, in other words Jean Moreau himself, entered to the sound of the Marseillaise. A great ball in the evening brought the festivities to a close.

The sociologists who were studying Auxerre as an example of a medium-sized French town in 1950 noted that the town had experienced a slower rate of economic development than the rest of France during the two preceding decades. They also observed that a large number of residents were suffering a housing crisis caused by the age of the housing stock and the lack of expansion outside the traditional city centre. Another worry for the authorities was an inadequate water supply. Indeed, for many years after the publication of the book, living conditions continued to be a matter of real concern for the authorities. Moreau and his team returned to office in 1947, at a time when the whole country was being rebuilt, and was experiencing an unprecedented economic boom: was Auxerre to ignore these developments, or should it go for modernisation? These were the alternatives. Thanks to his position in the government, the mayor was able to obtain a subsidy to build 400 new dwellings at the beginning of the fifties. His efforts continued and greatly expanded in the early sixties; by the time Moreau retired in 1971, 7,300 homes had been built, and Auxerre had an Urban Expansion Zone where large numbers of council flats were thrown up without too much attention being paid to the environment.

So far as industry was concerned, caution was the order of the day. The town council was still closely linked to Guilliet's; one of Moreau's principal assistant mayors was an engineer from the School of Applied Arts and Crafts in charge of production at the factory. The first assistant mayor, Mlle Hérold, was the daughter of a family of prominent local manufacturers. The councillors displayed no great urge to attract new industries to Auxerre. Some people said they were afraid such a move would bring a wages explosion which would harm their businesses. However, Guilliet's never recovered its former dynamism, and in the end the council took advantage of the policy of industrial dispersal to attract several new firms to Auxerre. The largest was Fruehauf–France, which moved there in 1957 and created about a thousand jobs. However, it met with resentment from Guilliet's, which had the sale of some land to Fruehauf cancelled. In the lawsuit that followed, one of the lawyers asked a question which faithfully translates the sentiments of the old local bourgeoisie: 'What is this firm that it feels the need, like M. Pierre Mendès France, to add the name of the country to its own name in order to feel French?'[21] Guilliet lost the lawsuit, and after Fruehauf other smaller firms moved into Auxerre, whose population doubled, though it never became the industrial centre to which it might have laid claim on the grounds of its geographical location. The end of Moreau's mayorship coincided with the collapse of Guilliet's.

Unlike the machine-manufacturers, however, the mayor of Auxerre always retained his popularity. Children liked the confectionery he manufactured, and Moreau gradually became a patriarchal figure who guided the destinies of the city. His ministerial career was not interrupted by Queuille's resignation, for he returned to power shortly afterwards under his great friend Pinay, mayor of Saint-Chamond. There were many similarities between the two men, such as their preference for 'management' as opposed to politics, their attachment to the province, their loyalty to the moderate position, their support for Pétain and of course their religion: control of public spending. Moreau was one of Pinay's closest colleagues, as Secretary of State for the Budget. Pierre-Etienne Flandin, another friend of the Prime Minister, was also an adviser, but an unofficial one. When in turn Pinay was ousted, Moreau kept his position as Minister in the cabinet formed by René Mayer, which was to last for six months, until June 1953. Moreau was never a Minister again after that; he was approached by Pflimlin in 1958, when the Fourth Republic was in its death throes, but on the advice of Antoine Pinay he declined the offer.

During all these years, he remained above all a local notable. He was president of the General Council, but devoted most of his energy to the town. As a spry seventy-year-old, Moreau lived in the boulevard Vauban, where the best Auxerre families are to be found. 'He used to run around all over Auxerre in his old Peugeot', one of the present-day councillors told me. 'We also used to meet him in the street sometimes, and my grandfather was proud to shake his hand. For me, Moreau was the classic grandfather-figure.' In 1954, a great ceremony was held to celebrate the award to Moreau of the rank of *grand-officier* of the Légion d'honneur. Marshal Juin came in person to pin the medal on his chest. Auxerre put out the flags, and all the local notables were present. Juin used the occasion to deliver a violent attack on the government's European policy.

Only one great figure was refused a welcome in Auxerre during Moreau's time: General de Gaulle. The leader of the RPR was refused access to the town hall, where he had hoped to make a speech, and had to withdraw to the small neighbouring commune of Monéteau. This was in 1947, admittedly, when memories of the Occupation were still fresh. Moreau never converted to Gaullism, and the Gaullists got their own back. In the general elections of 1958, after the General's return to power, Moreau stood against a candidate from the Union pour la nouvelle république and lost his seat in the National Assembly. In his fury at this desertion by the voters, Moreau renounced his two mandates as mayor and member of the General Council. He never returned to the General Council, but his withdrawal from the town council did not last long. A month later, in the 1959 municipal elections, he stood again and easily recovered the office of mayor, which did not prevent him from being beaten again three years later in the general election by the UNR candidate, a lawyer named Lemarchand. The latter made an unsuccessful attempt at becoming mayor of Auxerre in 1965, advocating a bolder style of management. Once again, Moreau was equal to the challenge, and then later Lemarchand was implicated in the Ben-Barka affair and faded from the political scene. The mayor of Auxerre served one more term, but decided not to stand in the municipal elections of 1971, by which time he was eighty-three years old. He died the following year.

There was a big change, of course, at the beginning of the seventies. In the previous thirty years, Auxerre's appearance had altered, because of the rapid growth in population, the rise of the tertiary sector, the emergence of new districts on the outskirts of the town and changes in lifestyle. What effect did these changes have on political life? The answer is a complex one.

Not such a drama after all

Auxerre, 4 July 1988

There is major excitment at the town hall, though it is just an ordinary council session. I have to fight my way through the crowd. It is impossible to get into the large room on the first floor where the council sits; the public benches are full. There is a big crowd of us squeezed into the doorway. The reason for this sudden interest is not on the agenda. All it mentions are debates on various items of public works: open spaces in the Sainte-Geneviève district or plans for a bowling-pitch hardly seem to justify such intense curiosity! No, the secret lies elsewhere: the fact is that the mayor has just been made a Minister in the Rocard government. Soisson has become a symbol of the *rapprochement* between the Socialists and the centre-right: the ex-colleague of Giscard, now one of Raymond Barre's supporters, has been offered a key post, which one would have thought reserved for a Socialist, the Ministry of Labour, Employment and Training. Up to now, things have been very clear in Auxerre; the mayor headed a right-wing list with assistant mayors from the UDF and the RPR. Yet here he is, just a year after the municipal elections, joining Mitterrand's government. The town is hitting the headlines. Is what we are seeing the breakdown of the old allegiances? Is Auxerre to be the testing-ground for future Socialo-Centrist coalitions?

In calling this emergency meeting of the council Jean-Pierre Soisson is offering a platform for the different political parties to comment on his move. Obviously, everyone is waiting to see the reaction from the RPR and the Socialists. To the RPR, which had supported Soisson shortly before, at the early general election, the mayor's decision may seem like a betrayal. Some of the local Socialists, on the other hand, have expressed their displeasure at seeing yesterday's adversary suddenly shot to power in the name of the new policy. Soisson opens by calling on one of his assistant mayors, who is also departmental secretary of the RPR, to speak. Everyone waits with bated breath to see if he will disown the mayor. The speaker mentions the heavy responsibility Soisson has accepted, and criticises 'solutions that try to glaze over vital differences'. The tone of the speech is somewhat harsh, but the summing up dispels anxiety. The RPR has in fact decided to stay faithful to its ally, while remaining ever-vigilant. The spokesman for the Socialist Party is none other than Bonhenry, Soisson's old adversary. His tone is moderate: basically, the Socialists hope to work more closely with the mayor, while retaining the freedom to criticise. Will they in fact form a joint team in the future, as the Communist councillor affirms when it is his turn to speak? Impossible to say, for the moment.

Suddenly an RPR councillor rises from his seat; he goes over to Soisson and presents him with a bouquet of red roses, on the occasion, as he puts it, of the mayor's engagement to Bonhenry. Laughter all round, and the tension in the air disappears. So we are all going to be able to get on . . . like one big, happy family! After a short response from the new Minister, clarifying his position and stating that he rejects the sterile confrontation between left and right and wishes to avoid tension and distrust, the session continues in a very relaxed fashion. Many of the proposals are passed unanimously. 'Where Jean-Pierre leads they follow', I hear someone comment at the reception which closes this memorable session. Certainly everyone except the Communist councillor seems to be under the spell of his charm. 'The storm did not break', wrote *L'Yonne républicaine* the next day. In fact, at the end of the session Soisson felt able to thank his councillors for coming and voting on such important plans. *Rapprochement* seemed to be working . . .

The scene I have just described is no doubt only the first phase of a subtle game which will be played out against the background of the great national shake-up begun by the election of President Mitterrand Mark II. Funny how things work out! The mayor of Auxerre had spent his whole career as leader of the right wing in Burgundy and the Yonne. Soisson was one of the young Turks urged on initially by President Pompidou and later to become the household cavalry of Giscard d'Estaing, like his friends Stirn and Stasi, with whom he wrote a criticism of the joint programme of the left in 1973: *Le Piège (The Trap)* warned of the dangers of the alliance between the Socialists and the Communists and the threat of a popular democracy. Soisson was a brilliant Secretary of State for the Universities at the beginning of Giscard's presidency, and won a reputation at the time for being open-minded. This did not necessarily endear him to all. When Raymond Barre succeeded Jacques Chirac, Soisson was replaced by Alice Saunier-Seité, while he went to the Ministry of Training. He earned a reputation there as an expert on employment issues. At the end of Giscard's presidency he was Minister for Youth and Sport. He had previously served as General Secretary of the Republican Party, which replaced the Independent Republicans in 1977: when his ministerial career ended, Soisson was under forty-five years old, with wide experience in the labyrinths of politics.

He was close to Giscard from the time of his first presidential campaign, and remained loyal to him; he was in the front line of the difficult struggle of 1978 in which the left was finally beaten; in other words, he had always stuck to the 'right' side, which made it all the more surprising when ten years later he popped up in the middle of the Socialists. Commentators have mentioned his personal friendship with Michel Rocard, but in this case anecdote is no substitute for analysis. Like all true politicians, Soisson is a complex figure. According to some, his membership of the Mitterrand team simply demonstrated the opportunism of a man taking advantage of the circumstances to return to prominence, with no thought for the principles on which he was elected. Others did not question his integrity, but felt he acted on impulse, without any long-term plan. Whether he was an opportunist, or merely overimpulsive, one thing is certain: many of his colleagues were secretly hoping he would come a cropper.

Soisson's case can be seen differently from an anthropological viewpoint. We must first of all listen to his discourse as he addresses different audiences, and try to grasp through it all the elements of a coherent pattern. Secondly, we must avoid the modern tendency to compartmentalise political behaviour. This tendency leads commentators to give pride of place to the 'national' stance adopted by a politician, then to attempt to evaluate the local 'repercussions' of that stance. I myself consider it vital to approach the problem from precisely the opposite direction and show that local factors are not just a reflection of national politics, but in fact shape a politician and determine the parameters within which he can operate; they determine his individual destiny and explain why at a particular moment he may be better placed than someone else to make an original contribution on the larger political stage.

Understanding the particular circumstances of this case is the key to fathoming the secrets of a very particular section of the population – what we might call the tribe of professional politicians, whose rituals and codes we are beginning to appreciate. The council session reported above is a good starting-point for an analysis of this kind. From the point of view of an external observer, it had one very odd characteristic: a man was leading the debate in the name of one political majority when he had just gone over to another. All the political parties had gathered, in the sacred spot represented by the town hall, to take a public stance on his change of direction. The other strange thing about the meeting was that the speeches were entirely self-contained, as though it were vital they should have no immediate practical consequences. The meeting had opened in an atmosphere of uncertainty and some tension; after the exchange of speeches and the presentation of the bouquet of roses, we were back on the old footing of partners practised in the respective roles of majority and opposition.

By the end of the parley, there was a return to the basic characteristics of local politics, familiarity and complicity, as demonstrated by various signals. For example, in the course of the debate on a particular project, an assistant mayor mentioned the rue des Tanneries, and that gave rise to some discussion: anyone who really knew Auxerre would know he had meant the rue des Tanneurs; actually there was also a rue des Tanneries; true, but it was hardly likely . . . and so on, with everyone putting their oar in. When the session was over, the comments flew thick and fast: 'Auxerre is the testing-ground for the policy of *rapprochement*', somebody said in the corridor. It was quite clear that 'the boss' was still in control. Far from resenting this fact, the participants seemed reassured that there was to be no breakdown in relations: the spectre of disorder had been exorcised. Taking it all in all, it was probably not such a bad thing for the man who held the reins of power in the town to be singled out by the government to the extent of being offered an important ministry; speculation began about who would be in his team of advisers, and some names of officials who had shown promise in the town were cited; complicity had given way to curiosity.

Heir to a name

The preceding observations provide some insight into the part played by our deputy and mayor in local political life. When Jean Moreau's time finally drew to a close, the choice of a young man anxious to bring new energies to running the town was seen as the sign of a profound change. After the long reign of a member of the old industrial bourgeoisie that had reached its height half a century before, the accession of Jean-Pierre Soisson seemed to mark a turning-point. Certainly the new mayor's style was very different from that of his predecessor. When he announced his candidature, Soisson emphasised the fact that he was only thirty-six years old, that he was a graduate of the prestigious Ecole nationale d'administration, where he was the best student of his year in political science, and that he had been an auditor at the Public Accounting Office. It was not his first campaign in Auxerre, for he had tried his luck at the general election in 1967, when, as we saw, he was beaten by Périllier, the FGDS candidate who was also at the Public Accounting Office. 'I have to admit it was a dreadful campaign – far too intellectual', Soisson told me. 'After my defeat, I went to see Périllier.

"My dear friend" he told me, "you have a great deal to learn." "My dear colleague", I replied, for this is how we address each other at the Public Accounting Office, "I will study your campaign." I studied his campaign, and the next year I beat him.'[22]

The next year, of course, was 1968. This election, which marked the lowest point in the fortunes of the left, was an unexpected stroke of luck for Soisson: he was a representative of the establishment, not of progressive ideas. He was a member of the group of Independent Republicans which broke away from Antoine Pinay's Independents and Peasants in 1962, when those who favoured the Gaullist position on Algeria and a number of other issues regrouped around Giscard d'Estaing. So at the start of his career, the future mayor of Auxerre represented the continuation of his predecessor's line. It is true that Moreau remained faithful to Pinay, and in fact when Soisson stood for the first time in a general election, the former mayor openly opposed him. Not only did he stand at the first round in the CNIP list, but when he was beaten by Soisson he did not withdraw in favour of his young rival, but simply stood down, which was a help to Périllier. Apart from these ups and downs, it is important to note that although he was the candidate of the presidential majority, Soisson chose not to stand under the colours of Gaullism. He was a member at the time of Edgar Faure's team, and defined himself as a supporter of Pompidou. The Prime Minister asked him if he wanted the nomination of the Union des démocrates pour la République, and when he declined it, advised him to join the Independent Republicans. That was where Soisson got to know Giscard.

Soisson's decisions were dictated above all by local considerations. Gaullism has never been popular in Auxerre, nor indeed has the Christian-Democrat current which gained such strength in the post-war period. Soisson was a native of Auxerre: he knew it inside out, and knew that the Pompidou line could only be successful if presented as a prolongation of the moderate tendency. His move to the Giscard Independents was the result, therefore, not only of a deliberate strategy, but of his personal background. 'Jean-Pierre,' as he is familiarly known in Auxerre, is the son of a well-known family. His father was president of the Chamber of Commerce, and more importantly, Soisson and James (from the name of a partner) was for a long time the biggest department store in Auxerre.

The Soissons have deep roots in the Avallonnais; in the nineteenth century, a member of this peasant family settled in Auxerre, where he was employed by M. Laurent-Lesseré, who had a department store in the town. The newcomer quickly showed an aptitude for business, and on the death of his employer took over the firm and expanded it. One of his three sons, Henri, born in 1872, also showed strong business acumen. His father sent him to study commerce in Paris, and, unusually for the time, to England to study the language, which he considered indispensable. From the beginning of the century until his death in 1949, Henri ran the business, which now comprised not only a large department store in the centre of the quartier de l'Horloge district, but also a wholesale supplier specialising in industrial clothing, and of course some workshops. At that time they were the biggest suppliers of woollen cloth, garments and similar merchandise in Auxerre. Henri Soisson, who had married the daughter of the owner of a well-known store in Dijon, Le Pauvre Diable, was famous for his courtesy and for the pleasant atmosphere which prevailed in his establishment.

Soisson was a well-known local figure; he had a house in the best district, and like Moreau, was a member of Auxerre society. Unlike the Guilliets, who had gradually distanced themselves from their modest beginnings, Soisson was to remain a popular figure throughout his life. For one thing, his business was not too large; moreover, he was essentially a merchant whose activity brought him into daily contact with his customers. So far as his employees were concerned, Henri Soisson was an enlightened employer who set up a system of social security and pensions for them. He also founded the Family Hearth, a credit organisation aimed at enabling workers and shop staff to buy their own homes. He was an open-minded man, passionately interested in social issues all his life. 'He was a man of the centre' is his daughter's verdict today. His children were all sent to the local *lycée*, but politically he remained faithful to the moderate tendency; one of his friends from the time of their military service together was Professor Larby, a famous heart-specialist, who was a convinced Radical, and whose father had been senator for the Yonne under the banner of anti-clericalism. They argued from time to time, Soisson accusing Larby of being an extremist, but it did not prevent them from being the best of friends.

The Soisson business was flourishing, when in 1940 the shop accidentally caught fire. Henri's son, who had also studied commerce in Paris, had been made a partner, and it was he who now had to face the financial difficulties occasioned by the fire. In the fifties, the Printemps chain took over the store, which had been rebuilt on the same spot. Shortly afterwards, the workrooms had to close down. Today the famous sign 'Soisson and James' has been replaced by that of Printemps, but many of the older residents of Auxerre still call the store by the name of its founders.

Jean-Pierre is Henri's grandson, and was no doubt influenced by his grandfather; but after school he departed from the family tradition. His father had been senator for the Yonne under the banner of anti-clericalism. They argued from time to time, Soisson accusing Larby of being an extremist, but it did not prevent them from being the best of friends.

> I have never regretted my break with our family's business tradition. My mother is from a Provence family, and my grandfather and great-grandfather and my uncles on her side were all naval officers. I too wanted to serve my country. I wanted to be a

prefect. My model was Louis XIV's intendant, Colbert, who incidentally had an estate not far from here, at Seignelay.[23]

Soisson defines his grandfather as a Radical, but one devoid of anti-clerical fervour. He saw himself as in the same line, or so he told me on one occasion when he was still a member of the opposition and was getting ready to set up the presidential campaign as a supporter of Raymond Barre.

Neither the grandfather nor the father of the present-day mayor of Auxerre ever stood for local political office. His aunt, however, was a member of Jean Moreau's team during his last term and has always been interested in social issues. She now runs the welfare bureau for the commune of Toucy. One could describe the Soissons as influential members of Auxerre society. This was in a way the mantle inherited by Jean-Pierre when he emerged on to the political scene in the department. The name Soisson was already a symbol: 'The most Parisian of all Auxerre's stores. Everything for all the family', their advertisement read. Everyone had shopped at some time or another at Soisson and James. Moreover, they had a reputation for honest trading and quality in the service of several generations. Even before he began his campaign, the young man bore the mark of eligibility. What about networks? In 1967, fresh from the offices of Ministers to whom he had been an adviser in Paris, he was without the advantage of the network of relationships essential to his success. In fact, he came up against a formidable obstacle: Moreau, who, as we saw, was advised by people close to him not to stand down. His attitude produced a sort of general paralysis, certain members of the moderate network being reluctant to betray the former mayor, and others waiting to observe the conduct of the new candidate.

The constituency of Auxerre covers not only the town, but also a considerable rural area, including the Puisaye. Soisson could not therefore rely on the votes of the town alone. If he wanted a solid basis, he had to win the favour of the councillors and other influential figures in these rural parts. The local figure who did most for Soisson was Senator Guillaumot. He suggested to Moreau that it might be a good idea to 'pass the reins to Soisson'. Moreau declined, but Guillaumot went on to recommend Soisson to the mayors of the smaller communes.

At one of these meetings with the mayors, one of them asked me in front of everyone: 'Paul, old chap, how come you're supporting one of the Auxerre bourgeoisie?' I introduced Jean-Pierre to him, the mayor liked him, and a week later he had taken up his pilgrim's staff and was going all round the Puisaye drumming up support for him.[24]

In 1968, it was the Puisaye, not Auxerre, that ensured Soisson's election to the National Assembly. 'I had got up a petition asking him to stand in the general election', Guillaumot recounted. 'I persuaded some mayors to sign it. Half the time, they had to rest the paper on the wing of their tractor in a field. I knew his father: he had been a prisoner with one of my uncles and they kept up a bit of a friendship.' Thanks to men like Guillaumot, who quickly came to see him as the 'natural' successor to Moreau, Soisson acquired a vital asset, control of a double network. He stood at the centre of two non-intersecting circles, for the Auxerre network and its rural counterpart are quite separate entities. His main asset was his ability to manipulate these two systems simultaneously.

'Jean-Pierre Soisson has done a lot for the Puisaye. It is thanks to him that the area got what it did', I was told by one councillor, who could hardly have made his meaning clearer. The area is a hard one to farm, and there has been a big drift away from the land. Various projects have been needed to keep some kind of economic activity alive. The deputy has fought hard to obtain the required subsidies. A development committee for the Puisaye has been in existence for several years, aimed at coordinating the activities of the different cantons, and more particularly at developing tourism in certain well-known spots, such as the château at Saint-Fargeau, the Bourdon reservoir and Colette's village of Saint-Sauveur. The most spectacular achievement, of course, was the Club Méditerranée development, with its tempting promise of two hundred new jobs; Soisson and the Crédit agricole claim the credit for this project, which caused a great stir in the region. The deputy's local strategy consists of a relentless quest for any prospect capable of galvanising this rather sleepy region. This strategy is backed up by the other members of the General Council. Over the years, Soisson has personally selected those who represent the Puisaye on the General Council today. To some extent, these are his delegates on the ground, and his job is to coordinate and inspire this smooth-running machine. He often goes to the Puisaye, where he holds surgeries and keeps an eye on 'his' councillors: 'Soisson is the Count of Auxerre, and the Marquis of the Puisaye', someone joked. Not that people hold out too much hope for the region, which has known bad times before, and has an ageing population. However that may be, the vertical political organisation which has grown up around Soisson keeps him safe from any storm, as was shown in 1981 when the left was so successful elsewhere. That year, the mayor of Auxerre did not have a majority in the town, so he concentrated his efforts on the country districts, and it was the votes of the Puisaye that gave him his slim advantage over his Socialist opponent.

Governing from the centre

The fact is that Auxerre presents a very different political profile from its rural surroundings. The commercial centre is traditionally loyal to the Soisson heir; the new districts, such as Sainte-Geneviève, les Rosoirs, Saint-

Siméon and les Piedalloues, tend to fluctuate. They voted left in the general election of 1981, but that did not prevent them voting for the mayor when it came to the municipal elections. We remarked earlier that the sociological make-up of Auxerre has been visibly altered by the rapid growth of the tertiary sector. By the end of Jean Moreau's reign, there had been an increase in the population, due mainly to the growth of the middle class. To give just one example, the town hall today employs some eight hundred people: the number of staff has doubled since Soisson's arrival on the scene, just as it has in other administrative offices in the city. Many middle managers and civil servants live in the new districts. These are the people who vote left in the general elections and elections to the General Council, yet remain faithful to their mayor in the municipal elections.

Soisson himself is perfectly aware of this situation. 'The balance of power is held in Auxerre by the trade union Force ouvrière', he told me. 'When I have them on my side, I take 62 per cent of the vote. If they are against me, I only take 52 per cent. We must never forget that Auxerre today is a town of civil servants.'[25] It must be said that the mayor's policies have favoured this development. Right from his first term, he showed a great desire to 'get the town moving'. His programme was an ambitious one, aimed at 'promoting, conserving and restructuring the town centre', while improving facilities in the outlying districts. He set to work in the euphoric aftermath of victory. Development was all the rage in the 1970s. People took the long-term view, and aimed high. Soisson's forecasts relied on a projected annual increase of 2 per cent in the population, which would have given Greater Auxerre a population of 65,000 in 1985 and 100,000 in 2010. The plans for the town centre included a number of traffic measures, such as the creation of a pedestrian precinct, a huge car-park on the site of the old market and an underground car-park near the boulevards. The quartier du Pont and the quartier de la Marine districts were objects of an urban renewal programme.

The second aspect of the plan related to the newer districts. The mayor made a point ot offering facilities to make life in the newly built council blocks of the Sainte-Geneviève district more attractive. The mixed public- and private-sector housing development of Saint-Siméon in the Hauts d'Auxerre district also dates from this period, with 1,300 dwellings built between 1974 and 1979; in 1975, work began at les Piedalloues, an area at the entrance to the town set aside for the construction of an estate of detached houses. In carrying out this vast programme, Jean-Pierre Soisson demonstrated the same ingenuity he had shown in the Puisaye. In 1974, a contract was signed between Auxerre and the government, by which the town benefited from a significant number of subsidies; it also received loans at reduced rates of interest. The town was thus getting into debt, which caused some agitation amongst Moreau's traditional voters. Moreau had actually said in his speech of farewell to the town hall: 'The doctrine of prudence in public spending . . . has been the rule since the Liberation.' He had also drawn attention to Auxerre's favourable position as one of the twenty towns with the lowest rates in France. This doctrine took some knocks during Soisson's first two terms in office. Admittedly, the town was the object of improvements the likes of which had not been seen since Surugue's days. However, certain developments were by no means universally welcomed, for example, the underground car-park and the improvements to the esplanades, which cost the mayor his seat on the General Council in 1976. Nevertheless, Soisson has fond memories of this period, which with hindsight he considers the most interesting of his career because of what he achieved.

From 1983, with the new austerity, the town no longer benefited from the same level of investment; the rates had to be kept down, and public spending more tightly controlled. Auxerre's municipal authorities opted at that time for efficiency rather than innovation, which did not prevent the mayor from pressing for the restoration of the old part of town, and improvements to the council flats in Sainte-Geneviève, a district that had been increasingly deserted by the middle class and now had a high percentage of immigrants. This move was strongly criticised by the right, particularly by the National Front. However, Soisson, who had no hesitation about accepting a compromise over plans for the city centre which were criticised by the residents, was also quite capable of fighting for welfare projects he considered vital. Here we see some of the complexity of the man: sprung from the middle bourgeoisie, he was above all a man of action, yet highly sensitive to the contradictory currents running through Auxerre society. Soisson governed from the centre, but was quite the opposite of a quietist. He could see new social trends in the town, and took steps to accommodate them. Hence his desire to turn Auxerre into a town suitable for its new middle class; similarly, the improvements to Sainte-Geneviève and the installation of certain basic facilities in 1984, another move which was criticised from the right, arose from his sharp awareness of the inequalities threatening the stability of local society.

The mayor's political allies on the municipal council were sometimes puzzled by these moves. They were united by anti-Communist sentiments, and for a long time the existence of a Union of the Left was enough to ensure agreement within the council. When drawing up his list in 1971, Soisson had been careful to surround himself with some of Jean Moreau's main colleagues. In this way, he signalled the fact that his policies would be a continuation of those of his predecessor; later, he brought in new men to the main assistant mayor positions. The new mayor showed from the beginning that he was 'the boss', taking charge of all the main dossiers on development plans, and building up a team to take care of administration. Rather like the councillors of the Puisaye, the municipal councillors had a representative mission in the first instance: they were spokesmen for the aims and objectives of their respective districts, and mediators between the residents and the mayor. Soisson's choice of assistant mayors from amongst the councillors also responded to his desire to have people with ample grass-roots experience around him. Four men were particularly important: first, the principal assistant mayor, who chaired the works committee. He acted to some extent as a shield for the mayor: his job was to make sense of the huge volume of public works-related information that rains down every day on a town like Auxerre; he also had to deal with people's complaints about the state of the pavements or other items requiring attention; finally, he had to face the storm of protests which improvement invariably provokes. Next in importance was the assistant mayor in charge of town-planning and development, a man respected for his expertise on the subject. Third was the assistant mayor in charge of sports facilities, a consultant in the casualty department of the Auxerre hospital who was also departmental secretary of the RPR; this man got on very well with Soisson. Finally, we should mention the assistant mayor in charge of finances, a lecturer in mathematics from the University of Paris: personal friendship and esteem were the main motives behind this particular appointment, though the general view is that the mathematician, who originally had nothing going for him except the mayor's support, is in fact just the man for the job.

We should note that apart from the RPR leader, the assistant mayors seem to be the mayor's men, rather than politicians as such. Soisson holds the levers of power, backed up by a small team of administrators. There is an inner circle of two key men who are always to be found at the town hall: the general secretary and Soisson's private secretary. The former worked originally in hospital administration before becoming Soisson's private secretary for a time. He was one of the main organisers of two successive campaigns, for the elections to the General Council in 1982 and to the municipal council in 1983. The young man became one of Soisson's closest colleagues; he belongs to an Avallonnais family, 'originally from the same village as Soisson's ancestors'.[26] The General Secretary feels his job is highly political. He is a member of the UDF and defines himself as a right-winger. So far as he is concerned, running Auxerre is not a simple matter of administrative efficiency, but also means ensuring the predominance of certain ideas, and safeguarding future election success. The General Secretary is a sort of one-man-band at the town hall; the mayor is often away from home, on trips to Paris or Dijon, but he keeps in contact by phone with his general secretary: 'Everything goes through him', I was informed by the assistant mayors and council employees. The other key figure in Soisson's entourage is his private secretary, a young woman who has worked with him for several years, and who organises his diary in the department, receives callers and follows up contacts with councillors and other local personalities. With her intimate knowledge of the town and the ins and outs of local politics, the private secretary is also an influential member of the council. She and the General Secretary are Soisson's 'watchdogs' while he is tied up with his government responsibilities.

Undivided power

The present mayor of Auxerre has thus managed to impose his authority on the municipal council, like his predecessor Jean Moreau. The two men's methods are different, for a very serious approach is not the fashion nowadays. An anecdote will illustrate the change in style: 'On the day of the transfer of powers', Soisson told me, 'Jean Moreau wore tails to welcome me to the town hall. I was wearing a lounge suit, and my hair was quite long. He wore the sash of the Légion d'honneur. I was rather embarrassed.'[27] The mayor and the councillors now address each other with an informality which would have been inconceivable in Moreau's time. 'Jean-Pierre' or even 'J.-P.', as he is known, is a man who enjoys meeting people: that is one of the secrets of his popularity. At election time his friendliness works wonders; the mayor can wander into a bar, order a glass of wine and chat to anyone he meets in just the right tone. 'Moreau commanded respect for his age and his heroic exploits', someone told me. 'Jean-Pierre is more like one of us – he's like a big kid, you want to please him.' Soisson symbolises several things at once for his fellow-citizens: the offspring of a respected family, the young man from the provinces who has made good in Paris, but who has not forgotton his native town. Nor should we overlook the prestige of his meteoric career in politics. Soisson is impatient, perhaps inclined at times to rush into things; but he has an enthusiastic approach which is in contrast to the rather stiff formality of his predecessor. He is a clear case of the 'young man who is ambitious, without being ruthless'. We might note the interest he has always shown in young people throughout the different ministerial posts he has occupied.

Although over fifty, Soisson is still considered a youthful mayor; people see him as having a creative streak, and they expect surprises from him. So recent events have not come as too much of a shock. Soisson's daring solo leap in the direction of the Socialists, and his airy acceptance of a high-risk ministry, accord with the image the people of Auxerre have of their mayor. On the other hand, when it comes to running the town, his informal style has the paradoxical effect of reinforcing his authority. In this atmosphere of intimacy with his councillors, it is obviousthat nobody can boast of greater legitimacy than he himself. Power is exercised, as we saw, through the mediation of the general secretary and the private secretary: again, a contrast with the Moreau regime, where the municipal council was not backed up in this way by a more overtly political team. The mayor governs, the council deliberates: one could find no apter summary of the principles underlying the structure of local government.

The left-wing opposition, which is a small minority, as it has only 7 councillors out of a total of 39, has never received any favours from the mayor. His inflexibility on this point contrasts with his advocacy of more liberal policies at national level, both as president of the coordinating committee for regional programmes of professional and vocational training, and as a supporter of Raymond Barre, who since 1987 has pledged himself to a policy of *rapprochement* with the Socialists in the event of his success. Yet in Auxerre at present there is not a single Socialist on any official body, such as the Council Housing Office or the mixed public- and private-sector housing corporation. Similarly, all the offices of assistant mayor or chairmen of committees are filled from the ranks of the majority. Soisson seems unwilling to compromise his position by ignoring a left–right divide important to the voters. Since he had a solid majority, he had no need of the Socialists to govern the town. If he attempted a *rapprochement*, he would run the risk of disappointing those who voted for him. There is another factor to be taken into consideration, which is the existence since 1983 of a dissident tendency within the majority. Several councillors are followers of the National Front: one of them even resigned from the Finance Committee. Obviously the mayor is not keen to provoke criticism from his own right-wing supporters by giving strategic positions to Socialists. His strategy of making no concessions to the left in council posts, and choosing a well-known right-winger as General Secretary, has proved successful: on the one hand, Soisson has reinforced his position as sole master of the ship, and on the other the extreme right has failed to make any significant headway in Auxerre.

By this means, the mayor has kept his freedom of manoeuvre, and has been able to promote a project close to his heart. While not wishing to turn Auxerre into a big university town, which would be an unrealistic aim, given the proximity of Paris and Dijon, he does want to turn it into a centre for education and training. There have been two concrete achievements recently in this field. A *lycée technique*, the first to be built in Burgundy in the aftermath of the decentralisation of education, was completed in record time. The mayor of Auxerre is also vice-president of the Regional Council for training needs, and was able to ensure that the town received financial assistance available through the region, to which specific responsibility for educational facilities had just been devolved. The new school was obtained on very advantageous terms, as the region furnished 80 per cent of the required investment. The municipal council agreed to the proposal at the end of 1986, and by September 1988, the school was opening its doors to pupils. A second project rounded off the operation, which even the mayor's opponents now recognise was a good idea: the setting up of a Master's degree in Science and Applied Technology at the University of Burgundy. The aim was to encourage the growth of specialised training for the industries in Auxerre and the surrounding area. With the municipal elections coming up in one year's time, these moves were not entirely disinterested. The fact remains that, as even one of his main critics admitted, Soisson is for the moment the only person capable of coordinating this kind of project, involving contributions from different levels of authority and the agreement of various bodies which are sometimes difficult to coordinate and synchronise.

Soisson is a man of action. He likes nothing better than taking on a challenge and succeeding. He sees it as a test of his power, and it must be admitted that the success of this type of operation is dependent on the fact that he holds several offices at once, and has real influence at regional level. However, power in this sense should be understood as the ability to anticipate public demand, and accept the risk implicit in putting forward an image of the town (up-to-date, well-provided with educational facilities) which its inhabitants have never even envisaged. These are rather extraordinary powers, and what the mayor seeks to win by his achievements is symbolic prestige. As Soisson knows full well, demonstrating his powers is the way to ensure the continuing popularity which is the main guarantee of his position in Auxerre. 'I run a permanent election campaign', he told me. 'As soon as an election is over, it is time to start getting ready for the next one. No one can ever be sure of victory. On the actual day of the election, I can't help it, I'm invariably worried sick.'[28] Soisson has been the big name in Auxerre political life for nearly twenty years now: it is no coincidence that the only man who can rival him in public esteem is from a totally different field of endeavour: 'Auxerre has two great men', I was assured by a local expert, 'Soisson and Guy Roux.' Roux is the manager of the local football team, Auxerre Juniors, which he has built up into a first-class team which has made a name for itself in the first division league championship.

'The team is a shop-window for the town', its manager proudly told me, and it must be admitted that for many Frenchmen, Auxerre means the football team. The municipal council has put a lot into the club's development; this was particularly the case when Soisson was Minister for Sport, but even since then, the club has received a large amount of help from the council. Some councillors have expressed reservations on this policy, complaining that the club is too expensive. Guy Roux responds that the council grant is only 10 per cent of the club's costs. It has a training policy which has proved particularly effective. Thanks to a training programme set up in 1982, and the manager's skill, the team has produced a number of great players who have made its reputation and who have on occasion fetched a high price from other teams to which they have been 'sold'. Guy Roux's local popularity is the reward for this remarkable success. We should not forget that he is a native of Auxerre, and has been with the team for the last twenty-five years. 'Auxerre Juniors', he declares, 'is a political force. A Communist leader admitted that: he said "Out of 10,000 fans at a given match, 2,000 are Communist supporters." The same is true for the other parties. Don't forget, the fans are in most cases ratepayers and voters.'[29]

So the team manager can talk to the mayor on equal terms. Guy Roux knows perfectly well that he is responsible for the club's success. He feels he has an important position in the community, as a spokesman for the club and its many fans. In his own way, he is a politician, fighting all the time to improve his club's situation. For example, the ground can now hold 20,000 spectators. Guy Roux explained to me how he had managed to get an extra stand built:

The idea of building the stand came from the left-wing list. I had a meeting with them and I got them to put out a pamphlet promising the stand would be built if they got in. When the right wing got to hear about it, they made the same promise, and had to stick to it after they were elected. You can get a lot in an election year!

In his own way, Guy Roux is a skilful politician. He is not shy about expressing his ideas, or defending his club against its denigrators, in a paper he has founded called *Come on the Blues*! He has always been quite a good writer, and his pen is feared on all sides. Yet he has no ambition to enter local politics: 'The only party I support is the round leather ball party', he jokes. He gets on very well with Soisson, and the two men respect each other. Each avoids encroaching on the other's territory, and both are keen to cash in on the advantages of fame: 'I'm a bit of a media-figure', Roux told me. 'I'm on telly more often than Soisson – once a week on FR3 Burgundy and twenty times a year on national telly; I'll be doing more of that in future. I was a guest on a Sunday night sports programme the other week, with Thierry Rolland. We were lucky, and got record viewing-figures: 9 million viewers between 10.00 and 10.30. That counts here.'

Basically this situation offers the advantage of preserving the mayor's dominant position so far as politics is concerned. He reigns supreme in Auxerre, mainly because of his roots in the moderate bourgeoisie of the town. Soisson belongs, sociologically speaking, on the right, and that leaves him free to occupy the political centre. He stays in power because the way he runs Auxerre, with the support of traditional right-wing sectors, is in fact very similar to the way a left-wing mayor would do it, hence the difficulty the left experiences in putting forward a real alternative. Opinions on the left are divided as to the best way of dealing with the mayor. Some insist on a critical stance, in the name of the familiar right–left opposition. Others, such as Guy Ferez, a young municipal councillor elected in 1983, who has become a leading spokesman for the opposition, advocate a more realistic strategy. They feel that the left should adopt a 'constructive' approach to large municipal projects, in order to present an image of managerial ability to the electorate. Otherwise the left is simply seen as a negative force, while the right is seen as 'people who get things done and don't shirk their responsibilities'. National developments within the Socialist Party have of course encouraged the latter attitude. Does this mean we are moving towards a policy of collaboration between the mayor and the Socialists? Once again, Soisson is the man in control: as we saw, he has put obstacles in the path of such a development, by refusing to invite Socialists to join the main public bodies in the town.

Politics and pragmatics

The fact is that the mayor of Auxerre has always liked to keep a card or two up his sleeve, and leave his options open: in his role as deputy, we saw him adopt a liberal policy towards his colleague Henri Nallet, whom he never ceased to praise. The two men were in regular contact, to the annoyance of the RPR deputy, Philippe Auberger, who represented the north of the department in the Assembly. This was before Mitterrand's re-election, when Jacques Chirac and his friends were in power, and Soisson, like the other followers of Barre, was fighting against the very idea of a co-existence between the right and a Socialist President. Are we to conclude that Soisson, like a large number of other politicians, was perfectly capable between 1986 and 1988 of practising either co-existence or its complete opposite, in each of the three types of territory he represented? It is certainly clear that he took a different attitude to the issue at municipal, departmental and national level. However, this is not so astonishing when we realise that there were different factors operating in each case. Certainly in all three types of constituency at the time there was a strong antagonism which could be described in schematic fashion using the terms 'left' and 'right'. However, to assume that this opposition operates in the same way at each of the three levels is to deny the existence of what I will call a 'pragmatics' of politics, rather as writers on linguistics talk of a 'pragmatics' of language.

The aim of party discourse in politics is to stress a simple notion, the idea that from top to bottom of the social edifice, political relations can be reduced to a single antagonism, fixed for all time, between the representatives of different ideologies. Closer examination reveals the limitations of this purely abstract formulation, forcing us to admit that although politics involves a web of relationships with ramifications, or networks in permanent competition, it also consists of individuals operating within a context, that is to say, adapting their discourse and their strategy to the constraints of a particular situation, which may call for forms of cooperation which apparently ignore the usual antagonisms. At the risk of being misunderstood if my statement is wrongly taken as a value judgement, I would be inclined to say that political activity, if pursued over the full range of territories, from local to national, is basically *equivocal.*

In this respect, our deputy and mayor is an excellent example of a man exercising several types of elective function simultaneously, and deploying skilfully the range of shade and colour this broad palette offers. This phenomenon of multiple office is of course characteristic of the French political system, and frequently produces a situation in which one person exercises several mandates and therefore represents several levels of community. A monolithic discourse (politics as a simple opposition) is contradicted, as it were, by the equivocal nature of multiple representation. In this sense, it could be argued, the French political system, though apparently fixed, not to say rigid, is in fact endowed with supreme flexibility, and the skill of the protagonists lies in giving due weight both to explicit ideological concerns and to the reality of the situation in which they find themselves. There is an internal balance in the system, so it is probably no coincidence that for some time now, as political discourse has grown more complex and has tried to free itself from the traditional confrontational model, there has been a parallel questioning of the phenomenon of multiple office, with a limit being placed on the number of simultaneous mandates a public figure may exercise.

Discrepancy and interaction: the local and the national

On 22 November 1986, François Mitterrand visited Auxerre for the ceremony marking the centenary of the death of Paul Bert. He used the occasion to recall how important it was that education should be available to all and to state that tolerance should be the keynote of government action. Welcoming the President to the town hall, Soisson referred to him in de Gaulle's famous formula as 'the man in charge of what is essential'. He went on to quote the following statement by Paul Bert: 'It is a fine task, and our traditional task as republicans, to induce an atmosphere of calm, by removing the causes of disorder.' This was more than just a casual quotation: it was the expression of a belief which was translated into action eighteen months later with Soisson's entry into the government. Here we see a discrepancy between the local and the national. Yet Soisson's position as mayor does not seem to have been affected in the least by his spectacular return to prominence in national politics. Auxerre remained faithful as ever, just as it had been faithful to Jean Moreau, before and after the Liberation. Should we be surprised by the town's strange constancy? Is it indifferent to events in the world outside? Is it used to keeping the same mayor for long periods? Has Auxerre, the stronghold of the Independents, perhaps been converted to the doctrine of *rapprochement* preached by a left-wing President?

Only a few days earlier, Soisson had won the largest majority of his career, against a Socialist, J.-P. Rousseau. His slogan had been a simple one: *Together*! 'I want people from different political tendencies to be able to work together', he explained in his campaign leaflet. The mayor was thus heralding the future, and once again his opponents were left looking sectarian and old-fashioned. Soisson won the right-wing vote, but it is clear that some left-wing voters also supported him, so he could boast of having at least achieved his aim of significantly enlarging his support within the town. This time he had no need of the reinforcements from the Puisaye. However, it was obvious that the *rapprochement* option might lose Soisson some of his traditional voters. As soon as he entered the government, he could be seen sounding out the local Socialists. He was well aware that here again he would have to govern from the centre. Thus we see the first outlines of a complete upheaval in local political habits, under the pressure of national events and the corresponding choices made by Soisson. I have mentioned the discrepancies between the different contexts in which he exercised political power. Here, we have a completely new situation at national level, which required a certain adjustment of the deputy's stance in Auxerre. He had to carry out this adjustment, bringing his local policies into line with his national strategy.

Discrepancies and interaction: what the anthropologist immediately notices here is the constant interweaving of the national and the local. Each acts upon the other, in a constant dialectical process. For example, the national on the local. We have just seen that the people of Auxerre are poised today on the brink of a new political formula, an alliance of the left and the moderate right, along the lines of the coalition which ran the town before the war. This combination, induced by Soisson's entry into the government, is only possible because of his influence over a large body of voters, which enables him to open up to his left without fearing for his right. The operation is probably made easier by the aura of Soisson's prestige on the national scene. This gives him a symbolic value, and brings with it a new image for Auxerre as a testing-ground for *rapprochement*, and an example of up-to-date political ideas. The image is a flattering one for the townspeople.

What about the other way round, the local affecting the national? This is the truly original feature of Soisson's political career. The man is a pure product of the provinces, the heartland of France, and of the moderate, bourgeois tradition which has traditionally prevailed in local society. Moreover, he agreed to represent the town but refused to be a hostage to one particular group of voters; instead, he managed to blend the three great ideological currents which succeeded each other historically: one, the old Radical and Jansenist tradition (Soisson often recalls that when he gave the name 'Republican Party' to the group of Giscard's followers, he had in mind the former name of the Radical Party, which was 'Republican, Radical and Socialist-Radical Party'); two, the Independent and moderate tendency which strongly influenced the department's politics through Flandin and Moreau; three, the progressive attitudes of the new middle classes. He therefore had much previous experience of what might truly be called 'Centrism', with his mingling of disparate elements, such as sociological roots on the right and innovatory moves in the direction of the Socialists. His political stature was based on this experience, which was also the source of his affinity with Raymond Barre, who embodies a similar mixture of provincial conservatism, suspicious of the subtleties of the political world of Paris, and an economic reformism which concentrates on essentials and is free of any kind of demogogy. This explains why, after François Mitterrand's re-election, Soisson presented exactly the right profile for the policy of *rapprochement*: a true man of the right, by his origins and the principles for which he had fought, but accustomed to deploying on the ground the foresight that had led him to govern with an eye on the left. This very deep experience of local politics turned Soisson into just the man for the new political circumstances.

What about Auxerre? Can we see our medium-sized town as in some way the echo or perhaps even the herald of great turning-points in the evolution of France? A bastion of Radicalism under old man Combes, it then sided with the Popular Front, supported a Pétainist mayor, and finally formed a passionate attachment to a follower of Giscard who is now leading it into the land of Mitterrand. My own feeling is that in choosing the men who govern her, Auxerre's first thought is for Auxerre. Then it is up to the lucky candidates to hold fast to the helm, battling against contrary winds, or steering close to the shores of central power. They are given a lot of leeway, and they use it as they see fit, one as a moderate and another as a progressive. Any failure of taste – a drift towards either extreme, a premature alliance – is to be severely punished. It needs to be stressed that this peaceful city is highly sensitive to any discord, even in the corridors of the town hall. Auxerre is demanding: it is not enough to have seduced her at the time of the elections, she must be attached to a man by stronger bonds than that. After 'old M. Moreau', she turned to a younger leader, 'the Soisson boy'. 'It's true love', says Soisson of his relationship with Auxerre. Perhaps that is a good note on which to end.

Conclusion

We have reached the end of our journey into the political life of a French department, and it is time now to draw some conclusions, and respond to any queries that may have arisen either about the approach taken in this book or about a number of observations whose significance seems to go well beyond the particular case of the Yonne. As I have stressed from the beginning, I observed local society and its representatives from the point of view of an anthropologist. This approach, inevitably, has affected the results obtained: data which are generally of interest to political science have been relegated to second place, whereas other aspects have received a great deal of attention. Despite the well-known difficulty of separating aims and approach, it might nevertheless clarify matters to distinguish and discuss three issues at some length: first the question of point of view in anthropology, second, the nature of French political culture, and third, anticipated developments.

Point of view in anthropology

What is anthropology? Let me pose the question as crudely as this, at the risk of answering it clumsily or imperfectly. The notion of anthropology is usually linked to the notion of the exotic. For most of the people I met, an anthropologist was someone who travelled far and collected large amounts of information to add to our knowledge of some distant tribe. This is the usual image of anthropology, and it was the one held by an informant who began our conversation with the warning, 'We are not savages here, you know . . .' Certainly, anthropological activity is very directly linked to the exploration of societies with very different customs from our own. Anthropology was born out of the fascination with these other cultures and the difficulty of understanding other human beings, a difficulty arising not only from lack of knowledge of their language, but also from ignorance of their everyday codes and the way they experience and envisage both their natural environment and their social relationships.

Anthropology is it is known today began to develop towards the end of the nineteenth century, with L. H. Morgan's comparative study of kinship relations in the most diverse kinds of society, and Franz Boas's work on the myths and traditions of the North American Indians. The first big 'field-trip' was Bruno Malinowski's contact with the Trobriand Islanders in Melanesia in 1915. He made several long-term stays, during which he applied himself to learning the language and sharing the life of the native islanders. This method enabled Malinowski to collect a large body of data on a wide variety of aspects of Trobriand society, such as the economy, the cycle of exchange between the inhabitants of the different islands, social organisation, kinship and sexuality. This is how the anthropologist's vocation began to be defined: the intensive study of a social microcosm, with the aim of understanding all its different aspects. Malinowski started it off, and the number of societies explored rapidly multiplied. From then on, the anthropologist was essentially someone who worked in the field: whether in the Amazon, India or Africa, the method was the same, namely a long-term inquiry, in which the researcher took the time to penetrate gradually into worlds which at first seemed essentially alien to him. The specialist nature of this type of task did not, however, imply that the researcher was completely enclosed in the world of 'his' tribe. Anthropological activity is by its nature comparative: to quote just one example, a major achievement in this realm has been Claude Lévi-Strauss's demonstration of the underlying rules governing kinship systems from the four corners of the earth, all apparently very different.

So the three indispensable ingredients of anthropology are: a willingness to engage seriously with societies different from our own, detailed observation, and a comparative approach. I do not believe many specialists would quarrel with this, so the image anthropology projects to a larger audience corresponds quite faithfully to its historic ambition. In the context of this tradition, the idea of practising anthropology within one's own society may cause problems, since the observer is no longer outside the object of his observations. 'We are not savages': we both belong to exactly the same culture. In short, the idea does not seem to work. Yet if we consider anthropology's comparative aim, it would seem logically inconsistent to look at all human societies except one's own. Surely that exception would invalidate the whole approach? In fact, anthropologists have recognised the need to take into account the world they know best. If we look just at the case of European societies, we see the beginnings of this type of research in the first years of this century, parallel to the expansion of exotic anthropology. But anthropologists who looked at Europe confined themselves to collecting information about customs and traditions relating to social phenomena which were already practically extinct. At that time, and even until comparatively recently, they were also mainly interested in rural populations, which were seen as the fundamental guardians of a folk culture assumed to be the basis of our societies.

Stay-at-home anthropology, as we might call it, continued into the 1950s with important works applying the precepts of Malinowski to peasant societies, and scrutinising every single element of local social life: the economy, kinship, institutions, symbolism, and so on. The implicit postulate in this kind of research was that the anthropologist should take as the object of his study an entity which was spatially and demographically limited (a town, a village, a district within a town), in order to acquire as much detail as possible about its workings; from this point of view, the ideal object of anthropological study was the type of society where 'everyone knows everyone else'. The interest aroused by these studies,[1] and their remarkable quality demonstrate, if a demonstration is necessary, that the anthropology of rural societies was a necessary development within the general growth of anthropology. Similarly, the growth of comparative studies on topics such as kinship and transmission gave rise to a fruitful dialogue with anthropologists specialising in 'exotic' societies.

In one of the chapters of *Anthropologie structurale* devoted to methods and teaching in anthropology, Lévi-Strauss asks whether the anthropological approach is different from that of the other social sciences. He makes it clear that it is quite valid to subject our own societies to anthropological scrutiny, but points out that whereas in sociology the predominant point of view is that of the observer, 'anthropology attempts to draw up a social science of the observed, either by voicing the point of view of the native inhabitant, when describing strange, remote societies, or, if it enlarges its field of study to include the observer's own society, by attempting to establish a frame of reference based on anthropological experience, and independent of both the observer and the object of his study'.[2] We have here a very clear conception of an anthropology of modern societies, which is simply the reverse side of a type of scrutiny traditionally turned on exotic societies. Moreover, Lévi-Strauss shows the complementary nature of the two approaches very clearly.

There is still an apparently almost irreducible difference between our societies and those worlds for which anthropologists have traditionally shown a preference. Lévi-Strauss insists that exotic societies should not be defined negatively by such terms as 'uncivilised, having no system of writing, pre- or non-mechanical'. What they have in common is a positive factor: 'these societies are based on personal relationships, on concrete connections between individuals, to a much higher degree than is the case in other societies'.[3] It is in fact our societies which should be described negatively, characterised as they are by the development of 'inauthentic' relationships, in which communication between individuals no longer offers a 'global experience', a 'concrete apprehension of one subject by another'.[4] To what extent, then, do our societies constitute a fit object of study for anthropology? Lévi-Strauss states that one can find even in our society, the society of the observer, what he calls 'strata of authenticity'. To reach these, it is vital to study what demographers call a 'self-contained unit', for example, a village, a particular district in a town, a factory. Taking as his example some studies which were being carried out at the time in France under the auspices of UNESCO, Lévi-Strauss notes that researchers came up against problems when they moved up the scale and turned their attention to medium-sized towns: 'Thirty thousand people cannot constitute a society in the same sense as five hundred. In the former case, communication does not take place primarily between individuals, or in an interpersonal mode; the social reality of "transmitters" and "receivers" . . . disappears in the complexity of "codes" and "relays".'[5]

I have brought in these quotations from Lévi-Strauss because they sum up the conception which underlay the practice of Europeanist anthropologists until fairly recently. In order to seize the totality of social life, its 'systematic entirety', to use the term introduced by Marcel Mauss, the anthropologist had to study collectivities which were limited in size and relatively closed. This was not simply an argument about method; it implied a more general conception of the nature and aims of anthropology, and gave overriding emphasis to manifestations of 'authenticity'. The important point was not so much the size or number of the population in question, but the non-mediated, 'interpersonal' nature of relationships between people.

The model of authenticity ,was the type of life 'perceived at first as traditional and archaic' which Lévi-Strauss observed among Amazonian tribes and which he describes so memorably in *Tristes tropiques*.[6] The object of anthropological study in modern societies is specific and restricted: specific, in that it concerns relationships inaccessible to sociology; and restricted in that the investigation is limited to a small enclave within our societies. There are signs here of an underlying philosophy of anthropology, which incidentally can also be traced in the craze for studying village communities. It is an ambiguous philosophy, based on nostalgia for a quality of transparency we are supposed to have lost. This 'country-fresh' anthropology had its attractions: the researcher could feel he was rediscovering levels of authenticity, without having to rush off to the ends of the earth. Though from the same world as the 'natives' he was studying, he was sufficiently distanced from them culturally to bring to bear the detached view which had proved so effective with exotic societies. Impressed above all by continuity, and constantly on the lookout for traditional customs, the anthropologist was in a way continuing the work of folklorists and students of popular crafts and traditions.

I have stressed the positive aspects of such a method – its contribution to certain classic domains of anthropology, such as the study of kinship and symbolism. Yet somehow this anthropology of the western world never really managed to make its mark, except as a pale, lacklustre copy of 'real' anthropology, which concerned itself with 'proper' savages. Moreover, the publication of numerous papers, the eagerness to apply to 'our' peasants the methods which had been so successful with other peoples, was not matched by a corresponding interest in the methodological and theoretical problems such an approach inevitably throws up. Hence the disappointing results of the enterprise, despite the advantage it might have enjoyed from being very much in line with the times: the aftermath of May 1968 saw, amongst other things, the emergence of a concern with ecology, and the rediscovery of a rural world on the brink of disappearance. This was also a period when there was great concern to preserve not only buildings, but also a whole human and cultural heritage, which was now seen as a part of the vital richness of old Europe. In this context, the ideas of 'emergency anthropology' and preservation of the 'anthropological heritage' came into their own. Yet the uneasy question lingered: was the anthropology of our societies necessarily tied to a philosophy of the traditional and the authentic, and inapplicable to the main expressions of modernity?

The other social sciences were only too happy to adapt to this division, sociologists and historians leaving anthropologists to work on the edges of their respective domains, on matters outside immediate concerns. Curiously, the questioning of the approach came from within the discipline itself. New issues arose when anthropologists began to take an interest in the social phenomena of towns. As Lévi-Strauss had indicated, it was perfectly valid to apply the methods of anthropology to a 'big city neighbourhood': the Americans had been trying out these techniques since the thirties, notably in Chicago.[7] But forty years were to pass before the appearance of an urban anthropology that investigated the suburbs, went into council flats, looked at ethnic minorities in the big cities and finally, more recently still, attacked (in the figurative sense only, of course) the middle classes in the posh areas. This is quite clearly an anthropology of the familiar, and the large number of fields to which attention has been turned, from factories to housing schemes, not forgetting the Métro, are an indication of the numerous applications of this new approach; it is like a sudden realisation of the potential uses of a hitherto neglected tool.

These new developments in anthropology have led to a clearer definition of the actual object of study. It is obvious that authenticity is no longer a sufficient criterion to define the type of social relations that are the concern of anthropologists. They are now exploring – not without a certain pleasure, it seems – the world of the inauthentic, the world of mediated communication. The nostalgic idealisation of transparent human relationships is pretty hard to reconcile with the reality of what have been called 'complex' societies, in opposition to the traditional chosen domain of anthropology, the 'primitive'. This is not to deny the profound difference between industrialised societies and other cultural universes: what is being questioned is the tendency to use this difference to separate the true domain of anthropology from other areas to which it can only be admitted on condition that it explores the last remnants of authenticity or primitiveness.

Modern anthropology is not content merely to mimic its exotic big sister more or less convincingly. To take just one example: the method of choosing as an object of study a self-contained unit, on the model of the village or the tribe, proves inadequate in the face of certain aspects of modern social life. Politics would be one very crude example. I will return to this point in greater detail, but it is obvious that political space in a centralised State cannot be divided up in the same way as in a leaderless society where kinship segments are juxtaposed. Local politics take their meaning from the existence of national politics, which implies that there is a constant toing and froing between the two dimensions. To seize that fluctuating movement, and grasp the different levels of local reality, demands care in the choice of appropriate methods. I myself was obliged to adopt a new approach, that is, give up the idea of proceeding in the Yonne in the same way I did in Ochollo. In other words, I had to explore a new intellectual territory: the method that governed my observations in Africa was not automatically valid in the case of France.

Does this perhaps signal a radical split in the discipline? Marc Augé refers to an 'anthropology of the familiar' and an 'anthropology of the remote'[8]: have these two branches anything in common? These questions need to be asked, at least. They bring us back to our original inquiry into the nature of anthropology. Let me turn again to Lévi-Strauss. 'Anthropology', he writes at the beginning of *Anthropologie structurale*,' is particularly interested in all those things that are not written, not so much because the peoples it studies are unable to write, but because the object of its attention is different from all those things that men normally think of committing to stone or paper.'[9] The aim of anthropology is thus defined by reference to a form of communication: non-written communication is given special status, not by reference to the peoples under observation (able or unable to write), but by reference to the actual aims of anthropological study. An important point is that Lévi-Strauss is careful not to identify this mode of communication with oral expression. It is true that the quality of the communication, its authenticity or transparency were awarded a no doubt debatable primary status in the texts cited earlier, but here the statement of principle concerns the object of study. It should be understood, apart from anything else, as a warning not to fall into the trap of giving too much importance to what is written when we examine societies like our own which build up mountains of paper, but it also announces a totally new approach to social phenomena. I have no doubt that if a crafty questioner were to ask Lévi-Strauss: 'So, what is it that people do not think to commit to paper?', the reply would demand considerable thought. Yet here we have precisely the nub of my own work, in the field of politics. As we know, in this particular sphere, written documents play an essential part; researchers are called upon to spend a great deal of their time amongst statute-books and archives. But anthropology must bring in another dimension, related to its interest, or perhaps one should say its obsession, with forms of behaviour and expression which the protagonists have no reason to commit to paper, of which they are perhaps not even aware. This factor alone differentiates anthropology from other disciplines concerned with politics. To invent a metaphor, I would say that unlike his colleagues in political science, the anthropologist peers into the cracks between the overt statements or the coded social relationships that govern the world of political action and decisions.

Here is the meeting-place for our two branches of anthropology: living with an Ethiopian people, in a totally alien situation, I would notice certain obvious features of collective life, such as gestures of politeness, ritual formulae, ways of commending or denigrating a meal, typical behaviour in a place of assembly. Little by little, I would attempt to give coherence to these elements, which might seem insignificant separately, but which had their place in a larger scheme which we might call the native 'culture'. Anthropology in this sense is quite simply a journey to the land of meaning; its ambition is to bring out the symbolic pattern which underlies men's words and actions and shapes their identity while creating the otherness of outsiders. For example, in Ochollo a particular dignitary led funeral cortèges: I asked 'Why him?' and they told me: 'He grew on the rock.' When I vainly protested that a man does not grow on a rock, they urged on me the etymology of the man's title, which came from the verb 'to grow'. For them this was proof enough, and that fact confirmed me in my role of stranger, close to them, since I shared their lives, yet sufficiently distanced by my cultural references to discern under these examples the important outlines of the symbolic pattern.

Here or elsewhere, anthropology is essentially a way of looking at societies: it is a 'distanced look', as Lévi-Strauss so aptly put it. This is the important thing, not the methods. Anthropology is the art of distancing within the everyday. It is, certainly, an art easier to practise amongst strangers than in one's own society. The anthropology of the familiar is constantly in danger of drowning in the tranquil waters of our symbolic certitudes, whereas foreign societies constantly remind us that we are intruders: we remain on the alert, eager to understand. Clifford Geertz has aptly compared a culture to a text we try to decipher. Finally, we should note that the unavoidable distance clarifies the contours of what we are examining.

This is not the case with our own society. The anthropologist accustomed to exotic worlds find himself facing an anthropology of the banal when he tries to apply his techniques to French society. Here there is no question of becoming familiar with an unknown culture: on the contrary, the task is to create an artificial distance between ourselves and the phenomena of our daily lives, to escape, in a sense, the blinding proximity of the object. 'Instead of a *de facto* distance, and a deliberate identification (in the exotic terrain), we have a *de facto* identification and a deliberate distancing', writes Jean Jamin.[10] This formula clearly suggests the difficulties faced by any conscientious anthropology of the modern. Hence the need to invent strategies of approach to the banal. One of the most successful studies of this type was not in fact the work of a professional anthropologist – which may be no coincidence – but of a semiologist: Roland Barthes presents in his *Mythologies* a masterly analysis of the collective representations that are the stuff of our daily life. Steak and chips, cars, popular heroes, advertisements for detergents, they are all in there; our culture stands revealed in all its most diverse manifestations. This is no intensive observation of a micro-society: Barthes's 'field' consists of all these scattered materials, from films to newspaper articles, posters, or overheard scraps of conversation in cafés. These are words and forms of behaviour which reveal a fundamental coherence, or in the words of the author of *Mythologies*, 'what we might call a public philosophy, that which governs everyday morality, public ceremonial, profane rites, in short, the unwritten rules of social life in bourgeois society'.[11] We are thus invited to a fantastic exploration of the banal manifestations that give our social life its spice. There is nothing we did not already know, since we share in these representations by the very fact of belonging to the society under observation, and yet how surprised we are at the discovery and display of a symbolic universe whose importance we failed (or were unable) to appreciate.

Here we see the explanatory possibilities of anthropology understood as 'observation from a distance' and alert to the real world. The distance, as should be clear by now, is not simply the result of the co-existence of an I (the researcher) and others (the objects of his study), but the fruit of a strategy or, more modestly, a makeshift response, as was the case in my observation of politics as I drifted down the Yonne. I had no hesitation in using the most diverse kinds of material – the local press, rumours, direct observation of public events – and in that sense the basic data in this study are of the same documentary order as those registered in *Mythologies*. The differences are, first of all, that my topic is purely political, and secondly that it covers a limited territory, in that respect following the classic precepts of anthropology. Delineating the territory in this way led me to attach great importance to my meetings with what one might call the 'main actors'. Here again, I have not followed Roland Barthes. His interest was drawn to collective manifestations, whereas my starting-point, as we have seen, was the individual in his confrontation with the phenomenon of politics in the course of his career. My own journey led in a sense from one individual to the next, regardless of geographical distance and in defiance of the sacrosanct tradition of community studies, so keen to define their famous 'self-contained units'.

As a political acquaintance of mine put it once, 'You are examining the local, but it is not a micro-study.' He meant that I had not settled in one precise spot to examine the political activity of a small collectivity, as he would have expected of an anthropologist. Why was I so reluctant to stay in one place, why wander all over the department? I must explain that my nomadism was not a whim; on the contrary, I considered it to be the best possible method in the circumstances. First of all, I was trying to take account of the nature of political space, which involved looking at the electoral divisions associated with the territory. If one is to show the relationship between the different spheres of local politics, the interweaving and possible overlap of powers, it is essential to avoid shutting oneself away in a territory whose limits are rigidly defined – the commune, for example. Moving around and ceaselessly questioning local definitions of the centre and the periphery were my method, the aim of which was to achieve a distanced vision of my own society. The other reason for my relative mobility, as I have said, derived from the importance I gave to individual interviews. Politics is basically a collective activity, but individual experience is an invaluable source of information about its different aspects. It demonstrates the complex interplay of symbolic meanings, causality and individual initiative in the organisation of local politics and the system of representation in France. The individual careers of real people can throw considerable light on a field defined and rendered banal by public discourse, be it the language of political parties or its paraphrase in journalism. The individual is what we might call a carrier, as Marc Augé has explained:

> The anthropologist in an industrial society where the media play an important role will gradually discover that although each individual is in himself a world of imaginary and symbolic meanings, there are levels of organisation at which individual meaning can no longer be distinguished from social meaning and where the relationship between the two is itself significant. All this the anthropologist tries to lay bare.[12]

So, begin with the individual, think in terms of meanings, try to uncover relationships: there are in fact a summary of the methods I used in my research. Sometimes one or other of my informants would ask what on earth he could tell me about a world which was largely familiar to me, as it was to any French citizen. Wouldn't it be easier if they were savages? In fact, all I required was that they should be involved in some way in the 'plot' of local politics. I am using 'plot' here in the literary or theatrical sense, to refer to what Paul Veyne defined as a 'human as distinct from "scientific" mixture of material causes, deliberate aims, and chance events, in short, a slice of human experience, which the historian cuts as he sees fit, and in which facts have both an objective and a relative significance'.[13] I immersed myself in this plot, so much so that I was asked by several 'informants' what meaning I myself attributed to such and such a situation in which they were involved. I even found myself dragged into a discussion of tactics on some occasions. The observations I was able to make acquired their solidity from this constant exchange of words, so characteristic of anthropological activity. I had to facilitate these exchanges, by frequent contact with different characters, each one firmly established in his role. I as the anthropologist had to be willing to ask the sort of naive, incongruous, even preposterous questions evoked inevitably by my position of detachment. This method, I believe, gave me an insight into certain aspects of the 'political culture' underlying this particular type of plot.

Aspects of a political culture

The anthropologist may not have the comforting security of being able to back up his findings with statistics and the use of what are called 'representative' samples, but he can at least boast that he sees the world 'from below'. This was the case in my view of politics in our society. In the majority of analyses of power, the State takes pride of place. The growing complexity of the modern State, and the crises it faces, have given rise to a number of interesting questions. However, we must surely recognise that on a broader view, the State is only the tip of the iceberg. The purely institutionalist view which tends to prevail in the investigation of modern political relations in the long run impoverishes our understanding of those relations. Michel Foucault has criticised this widespread tendency: 'If we make institutions the starting-point for our analysis of power relations, we run the risk of seeking in the former the origin and explanation of the latter, in other words, of explaining power in terms of power.'[14] In the course of my research, I naturally encountered the State, or at least the discourse of the State in the mouths of its servants, that mixture of abstract reasoning, conformism and utopianism that characterises the language of the technostructure. This discourse reveals the weight of everyday existence and the resistance encountered by any more or less serious attempt at administrative reform. To take two examples among thousands: all efforts to modernise municipal structures by fusing or associating often tiny communes have failed; and more recently, in the context of decentralisation, it has proved extremely difficult to set up any kind of meaningful structure at regional level. The apparent irrationality shown here takes us into the shadowy zone of that 'French disease' whose existence is recalled from time to time in politicians' homilies. Leaving aside the moralistic overtones of the phrase, it is clear that we have here certain elements of continuity and certain basic principles which define the essential character of our political culture, in the very general sense of the way we envisage and act out politics. In the course of my prolonged immersion in the political life of the department of the Yonne, I have been able to identify a number of these. The keystone of French political culture, it seems to me, is the point where a *logic of political space* meets a *logic of political representation*. I say a logic, but perhaps it would be better to say an ideologic,[15] which guides the behaviour of the protagonists, and which the latter translate and manipulate according to their situation at a given time. So far as political space is concerned, we have observed that the eternal disquisition on the centralist nature of modern France has in fact tended to mask the real nature of our concept of territorial arrangement. Politics has always a close and yet complex relationship to territory. E. E. Evans-Pritchard, in the introduction to his political anthropology of the Nuer of Sudan, defines political relationships as 'relations within a territorial system between groups of persons who live in spatially well-defined areas and are conscious of their identity and their exclusiveness'.[16]

French centralism is in this sense no more and no less than a method of territorial segmentation. It cannot be reduced to a simple opposition between Paris and the provinces. By going back to the debates in the Assembly on the reorganisation of the kingdom in 1789–90, we saw how a truly hierarchical principle was put into effect all over the country. It proposed an opposition between centre and periphery, biased in that it uniformly favoured the former at the expense of the latter. However, this biased opposition was present at all levels of territorial division. I prefer to call this a polycentric rather than a centralist system. We should note that in the two hundred years that have passed since then, this polycentric representation of political space has not been seriously contested; the failure in 1971 of attempts to amalgamate small communes is highly significant in this context. In attempting to reduce the number of communes, the reformers clashed with a deep-rooted concept: they were airily trying to abolish entities which were admittedly very small, but which at their own level occupied the position of centre. Hence the outcry from mayors, the main spokesmen for this polycentric conception of political space. We have seen that the mayor embodies the political unity of his community: he is the centre, while the municipal councillors essentially have an intermediary role.

The most spectacular demonstration of the continuity of this idea of political space was seen, however, during decentralisation in 1982. This alarming spectre had regularly haunted the national political agenda. There was no shortage of projects, so the administrative reforms which were eventually implemented bore the traces of earlier suggestions. The nub of the reform consisted of the transfer of powers and responsibilities to the various levels of local authority: great discretion was exercised, however, in one particular area, which was the overall organisation of the national territory. The elevation of the region into a full-blown entity did not interfere in any way with the division of the country into departments. To the great disappointment of the two sorts of regionalists – modernising technocrats and intellectuals attracted to local cultural forms – successive governments took great care to avoid getting involved in a debate on the regionalist issue. It was decided instead of promote a sort of peaceful co-existence between the region and the department, sometimes reaching a stage more akin to cohabitation. In the case of Burgundy, for example, our study of the Yonne demonstrates the extent to which decentralisation has increased the importance of the department and its elites, so that there has been no real opportunity for a regional government to assert itself. Once again, a temperate polycentrism has triumphed.

I now come to the logic of representation which informs the French system at a very deep level. Here again, anthropological observation is particularly fruitful. It will be recalled that my starting-point was a very simple question, which can be expressed as: 'How does one gain access to political office in France?' Initially, the answer seemed straightforward: 'As it is a democracy, one need only obtain the votes of one's fellow-citizens.' However, that led to a more complex question: 'Why do people vote for one candidate rather than another?' This is where my research in the villages of the Morvan and then in larger communes led me to introduce the notion of *eligibility* as a sine qua non of any political career. It became clear by the end of my inquiry that in our system this quality of eligibility is available only to a minority of candidates. Thus the original question can be refined to the following: 'Under what conditions does a candidate achieve eligibility?' It was at this point that I introduced the question of *networks*. In other words, I posited that eligibility was primarily a question of relationships.

On this point, the canton of Quarré-les-Tombes offered an almost pure example, a sort of degree zero of political representation. I was able to observe how the quality of eligibility was transmitted over long periods within networks in which kinship relations and matrimonial strategies were vital. These processes are described in the first two chapters, and I do not want to repeat the details of the research. To avoid any misunderstanding, and in answer to a question I have been asked many times, I would like to make it clear that the webs of relationships one can point to, and which merit the term 'network', should be seen as what Max Weber called 'ideal types', or, to use another term he favoured, 'mental constructs'.[17] One of the tasks of the researcher is in fact to reconstruct the web of relationships, as local informants will afford him only a partial and often biased account of it. This reconstruction is only possible as the result of extensive travel around the area of local power, frequent conversations, observation, and use of the valuable information contained in documentary archives.

Even then the ideal type thus hypothesised may not exhaust the complex reality of the network. All we can say is that the anthropological approach offers an excellent means of distinguishing the main outlines of these patterns of relationships. It cannot be over-emphasised that the networks are not fixed entities. There can be no question of simply listing the connections between an individual and other people in the vague general context of local life. Political networks must be seen as an essentially dynamic phenomenon: what we are looking at here is not a series of more or less identifiable groups, but a series of potentialities, which can be activated in response to concrete situations. Elections are one of the moments at which this system of relationships comes into play. A candidate for political office may deliberately use his network potential by displaying signals calculated to evoke it in the eyes of the community. Such a strategy is observable in cases where the candidate is closely related to key figures in the network: the Flandins are an excellent illustration of such a situation. But we also observed how, in the absence of overt signals, the inhabitants of a commune will nevertheless spontaneously attribute to a candidate affiliation to one or other of the networks. Under these conditions, the network stands revealed, not as an inert reality, but as a potentiality brought to realisation by the gaze of others. The members of the local community are in a sense the guardians of a memory which can restore the clarity of affiliations which have grown blurred with time.

For we must not forget that political representation is a phenomenon which achieves its full meaning through continuity. 'Talking politics' is in a way stating one's position in relation to certain key polarisations which go back a long way but whose effects are still felt. I believe that French politics is still marked by the three great founding events of the Revolution, the Separation of Church and State, and the Resistance: turning-points in history which were also periods of intense conflict and which continue to impress the collective imagination. We have seen how, as relations between the Church and the new Republic soured, the political networks took up a position on either side of the line. As the years passed, the ideological enmity gradually grew less, but it still underlies many of today's electoral rivalries; even in situations where the candidates stoutly proclaim their apolitical stance, each candidate is immediately classified in terms of this ancestral divide. The founding event has left its mark, and the behaviour of voters is strongly affected by this sort of imprint transmitted from generation to generation. Though tied to the social and historical context of a particular time, the great ideological divisions (clericalists versus anti-clericalists, right versus left) have an influence well beyond that context. They leave in their wake what Maurice Agulhon has called 'philosophical allegiances';[18] the battle continues, as it were, on the ideas front, though still with no apparent hope of a reconciliation between the two camps.

An illustration of the continuity of ideological cleavages can be seen in the rivalry between Radicals and moderates, not only in the Yonne, but in the majority of other departments: neither changes of personnel nor the evolution of the surrounding society really alter the basic premises. French politics is a terrain of long memories. The political class is the guardian of those memories, which it feeds in turn in the ritual observances it constantly carries out, those acts of commemoration that are the sign of its loyalty to its vocation of acting on behalf of others, while also embodying them. I am not thinking only of the liturgy that came to be accepted under the Third Republic, or all those monuments illustrating the Triumph of Reason and Progress over Obscurantism. In more recent times, the Resistance has offered the basis of an edifice of symbolism whose chief architects have been the Communists. It was not enough that the population of the department had the chance to appreciate on the spot the exemplary actions of militants prepared to sacrifice their lives to a particular vision of France and its future. As soon as the war was over, a picture began to be built up of the liberating hero, the Communist patriot; it had its own monuments and rituals, and made a considerable political impact, in the sense that it helped the party to put down deep roots in local life and traditions.

Legitimacy is certainly one of the key words in French political vocabulary. To enjoy legitimacy is to belong to the world of eligible individuals, those to whom responsibilities can be entrusted. Legitimacy is an elusive quality at first glance: certain individuals canvassing the votes of their fellow-citizens are immediately recognised as legitimate, while others, despite repeated efforts, are doomed to failure. 'What did you expect?' 'It was obvious': these comments are heard again and again when the results of an election are announced. It is as though a candidate's legitimacy is something people instinctively recognise. Suppose I wanted to be mayor of Quarré-les-Tombes; no sooner has the idea entered my head than I realise I haven't a chance. In a way there is nothing to stop me: as an individual I am no more or no less fit to perform such a function than anyone else, and yet it is perfectly obvious that I haven't a chance. Why not? Because I cannot by any stretch of the imagination be said to belong to the world of local political networks. It is a serious handicap. That does not, of course, mean that it is insurmountable. We have seen that under certain conditions it is possible to achieve political office without the advantage of local roots, but only if one can reach some kind of agreement with the existing networks, with a view to finding a place within them.

This system fits admirably with the logic of political spaces as we discerned it. It implies, for example, placing a high value on territorial roots. Legitimacy is rooted in the soil. The first question asked of a candidate concerns his provenance: whether or not he is 'from around here' will be a major influence on his future. Professional politicians take great pains to emphasise their roots in their respective constituencies. In the absence of roots they eagerly display 'local connections'. Having relatives in the area, however distant, is no small asset to a Parisian in search of an elusive legitimacy. This local dimension can be appreciated in the various conversations I have relayed: my informants volunteered such information in advance of the question, often dwelling at length on their geographical origins. We have also seen how all the main political parties give great importance to local activity: everyone from the Communists to the RPR devotes themselves to 'constituency spadework', to use a metaphor which is revealing in itself. The Socialists, who were ill at ease in this kind of situation for a long time, have learned to revise their strategy and give due importance to the local dimension.

While emphasising the importance of local factors in our political practice, we must not minimise the 'national' factor, or of course the role of the parties, notably in the selection of candidates to the General Council and the National Assembly. The arrival in the department of the Minister for Agriculture was significant in this respect. Henri Nallet's candidature initially looked like the work of the national leadership of the Socialist Party. Without that nomination, the newcomer would have had no political existence. It is clear, however, that the support of the party was not in itself sufficient to invest the candidate with a real status in the department, as Henri Nallet himself realised only too well. We saw that the success of this parachute landing was due in great measure to the Minister's own efforts in travelling all round the constituency, meeting large numbers of people, and promptly acquiring a house in one of the chief towns. No doubt his journey was like an assault course in places, but by the end the traveller was captivated by the area, to the extent of being completely integrated into it. The candidate's task was to take over a network, and win the loyalty of groups well beyond the orbit of his own party. It is an unending task, in the sense that he has to cultivate this network, constantly widening his basis of support and forming new links within his chosen territory. This is the surest way to build a really solid political legitimacy.

What makes local political life so interesting in a country like France is the margin of play between the formal aspects of political activity – membership of a party, the well-ordered antagonism between the main parties – and the whole world of relationships that forms the indispensable and ubiquitous backdrop to that activity. For example, to define the position of Jean-Pierre Soisson in the political set-up, it would initially seem sufficient to state that he is one of the leaders of the right, and has frequently been elected in preference to a Socialist candidate. In other words, in view of the political tenor of the population of Auxerre, with its majority of right-wing voters, it is no surprise to a political scientist that Soisson should enjoy such a stable position. Yet things are not quite this simple, since we noticed that the voters swung to the left in the general election, yet had no hesitation in electing Soisson at the local elections. He is what is called a 'local personality'. Everyone in Auxerre knows that the deputy's political colours, his party label, are but one element among many of his personality. Other qualities are just as vital in ensuring his continuity in office: the fact that he is the heir to a well-known name, that he represents youth and new ideas, that he has forged, and maintains, links with the mayors of the Puisaye and the elite of Auxerre, that he has been a Minister.

Here we begin to appreciate that an elected representative is not simply the embodiment of an idea or a party. What wins him the support of his fellow-citizens is above all the fact of incarnating a series of qualities which make him a being at once similar to, yet different from, others. Soisson is the offspring of an old Auxerre family, the embodiment of a familiar sociological reality, but he is also a man who has succeeded in the world, who has distinguished himself from the common herd, who shows ambition. A potent mixture of similarity and difference: that is the characteristic image of the 'representative' personality in our democratic societies. And this is valid for all parties. We noticed it in the case of the Communist members of the General Council: their participation in situations of social conflict and demonstations and the periodic reaffirmation of their links with the working class in no way contradicted a symbolism designed to establish a distance between the representative and those he represents. Within our concept of fitness to represent, the politician occupies a special place: he is both the product of ordinary society – and in this sense the distinction people have tried to bring in at government level between those Ministers representing ordinary society and 'political' Ministers seems unconvincing – and an image supporting the most varied beliefs. A person and a symbol: that is the definition of a public figure, and it is true at both ends of the scale, the local and the national. By analysing electoral habits, and following the representatives in their daily lives, we have gained some idea of the importance of the symbolic and the imaginary in the world of politics.

That leads us to qualify the old cliché which says that action is the key word in politics. Politicians, we are told, are men and women of action, or at least they have the extraordinary privilege of being able to affect the actions of others. I would be inclined to add that politicians also have the power of *evocation.* Think of the great ceremonies presided over from time to time by the President of the Republic, which serve to remind us periodically that we belong to a community symbolised in the person of the Head of State, occasions such as the military parade on 14 July or the Armistice Day ceremonies on 11 November . . . France does not merely need to be governed, as we are reminded from time to time; she also needs to be given an identity, both in the person of the wielder of supreme power and in the signs he handles. The dimension of the sacred in relation to power has lost nothing of its strength in the modern world. François Mitterand has shown a remarkable ability to cultivate this power of evocation, just as General de Gaulle did before him, though in a different register. Far from weakening the symbolism of power, the development of the media has given it new life. Images incite new forms of identification; with these images, politics, faithful to its vocation, makes people dream. On a much more local level, my research showed quite clearly the dominant role of symbol and ritual in the political life of a department.

Many rituals are intended to express in a material form the continuing identification of the elected representative with his community. Some commemorate events which have significantly marked the community, and here the elected representatives must speak and behave in a way which magnifies their personalities, the incarnation of the common heritage: others are ceremonies of inauguration which permit the display of improvements to the common heritage to which the elected representative has contributed. One of the essential activities of a deputy consists, as we have seen, in repeated weekly journeys around his constituency. These ceremonies are not so very different from those which anthropologists have observed in remote societies. There is, of course, no ritual sacrifice: instead, monuments are unveiled, a minute's silence is observed, and so on, but the meaning of the ceremony, the affirmation of local roots and a common territory, is just as basic. The public figure is participating in a ceremonial marking of territory. Those who refuse to devote the required time to these political rituals will sooner or later learn to their cost that it is a mistake to neglect this aspect of political representation. Evocation, symbols, rituals. Should we see the observance of these ceremonies, faithfully reported week by week in the local press, as an example of archaic practices? Surely the idea of localised power, consecrating the identity of an individual and a territory, will inevitably disappear in favour of a more rational and efficient system? Certainly the general evolution of French society, which is more and more urbanised, and taken up with the restructuring of the economy, would invite such a reflection. Moreover, the persistence of a memory of networks and old ideological divisions coming into play in local elections might be seen as an obstacle to modernisation and the attempt to open up the political spectrum. Is it possible to go beyond mere talk and modernise French political life – to 'do things differently' or 'improve the system', as people are always saying – when in this realm as in no other the continuity of networks and memory, of rituals and symbols, seems all-powerful and omnipresent?

Future developments

It is worth stressing that the department as an entity offers one of the best examples of such continuity. An inheritance of the Revolution, it is still an obligatory staging-post in every political career even today. It is also the principal administrative division; its chief town is the location of most of the important offices, such as the public works, finance, health and agriculture offices. From the point of view of local political relations, the department is a sort of microcosm, and one could say that there is a political class that takes its identity from the department, whatever its ramifications may be at regional or national level. The polycentric conception which lies at the heart of our political system finds its ideal expression in the organisation of the department. The sub-division of the department into cantons, each centred around its chief town and embodied in the person of a notable or 'messenger', the member of the General Council, is what gives the department its special character. The office of member of the General Council certainly represented the quintessence of our concept of political representation: acquiring their influence from their role of intermediaries between the population, their mayors and the administration, the members of the departmental assembly always formed a small elite, aware of their prerogatives, yet willing to accept without too much complaint the superior authority of the prefect in running things. The fact is that until the administrative reforms introduced in 1982, polycentrism was narrowly constituted by the *co-existence* of the councillors within the departmental assembly: they did not strictly speaking form a local government. The gathering of councillors *embodied* the unity of the department, but the expression of that unity in the day-to-day administration was the responsibility of the prefect. In this way, the principle of polycentric representation was respected, yet did not constitute an obstacle to action.

This remarkably close fit between the logic of representation and that of political space no doubt explains the extraordinary stability of a system which has lasted right down to the present, apparently unaffected by the legislative and constitutional ups and downs France has known since the Revolution. The transfer of departmental executive power from the prefects to the Presidents of General Councils in response to the laws on decentralisation upset this tradition. While not contesting the role of the department, the law of 1982 nevertheless had a direct effect on the workings of local institutions: as the prefect faded into the background, members of the General Council became full-blown administrators. Local government was formed around the President of the General Council. The term 'representative' is no longer a satisfactory description of the member of the General Council. It is is no longer sufficient for them to meet together: an overall policy must be made to prevail. Thus we see the replacement of the *polycentrism* which had prevailed up to that point by a *concentrism* embodied in the authority of the President of the General Council backed up by a political majority. There was undeniably a change in this respect, relating not only to the general conception of political space, but also to power relations between the big names in the department; to be President of the General Council under the new system has become a worthwhile venture, while at the same time it is becoming more and more difficult to combine this office, and its increased burden of responsibility, with a national or municipal mandate. This is not the result simply of the legal dispositions aimed at curbing the simultaneous exercise of several mandates; it also reflects the increased investment now required in time and energy.

One might reasonably predict that one of the results of this development will be a notable increase in the technical skills required in local government, with local councillors – or the majority of them at least – gradually acquiring the wider skills required to deal with the issues now coming within their remit. Thus one might expect to see the emergence of a generation of councillors more expert than their predecessors, and more concerned to grasp the economic problems facing the whole department than with parish-pump issues. Instead of the 'heritage' profile of the notable with strong local roots, a more 'professional' type of councillor may emerge, one whose legitimacy will be based on technical knowledge and ability to take decisions and lead others. Under these conditions, membership of a network will seem less vital than in the past; membership of one of the political parties which are strong in the area, or even a discreet apoliticism, will be a help in getting started. Thus at a time when our society is changing very rapidly, we may see the waning of the 'archaic' methods of transmitting power and the ideological heritage that went with it. Under these conditions, legitimacy may come rather from the concrete activity of public figures. We have seen the importance given to technical competence and the ability to generate new ideas in the fields of town planning and urban renewal amongst councillors who see themselves as the partisans of up-to-date ideas.

It is difficult to give a time-scale for this process, but it is quite clear that it has already begun. Decentralisation favours it, at the same time strengthening and rejuvenating the department as an entity. At least, that is what my observations suggest, which leads me to wonder whether this new approach to local politics, with its emphasis on the spirit of enterprise, will lead as an indirect result to substantial modifications in two areas of local life: one, the reproduction of the political class through its own networks, and two, the relationship between councillors and their fellow-citizens. Will the latter be more and more influenced by the concrete success of councillors in attracting investment to the area? Will they be less obsessed with the here and now, with the kerb that needs repairing or exemption from military service for their son in response to the councillor's intervention? Will the councillor become something more, and something better, than simply an effective intermediary? We have seen how vital this practical role of the elected representative still is: the demands made of present-day deputies are exactly akin to those made on Pierre-Etienne Flandin. Similarly, we have noted that the ideological oppositions which presided over the formation of the networks, approximately a hundred years ago, are still very much alive, even if they hardly correspond any longer to present-day realities and needs.

Certainly neither left nor right can afford to despise local networks: there can be no possibility of a political career that is not inscribed in the workings of local relationships. And yet one sees a rearrangement of the networks, helped by the appearance of new personalities. The achievements of Henri Nallet in this respect, opening up the traditional anti-clerical republican network to other currents closer to the real economy, are typical of this development. What about a more profound shake-up in the landscape of local politics? Jean-Pierre Soisson's spectacular adhesion to the Socialist government is still a source of excitement in Auxerre and throughout the whole department. Many people are banking on a *rapprochement* between Soisson and the local Socialists for the municipal elections. It is not so strange that Auxerre should be one of the testing-grounds for the new centre–left alliance. Just as the Socialists and the centre have been working together for some time now on projects for the good of the whole department, so one can easily imagine them getting together to run one or two communes. That would be on condition, however, that as one of my informants put it, 'people are still themselves': the alliance could not accommodate any changes of identity. There must be respect for the outlines of the networks and the memory of old loyalties. Here again, the strategies of the different parties must take account of past history, the sediment of which forms the base of local political life.

This forces me to qualify my vision of future developments in French political culture. True, we must not underestimate the importance of factors like the growth in professionalisation of political activity and the development of alliances bridging the traditional ideological divides. Like other aspects of society, French politics is changing; but it would certainly be a mistake to see this as the triumph of the rational over archaic beliefs, with as its counterpoint the emergence of a new class of entrepreneurial politicians, resolutely modernist and with their gaze fixed on the future. The anthropologist is well placed to tell what exactly distinguishes a public figure from the entrepreneur or 'manager' that he sometimes boasts of emulating. The nub of the question is the one word 'election'; one is a representative, the other is not. Political representation brings in its wake a whole world of values, relationships, overlapping histories and tangled signs. The real professional politician, as we have seen, is one who plays continually and subtly with these different registers. Local political life provides a fine demonstration of the adaptability of the leading protagonists, who can combine elements of a distant past with the needs of the present as required. The continuity of rituals, and people's attachment to symbols remind us once again that memory and imagination go hand in hand with reason to make politics a job apart, where the limit of power is always the horizon of legitimacy.

'What is politics like in your country?'

Coming to the end of these quiet days in the department of the Yonne, I felt that I had finally glimpsed the beginning of an answer to the question I had been asked by the Ochollo . . .

Notes

Preface to the French edition

1 See Marc Abélès, *Le Lieu du politique* (Paris, Société d'Ethnographie, 1983).

1 Who is eligible?

1. In relation to the Morvan, I consulted the following works: J. Levainville, *Le Morvan. Etude de géographie humaine* (Paris, Armand Colin, 1909); Jacqueline Bonnamour, *Le Morvan, la terre et les hommes* (Paris, PUF, 1966); Marcel Vigreux, *Paysans et notables du Morvan au XIXe siècle jusqu'en 1914* (Château-Chinon, Académie du Morvan, 1987).
2. Louis Devoir, *Au fil des jours et des ans* (Saint-Germain-des-Champs, 1984), pp. 46–7.
3. *Ibid.*, p.6.
4. *Ibid.*, p.50.
5. Municipal Archive, Saint-Germain-des-Champs.
6. Devoir, *Au fil des jours*, p. 73.
7. *Ibid.*, p.56.
8. *Ibid.*, p.52.
9. *Ibid.*, p.82.
10. Tract distributed during the municipal campaign in 1983.
11. Municipal Archive, Saint-Germain-des-Champs.
12. V. B. Henry, *Mémoires historiques sur le canton de Quarré-les-Tombes* (2 vols., Auxerre, Imprimerie Albert Gallot, 1875).
13. J. F. Baudiau, *Le Morvan, ou essai géographique, topographique et historique sur cette contrée* (2 vols., Nevers, Fay, 1854).
14. National Archive, D4 bis 1.
15. On this period, see Claude Hohl, 'Autour d'une élection cantonale:le parti légitimiste dans l'Avallonnais au début du second Empire, *Bulletin de la Société des sciences historiques et naturelles de l'Yonne*, 114 (1982), 71–86.
16. Archive of the department of the Yonne, 2Z5, 5 August 1853.
17. Archive of the department of the Yonne, 2Z6, 12 August 1853.
18. *Ibid.*, May 1855.
19. National Archive, F1 C3 Yonne, April 1859.
20. National Archive, F1 B2 Yonne 18, letter from the mayor of Saint-Léger to the schools inspector.

21. *Ibid.*, sub-prefect's report, 30 October 1871.
22. *Ibid.*, police sergeant's report, 22 December 1871.
23. *Ibid.*, sub-prefect's report, 3 October 1871.
24. Petition published in *Le Nouvelliste de l'Yonne* (12 March 1877), from which I have also taken the quotation from *Le Pays*.
25. National Archive, F1 B2 Yonne 18, letter from the mayor to the Prime Minister and Minister of the Interior, 16 March 1877.
26. *Ibid.*, 8 April 1877.
27. *Ibid.*, 8 August 1877.
28. Archive of the department of the Yonne, 3M1 301.
29. *Ibid.*
30. Municipal Archive, Saint-Brancher, debate of 7 August 1902.
31. Municipal Archive, Saint-Léger-Vauban, debate of 4 June 1899.
32. Archive of the department of the Yonne 2M5 262, municipal elections (5 May 1912).
33. *Ibid.*
34. *Ibid.*

2 Dynasties

1. For the Flandin family history, apart from archive material, I have mainly used the *Recueil généalogique de la bourgeoisie ancienne*, ed. André Delavenne, preface by the duc de Brissac (Paris, 1954) and Dom Bénigne Defarges, *Mon village sur Cure*, 2nd edn (La-Pierre-qui-Vire, Editions de La-Pierre-qui-Vire, 1979). I am grateful to have received invaluable information from M. Paul Flandin and Mme Régine Pujo, who allowed me to consult the Flandin private family archive.
2. Of Paul's four children, the two girls had no issue. Their brothers Gilbert and Bernard had one son each: Gilbert's son entered holy orders, and Bernard's was killed in 1940. We should note that this branch of the family had inherited the properties situated in Lormes and its surroundings.
3. National Archive, F1 C3 Yonne.
4. *Ibid.*
5. Charles Girard, 'Les Elections dans l'Yonne sous la IIIe République', series of articles published in *L'Yonne* (January–March 1924).
6. François Goguel, 'Un siècle d'élections législatives dans l'Yonne (1848–1946)', in *Du jansénisme à la laïcité. Le Jansénisme et les origines de la déchristianisation*, Ed. Léo Hamon (Paris, Editions de la Maison des Sciences de l'Homme, 1987), pp. 191–216.
7. Girard, *L'Yonne* (15 February 1924).
8. See Pierre Ordioni, 'Sur l'anticléricalisme de Paul Bert et ses racines jansénistes', in Hamon (ed.), *Du jansénisme*, pp. 167–89.
9. National Archive, F1 C3 Yonne 7, report of 1869.
10. Archive of the department of the Yonne 3M1 301, quoted in *Les Paysans de l'Yonne au XIXe siècle*, ed. Jean-Pierre Rocher (Archives de l'Yonne, service éducatif 1978), p. 91.
11. Information taken from Defarges, *Mon village*, pp. 114–16.
12. See J. P. Rocher, 'Auxerre pendant la première moitié du XIXe siècle', in *Histoire d'Auxerre des origines à nos jours*, ed. J. P. Rocher (Auxerre, Editions Horvath, 1984), pp. 303–41.

13. Archive of the department of the Yonne, Ribière Papers, Manifesto dated 12 December 1881.
14. Archive of the department of the Yonne, 2M5 214.
15. *Ibid.*
16. *Annuaire de l'Yonne* (1869).
17. *Dictionnaire des parlementaires français* (Paris, PUF, 1960), p. 2843.
18. Goguel, 'Unsiècle d'élections législatives', p. 203.
19. Girard, *L'Yonne* (28 March 1924).
20. *Le Petit Parisien* (18 April 1936).
21. *Revue de l'Yonne* (19 April 1928).
22. Letters from M. Marceau, undated, and M. Colas, 4 April 1928, private archives.
23. *Revue de l'Yonne* (19 April 1928).
24. Undated statement. Private archives.
25. *Ibid.*
26. *Ibid.*
27. *Ibid.*
28. *Ibid.*
29. Letter from the mayor of Merry-sur-Yonne, 10 April 1928. Private archives.
30. Letter from M. Soulebeau, 27 March 1928. Private archives.
31. Letter from Maître Guimard, notary at Chatel-Censoir, 2 April 1928; reply, 3 April 1928. Private archives.
32. Letter from M. Hamelin, distiller, of Monétau, 17 April 1928. Private archives.
33. Reply from P.-E. Flandin, 18 April 1928. Private archives.
34. Goguel, 'Un siècle d'elections législatives', p. 209.
35. *Journal officiel*, Débats de la Chambre (12 March 1931), 1990ff.
36. Jean Zay, *Souvenirs et solitude*, quoted in Edouard Bonnefous, *Histoire parlementaire de la IIIe République*, V, *La République en danger: des ligues au Front Populaire (1930–1936)* (Paris, PUF, 1962), p. 388.
37. *L'Air de Paris* (18 April 1936).
38. *Le Petit Journal* (18 April 1936).
39. Manifesto, undated. Private archives.
40. *Le Provençal* (23 April 1936).
41. *L'Avenir du Tonnerrois* (24 April 1936).
42. *Ibid.*
43. Letter of 14 November 1945.
44. Devoir, *Au fil des jours*, p. 55.
45. Eugen Weber, *Peasants into Frenchmen* (Stanford, Stanford University Press, 1976), Fr. trans. *La Fin des terroirs* (Paris, Fayard, 1983), 839pp.
46. Vigreux, *Paysans et notables*, ch. 1, esp. p. 588. See also Maurice Agulhon, *Histoire vagabonde* (Paris, Gallimard, 1988). For an anthropological and historical approach to local political dynasties, see Yves Pourcher, *Les Maîtres de granit. Les Notables en Lozère du XIIIe siècle à nos jours* (Paris, Olivier Orban, 1987).

3 Ups and downs in politics

1. *Théorie des pouvoirs et idéologie. Etudes de cas en Côte-d'Ivoire* (Paris, Hermann, 1975).
2. Conversation with Michel Bonhenry.

3. *L'Yonne républicaine* (26–7 February 1977).
4. We will return in Chapter 7 to the political role and personality of Jean Moreau.
5. Conversation with Daniel Dollfus.
6. Conversation with Grégoire Direz.
7. *L'Yonne-Sud* (3 December 1982).
8. *Ibid.*
9. *Ibid.* (9–10 December 1984).
10. Interview published in *L'Yonne républicaine* (30 April 1987).
11. In the general election in June 1988, Grégoire Direz was beaten by a large majority in the constituency of Avallon–Tonnerre by Henri Nallet.
12. Gilles Dauxerre, *L'Yonne républicaine* (30 April 1987).
13. Michel Marié, *Un territoire sans nom* (Paris, Librairie des Méridiens, 1982).

4 The new deal: decentralisation

1. On the whole of this reorganisation of the country, see the helpful article by Marie-Vic Ozouf-Marignier, 'De l'universalisme constituant aux intérêts locaux: le débat sur la formation des départements en France (1789–1790)', *Annales ESC*, 6 (1986), 1193–1213.
2. The creation of the department of the Yonne is examined in depth in Charles Porée, 'La Formation du département de l'Yonne en 1790', *Bulletin de la Société des sciences historiques et naturelles de l'Yonne*, 63 (1909), 5–195.
3. *Ibid.*, 30–1.
4. Archive of the department of the Yonne, C190, fol. 46. Debate of 19 October 1788.
5. *Moniteur* I, p. 246. Session of 24 September 1789.
6. *Ibid.*, p.336. Session of 3 November 1789.
7. National Archive, D4 bis 300.
8. *Ibid.*, D4 bis 448.
9. *Ibid.*, D4 bis 91.
10. *Ibid.*, D4 bis 300.
11. Archive of the department of the Yonne, L272, quoted in Porée, 'La Formation du département de l'Yonne', 83–4.
12. As we saw in the previous chapter.
13. For the reforms of Year 3 and their failure, see Jacques Morange, *L'Idée de municipalité de canton de l'an III à nos jours* (Paris, PUF, 1971).
14. Tocqueville, *Souvenirs*, Part 2, XI, (Paris, 1895).
15. Pierre Grémion, *Le Pouvoir périphérique* (Paris, Seuil, 1976).
16. Pierre Richard, 'La Réforme des collectivités locales', in *Décision et pouvoir dans la société française*, ed. Lucien Sfez (Paris, UGE, 10/18, 1979).
17. Christian Pineau, *Mon cher député* (Paris, Julliard, 1969), pp. 67–8.
18. Robert de Caumont, *Des conseillers généraux, pour quoi faire*? (Paris, Editions Téma, 1973), p. 103.
19. Grémion, *Le Pouvoir périphérique*, p. 305.
20. Archive of the department of the Yonne, 2M3 161.
21. Conversation with Raymond Janot.
22. Conversation with Jean Pélissier.
23. *L'Yonne républicaine* (3 July 1987).
24. Conversation with Jean Chamant.

5 Parachuting in

1. *L'Yonne républicaine* (11 May 1897).
2. Conversation with Henri Nallet.
3. Conversation with Jean-Paul Rousseau.
4. Conversation with Roland Enès.
5. *L'Yonne républicaine* (28 September 1973).
6. *L'Yonne républicaine* (1 October 1973).
7. See Calliope Beaud, *Combat pour Vézelay ou Péchiney Pollution* (Paris, Editions Entente, 1976).
8. Conversation with André Fourcade.
9. *La Lettre d'Henri Nallet*, No. 9 (December 1987).

6 The Communist Party and real life

1. Conversation with Armand Simonnot.
2. Mugnier's report is cited by Robert Bailly in his *Les Feuilles tombèrent en avril* (Editions Sociales, 1977), pp. 117–18.
3. Written account by A. Simonnot, cited in Jacques Canaud, *Les Maquis du Morvan (1943–1944). La vie dans les maquis*, Preface by René Rémond (Château-Chinon, Académie du Morvan, 1981), p. 41.
4. In the nineteenth century, the figure of the poacher symbolised a rejection of the law, a break with the established order and a dissident activity which found sympathy with the poorer classes: 'A group of men whose behaviour vis-à-vis the law and their masters is at heart admired by the poorer groups in society. The move or transfer to a political attitude is easily made in a period of revolution such as 1848–1852: poachers become "reds", they do not accept authority, and they are very ready to enter into secret groups or societies' (Vigreux, *Paysans et notables*, p. 592).
5. Archive of the department of the Yonne, 3M1 337. Correspondence of 13 February 1885.
6. *Annuaire de l'Yonne* (1852), Ch. 2, 423.
7. Conversation with André Durand.
8. Cited in Rocher (ed.), Ch. *Histoire d'Auxerre* 2, p. 311. See on the same subject J. P. Rocher, 'Auxerre et le chemin de fer', *Bulletin de la Société des sciences historiques et naturelles de l'Yonne* (1977).
9. Conversation with Guy Lavrat.
10. Conversation with Jean Cordillot.

7 Deputy and mayor

1. C. Bettelheim and S. Frère, *Une ville moyenne: Auxerre en 1950. Etude de structure sociale et urbaine*, Cahiers de la Fondation nationale des sciences politiques (Paris, Armand Colin, 1952).
2. National Archive, F1C3 1253. Report of Prefect Gibaud, 28 May 1945.
3. Decision No. 102, 5 June 1945. Honour Jury chaired by René Cassin.
4. National Archive, F1C3 1253. Report of Prefect Gibaud, 25 June 1945.
5. *Ibid.* Report of 25 July 1945.
6. See Jean-Charles Guillaume, *Guilliet. Histoire d'une entreprise (1847–1979)* (Auxerre, Société des sciences historiques et naturelles de l'Yonne, 1986).
7. Archive of the department of the Yonne, 2M2 91. Municipal elections (13 November–7 December 1919).

8. Archive of the department of the Yonne, 2M5 315. Municipal elections (3–10 May 1925). Election manifesto of Bloc ouvrier et paysan.
9. Quoted in *L'Yonne républicaine* (17 March 1971).
10. Speech by Mgr Deschamps on the centenary of the founding of Guilliet's, 17 April 1948. See Guillaume, *Guilliet*, p. 128.
11. Archive of the department of the Yonne, 2M5 341. Municipal elections (5–12 May 1929). Correspondence of 6 May 1929.
12. *Ibid.* Municipal elections (5–12 May 1935). Correspondence of 16 May 1929.
13. *Ibid.* Letter from the prefect to the president of the General Council, P.-E. Flandin, 7 May 1935.
14. Municipal Archive, Auxerre. Ballot, 12 May 1935. Objection by M. Moreau and colleagues, Interdepartmental Prefectural Council, Dijon, No. 61, Yonne.
15. *Le Bourguignon* (8 May 1941), report of Auxerre municipal council taking office, 5 May 1941.
16. Municipal Archive, Auxerre. Extract from minutes of council.
17. See Antoine Demaux, *Une république à chaque bras . . .*, Preface by J.-P. Soisson (Auxerre, Editions F. P. Lobies, 1981), pp. 58–9.
18. Municipal Archive, Auxerre. Elections to General Council, 23 September 1945. Pamphlet by the Socialist and Communist sections.
19. *L'Yonne républicaine* (17 March 1971).
20. *L'Eclaireur de l'Yonne* (September 1948), quoted in Demaux, Une *république*, p. 77.
21. Quoted in Guillaume, *Guilliet*, p. 203.
22. Jean-Pierre Soisson, *La Victoire sur l'hiver* (Fayard, 1978), p. 33.
23. Conversation with Jean-Pierre Soisson. For other extremely useful information on the history of the Soisson family, I have to thank Mme Marie-Thérèse Laubry.
24. Conversation with Paul Guillaumot.
25. Conversation with Jean-Pierre Soisson.
26. Conversation with the General Secretary of the town hall, Auxerre.
27. Conversation with Jean-Pierre Soisson.
28. *Ibid.*
29. Conversation with Guy Roux.

Conclusion

1. For developments in Europeanist anthropology, see *Ethnologies en miroir*, ed. Isac Chiva and Utz Jeggle (Paris, Editions de la maison des sciences de l'homme, 1987).
2. Claude Lévi-Strauss, *Anthropologie structurale* (Paris, Plon, 1958), p. 397.
3. *Ibid.*, p. 400.
4. *Ibid.*
5. *Ibid.*, p. 402.
6. *Ibid.*
7. See *L'Ecole de Chicago. Naissance de l'écologie humaine*, translated and introduced by Y. Grafmeyer and I. Joseph (Paris, Champ Urbain, 1979).
8. Marc Augé, 'Qui est l'autre? Un itinéraire anthropologique', *L'Homme*, 103 (1987), 25.
9. Lévi-Strauss, *Anthropologie*, p. 38.

10. Jean Jamin, 'Le Texte ethnographique. Argument', *Etudes rurales*, 97–8 (1985), 20.
11. Roland Barthes, *Mythologies* (Paris, Editions du Seuil, 1957), p. 227.
12. M. Augé, 'Qui est l'autre', 25.
13. Paul Veyne, *Comment on écrit l'histoire* (Paris, Editions du Seuil, 1971), p. 38.
14. Michel Foucault, 'Deux essais sur le sujet du pouvoir', in H. Dreyfus and P. Rabinow (eds.), *Michel Foucault: un parcours philosophique* (Paris, Gallimard, 1985), p. 315.
15. I have borrowed this notion from Marc Augé: see in particular *Pouvoirs de vie, pouvoirs de mort* (Paris, Flammarion, 1977), Ch. 2.
16. E. E. Evans-Pritchard, *The Nuer* (Oxford, Clarendon Press, 1940), p. 4.
17. Max Weber, 'L'Objectivité de la connaissance dans les sciences et la politique sociales' (1904) (French translation) in *Essais sur la théorie de la science* (Paris, Plon, 1965), p. 190.
18. 'There have been class conflicts, but there have also been philosophical loyalties which have lasted through or against the currents of history', Maurice Agulhon, *Histoire vagabonde*, Vol. II (Paris, Gallimard, 1988), p. 241.

Cambridge Studies in Social and Cultural Anthropology

Editors: JACK GOODY, STEPHEN GUDEMAN, MICHAEL HERZFELD, JONATHAN PARRY

1 The Political Organisation of Unyamwezi
R. G. ABRAHAMS

2 Buddhism and the Spirit Cults in North-East Thailand*
S. J. TAMBIAH

3 Kalahan Village Politics: An African Democracy
ADAM KUPER

4 The Rope of Moka Big-Men and Ceremonial Exchange in Mount Hagen. New Guinea*
ANDREW STRATHERN

5 The Majangir Ecology and Society of a Southwest Ethiopian People
JACK STAUDER

6 Buddhist Monk, Buddhist Layman: A Study of Urban Monastic Organisation in Central Thailand
JANE BUNNAG

7 Contexts of Kinship An Essay in the Family Sociology of the Gonja of Northern Ghana
ESTHER N GOODY

8 Marriage among a Matrilineal Elite. A Family Study of Ghanaian Civil Servants
CHRISTINE OPPONG

9 Elite Politics in Rural India Political Stratification and Political Alliances in Western Maharashtra
ANTHONY T CARTER

10 Women and Property in Morocco. Their Changing Relation to the Process of Social Stratification in the Middle Atlas
VANESSA MAHER

11 Rethinking Symbolism*
DAN SPERBER. Translated by Alice L. Morton

12 Resources and Population: A Study of the Gurungs of Nepal
ALAN MACFARLANE

13 Mediterranean Family Structures
EDITED BY J. G. PERISTIANY

14 Spirits of Protest: Spirit-Mediums and the Articulation of Consensus

among the Zezuru of Southern Rhodesia (Zimbabwe)
PETER FRY

15 World Conqueror and World Renouncer. A Study of Buddhism and Polity in Thailand against a Historical Background*
S. J. TAMBIAH

16 Outline of a Theory of Practice*
PIERRE BOURDIEU. Translated by Richard Nice

17 Production and Reproduction: A Comparative Study of the Domestic Domain*
JACK GOODY

18 Perspectives in Marxist Anthropology*
MAURICE GODELIER. Translated by Robert Brain

19 The Fate Shechem, or the Politics of Sex: Essays in the Anthropology of the Mediterranean
JULIAN PITT-RIVERS

20 People of the Zongo: The Transformation of Ethnic Identities in Ghana
ENID SCHILDKROUT

21 Casting out Anger: Religion among the Taita of Kenya
GRACE HARRIS

22 Rituals of the Kandyan State
H. L. SENEVIRATNE

23 Australian Kin Classification
HAROLD W. SCHEFFLER

24 The Palm and the Pleiades: Initiation and Cosmology in Northwest Amazonia
STEPHEN HUGH-JONES

25 Nomads of Southern Siberia: The Pastoral Economies of Tuva
S. I. VAINSHTEIN. Translated by Michael Colenso

26 From the Milk River: Spatial and Temporal Processes in Northwest Amazonia*
CHRISTINE HUGH-JONES

27 Day of Shining Red: An Essay on Understanding Ritual*
GILBERT LEWIS

28 Hunters, Pastoralists and Ranchers: Reindeer Economies and their Transformations*
TIM INGOLD

29 The Wood-Carvers of Hong Kong: Craft Production in the World Capitalist Periphery
EUGENE COOPER

30 Minangkabau Social Formations: Indonesian Peasants and the World Economy
JOEL S. KAHN

31 Patrons and Partisans: A Study of Two Southern Italian Communes
CAROLINE WHITE

32 Muslim Society*
ERNEST GELLNER

33 Why Marry Her? Society and Symbolic Structures
LUC DE HEUSCH. Translated by Janet Lloyd

34 Chinese Ritual and Politics
EMILY MARTIN AHERN
35 Parenthood and Social Reproduction. Fostering and Occupational Roles in West Africa
ESTHER N. GOODY
36 Dravidian Kinship
THOMAS R. TRALTMANN
37 The Anthropological Circle: Symbol, Function, History*
MARC AUGE. Translated by Martin Thom
38 Rural Society in Southeast Asia
KATHLEEN GOUGH
39 The Fish-People: Linguistic Exogamy and Tukanoan Identity in Northwest Amazonia
JEAN E. JACKSON
40 Karl Marx Collective: Economy, Society and Religion in a Siberian Collective Farm*
CAROLINE HUMPHREY
41 Ecology and Exchange in the Andes
Edited by DAVID LEHMANN
42 Traders without Trade: Responses to Trade in two Dyula Communities
ROBERT LAUNAY
43 The Political Economy of West African Agriculture*
KEITH HART
44 Nomads and the Outside World
A. M. KHAZANOV. Translated by Julia Crookenden
45 Actions, Norms and Representations: Foundations of Anthropological Inquiry*
LADISLAV HOLY AND MILAN STUCKLIK
46 Structural Models in Anthropology*
PER HAGE AND FRANK HARARY
47 Servants of the Goddess: The Priests of a South Indian Temple
C. J. FULLER
48 Oedipus and Job in West African Religion*
MEYER PORTES
49 The Buddhist Saints of the Forest and the Cult of Amulets: A Study in Charisma. Hagiography, Sectarianism, and Millennial Buddhism*
S. J. TAMBIAH
50 Kinship and Marriage: An Anthropological Perspective (available in paperback/in the USA only)
ROBIN FOX
51 Individual and Society in Guiana. A Comparative Study of Amerindian Social Organization*
PETER RIVIERE
52 People and the State: An Anthropology of Planned Development*
A. F. ROBERTSON
53 Inequality among Brothers. Class and Kinship in South China
RUBIE S. WATSON
54 On Anthropological Knowledge*
DAN SPERBER

55 Tales of the Yanomami: Daily Life in the Venezuelan Forest*
JACQUES LIZOT, Translated by Ernest Simon

56 The Making of Great Men: Male Domination and Power among the New Guinea Baruya*
MAURICE GODELIER. Translated by Rupert Swyer

57 Age Class Systems: Social Institutions and Politics Based on Age*
BERNARDO BERNARDI, Translated by David I. Kertzer

58 Strategies and Norms in a Changing Matrilineal Society. Descent, Succession and Inheritance among the Toka of Zambia
LADISLAV HOLY

59 Native Lords of Quito in the Age of the Incas. The Political Economy of North-Andean Chiefdoms
FRANK SALOMON

60 Culture and Class in Anthropology and History. A Newfoundland Illustration
GERALD SIDER

61 From Blessing to Violence: History and Ideology in the Circumcision Ritual of the Merina of Madagascar*
MAURICE BLOCH

62 The Huli Response to Illness
STEPHEN FRANKEL

63 Social Inequality in a Northern Portuguese Hamlet: Land, Late Marriage, and Bastardy, 1870–1978*
BRIAN JUAN O'NEILL

64 Cosmologies in the Making. A Generative Approach to Cultural Variation in Inner New Guinea*
FREDRIK BARTH

65 Kinship and Class in the West Indies. A Genealogical Study of Jamaica and Guyana*
RAYMOND T. SMITH

66 The Making of the Basque Nation
MARIANNE HEIBERG

67 Out of Time: History and Evolution in Anthropological Discourse
NICHOLAS THOMAS

68 Tradition as Truth and Communication
PASCAL BOYER

69 The Abandoned Narcotic: Kava and Cultural Instability in Melanesia
RON BRUNTON

70 The Anthropology of Numbers
THOMAS CRUMP

71 Stealing People's Names: History and Politics in a Sepik River Cosmology
SIMON J. HARRISON

72 The Bedouin of Cyrenaica: Studies in Personal and Corporate Power
EMRYS L. PETERS edited by Jack Goody and Emanuel Marx

73 Property, Production and Family in Neckerhausen
DAVID WARREN SABEAN

74 Bartered Brides: Politics, Gender and Marriage in an Afghan Tribal Society
NANCY TAPPER

75 Fifteen Generations of Bretons: Kinship and Society in Lower Brittany, 1720–1980
MARTINE SEGALEN, translated by J. A. Underwood

76 Honor and Grace in Anthropology
Edited by J. G. PERISTIANY and JULIAN PITT-RIVERS

77 The Making of the Modern Greek Family: Marriage and Exchange in Nineteenth-Century Athens
PAUL SANT CASSIA and CONSTANTINA BADA

78 Religion and Custom in a Muslim Society: The Berti of Sudan
LADISLAV HOLY

*available in paperback